Cher Philip — a la
recherche
de Paris.

December '98

Raymond

Les Chats

Photographies et poèmes

Bibliothèque de l'Image

Conception graphique : Alessandra Scarpa.

photo : Terry deRoy Gruber

Le chat

I

Dans ma cervelle se promène,
Ainsi qu'en son appartement,
Un beau chat, fort, doux et charmant.
Quand il miaule, on l'entend à peine,

Tant son timbre est tendre et discret;
Mais que sa voix s'apaise ou gronde,
Elle est toujours riche et profonde.
C'est là son charme et son secret.

Cette voix, qui perle et qui filtre
Dans mon fonds le plus ténébreux,
Me remplit comme un vers nombreux
Et me réjouit comme un philtre.

Elle endort les plus cruels maux
Et contient toutes les extases;
Pour dire les plus longues phrases,
Elle n'a pas besoin de mots.

Non, il n'est pas d'archet qui morde
Sur mon cœur, parfait instrument,
Et fasse plus royalement
Chanter sa plus vibrante corde,

Que ta voix, chat mystérieux,
Chat séraphique, chat étrange,
En qui tout est, comme en un ange,
Aussi subtil qu'harmonieux!

II

De sa fourrure blonde et brune
Sort un parfum si doux, qu'un soir
J'en fus embaumé, pour l'avoir
Caressée une fois, rien qu'une.

C'est l'esprit familier du lieu;
Il juge, il préside, il inspire
Toutes choses dans son empire;
Peut-être est-il fée, est-il dieu?

Quand mes yeux, vers ce chat que j'aime
Tirés comme par un aimant,
Se retournent docilement
Et que je regarde en moi-même,

Je vois avec étonnement
Le feu de ses prunelles pâles,
Clairs fanaux, vivantes opales,
Qui me contemplent fixement.

Charles Baudelaire, *Les fleurs du mal.*

Ernesse

«C'est mézigue, Ernesse, le greffier du bistro. La pompe à bière, é m'sert de piédestal artistique, et je peux dire que là-haut j'en jette un jus. Visez mes bacchantes, visez mes grandes feuilles! La greffière de l'épiceman, quand é m'voit, c'est tout juste si elle tombe pas en dig-dig, comme la celle de la concierge. Toutes pour Ernesse! C'est le quartier qui veut ça. Les gosses n'osent pas me tirer la queue. "Ah! qu'ils disent, il en riboule, des calots, Ernesse! Sans char, i'nous fout les foies!»

«Primo, c'est vrai que j'ai des beaux châsses. Aussi je les ouvre, et je cligne pas. Entre nous, si je clignais de l'œil, j'ai peur que la tache que j'ai sur le blair é m'fasse loucher...!»

Colette, *Autres bêtes, Chats de Paris.*

La chatte au miroir

«Est-elle plus jolie que moi? Je ne crois pas. D'ailleurs quelle chatte est plus jolie que moi? Je voudrais regarder cette intruse à loisir, pendant qu'elle me tourne le dos. Mais chaque fois, juste à ce moment-là, juste en même temps que moi... Elle se retourne et me regarde.»

Colette, *Autres bêtes, Chats de Paris.*

photo : Jane Bown

Chanson du chat

Chat, chat, chat,
Chat noir, chat blanc, chat gris
Charmant chat couché
Chat, chat, chat,
N'entends-tu pas les souris
Danser à trois des entrechats
Sur le plancher?

Le bourgeois ronfle dans son lit,
De son bonnet de coton coiffé,
Et la lune regarde à la vitre.
Dansez souris, dansez jolies,
Dansez vite
En remuant vos fines queues de fées.

Dansez sans musique tout à votre aise,
A pas menus et drus,
Au clair de lune qui vient de se lever,
Courez; les sergents de ville dans la rue
Font les cent pas sur le pavé;
Et tous les chats du vieux Paris
Dorment sur leurs chaises,
Chats blancs, chats noirs ou chats gris.

Tristan Klingsor, *Florilège poétique*.

Capucin et Adimah

(...)

Capucin: Qu'est-ce que tu regardes dans le jardin?
Adimah: Rien.
Capucin: Alors pourquoi regardes-tu le jardin?
Adimah, *agacée*: Je ne regarde pas le jardin! Je regarde, je ne sais pas, moi... Le ciel, une apparition, tout ce qui n'existe pas... Mon rêve...

Silence.

Capucin: Veux-tu m'épouser?
Adimah, *après un silence*: C'est drôle, j'ai entendu cette phrase-là quelque part...

Dans le jardin, le lierre qui couvre le mur de clôture s'agite. D'un remous de feuilles émerge un long matou rayé qui se laisse couler jusqu'en bas du mur et rampe vers le massif de rhododendrons.

Adimah, *léger cri*: Ah!...
Capucin, *qui n'a rien vu*: Qu'est-ce que tu as?
Adimah, *rêveuse*: Lèche-moi l'oreille droite, veux-tu?

(...)

Capucin, *près d'Adimah qui dort profondément*: Adimah!... Adimah!...
Adimah, *ronron très faible*: ....
Capucin, *à mi-voix*: Veux-tu m'épouser?
Adimah, *même jeu*: ....
Capucin, *vexé*: Ce n'est pas une existence. Tu t'es absentée pendant trois jours, et depuis ton retour tu dors tout le temps!... Adimah!... Viens à la fenêtre! Viens regarder dans le jardin!
Adimah, *d'une voix à peine distincte*: ...rder...rdin?
Capucin, *littéraire*: Oui, tu sais bien... Le ciel... Une apparition... Ton rêve...
Adimah, *s'éveillant à demi*: Mon quoi?... Ah! oui, je sais... Va donc dire à Emilie qu'elle le flanque dehors à coup de balai.
Capucin: Qui?
Adimah: Baba, le matou du voisin. Je l'ai assez vu.

Elle se rendort.

Colette, *Autres bêtes, Chats.*

La java des pussy-cats

Sur un vieux toit en zingue
Y avait des pussy-cats
Qui dansaient comme des dingues
En f'sant du bruit avec leurs pattes

Alertés, les voisingues
S'écriaient ça n'a rien d'bath
Y a d'quoi dev'nir sourdingue
On peut plus travailler ses maths

Le matou du marchand d'volailles
Une sardine en bandoulière
Avait enlacé par la taille
La chatte de la cuisinière

Chacun faisait du gringue
A la siamoise de l'épicier
C'était un vrai dancingue
A tout l'monde ils cassaient les pieds

Au bout d'une demi-plombe
Ecœurés par ce raffut
Les flics s'amènent en trombe
En faisant tourner leurs massues

Et c'est une hécatombe
Les ardoises volent en éclats
On aurait cru des bombes
Mais y avait déjà plus un chat

Réfugiés au fond d'une cave
Les pussy-cats pas dégonflés
Sirotant d'l'alcool de betterave
S'étaient remis à gambiller

Toute la nuit ils dansèrent
En usant des kilos d'savates
Pour leur anniversaire
La java des pussy-cats

Boris Vian.

Le Chat noir

Un fantôme est encor comme un lieu
où ton regard se heurte contre un son;
mais contre ce pelage noir
ton regard le plus fort est dissous:

ainsi un fou furieux, au paroxysme
de sa rage, trépigne dans le noir
et soudain, dans le capitonnage sourd
de sa cellule, cesse et s'apaise.

Tous les regards qui jamais l'atteignirent,
il semble en lui les recéler
pour en frémir, menaçant, mortifié,
et avec eux dormir.
Mais soudain, dressé vif, éveillé,
il tourne son visage – dans le tien:
et tu retrouves à l'improviste
ton regard dans les boules d'ambre
jaunes de ses yeux: enclos
comme un insecte fossilisé.

Rainer Maria Rilke, *Nouveaux poèmes.*

La Chanson du chat noir

L'entrée – célèbre – sur la cour
S'appelle «escalier de service»,
Dans cette entrée, comme en son fief,
Habite le Chat Noir.

L'obscurité le protège, il cache
Son rire moqueur dans sa moustache...
Tous les chats chantent ou pleurent,
Mais le Chat Noir, lui, se tait.

Il n'attrape plus les rats depuis belle lurette;
Ricanant dans sa moustache,
Il nous attrape aux belles paroles,
A la rondelle de saucisson.

Il n'exige, ni ne prie;
Et seul son œil jaune brille
Chacun vient le servir de lui-même
Et de surcroît lui dit merci.

Il ne lâche pas un mot
Ne fait que manger et boire.
Quand ses griffes râclent le sol
On dirait qu'il vous fend la gorge.

C'est pour ça, faut croire, qu'est triste
La maison où nous habitons.
Il faudrait y mettre une lampe...
Mais pas moyen qu'on se cotise.

Boulat Okoudjava.

photo : Jane Bown

Le petit chat noir

J'ai peu vécu de la vie terrestre, où j'étais noir. Noir entière-ment, sans tache blanche au poitrail, ni étoile blanche au front. Je n'avais même pas ces trois ou quatre poils blancs, qui poussent aux chats noirs dans le creux de la gorge, sous le menton. Robe rase, mate, drue, queue maigre et capricieuse, l'œil oblique et couleur de verjus, un vrai chat noir.

Mon plus lointain souvenir remonte à une demeure où je ren-contrai, venant à moi du fond d'une salle longue et sombre, un petit Chat blanc. Quelque chose d'inexplicable me poussa au-devant de lui, et nous nous arrêtâmes nez à nez. Il fit un saut en arrière, et je fis un saut en arrière en même temps. Si je n'avais pas sauté ce jour-là, peut-être vivrais-je encore dans le monde des couleurs, des sons et des formes tangibles...

Mais je sautai, et le Chat blanc crut que j'étais son ombre noire. En vain j'entrepris, par la suite, de le convaincre que je possédais une ombre bien à moi. Il voulait que je ne fusse que son ombre, et que j'imitasse sans récompense tous ses gestes. S'il dansait je devais danser, et boire s'il buvait, manger s'il mangeait, chasser son propre gibier. Mais je buvais l'ombre de l'eau, et je mangeais l'ombre de la viande, et je me morfondais à l'affût sous l'ombre de l'oiseau...

Le Chat blanc n'aimait pas mes yeux verts, qui refusaient d'être l'ombre de ses yeux bleus. Il les maudissait, en les visant de la griffe. Alors je les fermais, et je m'habituais à ne regarder que l'ombre qui régnait derrière mes paupières.

Mais c'était là une pauvre vie pour un petit Chat noir. Par les nuits de lune je m'échappais et je dansais faiblement devant le mur blanc, pour me repaître de la vue d'une ombre mienne, mince et cornue, à chaque lune plus mince, et encore plus mince, qui semblait fondre...

C'est ainsi que j'échappai au petit Chat blanc. Mais mon éva-sion est une image confuse. Grimpai-je le long du rayon de lune? Me cloîtrai-je à jamais derrière mes paupières verrouillées? Fus-je appelé par l'un des chats magiques qui émergent du fond des miroirs? Je ne sais. Mais désormais le Chat blanc croit qu'il a per-du son ombre, la cherche, et longuement l'appelle. Mort, je ne goû-te pourtant pas le repos, car je doute. Peu à peu s'éloigne de moi la certitude que je fus un vrai chat, et non pas l'ombre, la moitié noc-turne, le noir envers du chat blanc.

Colette, *Autres bêtes, Chats.*

photo : Jane Bown

photo : Jane Bown

Les esclaves

Au commencement, Dieu créa le chat à son image. Et, bien entendu, il trouva que c'était bien. Et c'était bien, d'ailleurs. Mais le chat était paresseux. Il ne voulait rien faire. Alors, plus tard, après quelques millénaires, Dieu créa l'homme. Uniquement dans le but de servir le chat, de lui servir d'esclave jusqu'à la fin des temps. Au chat, il avait donné l'indolence et la lucidité; à l'homme, il donna la névrose, le don du bricolage et la passion du travail. L'homme s'en donna à cœur joie. Au cours des siècles, il édifia toute une civilisation basée sur l'invention, la production et la consommation intensive. Civilisation qui n'avait en réalité qu'un seul but secret: offrir au chat le confort, le gîte et le couvert.

C'est dire que l'homme inventa des millions d'objets inutiles, généralement absurdes, tout cela pour produire parallèlement les quelques objets indispensables au bien-être du chat: le radiateur, le coussin, le bol, le plat à sciure, le pêcheur breton, le tapis, la moquette, le panier d'osier, et peut-être aussi la radio puisque les chats aiment la musique.

Mais, de tout cela, les hommes ne savent rien. A leurs souhaits. Bénis soient-ils. Et ils croient l'être. Tout est pour le mieux dans le meilleur des mondes des chats.

Jacques Sternberg, *Contes glacés.*

photo : Martine Franck

Le chat qui ne ressemble à rien

Le chat qui ne ressemble à rien
Aujourd'hui ne va pas très bien.

Il va visiter le Docteur
qui lui ausculte le cœur.

Votre cœur ne va pas bien
Il ne ressemble à rien,

Il n'a pas son pareil
De Paris à Créteil.

Il va visiter sa demoiselle
Qui lui regarde la cervelle.

Votre cervelle ne va pas bien
Elle ne ressemble à rien,

Elle n'a pas son contraire
A la surface de la terre.

Voilà pourquoi le chat qui ne ressemble à rien
Est triste aujourd'hui et ne va pas bien.

Robert Desnos, *La ménagerie de Tristan.*

Le chat

Pour ne poser qu'un doigt dessus
Le chat est bien trop grosse bête.
  Sa queue rejoint sa tête,
  Il tourne dans ce cercle
  Et se répond à la caresse.

Mais, la nuit l'homme voit ses yeux
  Dont la pâleur est le seul don.
Ils sont trop gros pour qu'il les cache
Et trop lourds pour le vent perdu du rêve.

  Quand le chat danse
C'est pour isoler sa prison
  Et quand il pense
C'est jusqu'aux murs de ses yeux.

Paul Éluard, *Les animaux et leurs hommes,*
les hommes et leurs animaux.

photo : Karen Tweedy-Holmes

photo : Jean Gaumy

photo : Terry deRoy Gruber

Noir

«Noir dans le noir. Plus noir que le noir. Plus noir que le combat de nègres à minuit dans une cave. Je n'ai pas besoin, pour disparaître, de me cacher; je cesse seulement d'exister, et j'éteins mes phares. Mais je fais mieux encore, je dépose mes deux phares d'or au ras du tapis, flottants dans l'air, visibles et insaisissables, et je m'en vais à mes affaires...

«C'est de la magie? Mais bien sûr. Croyez-vous qu'on soit noir à ce point, sans être sorcier?»

Colette, *Autres bêtes, Chats de Paris.*

Lettre à Mlle Olga Lagrené

Mademoiselle,

Mon chat aurait mis la patte à la plume, s'il n'était pas si paresseux, pour vous remercier de l'offre tout aimable que vous voulez bien lui faire. Il me charge de vous présenter ses très humbles hommages et de vous dire qu'il accepte avec empressement. Il craint seulement que la gravité de son caractère, fort en rapport avec la couleur de sa robe, ne vous ennuie bientôt. De méchantes langues lui ont parlé de vos coquetteries et de votre besoin de mouvement. On lui a dit que vous vouliez plaire à tout le monde et que vous n'y réussissiez que trop bien, sur quoi, lui qui est une personne sérieuse pesant 15 kg et compagnon ordinaire d'une tortue, craint que vous le dérangiez de ses habitudes méditatives qui lui ont attiré une grande considération dans toutes les gouttières de la rue de Lille. Il offre à sa dame de compagnie la queue de toutes les asperges qu'il prendra comme appointements, mais il exige qu'elle lui prête ses genoux sans bouger pendant deux heures quand il a envie de dormir. Je crains bien que le marché ne se puisse faire à ces conditions, car je lui ai dit que ne je vous avais jamais vue deux minutes immobile. Sur quoi il a hérissé sa moustache et est allé se coucher sur le coton où loge son amie la tortue.

3 juillet 1853

Prosper Mérimée, *Correspondance.*

photo : Ferdinando Scianna

photo : Edouard Golbin

Prrou

Quand je l'ai connue, elle gîtait dans un vieux jardin noir, oublié entre deux bâtisses neuves, étroit et long comme un tiroir. Elle ne sortait que la nuit, par peur des chiens et des hommes, et elle fouillait les poubelles. Quand il pleuvait, elle se glissait derrière la grille d'une cave, contre les vitres poudreuses du soupirail, mais la pluie gagnait tout de suite son refuge et elle serrait patiemment sous elle ses maigres pattes de chatte errante, fines et dures comme celles d'un lièvre.

Elle restait là de longues heures, levant de temps en temps les yeux vers le ciel, ou vers mon rideau soulevé. Elle n'avait pas l'air lamentable, ni effaré, car sa misère n'était pas un accident. Elle connaissait ma figure, mais elle ne mendiait pas, et je ne pouvais lire dans son regard que l'ennui d'avoir faim, d'avoir froid, d'être mouillée, l'attente résignée du soleil qui endort et guérit passagèrement les bêtes abandonnées.

Février vient, et le vieux jardin ressembla, derrière sa grille, à une cage pleine de petits fauves. Matous des caves et des combles, des fortifs et des terrains vagues, le dos en chapelet, avec des cous pelés d'échappés à la corde – matous chasseurs, sans oreilles et sans queue, rivaux terribles des rats –, matous de l'épicier et de la crémière, allumés et gras, lourds, vite essouflés, matous noirs à collier de ruban cerise, et matous à collier de perles bleues...

La bourrasque tragique et voluptueuse se calma enfin. Je revis la chatte grise, étique, décolorée, plus farouche que jamais et tressaillant à tous les bruits. Dans le rayon de soleil qui plongeait à midi au fond du jardin noir, elle traîna ses flancs enflés, de jour en jour plus lourds – jusqu'au matin humide où je la découvris, vaincue, fiévreuse, en train d'allaiter cinq chatons vivaces, nés comme elle sur la terre nue.

Colette, *La paix chez les bêtes.*

Alice demeura quelques instants aux aguets, s'attendant presque à le voir réapparaître, mais il n'en fit rien, et au bout d'une ou deux minutes elle dirigea ses pas vers le lieu où on lui avait dit qu'elle trouverait le Lièvre de Mars. «Des chapeliers, se dit-elle, j'en ai déjà vu; le Lièvre de Mars sera le plus intéressant des deux, et, comme on est en mai, peut-être ne sera-t-il pas fou furieux... ou, du moins, peut-être ne sera-t-il pas tout à fait aussi fou qu'il l'était en mars.» Ce disant, elle leva les yeux vers l'arbre, et voilà que le chat, perché sur une branche, s'y trouvait de nouveau.

«Avez-vous dit cochon ou pochon?» demanda le chat.

«J'ai dit cochon, répondit Alice, et j'aimerais que vous ces-siez un peu d'apparaître et de disparaître d'une manière si sou-daine: vous me donnez le tournis!»

«Entendu», dit le Chat; et, cette fois, il s'effaça très lente-ment, en commençant par le bout de la queue et en finissant par un sourire, qui persista quelque temps après que le reste de l'animal eut disparu.

«Ma foi! pensa Alice, il m'était souvent arrivé de voir un chat sans souris (ou sourire); mais ce souris de chat sans chat! c'est bien la chose la plus curieuse que j'aie contemplée, de ma vie!»

Lewis Carroll, *Alice au pays des merveilles.*

A une chatte

Chatte blanche, chatte sans tache,
Je te demande, dans ces vers,
Quel secret dort dans tes yeux verts,
Quel sarcasme sous ta moustache.

Tu nous lorgnes, pensant tout bas
Que nos fronts pâles, que nos lèvres
Déteintes en de folles fièvres,
Que nos yeux creux ne valent pas

Ton museau que ton nez termine,
Rose comme un bouton de sein,
Tes oreilles dont le dessin
Couronne fièrement ta mine.

Pourquoi cette sérénité?
Aurais-tu la clé des problèmes
Qui nous font, frissonnants et blêmes,
Passer le printemps et l'été?

Devant la mort qui nous menace,
Chats et gens, ton flair, plus subtil
Que notre savoir, te dit-il
Où va la beauté qui s'efface,

Où va la pensée, où s'en vont
Les défuntes splendeurs charnelles?...
Chatte, détourne tes prunelles;
J'y trouve trop de noir au fond.

Charles Cros, *Le coffret de santal.*

photo : Karen Tweedy-Holmes

Le chat

Viens, mon beau chat, sur mon cœur amoureux;
   Retiens les griffes de ta patte,
Et laisse-moi plonger dans tes beaux yeux,
   Mêlés de métal et d'agate.

Lorsque mes doigts caressent à loisir
   Ta tête et ton dos élastique,
Et que ma main s'enivre du plaisir
   de palper ton corps électrique,

Je vois ma femme en esprit. Son regard,
   Comme le tien, aimable bête,
Profond et froid, coupe et fend comme un dard,

   Et, des pieds jusques à la tête,
Un air subtil, un dangereux parfum
   Nagent autour de son corps brun.

Charles Baudelaire, *Les fleurs du mal.*

photo : Walter Chandoha

photo : Guy le Querrec

Le matou

«Je suis le matou. Je mène la vie inquiète de ceux que l'amour créa pour son dur service. Je suis solitaire et condamné à conquérir sans cesse, et sanguinaire par nécessité. Je me bats comme je mange, avec un appétit méthodique, et tel qu'un athlète entraîné, qui vainc sans hâte et sans fureur.

«C'est le matin que je rentre chez vous. Je tombe avec l'aube, et bleu comme elle, du haut de ces arbres nus, où tout à l'heure je ressemblais à un nid dans le brouillard. Ou bien, je glisse sur le toit incliné, jusqu'au balcon de bois; je me pose au bord de votre fenêtre entrouverte, comme un bouquet d'hiver; respirez sur moi toute la nuit de décembre et son parfum de cimetière frais! Tout à l'heure, quand je dormirai, ma chaleur et la fièvre exhaleront l'odeur des buis amers, du sang séché, le musc fauve...

«Car je saigne, sous la charpie soyeuse de ma toison. Il y a une plaie cuisante à ma gorge, et je ne lèche même pas la peau fendue de ma patte. Je ne veux que dormir, dormir, dormir, serrer mes paupières sur mes beaux yeux d'oiseau nocturne, dormir n'importe où, tombé sur le flanc comme un chemineau, dormir inerte, grumeleux de terre, hérissé de brindilles et de feuilles sèches, comme un faune repu...

«Je dors, je dors... Une secousse électrique me dresse parfois, – je gronde sourdement comme un tonnerre lointain, – puis je retombe... Même à l'heure où je m'éveille tout à fait, vers la fin du jour, je semble absent et traversé de rêves; j'ai l'œil vers la fenêtre, l'oreille vers la porte...

«Hâtivement lavé, raidi de courbatures, je franchis le seuil, tous les soirs à la même heure, et je m'éloigne, tête basse, moins en élu qu'en banni... Je m'éloigne, balancé comme une pesante chenille, entre les flaques frissonnantes, en couchant mes oreilles sous le vent. Je m'en vais, insensible à la neige. Je m'arrête un instant, non que j'hésite, mais j'écoute les rumeurs secrètes de mon empire, je consulte l'air obscur, j'y lance, solennels, espacés, lamentables, les miaulements du matou qui erre et qui défie. Puis, comme si le son de ma voix m'eût soudain rendu frénétique, je bondis... On m'aperçoit un instant sur le faîte d'un mur, on me devine là-haut, rebroussé, indistinct et flottant comme un lambeau de nuée – et puis on ne me voit plus...

«Les nuits d'amour sont longues... Je demeure à mon poste, dispos, ponctuel et morose. Ma petite épouse délaissée dort dans sa maison. Elle est douce et bleue, et me ressemble trop. Ecoute-t-elle, du fond de son lit parfumé, les cris qui montent vers moi? Entend-elle, rugi au plus fort d'un combat par un mâle blessé, mon nom de bête, mon nom ignoré des hommes?

«Oui, cette nuit d'amour se fait longue. Je me sens triste et plus seul qu'un dieu... Un souhait innocent de lumière, de chaleur, de repos, traverse ma veille laborieuse... Qu'elle est lente à pâlir, l'aube qui rassure les oiseaux et disperse le sabbat des chattes en délire! Il y a beaucoup d'années déjà que je règne, que j'aime et que je tue... Il y a très longtemps que je suis beau... Je rêve, en boule, sur le mur glacé de rosée... J'ai peur de paraître vieux.

Colette, *La paix chez les bêtes.*

photo : Cecil Beaton

photo : Edward Weston

Le trésor

«Pauvre? Vous croyez que mon maître est pauvre, parce que ses contrevents vont choir au premier orage, parce que son mur chancelle, et que les vitres n'empêchent plus la bise d'entrer?

Détrompez-vous, mon maître est riche. Ne voyez-vous pas qu'il a, fidèle et fourrée d'hermine, lumière d'un logis sans feu, chaleur d'un lit sans duvet – qu'il a sur sa fenêtre ce bien inestimable, cet éclatant démenti: une chatte blanche?»

Colette, *Autres bêtes, Chats de Paris.*

photo : Jane Bown

Le chat bourgeois

Un chat tuait sans vrai désir.
C'était un chat très riche et il n'avait pas faim.
Il faut bien se distraire, enfin:
Chat bourgeois a tant de loisirs...
On ne peut pas toujours dormir sur un coussin.
De souris, il ne mangeait guère;
Son pedigree fameux l'ayant mis au-dessus
Des nourritures du vulgaire.
Son régime était strict. Cet immeuble cossu,
En outre visité, à dates périodiques,
Par les services de la dératisation,
Gens aux procédés scientifiques,
Tuant sans joie ni passion,
Au nom de l'administration,
De rat, de vrai bon rat, qui fuit et qu'on rattrape
Négligemment, ne le tuant qu'à petits coups
Sans tuer son espoir – vrai plaisir de satrape –
Il n'y en avait plus du tout
Avec leurs poisons et leurs trappes.
Restaient quelques moineaux bêtes et citadins,
Race ingrate
Qu'on étendait d'un coup de patte:
Assez misérable fretin.
Oubliant les rats,
L'employé du service d'hygiène ne vint pas.
On l'avait convoqué
Sur une autre frontière,
Pour tuer cette fois des hommes. Et la guerre,
Approchant à grands pas des quartiers élégants,
Les maîtres de mon chat durent fuir sans leurs gants,
En un quart d'heure, sur les routes incertaines.

Dans l'impérieux souci de sauver leur bedaine
Ils oublièrent tout, les bonnes et le chat.
Les bonnes changèrent d'état.
Loin de Madame, violées par des militaires,
Elles si réservées, elles se révélèrent
Putains de beaucoup de talent.
Leur train de vie devint tout à coup opulent
Et elles prirent une bonne.

Après un temps de désarroi,
Le chat, devenu chat, comprit qu'il était roi;
Que la faim est divine et que la lutte est bonne.
D'un œil blanc, d'une oreille arrachée aux combats
Dont il sortit vainqueur contre les autres chats,
Il paya ses amours royales sous la lune.
Sans régime et sans soin, ne mangeant que du rat
Il perdit son poil angora
Qui ne tenait qu'à sa fortune
Et auquel il ne tenait pas;
Il y gagna la mine altière
Et l'orgueil des chats de gouttière,
Et bénit à jamais la guerre
Qui offre aux chats maigris des chattes et des rats.

Jamais ce que l'on vous donne
Ne vaudra ce que l'on prend
Avec sa griffe et sa dent.
La vie ne donne à personne.

Jean Anouilh, *Fables.*

Les chats

Les amoureux fervents et les savants austères
Aiment également, dans leur mûre saison,
Les chats puissants et doux, orgueil de la maison,
Qui comme eux sont frileux et comme eux sédentaires.

Amis de la science et de la volupté,
Ils cherchent le silence et l'horreur des ténèbres;
L'Érèbe les eût pris pour ses coursiers funèbres,
S'ils pouvaient au servage incliner leur fierté.

Ils prennent en songeant les nobles attitudes
Des grands sphinx allongés au fond des solitudes,
Qui semblent s'endormir dans un rêve sans fin;

Leurs reins féconds sont pleins d'étincelles magiques,
Et des parcelles d'or, ainsi qu'un sable fin,
Etoilent vaguement leurs prunelles mystiques.

Charles Baudelaire, *Les fleurs du mal.*

Le chat et l'oiseau

Un village écoute désolé
Le chant d'un oiseau blessé
C'est le seul oiseau du village
Et c'est le seul chat du village
Qui l'a à moitié dévoré
Et l'oiseau cesse de chanter
Le chat cesse de ronronner
Et de se lécher le museau
Et le village fait à l'oiseau
De merveilleuses funérailles
Et le chat qui est invité
Marche derrière le petit cercueil de paille
Où l'oiseau mort est allongé
Porté par une petite fille
Qui n'arrête pas de pleurer
Si j'avais su que cela te fasse tant de peine
Lui dit le chat
Je l'aurais mangé tout entier
Et puis je t'aurais raconté
Que je l'avais vu s'envoler
S'envoler jusqu'au bout du monde
Là-bas où c'est tellement loin
Que jamais on n'en revient
Tu aurais eu moins de chagrin
Simplement de la tristesse et des regrets

Il ne faut jamais faire les choses à moitié.

Jacques Prévert,
Histoires et d'autres histoires.

Le petit chat

C'est un petit chat noir effronté comme un page,
Je le laisse jouer sur ma table souvent,
Quelquefois il s'assied sans faire de tapage,
On dirait un joli presse-papier vivant.

Rien en lui, pas un poil de son velours ne bouge;
Longtemps, il reste là, noir sur un feuillet blanc,
A ces minets tirant leur langue de drap rouge,
Qu'on fait pour essuyer les plumes, ressemblant.

Quand il s'amuse, il est extrêmement comique,
Pataud et gracieux, tel un ourson drôlet.
Souvent je m'accroupis pour suivre sa mimique
Quand on met devant lui la soucoupe de lait.

Tout d'abord de son nez délicat il le flaire,
Le frôle, puis, à coups de langue très petits,
Il le happe; et dès lors il est à son affaire
Et l'on entend, pendant qu'il boit, un clapotis.

Il boit, bougeant la queue et sans faire une pause,
Et ne relève enfin son joli museau plat
Que lorsqu'il a passé sa langue rêche et rose
Partout, bien proprement débarbouillé le plat.

Alors il se pourlèche un moment les moustaches,
Avec l'air étonné d'avoir déjà fini.
Et comme il s'aperçoit qu'il s'est fait quelques taches,
Il se lisse à nouveau, lustre son poil terni.

Ses yeux jaunes et bleus sont comme deux agates;
Il les ferme à demi, parfois, en reniflant,
Se renverse, ayant pris son museau dans ses pattes,
Avec des airs de tigre étendu sur le flanc.

Edmond Rostand, *Musardises.*

La fleur

«Oh! la jolie fleur dans la vitrine!
– Oui. C'est un petit pavot blanc.
– Je ne vous parle pas des petits pavots, je vous montre la fleur d'en bas, tachetée de clair et de sombre, veloutée, avec deux gouttes de rosée qui brillent, et de grandes éta-mines blanches pointues... Tiens, je me trompais: ce n'est pas une fleur, c'est un chat.
– Non, non, vous aviez raison, poète: c'est une fleur.»

Colette, *Autre bêtes, Chats de Paris.*

Poum

«Je suis le diable. Le diable. Personne n'en doit douter. Il n'y a qu'à me voir, d'ailleurs. Regardez-moi, si vous l'osez! Noir, d'un noir roussi par les feux de la géhenne. Les yeux vert poison, veinés de brun, comme la fleur de la jusquiame. J'ai des cornes de poils blancs, raides, qui fusent hors de mes oreilles, et des griffes, des griffes, des griffes. Combien de griffes? je ne sais pas. Cent mille, peut-être. J'ai une queue plantée de travers, maigre, mobile, impérieuse, expressive – pour tout dire, diabolique.

«Je suis le diable, et non un simple chat. Je ne grandis pas. L'écureuil, dans sa cage ronde, est plus gros que moi. Je mange comme quatre, comme six – je n'engraisse pas.

«J'ai surgi, en mai, de la lande fleurie d'œillets sauvages et d'orchis mordorés. J'ai paru au jour, sous l'apparence bénigne d'un chaton de deux mois. Bonnes gens! vous m'avez recueilli, sans savoir que vous hébergiez le dernier démon de cette Bretagne ensorcelée. «Gnome», «Poulpiquet», «Kornigaret», «Korrigan», c'est ainsi qu'il fallait me nommer, et non «Poum»! Cependant, j'accepte pour mien ce nom parmi les hommes, parce qu'il me sied.

«Poum!» le temps d'une explosion, et je suis là, jailli vous ne savez d'où. «Poum!» j'ai cassé, d'un bond exprès maladroit, le vase de Chine, et «poum!» me voilà collé, comme une pieuvre noire, au museau blanc du lévrier, qui crie avec une voix de femme battue... «Poum!» parmi les tendres bégonias prêts à fleurir, et qui ne fleuriront plus... «Poum!» au beau milieu du nid de pinsons, qui pépiaient, confiants, à la fourche du sureau... «Poum!» dans la jatte de lait, dans l'aquarium de la grenouille, et «poum!» enfin, sur l'un de vous.

«Ce soir, tandis que le jardin arrosé sent la vanille et la salade fraîche, vous errez, épaule contre épaule, heureux de vous taire, d'être seuls, de n'entendre sur le sable, quand vous passez tous deux, que le bruit d'un seul pas...

«Seuls? de quel droit? Cette heure m'appartient. Rentrez! La lampe vous attend. Rendez-moi mon domaine, car rien n'est vôtre, ici, dès la nuit close. Rentrez! Ou bien «poum!» je jaillis du fourré, comme une longue étincelle, comme une flèche invisible et sifflante.

«Faut-il que je frôle et que j'entrave vos pieds, mou, velu, humide, rampant, méconnaissable?... Rentrez! Le double feu vert de mes prunelles vous escorte, suspendu entre ciel et terre, éteint ici, rallumé là. Rentrez en murmurant: «Il fait frais» pour excuser le frisson qui désunit vos lèvres et desserre vos mains enlacées. Fermez les persiennes, en froissant le lierre du mur et l'aristoloche.

«Je suis le diable, et je vais commencer mes diableries sous la lune montante, parmi l'herbe bleue et les roses violacées. Je conspire contre vous, avec l'escargot, le hérisson, la hulotte, le sphinx lourd qui blesse la joue comme un caillou.

«Et gardez-vous, si je chante trop haut, cette nuit, de mettre le nez à la fenêtre: vous pourriez mourir soudain de me voir, sur le faîte du toit, assis tout noir au centre de la lune!...»

Colette, *La paix chez les bêtes.*

La mère chatte

«Un, deux, trois, quatre... Non, je me trompe. Un, deux, trois, quatre, cinq, six... Non, cinq. Où est le sixième? Un, deux, trois... Dieu, que c'est fatigant! A présent, ils ne sont plus que quatre. J'en deviendrai folle. Petits! petits! Mes fils, mes filles, où êtes-vous?

«Quel est celui qui se lamente entre le mur et la caisse de géraniums? Je ne dis pas cela parce que c'est mon fils, mais il crie bien. Et pour le seul plaisir de crier, car il peut parfaitement se dégager à reculons. Les autres?... Un, deux, trois... Je tombe de sommeil. Eux, ils ont tété et dormi, les voilà plus vifs qu'une portée de rats. Je m'enroue à répéter le roucoulement qui les rassemble, ils ne m'obéissent pas. A force de les chercher, je ne les vois plus, ou bien mon souci les multiplie. Hier n'en ai-je pas compté, effarée, jusqu'à neuf? Ce jardin est leur perdition.

«Où sont-ils? où sont-ils? Un, deux... Deux seulement! Et les quatre autres? Répondez, vous deux; sottement occupés l'un à manger une ficelle, l'autre à chercher l'entrée de cette caisse qui n'a pas de porte! Oui, vous n'avez rien vu, rien entendu, laids petits chats-huants que vous êtes, avec vos yeux ronds!

«... Ni dans la cuisine, ni dans le bûcher! Dans la cave? Je cours, je descends, je flaire... rien... Je remonte, le jardin m'éblouit... Où sont les deux que je gourmandais tout à l'heure? Perdus aussi? Mes enfants, mes enfants! Au secours, ô Deux-Pattes, accourez, j'ai perdu tous mes enfants! Ils jouaient, là, tenez, dans la jungle de fusains: je ne les ai pas quittés, tout au plus ai-je cédé, une minute, au plaisir de chanter leur naissante gloire, sur ce mode amoureux, enflé d'images, où ressuscitent mes origines persanes... Rendez-les-moi, ô Deux-Pattes puissants, dispensateurs du lait sucré et des queues de sardines! Cherchez avec moi, ne riez pas de ma misère, ne me dites pas qu'entre un jour et le jour qui vient je perds et je retrouve cent foix mon sextuple trésor! Je redoute, je prévois un malheur pire que la mort, et vous n'ignorez pas que mon instinct de mère et de chatte me fait deux fois infaillible!...

«Tiens!... D'où sort-il, celui-ci? C'est, ma foi, mon lourdaud de premier, tout rond, suivi de son frère sans malice. Et d'où vient celle-ci, petite femelle impudente, prête à me braver et qui jure, déjà, en râlant de la gorge? Un, deux, trois... Trois, quatre, cinq... Viens, mon sixième, délicat et plus faible que les autres, plus tendre aussi, et plus léché, toi pour qui je garde l'une de mes lourdes mamelles d'en bas, inépuisable, dans le doux nid duveté de poil bleu que te creusent mes pattes de derrière... Quatre, cinq, six... Assez, assez! Je n'en veux pas davantage! Venez tous dans la corbeille, à l'ombre fine de l'acacia. Dormons, ou prenez mon lait, en échange d'une heure de répit – je n'ai pas dit de repos, car mon sommeil prolonge ma vigilance éperdue, et c'est en rêve que je vous cherche et vous compte: un, deux, trois, quatre...»

Colette, *La paix chez les bêtes.*

Les souvenirs

Il siège au coin du feu, les paupières mi-closes,
Aspirant la chaleur du brasier qui s'éteint;
La bouilloire bouillone avec des bruits d'étain;
Le bois flambe, noircit, s'effile en charbons roses.

Le royal exilé prend de sublimes poses;
Il allonge son nez sur ses pieds de satin;
Il s'endort, il échappe au stupide destin,
A l'irrémédiable écroulement des choses.

Les siècles en son cœur ont épaissi leur nuit,
Mais au fond de son cœur, inextinguible, luit
Comme un flambeau sacré, son rêve héréditaire:

Un soir d'or, le déclin empourpré du soleil,
Des fûts noirs de palmiers sur l'horizon vermeil,
Un grand fleuve qui roule entre deux murs de terre.

Hippolyte Taine.

Remerciements

Les éditions Bibliothèque de l'Image sont particulièrement redevables à Mr Jean Claude Suarès pour son aide et ses conseils et lui expriment toute leur reconnaissance.

Crédits photographiques

Copyright des textes

The Daily Telegraph
sports yearbook
1999

Australian hockey player •Gary Prior ★14/5/98

The Daily Telegraph
sports yearbook
1999
Edited by David Welch

HAYDEN
PUBLISHING

Stevenage FC captain Robin Trottt hoping for divine inspiration as the FA Cup clash with Newcastle United approaches •**Russell Cheyne** ★**20/1/98**

First Published in Great Britain in 1998
Hayden Publishing Limited
32 Winifred Road, Hemel Hempstead HP3 9DX

Copyright © The Telegraph
Edited and compiled by David Welch and Martin Smith

Picture research and direction by Russell Cheyne

Designed by Wherefore Art?
Colour reproduction by PDQ Repro Ltd, Bungay, Suffolk

A CIP catalogue record for this book is available from the British Library

ISBN 0 9533683 0 0

Printed and bound by Jarrold Book Printing, Thetford, England

CONTENTS

7

Foreword by David Welch, Sports Editor of The Daily Telegraph

9

Introduction by Paul Hayward, Chief Sports Writer

12

Sports Review of 1998
A month-by-month review of the sporting year with the writers and photographers of The Daily Telegraph Sport team

98

1998 Interviews
A collection of the best interviews taken from the 1998 Telegraph Sport pages

110

1999 In Focus
A look forward to the next sporting year with five of the Telegraph's top writers: Christopher Martin-Jenkins, Henry Winter, Mick Cleary, Sue Mott and Martin Johnson.

120

1999 International Sports Calendar
A week-by week guide to sports fixtures and events around the world

196

1999 Fixtures
A listing by sport of major fixtures and events

203

Directory
A list of contact details of sports organisations

Dominic Cork *in extremis* during the Headingley Test Match •**Russell Cheyne** ★**9/8/98**   5

World Superbike Championship, Brands Hatch •Russell Cheyne ★2/8/98

FOREWORD

With Hearts accusing Spanish side, Real Mallorca, of fielding an 'ineligible goal-post' in a UEFA Cup match; England's footballers still claiming they were moral victors of the World Cup despite winning only two matches; and England's cricketers actually landing a Test series: 1998 represented an even more bizarre year for sport than usual.

The sight of our rugby players doing a lap of honour after their 25-8 defeat by the All Blacks, and David Lloyd's "we flippin' murdered 'em" after his side's drawn Test against mighty Zimbabwe, took some beating a year earlier, but sport never fails to trump its earlier excesses.

Who, for example, could have forecast that David Davies, the man in charge of the FA's press relations department, would find it possible to keep for himself many of the best bits from France 98, produce a World Cup diary with Glenn Hoddle, and remain in a job; and that Damon Hill would somehow manage to add some spice to an otherwise fairly stagnant Grand Prix season by winning a race in Belgium?

Somethings, though, made much more sense... Michael Parkinson was named Sports Writer of the Year; Giles Smith, Sports columnist; Martin Johnson, Sports feature writer; Russell Cheyne, Sports photographer; and Mihir Bose was judged to have produced the sports story of the year. These award winners - and many of their equally-talented colleagues - look back on the sporting year (and ahead to 1999) with great passion in the pages which follow....

David Welch was appointed Sports Editor of The Daily Telegraph in 1989 and was given the task of launching the country's first weekly sports supplement on behalf of the paper the following year. In 1995 he was made an assistant editor of the Telegraph and this year joined with his colleagues in producing a separate Saturday Sports supplement to go alongside its Monday stablemate.

His priority has been to widen the appeal and accessibility of the newspaper's sports section by introducing more quality writers, sports personalities, comment, analysis and humour to its pages while protecting the paper's reputation of providing the most comprehensive coverage of the sporting scene.

Michael Owen, England v Bulgaria European championship qualifier at Wembley Stadium •**Russell Cheyne** ★**10/10/98**

Paul Hayward

Owen offers enchantment from a mad world of sport

Sport is a release from the cares and worries of everyday life. But it is also a multi-billion entertainment industry. The Daily Telegraph Chief Sports Writer examines the changing nature of sport and looks forward to some of the highlights of 1999

Sport used to imitate life. Now life imitates sport. As we glimpse the white light of the millennium sport seems to fill up our senses more than any other cultural form. It takes a *Saving Private Ryan* for it to return to its proper proportions. It is television's most valuable sales pitch, the planet's foremost form of escapism and a laboratory for the best and worst of human endeavour.

It has drugs, ear-biting, corruption, greed, systematic lying, global takeover battles and death. The demise of Florence Griffith-Joyner at 38 may come to be remembered as nature's revenge for performance-enhancing drugs. But sport is also a release from all those things; a symphony of possibilities, what one observer has called, in a different context, 'a state of enchantment'.

Michael Owen's goal against Argentina in the World Cup was one such moment. For many in England it was the abiding image of 1998, and the principal source of hope for the coming year. Sport renews itself. Its natural season is springtime. Owen's goal was athletically sublime but it carried a significance much deeper than mere gymnastic prowess. It was a triumph of the mind. Eighteen-year-olds in flight are supposed to stop, look around, hesitate, lose their nerve, seek sanctuary in the advancing pack of elders. Owen, though, kept going. His angled shot into the attic of the Argentinian net was a comet that he may end up riding into legend. It is the masterpieces rather than the mendacity that we remember.

In Don DeLillo's literary masterwork, *Underworld*, the Soviet Union detonated its first nuclear test on the day Bobby Thomson hit his famous home run to give the New York Giants victory in baseball's World Series - 'the shot that was heard around the world'. The image is haunting. Part of DeLillo's inference is that America has measured out its days in sports scores. In the USA, certainly, sport is an anchor against national crisis. DeLillo's next work could be to examine what significance can be attached to the great home-run race between Sammy Sosa and Mark McGwire being enacted while the myth of the Whitehouse and presidential rectitude were being destroyed.

....

Owen's goal was athletically sublime but it carried a significance much deeper than mere gymnastic prowess

....

Baseball gave the country something to believe in, a way of looking back to a time before family life was ritually fractured, and the President was the rock on which an anti-Communist America was built. So much of sport is about memory. So much of it is an attempt to recreate the certainties of childhood. Allegiance is handed down through the generations.

Sport has these dimensions. It is not played in a social vacuum. That is why the proposed takeover of Manchester United by BSkyB was such seismic news. Many Manchester United supporters felt as if Murdoch had tried to buy a job lot of their souls. Look at people in stadiums - the way they do the same things every week on the way to the ground; the familial feelings they express towards the club; the language of 'second homes'; the way they mount the barricades at the thought of their own equilibrium being disturbed by takeovers or moves to new sites.

Many of the forces and currents of the new century pass through British sport. In 1999, two World Cups will be staged across the country and there are those who are desperate for the football World Cup and Olympics to run up these shores. In October and November, rugby union will attempt to reverse the political implosion of the last two years. Before that, the thwack and dash of cricket's World Cup will hasten the plink-plonk rhythms of the English sporting summer. Both events will be a test of our motorways, hotels, communications systems and above all our ability to find joy in the comfort of strangers - a capacity that was grievously absent during the rampages across France by England fans surfing a lamentable tradition of tribal enmity

As the 20th century burns to the filter, sport throws up new questions. Are we prepared to pay what the corporations who control it demand? Is love of the game and the chase an infinitely exploitable emotion? Will British governing bodies continue to be in thrall to TV companies and tycoons? Will anyone stop to point out that the value of sport is measured by more than how high the money and contracts are piled? Will it, in the end, sicken us, create monsters and

Introduction

mercenaries of the performers themselves, make us turn our backs on the storehouse of sporting memory and seek pleasure in other pursuits? Probably not, but you do not have to be a hair-shirted puritan to believe that sport is in danger of becoming irredeemably debased - something you might have to tell your children to keep away from, like the dual-carriageway or the amusement arcade.

Paradise or Pompeii? Whatever the joys and frustrations of sport plenty of changes are racing towards us. The age of 'free' TV is drawing to a close. Boxing smashed its glove into the pay-per-view era and other sports are certain to follow. Digital technology will enable clubs and governing bodies to control and sell their own rights. The 'TV station' of old will merely be an electronic postal service carrying the pictures to our homes. This will mean more money for sport and less for TV companies, unless they can find a new formula to keep control of the rights - which Murdoch and BSkyB have already endeavoured to do with the proposed Manchester United deal. This is merely step one in a hundred.

So much of sport is about memory. So much of it is an attempt to recreate the certainties of childhood. Allegiance is handed down through the generations

Cricket is trying to emerge from its dusty library. Rugby union is trying to achieve the first reverse-suicide by bringing itself back to life. Are these people for real? One of the enduring mysteries of the 1990s is how the simplest and most unpretentious of sports plunged a dagger in its own heart. If only they could hear themselves - splashing around in an alphabet stew of acronyms, an asylum of selfish demands. As things stand only New Zealand, South Africa, Australia and France will provide credible challenges for the 1999 World Cup. Unless some sanity is restored they might as well cut straight to the semi-finals.

Lawrence Dallaglio, an all-English hero, deserves better than to have his career wrecked by squabbling suits.

All sports need to launch a counter-offensive against football. There are signs that soccer's technicolour explosion is about to level out. Fashion is one element, the financial strain that is being put on supporters, unquestionably another. Over-supply and hubris may also bring the balloon down. The money-shovellers of the 21st century have risen more precariously than they know. A template for a European Super League with contrived matches and astronomical pay-per-view charges looks fine on the boardroom table of a merchant bank. But it would not survive long in the emotional melee of a Merseyside Derby or a meeting of Man Utd and Leeds on a cold Saturday in January.

Away from football, prospects for British sport are good. That other weekly flaunting of a dream - the National Lottery - is channelling millions into the areas where British sport needs it most: training facilities, clubhouses, sports science and stadiums. Travelling through France or Germany has made us cringe. Every one-horse town has its municipal stadium, its swimming pool, its floodlit tennis courts. For so long British success - and there has been much of it, across a staggering array of sports - has been achieved despite rather than because of the system. With a rebuilt Wembley, Manchester in full sporting bloom for the 2002 Commonwealth Games, and proper investment in the infrastructure of sport, Britain can finally shed the image of a well-meaning but bumbling presence forever chained at the ankle to the description plucky.

This, too, raises encouraging thoughts. Watching sport is fun, participating is even better. It would be nice to think that if some manufactured Euro-clash was available only on pay-per-view it would be possible to go to the municipal athletics track or Olympic-sized pool instead; to watch lower-league football in a prim and proper ground at which people from the same town were immediately recognisable and the players mixed with the fans.

It is not the people who own or stage sport who give it meaning. It is the people who watch and play. The starting whistle is the release from all the madness that surrounds the business of sport. They can never defile the game itself. Can they?
★October 1998

The dream is over... David Batty walks back after

10

missing the penalty which marked England's exit from the World Cup. The victorious Argentinian players celebrate •**Russell Cheyne ★30/6/99**

DAY BY DAY REVIEW

2: Helen Wills Moody, eight-times Wimbledon winner between 1927-38, dies in Carmel, California, aged 91.

3: Stevenage perform another FA Cup giant-killing by winning 2-1 at Swindon.

5: Shane Warne claims his 300th Test wicket after taking six for 34 in bowling out South Africa for 113 in Sydney, for an innings victory. Wasim Akram gives up the Pakistan captaincy after death threats against him and his family. David Bairstow, the former Yorkshire and England wicketkeeper, is found dead, aged 46.

7: West Indies appoint Brian Lara as captain for the five-Test series against England.

8: Yuan Yuan, the Chinese breast-stroke swimming, is sent home from the World Championships, along with her coach, after phials containing human growth hormones are found in her luggage at Sydney airport.

10: Simon Fenn, an Australian making his debut for London Scottish, has part of his left ear-lobe almost severed in a biting incident during a scrum at Bath in the Tetley's Bitter Cup. Stoke City fans stage a riot on the Britannia Stadium pitch after a 7-0 home defeat by Birmingham.

12: Terry Venables's spell as chairman of Portsmouth ends as he is bought out by director Martin Gregory.

13: Bath suspend prop forward Kevin Yates but do not state categorically that he was responsible for biting Simon Fenn's ear.

14: Four Chinese swimmings - Luna Wang, Zhang Yi, Cai Huijue and Wang Wei - test positive for drugs at the World Championships.

15: Faustino Asprilla moves back to Parma from Newcastle United. David Pleat is appointed director of football at Tottenham.

17: Tim Henman is beaten 7-5, 6-4 by Karol Kucera in the final of the Sydney International tournament. Alan Shearer comes on as a 73rd-minute substitute for Newcastle against Bolton, his first game of the season.

22: The FA charge Brian Clough, Ronnie Fenton and Steve Burtenshaw with misconduct following the "bungs inquiry".

24: Italy beat Scotland 25-21 in Treviso to push their case for inclusion in an expanded Six Nations Championship.

25: Despite Alan Shearer's third-minute goal, Newcastle are held 1-1 at Stevenage in the FA Cup fourth round. England draw their match against West Indies A, Angus Fraser taking five for 99. Denver Broncos beat Green Bay Packers 31-24 to win Super Bowl XXXII, John Elway successful at his fourth attempt.

26: England A decide to continue their tour of Sri Lanka after a bomb goes off in Kandy.

27: Three jockeys - Jamie Osborne, Dean Gallagher and Leighton Aspell - along with another man, are arrested by police investigating doping and race-fixing on British courses.

29: The first Test in Kingston is abandoned after an hour's play because the wicket is deemed dangerous; England had reached 17 for three.

31: Martina Hingis wins the Australian Open, beating Conchita Martinez 6-3, 6-3 in the final. Bath win rugby's European Cup with a 19-18 success against Brive in Bordeaux. Linesman Edward Martin is knocked unconscious by a fan during Portsmouth's match against Sheffield United.

Trevor McDonald

Trouble in paradise

Cricket lends itself to hyperbole perhaps as no other sport. The greatest teams can sink to abysmal depths. The finest batsmen can fail miserably, and bowlers once regarded as unplayable can be carted all round the park. Part of cricket's charm is its glorious uncertainty, its never-ending sense of fluctuating fortunes.

Nowhere is the change in fortune more evident than the Caribbean, where there are reasons to suggest that cricket in the West Indies, once the pride and passion of the region, is approaching something close to serious decline. So dismal is the outlook that Sir Gary Sobers has been contemplating the unthinkable: that England might be victorious in the Caribbean this winter. And as a pointer to a future West Indians have come to fear, Sobers adds that should England win, interest in West Indian cricket among its staunchest fans will wither and may never recover. Other commentators in the region see no other possible outcome.

It is always possible that England might lose, but they will surely never have a better chance of winning. And not because, as has often been suggested, young West Indians, attracted by thoughts of making big money in the United States, are turning away from cricket and towards basketball or football in droves. West Indians have always looked abroad in the professions and in sport as a way of achieving upward mobility. What is happening to West Indian cricket stems from much deeper causes.

The result is a team racked by divisions, openly at war with the selectors and the cricket authorities; a team dominated by selfish, material interests. One senior official told me: "The players have lost their pride. Their only interest now is in themselves and how much money they can make." To those who know, it is no surprise that the West Indies continue to under-perform. The biggest problem is what the chairman of selectors, Wes Hall, describes as the prevailing atmosphere of "spiteful insularity".

Every one of the six cricket-playing nations - Jamaica, Trinidad and Tobago, Barbados, Antigua, Guyana and St Vincent - seems hell bent on sacrificing the regional dimension of the West Indian game on the altar of narrow self-interest.

At its best, West Indies cricket has always been something of an article of faith, an acknowledgement that to compete at the highest levels, different islands must ignore the tensions of political disunity and set aside their differences, if only temporarily. They still do, but increasingly these days with obvious bitterness and with a conspicuous lack of grace.

The island constituents of the West Indies team fight openly among themselves about almost everything. They have battles about who should captain the side. The selectors suggested that Trinidadian Brian Lara was the man for the job for the recent tour of Pakistan, but the board, with the presidency based in Jamaica, overruled the selectors in favour of keeping Jamaican-born Courtney Walsh. They disagree over who should play in the team, who should be coach, who should be the manager. They fight at every level about how the game should be run.

It was put to me recently by one Barbadian observer that whereas Worrell, Sobers, Lloyd and Richards saw themselves as West Indian, Lara sees himself as Trinidadian, Curtly Ambrose as Antiguan. This was no criticism of Ambrose or Lara. It is simply the way it is. The Trinidad authorities mirror the attitude of their top batsman. Confronted with the evidence of the declining fortunes of West Indian cricket - Walsh and his team were humiliated by Pakistan in November and December, and the West Indies then managed to snatch defeat from the teeth of victory in the one-day final against England in Sharjah - Trinidad cricket officials talk about how well the island's prospects look in the domestic Red Stripe competition. The very name of that tournament has begun to engender controversy. Jamaica is the home of Red Stripe Beer - the competition's sponsors - and there is a widely held view among the smaller islands that Jamaica uses that fact as a way of exercising a kind of hegemony over West Indies cricket. Among officials in many smaller islands, the finger of suspicion is pointed at none other than the president of the West Indies board, Jamaican Pat Rousseau.

None of this would amount to anything were it not for the fact that recent West Indies performances suggest the Jeremiahs may be on to something. A situation resembling civil war existed on the tour of Pakistan, where the West Indies lost the three-match series 3-0, twice losing Tests by an innings and once by 10 wickets. Players were brought into the team by the selectors and dropped, although the captain was consulted only intermittently and the manager, Clive Lloyd, and the coach, Malcolm Marshall, not at all. The selection procedure operates as an independent arm, a long way from the team, and external to it. It might just be possible for other cricketing powers to operate in this way, but for the West Indies it is rank insanity. Manager and coach are known to feel that players are brought into the squad more in the hope that they would do well, than on the basis of having deserved their places.

Opposition bowlers have begun to expose

fundamental flaws in the technique of the West Indies' top batting order. The former Indian opening batsman, Sunil Gavaskar, talks about their tendency to play across the line, making them vulnerable to the swinging ball. Gavaskar feels that Pakistan ruthlessly exploited that failing, even though at times Wasim Akram bowled barely at half pace, and on the best pitches the West Indies have encountered on the subcontinent. That should be good news for Andy Caddick and Dean Headley, and for the ever-reliable Angus Fraser.

Most alarming is what some West Indian commentators see as a loss of pride in playing for the team. Losing Test matches is no longer the humiliation it once was. The will to fight and win has been replaced by the reckless gamble of the one-day shot. Of this criticism, not even the great Lara is immune. Shivnarine Chanderpaul is perhaps the honourable exception.

Surprisingly, in assessing this loss of pride, the University of the West Indies offer an interesting opinion. For some time now, they have been tracking what they call "contours of paradigmatic shifts in West Indian cricket culture". They have done so by making serious academic observations about the role of West Indies cricket in the life of the region with lectures and dissertations on subjects like: "Imperialism", "Colonial Education" and the "Origins of West Indian Cricket". In addition to pondering such lofty matters, undergraduates at the Centre for Cricket Research at the Cave Hill campus, Barbados, which was set up in 1994, have come up with a number of damning conclusions about the current state of the game in the Caribbean. Hilary McD Beckles, director of the research centre and professor of history at Cave Hill, believes the crucial factor in understanding what is happening to West Indian cricket is that the players have lost all respect for the governments in the region, which they regard as politically corrupt, bankrupt and dishonest.

They believe politicians have lost touch with the passions of average people and as a consequence players no longer wish to be West Indian ambassadors in the way Worrell, Sobers, Lloyd and Richards felt honoured to be. Beckles feels that the players are deeply suspicious of being "commodified" by sponsors like Red Stripe or Cable and Wireless, who, he said, were forced to demand legislation to ensure that the players agreed to compete. Beckles said his centre's research found that West Indian players consider the cricket authorities "old fashioned and primitive" and have little regard for them.

This would explain the way some players conduct themselves. When the West Indies were last in England, Lara absented himself from the team for four days, and on England's last tour of the West Indies, pace bowler Winston Benjamin came close to blows with an Antiguan cricket official over the seminal point of whether or not the player was allowed to park his car inside the ground.

Players despise these officials and see themselves as mercenaries fighting for themselves in the turbulence of the globalisation of sport. They have observed with scorn the inability of agencies in the region to provide any kind of living for them when their playing days are over. Sobers has a Barbados roundabout named after him, but has been able to find little serious work in the Caribbean. Viv Richards does some, but has had more lucrative contracts in Brunei. It took years for the West Indies to decide how to get Lloyd involved again in the game at home.

One sad consequence of this, according to Cave Hill research, is that some players are no longer concerned if they play cricket in the West Indies again. Their hearts and their minds are elsewhere. Playing for Kent or Gloucestershire seems infinitely preferable to playing the game at home.

None of this makes an England victory a certainty. Lara's captaincy could be a tonic to West Indies' chances of success, especially as some colleagues regard him as a more astute tactician than Walsh. Wasim Akram, who watched Lara struggle to make runs in Pakistan, believes the responsibility of leadership may inspire him to great batting again. And Lara may just be the man to mould the West Indies team into a func-

The players have lost their pride. Their only interest now is in themselves and how much money they can make

tioning unit. Those who disagree with that analysis point to Lara's volatile personality, his tendency to be a disruptive influence and the fact he has been reprimanded by the board on more than one occasion.

Trinidadians, who have named a public square after him and given him a mansion, will support him to the hilt. Jamaicans may not and Walsh might have to be persuaded to play under Lara. Lara's other big problem will be to persuade Ambrose not to chuck it all in and give of his best again against Mike Atherton and his England team. If Lara fails, the consequences for West Indies cricket could be terminal.
★10/1/98

Robert Philip

Salmon rising to the challenge

Brian Clough accused of financial misconduct, Terry Venables banned from the boardroom... Chinese women swimmers pumped so full of drugs they resemble Mao Tse-tung... cannibals running amok on the rugby field; every day, it seems, sport is assailed by yet another scandal. Disheartened? If so, by way of an antidote, may I offer the tale of a genuine sporting hero...

Graham Salmon was six months old when he lost his right eye; a year later, doctors discovered the cancer had spread to the retina of his left eye. They tried blasts of radium, but his tiny eye shrivelled up and it, too, had to be removed. Aged 18 months, he was too little to register the impact of his predicament and grew up never realising others might somehow regard him as handicapped. He wanted to be a runner, so he went out and broke the 100 and 400 metres world records. . . he wanted to be an Olympian, so he skied for Britain in the inaugural Winter Paralympics. . . he wanted to play golf, so he became good enough to beat the Americans at Wentworth in the Stewart Cup (the Ryder Cup for the blind) . . . he wanted to play cricket, so he appeared in an exhibition match at Lord's during the lunch interval of an England-Australia Test match. . . he wanted to be an inspiration to blind children, so he came to be awarded an MBE. . . he wanted to learn the Fosbury Flop, so he developed into an international-class high-jumper. . . he wanted a new challenge, so he ran in - and completed - the London Marathon. . . and all the while he wanted to go on playing football, which is what he was doing with his nephew in the back garden last week even though, having lost both eyes over 40 years ago, he surrendered his left leg to cancer last spring.

"I don't know what pleasure he gets from beating me," grins Salmon mischievously. "Imagine telling your classmates you play football against a 45-year-old one-legged blind man". That grin, a huge, 100-megawatt beam of delight which lights up a room and sends the heart soaring, accompanies Salmon throughout life. "You've put on a bit of weight," I inform him while idly leafing through a scrapbook detailing his greatest triumphs. "I'm exactly the same weight today as I was back then," he replies in a tone of outrage, "ten-and-a-half stones. I'm missing a leg, of course, but my weight has remained steady. . ." "So you're a keen football fan. Who do you support?" "Arsenal - and don't dare say it, I've used the line myself a million times; when you spend your Saturday afternoons at Highbury, being blind can be a blessing."

Being a blind Arsenal fan is one of the few blessings fate has seen fit to bestow upon Graham Salmon; deprived of sight almost from birth, in 1993 he was found to be suffering from leukaemia (the disease is presently in remission), before his next great battle with cancer began. His left leg and part of his pelvis have already been amputated, and he has just finished a course of chemotherapy to combat a tumour in his right leg and cancerous nodules on his lung.

Reduced to moving around his home in Loughton, Essex, on crutches when his wife, Marie, is at work, Salmon is temporarily housebound - "I don't have a free hand at the moment to hold my white stick so I can't get out unless there's someone here to push my wheelchair" - but refuses to accept the notion that the cancer has finally succeeded in terminating his sporting career. "I'll definitely play golf again," insists Salmon, the only blind player to shoot a hole-in-one in competition, and with a best round of 103 to his credit. "But because I've lost part of my pelvis, I may have to learn to play all over again on one leg. My coach is tinkering with the idea of building me a modified Zimmer frame, but the R & A may construe that as constructing a stance. I may even return to high jumping but I won't know how easy or difficult things will be until I

get fitted with my artificial leg next month. I'd like to think I can add a few more medals to my collection, however."

To date, that collection comprises: 1980 Paralympics - 400 metres bronze; 1981 European Championships - 100m bronze, 400m silver, high jump silver; 1983 European Championships - 400m gold; 1984 Paralympics - 400m bronze; 1985 European Championships - 400m silver. He also set a world record of 11.4sec for the 100m in 1983 and established six world records over 400m.

Behind every medal is the story of Salmon's indomitable will, his courage, his defiance, his cussedness and, above all, his laughter. "I should have won the 400m gold at the '81 Europeans. I broke the world record in the semi-finals, lowering it from 57 seconds to 56.16 in only my third run over the distance. My guide was a German 800m runner who I'd only just met, and when we lined up for the final, he said: 'You went off a bit quick for me in the semis. . . would you mind not going off quite so fast?' And I reckon that's why I finished second to one of the Russians." Salmon was pipped for gold again at the 1985 European Championships in Rome when he rounded the last bend locked in a three-way tussle for the medals. "Cracking race that was. If you can imagine it, there were three of us plus our three sighted guides - that's six of us abreast - coming down the home straight. The Pole on my inside reckoned his guide was slowing him down, so he let go of the strap and ran straight off the track. That left me and a German called Gerd Franke who won by a whisker in a photo-finish. I don't mind now, because Gerd and his family have been over here for a holiday and we've been over to Germany to stay with them. We've become really close friends."

He was an athlete who happened to be blind, not a blind athlete

An avid sports fan from childhood - "although I went to a boarding school for the blind, my parents never, ever let me behave like a blind child so I was encouraged to try everything all the other kids did" - Salmon's early track outings offered little hint of the triumphs to come. "When I left school, physically and mentally handicapped youngsters were expected to throw bean-bags at one another for exercise. The whole thing was a joke, a cruel joke in this country.

"No one had any idea what blind athletes wanted. At the first multi-disabled World Championships at Stoke Mandeville, the 100 metres was run on concrete which was bad enough. But if you're trying to listen to the voice of your caller who's guiding you and suddenly over the Tannoy booms another voice, 'Will the competitors in the paraplegic table-tennis competition please report to the main hall', I don't need to tell you what happens. The 100 metres runners went hurtling all over the place. I think two nearly drowned in the steeplechase water-jump."

Insistent he was an athlete who happened to be blind, not a blind athlete, Salmon employed Ron Murray at Crystal Palace as his coach and launched himself on an unsuspecting sport. "Being blind was almost an irrelevance. I wanted to run and I wanted to run like a 'normal' athlete. I didn't want people thinking here was some poor blind chap out for a bit of exercise because he'd been told it was good therapy. I wanted to be a world record holder and I hope I'm not boasting when I say I was a bit of a pioneer. Before me, no one went to proper coaches. I think seeing what I was achieving and how much I'd improved encouraged the authorities to bring in top coaches like John Bailey and John Anderson."

And so a runner he became; the fastest in the world over 100 and 400 metres before age - not blindness - began to slow him down and he turned to golf in 1987. Now the return of the disease which has tracked him remorselessly since birth has restricted his athletic activity to gentle work-outs in the gym at the bottom of his garden." It sounds funny, but I'm more mobile since I had the leg off. The tumour was so huge, I used to lie in bed all day. Also, the pain was pretty horrendous. I lived for my painkillers, which I took every four hours. Unfortunately, they wore off after two hours so the next couple of hours could be fairly traumatic. Now I'm free of pain, at least I can hop around."

A financial adviser with Abbey National ("who've been absolutely brilliant to me throughout all this"), Salmon divides the long hours of his enforced recuperation either writing his autobiography or completing a CD of his own compositions ("part Eric Clapton, part Mark Knopfler, I like to think") in his recording studio. "So I'm looking for a publisher and a record company willing to take a risk on a complete unknown."

Next month doctors will know whether the latest course of treatment has beaten back the cancer in his right leg and lung. "If it hasn't gone, then they'll need to decide what happens next. But I feel good, I feel healthy and that's the main thing. I've been told that a lot of amputees prefer a wheelchair to an artificial leg but that's no use to a blind person. "I want my new leg to work - it's got to work, because I sure as hell intend playing golf again. I love sport, and just like I've always done I'll make the most of my situation; make the most of what I have got. And a bit more."

★26/1/98

Sue Mott

"I think the media has been very unfair to us and our swimming team" - Chinese swimmer Shan Ying.

The River Runs Red, says the old song. But maybe not anymore. Not at the World Swimming Championships in Perth anyway, where competition got underway with the Chinese team perhaps less the favourites than they were. This has everything to do with the discovery by an alert customs officer at Sydney airport (perhaps long used to checking Ian Botham's luggage before Test tours) of 13 phials of human growth hormone in a Chinese breaststroker's bag.

He is a hero in more ways than he knows. First, he confirmed solid suspicion. When swimmer Chen Yan, in the women's 400m individual medley, lopped 1.31 seconds off the world record at the national championships in Shanghai last October, her coach, Yan Bingyan explained his technique. You just take a swirl of date soup, a pinch of ginseng root and add a gelatin extract from a donkey hide, he said. Oh yeah, that one. Delia Smith recommends it on Christmas pudding. I'm afraid that the world added a pinch of salt to the mixture and now it would seem we were right. For along with a magic of turtle blood and fricassee of caterpillar eyeball, or whatever it was, it seems the Chinese have been dabbling in that least romantic of substances - the performance-enhancing drug.

Despite official (and very belated) Chinese denials - "sheer fabrication" - that this must explain why Chinese women came from nowhere to win 12 of 16 medals at the 1994 World Championships in Rome, you'd have to be a contortionist to twist yourself into a position to believe them. Most of their rival swimmers don't. So, good, cheats are exposed but that is not the end of our customs officer's heroic contribution. As more and more Stasi files reveal their vile secrets, the full consequences of drug enhancement in women becomes apparent. For reasons certainly too medically complicated for my unenhanced brain, the female body responds more dramatically to hormone treatment.

This explains why Chinese men have lagged behind their women and why a succession of horror stories from behind the old Iron Curtain have predominantly involved women. One former East German athlete fell down the stairs and broke her leg in 100 places following the early onset of osteoporosis. Three former athletes all produced children with physical deformities. Heidi Krieger has just undergone a sex change. Together, it is evidence of a rampant abuse of women of which poor Yuan Yuan, the phial carrier, is the latest example. And how many girls will it deter from sport? If losing to a bunch of doped-up Power Rangers is the only challenge swimming represents you can hardly be surprised if the sport gets relegated to what you do on your summer holidays in an unsuitable bikini.

The villain of the piece has not yet stood up: the particular 'piece' being the rather large and bloodied chunk of earlobe that the London Scottish flanker, Simon Fenn, found missing from his person during the match with Bath. I mean, he must have noticed, the perpetrator. It's not every day you tuck into your opponent even if tea is a long way off. Perhaps he is planning a joint venture with Mike Tyson to open a trendy eaterie for cannibals and wants to keep the thing quiet. Anyway, efforts should be made to trace him if only because he might be straying from the healthy, high-energy diet recommended by the club's nutritionist. If rugby doesn't find him, it will be a shambles.

....

It seems the Chinese have been dabbling in that least romantic of substances - the performance-enhancing drug

....

When poor old Carrick of the Glasgow and District Division One ("not quite as low as you can get, but not far off", said a member of their committee) are being threatened with a ban for the rest of the season for a player blowing a kiss at an opponent, it is clear the disciplinary structure is askew. Carrick only had four players sent off between 1994 and 1997. Unfortunately, of course, in 1991, all 16 forwards were sent off during a match-cum-Armageddon with Glasgow University and last month the kiss-blowing incident against Birkmyre was not entirely unrelated to the 77 minutes' worth of ballistics that had gone before. Nevertheless, they have every right to feel aggrieved if the SRU are heavy-handed in their punishment. "We're no more aggressive than a lot of clubs," said the Carrick hooker Jim McGill. "A few weeks back I turned out against Strathclyde Police and it was bloody murder. What's a kiss after all?" If I know the women who play for Wests Rugby Club in Glasgow that's the very least they expect from their referees. In fact, there's probably not an officiator of their matches in all Scotland who wouldn't regard a mutilated earlobe as a lucky escape.

★12/1/98

January 1998

Teddy Sheringham stretches to dispossess Chelsea's Andy Myers during Manchester United's 5-3 FA Cup victory at Stamford Bridge •**Russell Cheyne**

John Parsons

Wills dominated the Wimbledon of her era

Helen Wills Moody, who so seldom showed emotion on court, even when winning Wimbledon eight times between 1927-38, that she became known as `Little Miss Poker Face', has died in a convalescence home in Carmel, California, aged 91.

The American, who was almost as invincible in her time as Suzanne Lenglen had been immediately before her, set a record at The Championships which lasted until Martina Navratilova won her ninth and last singles title there in 1990. One could almost sense a note of relief from the last surviving pre-war women's champion when it happened. Mrs Roark, as she had become in 1939, mainly kept in touch with tennis from what she was able to follow on television at home.

When I telephoned her a few days before that Navratilova triumph, she said: "Records are made to be broken, and I'm surprised this one has lasted so long. Martina is a splendid player and if she can win once again on what is such a specialised surface, she'll certainly deserve it."

Helen learnt her tennis at the Berkeley Tennis Club after her father, a physician, decided that a membership there would be a suitable 14th birthday present. It was not long before her studious, disciplined approach to life and her exceptional qualities of concentration blossomed.

From the earliest days as a junior champion to her many battles with "the other Helen" - Jacobs - her on-court appearance seldom changed: white sailor suit, white eyeshade, white shoes and stockings. She first played at Wimbledon in 1924, won five matches, but then lost the final to Britain's Kitty McKane, whose extra experience tamed the right-handed groundstroke power Wills was developing from practising almost exclusively against men.

"I never remembered any of the matches I won, only those I lost"

Although contemporaries, Lenglen and Wills met only once. It was in 1926, when Lenglen was thought to be at her peak. Lenglen won one of the most famous matches ever, but it effectively marked the end of her career and confirmed Wills, the Californian, still only 20, as the rightful successor as the finest player in women's tennis. In those days, as Wills recalled, it took a week to travel by train from California to New York, and another five days on the boat on which she said: "We would dance all the way across the Atlantic."

Helen Wills at Wimbledon in 1935 •**Popperfoto**

James Thurber, the American humorist, once described the Lenglen-Wills showdown on the French Riviera in February that year as "the battle of the century". Journalists poured in from all over the world. People living nearby sold space on the roofs of their homes overlooking the Carlton Club in Cannes to those who could not get seats. It is thought to have been the first tennis match to fetch blackmarket prices. The film rights were sold for £60,000. Lenglen won 8-6, 6-3, but was so exhausted that she sat down and cried with relief. Wills went on to dominate women's tennis for the next nine years.

In a six-year spell she did not lose a set in the French, US or Wimbledon championships. In 1935 she was match point down at 2-5 in the third set against Jacobs who, distracted by a gust of wind, lost the point, her nerve and the final. Not that Wills recalled the incident. "I never remembered any of the matches I won, only those I lost," she told me. Besides Wimbledon, Wills won the US title seven times and the French four. It was once said of her: "She never smiled - but nor did she ever frown." Tennis today did not seem to her to be as much fun."

"I kept on for so many years because I enjoyed it," she said not too long ago. "I often ask myself whether I'd have been so happy playing tennis today."

★3 / 1/ 98

END COLUMN

Giles Smith

Many sheepish returns

Football Diary:

●Another Mark Twainesque moment this week when the premature demise of Eoin Hand, the former Republic of Ireland manager, was exaggerated out of all proportion in an evening newspaper on the south coast. The newspaper had wrung heart-felt eulogies from associates to compile a page of tributes.

The Daily Telegraph, always keen for accuracy, telephoned Hand's address to check the story. "Is this a social call or are you telling me I'm up for the Manchester United job?" asked the voice at the other end of the phone, unaware that he had been written off in a big way.

Our reporter hastily moved on to a discussion about the weather, and it was not until later that Hand discovered the true nature of the call when other messages of condolence started to filter through. Like Twain, Hand, 52, laughs off the incident: he is in rude health and contines as an analyst for RTE television's football coverage.

●The announcement of the sponsors' man of the match is often greeted with derision: the selection for Swindon's match against Ipswich merely caused bewilderment. Littlecote Farm Partners chose Kevin Watson. One problem: Kevin Watson wasn't playing.

Apparently some of the women in the sponsors' lounge had seen Watson's photograph in the programme and thought he looked "cute". Fortunately Sir Seton Wills, a club director who is involved with the sponsors, spotted the error and persuaded them to nominate George Ndah instead.

Sport Around The World:

●Evel Knievel, the world's most famous daredevil motorcycle rider, has undergone hip replacement surgery in Florida three weeks after being injured. No, he was not hurt trying to jump over a row of buses or riding the wall of death. . . he was playing golf. Knievel, 59, stumbled into a creek bed somewhere on the back nine.

●Gridiron lost one of its few intellectuals, as well as a top coach, when Marv Levy, 72, retired at the Buffalo Bills. When Dallas coach Jimmy Johnson gloated over Levy's fourth Super Bowl loss, a thrashing by the Cowboys, that: "My players are belly-laughing to the Flintstones while he's reading his guys Shakespeare", Levy replied: "There should never be any shame in intelligence."

●A contender for the United States Olympic team was disqualified from a college race when he finished naked. As soon as Matt Zelen dived into the pool at Collegeville, Minnesota, to start the 100-yard butterfly, he realised he had forgotten to tie his trunks. They were soon around his ankles, and he kicked them off before racing on to finish two seconds clear of his rivals. But Zelen was stripped of his victory for not wearing the correct attire. Zelen would have won more easily - he was laughing so hard he forgot to breathe for almost the whole first length. "It was hilarious, but it's too bad so many people were there," Zelen said. He carried on because it was the butterfly, and added: "If it had been the backstroke, I obviously would have stopped."

Letters To The Sports Editor:

●SIR - I am in full agreement with Henry Winter in his description of the unusually powerful effect that gravity seems to have on David Ginola while indulging in the lightest of contacts with opponents. Curiously, an anagram of David Ginola is: "O! A lad diving." - MICHAEL TULLY, Northolt, Middlesex.

This week one man and his dog celebrated the beginning of its twenty-first series. Just think of it: 21 years. If the sheep aren't knackered by now, they never will be.

At the top of the programme, Robin Page, our presenter, had a little semi-rehearsed exchange with Gus Dermody, the Alan Hansen of sheepdog trialling, in order to bring into focus some of the changes witnessed by the sport and the world around it in those two decades. And who better to fill us in than these two men of the country, as signalled immediately by their garb? Robin was wearing a leather jerkin which could probably have stopped bullets, while Gus stood before us in a thick tweed suit which seemed to have been woven from a selection of pickles and chutneys.

Gus mentioned "the improvement in the dogs" in the lifetime of the programme and congratulated the series for "bringing sheepdog trialling right into everybody's home". Not literally, of course, which could play havoc with the carpets, but one took the point. Gus also happily noted how the sport had been largely unaffected by the increasing sophistication of rough-terrain vehicles, a development which some feared would limit the work for dogs, not to mention bringing sheep house prices down to new lows.

To no small extent, the programme itself embodies a sterling resistance to the advance of technology. Traditional crafts inform it through and through. This is not just because it invites us to take pleasure in watching a dog cause seven sheep to pass through a gate, though, as on-screen spectacles go, this is bound to look ambitiously under-stated in the age of the computer game.

Consider in addition its method for showing us the intended course - this one was a small green slice of Wildboarclough in Cheshire. Not for *One Man and His Dog* one of those Formula One-style computer-generated simulations, offering us a sheep's eye view of three-dimensional fetch gates and shedding rings. Gus just points with a pen at a drawing on an easel. The drawing, you may notice, has a rather nice, bevelled wooden frame. But the world is out there, and Gus and Robin know it. Word is the sport has been all but obliterated in highly litigious America because of the increasing likelihood that a sheep will sue for harassment. Also, Robin and Gus were tastefully silent on the whole controversial topic of sheep-cloning, whose repercussions for *One Man and His Dog* are potentially myriad. And if the scientists move on to sheepdog-cloning, then it is clear that both the sport and the programme are going to be in big trouble.

Yet Robin asked a question behind which one sensed in advance a slight tinge of despair. "So when people say sheepdog trialling is dead on its feet, they're wrong?" "Yes," Gus replied, as somehow one knew he would. "Most definitely."

These days the sport does not exist which isn't worried for its profile, its public image, its share of the market-place. Big, unwieldy - and perhaps, finally, unhelpful - questions about 'the state of the game' hang over sheepdog trialling in the same way that they hang over darts. These two sports have more in common than you might think, in fact, with their television-inspired boom years receding into the past and no sign of another explosion. Darts and sheepdogs both once tweaked the nation's curiosity, but then the nation moved on to other things. "Darts has become so popular in Holland," observed Tony Green, with just the hint of a sigh in his voice, commentating for the BBC at the Lakeside Country Club and Sky Sports have just checked out at Purfleet. Whatever the broader issues, darts occupies our screens at this time of year like at no other.

As ever, the contrast is educational. With the weather outside playing up wildly, Dougie Donelly for the BBC referred briefly to "windswept Surrey" and left it at that. Jeff Stelling, for Sky, meanwhile, was telling us: "If you're not coming here, please heed that police advice. Stay at home. Because these semi-finals will be worth watching." Which was a slightly loose interpretation of the police warning, but driven, one felt, by uncontainable enthusiasm.

Sky also have Sid Waddell, who is a one-man argument for purchasing a satellite dish. Hyperbolic and over-excited a lot of the time, Sid yet retains a sense of proportion about his role. He brought to an end a lengthy spell of

·····································

Gus stood before us in a thick tweed suit which seemed to have been woven from a selection of pickles and chutneys

·····································

being wise after the event - the commentator's curse - with his partner, John Gwynne, by suddenly saying: "We'd be in the first team at the Retrospective Arms." That showed class.

At the BBC's Frimley Green, there's no amplified thud when the dart hits the board and the noise from the crowd is mixed low. It's not hard to work out which party you would rather be at. Sky Sports and darts go together like a horse and carriage. The sport itself is so doggedly bare of embellishment, and Sky so keen to embellish it with smoke, music and girls in bikinis carrying flags, that the resulting television, as well as being permanently on the edge of comedy, starts to look like an act of defiance. As Robin Page might have said: "So when people say darts is dead on its feet, they're wrong?" And Gus Dermody would have shaken his walking stick and said: "Yes. Most definitely."

★5/ 1/ 98

Martin Johnson

Harry Ganja, a lay double tuck and arbiters from Azerbaijan

The Winter Olympics may lack the glamour of the summer Games, but Nagano certainly had its moments

The first in-flight video on the All Nippon Airways flight out of Heathrow featured a classroom of Japanese schoolchildren engaged in such an orgy of celebration you could only assume that either double maths had been cancelled, or the headmaster had performed a triple toe-loop on a banana skin. However, it soon became apparent that their riotous applause was directed at a former pupil who had just won a bronze medal in the Olympic ski jumping. This promptly conjured up a vision of an equivalent presentation on British Airways, namely, a man slumped comatose in front of a TV set at three o'clock in the morning, while the grey silhouette of a Norwegian biathlete flickered dimly through a blizzard, accompanied by intermittent hooting on an alpine horn.

The BBC will have broadcast 100 hours of Winter Olympics after the closing ceremony, conceivably in the belief that a sleeping army of curling addicts lurked somewhere out there, but more probably because satellite and ITV have made so many raids on the sporting vaults that there was precious little else left for them. Even for the biggest TV players of them all, the United States, viewing figures are down, largely due to the fact that these Games have been conspicuously short on soap opera.

Four years ago, in Lillehammer, the Nancy Kerrigan-Tonya Harding feud climaxed with a US TV audience bettered only by two Super Bowls and the final episode of *MASH*. Anxious for more of the same, attempts to build up a Michelle Kwan-Tara Lipinski rivalry have foundered on the fact that both girls exude more saccharin than a three-year-old Shirley Temple. The American media have thus been reduced to in-depth revelations about the 15-year-old Lipinski's experiments with make-up, and her off-ice relaxation sessions in the Olympic Village's embroidery class.

In an era in which gold medals are as much the work of the pharmaceutical industry than the training ground, the only hint of scandal in Nagano has been the marijuana-related exploits of a Canadian snowboarder. And even this has raised nothing more than a giggle, not least because Canada's freestyle skiing judge goes by the name of Harry Ganja.

Apart from the lopsided influence of technology - hinged skate blades, parabolic skis and aerodynamic bits of rubber stuck on to skate suits - one thing that makes the Winter Olympics less of a turn on than its summer counterpart is the fact that so many events are decided by judges. Not so much *Citius, Altius, Fortius*, as what some anonymous arbiter from Azerbaijan thinks of your mid-air separation, or whether the sequins on Michelle's dress are more eye-catching than Tara's.

Nevertheless, the on-site enthusiasm here has been overwhelming. Huge parties of Japanese make two to three-hour bus trips into the mountains (generally to be informed that the giant slalom has been postponed again) and touts, including a well co-ordinated outfit from Liverpool shouting "ticketo!" as each bus disgorges its passengers, have been asking treble for tickets costing as much as £180 for the ice hockey final. Just about everything in Nagano is recyclable, there is no litter, and a ski-run was moved in order not to disturb the local buzzard population. Their official Games motto is "Homage to Nature", the theme of which is "caring about plant and animal life", although how these laudable sentiments quite square with Japan's ambition to harpoon every whale in the ocean is not entirely apparent.

Mind you, in terms of slow death,

DAY BY DAY REVIEW

1: Petr Korda moves to No 2 in the world after comfortably beating Marcelo Rios in straight sets in the Australian Open final.

4: Two goals by Alan Shearer end Stevenage's resistance in the FA Cup, though the non-Leaguers are far from humiliated in a 2-1 defeat at Newcastle.

5: Chris Sutton withdraws from the England B squad to play Chile, thus leaving his international future in doubt.

7: England open their Five Nations campaign with a 24-17 defeat in Paris, while Scotland win 17-16 in Dublin.

8: Greg Norman wins the tournament which bears his name, by two shots from Jose-Maria Olazabal, in Sydney. Greg Rusedski maintains his two-year record of never having his serve broken, but still loses in the Croatian Open final to Goran Ivanisevic.

9: Carl Hooper hits an unbeaten 94 to carry the West Indies to a three-wicket victory over England in the second Test. Lawrie McMenemy is appointed manager of Northern Ireland.

10: The RFU ban Bath's Kevin Yates for six months for the incident in which Simon Fenn, of London Scottish, had his earlobe bitten; Yates maintains his innocence.

11: Michael Owen becomes, at 18 years 59 days, the youngest player to be capped by England, who lose 2-0 to Chile at Wembley.

12: Chelsea sack manager Ruud Gullit, obstensibly over a contract dispute, and replace him with the Italian Gianluca Vialli. Ross Rebagliati is reinstated as winner of the snowboarding Olympic gold on a legal technicality.

13: Andy Caddick and Angus Fraser take five wickets apiece as England dismiss West Indies for 159 on the first day of the third Test in Port of Spain.

15: South Africa's Pat Symcox (108) becomes only the third No 10 batsman to score a century in a Test match, and his ninth-wicket partnership of 195 with Mark Boucher, against Pakistan in Johannesburg, is a Test record. Rangers announce that Dick Advocaat will take over as manager from Walter Smith in May.

17: England square the Caribbean series with a three-wicket win in Port of Spain, their 226 for seven the 11th time in Test history that the largest score in a Test has come in the fourth innings.

19: Lou Macari loses his breach of contract claim against Celtic after they sacked him as manager in 1994.

20: Tara Lipinski becomes the youngest Winter Olympic champion when she wins the figure skating title. The Five Nations agree to become six with Italy voted on board.

21: Britain claim their first medal at the Winter Olympics, a bronze in the four-man bobsleigh. England record their highest points total in a Five Nations match in beating Wales 60-26 at Twickenham, while France are 51-16 winners against Scotland at Murrayfield.

23: The FA suspend referee Dermot Gallagher for one match because his performance in the Arsenal v Chelsea game was not up to standard.

24: On a day of departures, Brian Little quits as manager of Aston Villa, and Brian Ashton resigns as Ireland's rugby coach.

25: John Gregory takes over as Aston Villa manager.

19

harpooning is marginally preferable to watching the 10,000 metres speed skating, which begins with a series of tension-building announcements ("Attention, the ice temperature is 5.5...") and is followed by sumo-thighed people dressed in Spiderman suits skating in circles for the thick end of a quarter of an hour.

The short-track skating is more exciting, not least because they race against people rather than a stop-watch, and when it comes to taking out opponents on a bend, there are one or two Michael Schumachers out there. Britain actually had a surprise heat qualifier in Matthew Jasper, who was gliding around in last place when three skaters in front all flew off the ice. It's dangerous too, and after a nasty accident some years ago, they now have to wear special neck and wrist guards to protect the major arteries against flying blades. This is in direct contrast to the 10,000 metres, where it is the spectators who need the protection in case they have an overpowering urge to open a vein.

In terms of excitement, though, there was nothing to match the women's aerials, where America, as usual, won the gold medal for naff banner of the Games: "We love you Nagano - go USA!" And the pressure on the Americans to "go!" was illustrated by a man in a Stars-and-Stripes anorak behaving as though he had just concluded a passive smoking session with the Canadian snowboarders. This turned out to be the fiance of the first-round leader, Nikki Stone, who was hyper-ventilating as Stone lined up her second jump. Fists clenched, sweating profusely, and shouting "C'mon girl", he then reacted to Stone's gold-medal leap by making a noise like a howling coyote and leaping the fence into the competitors' enclosure. Turning to the crowd he bellowed "Ar-some! Ar-some!" It was unclear whether he was referring to Stone or himself, but in either case, ar-some was right.

The boyfriend was then besieged by American reporters, while Stone's parents were hauled in front of the CBS cameras. Stone blubbed so hard she melted the snow, before finally giving the media the quotes all America was waiting for. "I just can't believe it," she sobbed. "It's just so impossible."

Stone's winning jump was something called a lay full double tuck, which involves a 40-foot leap into the air, a series of backward flips, twists and somersaults and, not least, landing the right way up. Other competitors wimped out with kids' stuff called the lay tuck and the lay lay, which is the sort of thing you and I can pull off in icy weather, merely by taking to an ungritted pavement wearing leather soles.

Having filed their Nikki Stone quotes, the Americans stampeded off to the ice rink, where the Olympic kissing championships, sponsored by Interflora, were taking place. Its official title was the ladies' ice skating short programme, in which Michelle and Tara were doing battle, partly on the ice, but mostly (after all, once you've seen one triple toe-loop you've seen them all) off it. First, there was the contest to see which girl would have most flowers thrown at them at the end of their programme (they're all recycled back to the audience, incidentally) after

which they kissed all the flower collectors, hugged their coaches, and retired to a booth containing even more flora in order to be judged for artistic impression. Blubbing uncontrollably can earn you a full set of 5.9s, while the compulsory element in the programme - waving at the camera while clutching a cuddly toy - is another crucial factor in the judges' deliberations.

Tara's performance led to a ferocious scrum in the interview room, where you could barely make out a squeaky voice somewhere behind a sea of bodies. You wouldn't have got a glimpse of Michael Jordan, never mind Tara, who towers to all of 4ft 10in out of her skates. One American reporter, arriving late, grabbed another as they dashed for the media centre. "What d'she say?"

After safely negotiating the first three gates, Carrick went one way, Anderson the other and the hyphen went straight through the pole

"Dunno. Something about being on a cloud."

Finally, there were the Brits. Their fortunes were summed up by the women's slalom, in which Emma Carrick-Anderson, having prepared for four years, lasted four seconds before wiping herself out on the fourth set of poles. After safely negotiating the first three gates, Carrick went one way, Anderson the other and the hyphen went straight through the pole.

The British Olympic Association issued their athletes with a list of helpful phrases, such as "kibun go varui desu", which means "I don't feel well" and is close enough to "I'm as sick as a parrot" to have proved highly useful. One glaring omission, however, was the Japanese for "Can you send for an ambulance and a plough? The pair of skis sticking out of that snowdrift belong to the British No 1".

Why anyone should expect Britain, with no funding or facilities to speak of, to win medals in the Winter Olympics is a mystery, and the biggest giggle of all is the BOA's tough new qualification policy, supposedly to weed out 'passengers'. At least we used to have some characters, as we were constantly reminded by the most-asked question of these Games. "Prease, where Eddie Eagroo?" Where indeed?
★21/ 2 / 98

Bryon Butler

Football League lay foundations for their celebration of 100 years

" Put any group of football fans together, and sooner or later, the conversation turns to who was the greatest player of all time," says Sepp Blatter. Well, here goes ....

By the time this season is over, 126 clubs will have played around 155,000 games and scored more than 450,000 goals in the Football League, and their promising offspring, the Premiership. Next season - and we can be precise about this - will also be their 100th.

The League, mindful of their seniority, jealous of their traditions and determined to emphasise their venerable place in sporting society, intend to raise a glass or two to the occasion. Jack the Ripper was lurking, Wyatt Earp shooting, Vincent Van Gogh painting and Florence Nightingale caring when the League kicked off on Sept 8, 1888 − since when, after being rudely interrupted by two world wars, they have retained their robust constitution, despite losing their head.

The 100th season will be marked, it has been decided, with dignity and charity in mind. There will be a match, a 'do' or two, a few souvenirs and, yes, some rolls of honour. Lists are currently very popular. In fact, Sepp Blatter, the general secretary of FIFA, the game's governing body, has just been extolling the fascination of lists. Great, greater, greatest . . .

"Put any group of football fans together," he says, "and sooner or later, the conversation will turn to the same subject: who was the greatest player of all time. It is a provocative exercise."

The Football League, undaunted, are in the process of selecting 100 national legends of their own - and then another 100 'local' legends. The difference is sometimes a little fine but always valid. 'Dixie' Dean, Stanley Matthews and George Best, for example, were undoubtedly national heroes, while John Trollope and Joe Payne are legends of the more local variety - and none bigger.

Trollope played 770 games for Swindon between 1960-80, a record total for one club, while Payne scored 10 goals, another record which still stands, in Luton's 12-0 walloping of Bristol Rovers on a bitterly cold Easter Monday in 1936. Payne was a reserve wing-half who was playing at centre-forward for the first time in his career on that famous afternoon; and, the following season, he scored 55 goals, one more record, in 39 games in the Third Division South. Sixty or so years on, Luton's sponsors now sip their ale or tea in the Joe Payne Lounge at Kenilworth Road.

Tom Finney, Billy Wright, Bobby Moore and Bill Nicholson are others who have stands or

Some players deserve to be on a list all by themselves. The splendidly named Albert Hall was one

suites named after them, while a few more are even venerated by statues. One is being planned for Duncan Edwards, who already figures in a stained-glass window of a church in Dudley. Selection of both kinds of legend is going to involve much argument; and the Football League hope to involve local papers, radio and club programmes in encouraging supporters to nominate their local heroes.

Some players deserve to be on a list all by themselves. The splendidly named Albert Hall was one - no relation to Festival Hall, Carnegie Hall or any Hall of Fame. He was Tottenham's top scorer in the last season before the Second World War. He managed 10 goals, which was one more than the brilliant Willie Hall (again no relation) who did, however, score seven in only five matches for England that same season. Albert Hall clearly had prospects. But then came war; and Hall, a Welshman, was captured by the Japanese and forced to work on the Burma railway. His ship was torpedoed while he was being transferred with 2,000 other prisoners to Japan, and he spent six days surviving shark attacks before becoming one of a small number rescued by an American submarine. At the end of the war, he played eight more League games for Tottenham and then nine for Plymouth - but never managed another goal. He has just died, aged 79.

Another list has closed, too. George Male, a member of Herbert Chapman's great Arsenal side of the Thirties, has died at the age of 87. Male, an East Londoner, was a defender of undentable stability and with Eddie Hapgood, a volatile character, formed one of the most famous full-back combinations of all. Both, in fact, captained England and both will be pushing for a place among the League's 100 legends. It says much for Chapman's side that Alex James, Cliff Bastin and David Jack will also be contenders - James, naturally, a certainty.

But the very first name on the list, chronologically, is bound to be a Londoner who made his name in Scotland and then played for Preston, Derby and England. He was Johnny Goodall, a centre-forward and star of the Preston side who won the first League championship of all without losing a game and, that same season, 1888-89, the FA Cup without conceding a goal. He has been described as "the pioneer of scientific professional play". Preston were known as the 'Invincibles' and Johnny Goodall himself was affectionately known as 'Johnny Allgood'. He'll do.

★25 / 2 / 98

League Legends

John Goodall	*Preston, Derby, New Brighton, Glossop, 1888–1904*
Billy Bassett	*West Brom, 1888–1900*
Archie Hunter	*Aston Villa, 1888–1891*
Steve Bloomer	*Derby, Middlesbrough, 1892-1915*
Billy Meredith	*Northwich, Man City, Man Utd, 1893-1925*
Bob Crompton	*Blackburn, 1896-1921*
Billy Foulke	*Sheffield Utd, Chelsea, Bradford, 1894-1908*
Alf Common	*Sunderland, Sheff Utd, Middlesbrough, Arsenal, Preston, 1900-1915*
Sam Hardy	*Chesterfield, Liverpool, Aston Villa, Nottingham Forest, 1902-1926*
Bill McCracken	*Newcastle, 1904-1924*
Viv Woodward	*Tottenham, Chelsea, 1908-1915*
Clem Stephenson	*Aston Villa, Huddersfield, 1910-1930*
Charles Buchan	*Sunderland, Arsenal, 1910-1929*
Elisha Scott	*Liverpool, 1912-1934*
Dixie Dean	*Tranmere, Everton, Notts Co, 1923-1939*
George Camsell	*Durham, Middlesbrough, 1924-1939*
Hughie Gallagher	*Newcastle, Chelsea, Derby, Notts County, Grimsby, Gateshead, 1925-1939*
Harry Hibbs	*Birmingham, Bristol C, 1925-1939*
Alex James	*Preston, Arsenal, 1925-1938*
Eddie Hapgood	*Arsenal, 1927-1939*
Cliff Bastin	*Exeter, Arsenal, 1927-1948*
Wilf Copping	*Leeds, Arsenal, 1930-1939*
David Jack	*Plymouth, Bolton, Arsenal, 1930-1935*
Stanley Matthews	*Stoke, Blackpool, 1931-1966*
Ted Drake	*Southampton, Arsenal, 1931-1939*
Joe Mercer	*Everton, Arsenal, 1932-1954*
Raich Carter	*Sunderland, Derby, Hull, 1932-1953*
Peter Doherty	*Blackpool, Man City, Derby, Huddersfield, Doncaster, 1933-1954*
Frank Swift	*Man City, 1933-1951*
Tommy Lawton	*Burnley, Everton, Chelsea, Notts Co, Brentford, Arsenal, 1935-1957*
Wilf Mannion	*Middlesbrough, Hull, 1936-1956*
George Hardwick	*Middlesbrough, Oldham, 1937-1956*
Johnny Carey	*Man Utd, 1937-1954*
Stan Mortensen	*Blackpool, Hull, Southport, 1938-1958*
Neil Franklin	*Stoke, Hull, Crewe, Stockport, 1946-1958*
Trevor Ford	*Swansea, Aston Villa, Sunderland, Cardiff, Newport, 1946-1961*
Nat Lofthouse	*Bolton, 1946-1961*
Tom Finney	*Preston, 1946-1960*
Alf Ramsey	*Southampton, Tottenham, 1946-1955*
Len Shackleton	*Bradford PA, Newcastle, Sunderland, 1946-1958*
Jimmy Dickinson	*Portsmouth, 1946-1965*
Arthur Rowley	*West Brom, Fulham, Leicester, Shrewsbury, 1946-1965*
Billy Liddell	*Liverpool, 1946-1961*
Billy Wright	*Wolves, 1946-1959*
Jackie Milburn	*Newcastle, 1946-1957*
John Charles	*Leeds, Cardiff, 1948-1966*
Ivor Allchurch	*Swansea, Newcastle, Cardiff, 1948-1968*
Danny Blanchflower	*Barnsley, Aston Villa, Tottenham, 1948-1964*
Bert Trautmann	*Man City, 1949-1964*

Jimmy McIlroy	*Burnley, Stoke, Oldham, 1950-1968*
Tommy Taylor	*Barnsley, Man Utd, 1950-1958*
Cliff Jones	*Swansea, Tottenham, Fulham, 1952-1970*
Johnny Haynes	*Fulham, 1952-1970*
Duncan Edwards	*Man Utd, 1953-1958*
Jimmy Armfield	*Blackpool, 1954-1971*
Terry Paine	*Southampton, Hereford, 1956-1977*
Bobby Charlton	*Man Utd, Preston, 1956-1975*
Jimmy Greaves	*Chelsea, Tottenham, West Ham, 1957-1971*
Denis Law	*Huddersfield, Man City, Man Utd 1956-1974*
Gordon Banks	*Chesterfield, Leicester, Stoke, 1958-1973*
Dave Mackay	*Tottenham, Derby, Swindon, 1958-1972*
Bobby Moore	*West Ham, Fulham, 1958-1977*
Alan Mullery	*Tottenham, Fulham, 1958-1976*
Geoff Hurst	*West Ham, Stoke, West Brom, 1959-1976*
Nobby Stiles	*Man Utd, Middlesbrough, Preston, 1959-1974*
Johnny Giles	*Man Utd, Leeds, West Brom, 1959-1977*
Billy Bremner	*Leeds, Hull, Doncaster, 1959-1982*
Frank McLintock	*Leicester, Arsenal, QPR, 1959-1977*
Alex Young	*Everton, Stockport, 1960-1969*
Martin Peters	*West Ham, Tottenham, Norwich, Sheff Utd, 1960-1981*
Tommy Smith	*Liverpool, Swansea, 1962-1979*
Norman Hunter	*Leeds, Bristol C, Barnsley, 1962-1983*
Pat Jennings	*Watford, Tottenham, Arsenal, 1962-1985*
Alan Ball	*Blackpool, Everton, Arsenal, Southampton, Bristol Rov, 1962-1984*
Colin Bell	*Bury, Man City, 1963-1979*
George Best	*Man Utd, Stockport, Fulham, Bournemouth, 1963-1983*
Peter Shilton	*Leicester, Stoke, Nottm For, Southampton, Derby, Plymouth, Bolton, Leyton Orient, 1965-1997*
Ray Clemence	*Scunthorpe, Liverpool, Tottenham, 1965-1988*
Malcolm Macdonald	*Fulham, Luton, Newcastle, Arsenal, 1968-1977*
Kevin Keegan	*Scunthorpe, Liverpool, Southampton, Newcastle, 1968-1984*
Trevor Francis	*Birmingham, Nottm For, Man City, QPR, Sheff Wed 1970-1995*
Graeme Souness	*Middlesbrough, Liverpool, 1972-1984*
Liam Brady	*Arsenal, West Ham, 1973-1990*
Glenn Hoddle	*Tottenham, Swindon, Chelsea, 1974-1996*
Bryan Robson	*West Brom, Man Utd, Middlesbrough 1974-1997*
Alan Hansen	*Liverpool, 1977-1990*
Kenny Dalglish	*Liverpool, 1977-1990*
Gary Lineker	*Leicester, Everton, Tottenham 1978-1993*
Ian Rush	*Chester, Liverpool, Leeds, Newcastle, 1978-1998*
Ossie Ardiles	*Tottenham, Blackburn, QPR, Swindon, 1978-1990*
Neville Southall	*Bury, Port Vale, Everton, Stoke, 1980-1998*
Paul McGrath	*Man Utd, Aston Villa, Derby, 1981-1998*
John Barnes	*Watford, Liverpool, Newcastle, 1981-1998*
Tony Adams	*Arsenal, 1983-1998*
Paul Gascoigne	*Newcastle, Tottenham, Middlesbrough, 1984-1998*
Alan Shearer	*Southampton, Blackburn, Newcastle, 1987-1998*
Ryan Giggs	*Man Utd, 1990-1998*
Eric Cantona	*Leeds, Man Utd, 1991-1997*
Peter Schmeichel	*Man Utd, 1991-1998*
Dennis Bergkamp	*Arsenal, 1995-1998*

February 1998

That's torn it... England's Garath Archer in the heat of battle against South Africa at Twickenham •**Russell Cheyne**★29/11/97

Andrew Baker

Holding retains art of perfect delivery

Sky's cricket coverage has been exemplary while the cameras have been focused on the pitch. But the cameramen are still afflicted with wandering eyes, and the director continues to encourage them. Thus, when there is a moment to spare between pacy off-cutters and blistering drives, the screen will suddenly be filled with racy cut-off tops and blistering thighs. Furthermore, when the players take a drinks break, the commentators reflect on their weekend breaks. We have been treated to the

....

His contributions are delivered in a wonderfully resonant, relaxed bass. The sound of hot, dark, spiced rum

....

sight of a bikini-clad lovely sashaying down a tropical beach accompanied, incongruously, by a voice-over from Bob Willis on the delights of his favourite Tobagan hideaway. (Tobagan as in the Caribbean island, that is, rather than the Alpine A-to-B device. For winter sports, see below). But we will forgive these passing aberrations, for they are more than compensated for by the diet of gripping cricket, especially when it is described in the delicious lilting tones of Michael Holding.

When Holding was in his pomp as a peerless fast bowler, his gloriously graceful run-up to the wicket and lethal pace earned him the nickname 'Whispering Death'. Luckily for the viewers, he does not whisper in the commentary box: his contributions are delivered in a wonderfully res-

onant, relaxed bass. The sound of hot, dark, spiced rum. Surely there will not be a sexier voice in sports commentary until the BBC see the error of their ways and sign up Mariella Frostrup to describe the ice dance at the Winter Olympics in Nagano.

Instead, the Corporation's coverage of the Games is fronted by Ray Stubbs, looking as ever like Bill Beaumont's more intelligent younger brother, and one Jane Hoffen. The pair deserve some kind of medal for grace under fire, not least because they are condemned to bind together coverage that is forever at the mercy of the elements and whimsical host broadcasters while seated in what must be the world's first virtual chalet.

Whizzy introductory graphics are always to be expected in Olympic broadcasts, but the Beeb's computer wizards must surely have been doing some passive inhaling among the snowboarders to come up with the opening sequences for Nagano. If we are to believe what their manipulated pixels represent, Stubbs and Hoffen preside over proceedings from the kind of mountain-top eyrie beloved of Bond villains.

But rather than visions of world domination they can conjure only plucky Brits out of their element. And sometimes not even that. Something of a nadir in the broadcasting of the games was marked when the men's downhill skiing was cancelled - no surprise there, since the sport is afflicted by the wrong kind of precipitation in much the same way as British trains are affected by the wrong kind of vegetation - but, to make matters worse, the host broadcasters had decided not to share with us coverage of the British men's crucial curling contest.

This was an odd omission on the part of the Japanese television types, because the Brits were taking on . . . the Japanese. Perhaps they are as bad at sliding lumps of rock along rinks as they are at, say, cooking fish, and just don't want the rest of us to find out. This shyness or secrecy left someone with a lot of filling in to do: Julian Tutt, in fact, our man on the mountain with the packet of Victory V lozenges and the Winter Olympics trivia handbook. The problem, Julian explained, was that while at the top of the mountain snow was falling, at the bottom it was

raining. Which might have made a more novel kind of combined event in which the racers started off snow-skiing and ended up water-skiing, but sadly the organisers were reluctant to seize the opportunity and decided instead to pause for thought and send all the competitors a few hundred yards down the mountain to a restaurant while they worked out what to do next.

Back in the studio, Stubbs asked Martin Bell (brother of the marginally more famous Graham, or is it the other way round?) what the skiers would be getting up to during the unscheduled lay-off. "Well," Bell revealed, "They'll get changed, play computer games, read a book, or learn to play the mouth organ or whatever . . ." The daredevils.

But enough of such revelations. Stubbs hailed Tutt once more, to discover that things were looking up. "You can see that the snow temperature is actually quite cold," Tutt somewhat desperately observed, "which is good news." Indeed: skiing on hot snow has never been easy. The organisers, however, remained uneasy, and before they would consent to starting the competition, sent down the course a local Japanese skier known as a forerunner.

No caption appeared to name this plucky amateur, nor, thankfully, was his nervous progress timed. But he got to the bottom, through the gloom, with only a wobble or two, and once you saw the expression on his face dumbstruck with absolute fear barely conquered, you knew there would be no official downhill run that day. And, although Tutt may have tutted, we felt good for the forerunner, who would one day be able to tell his descendants that he skied the mountain the Olympians didn't.

One would love to be able to report that matters improved for the hard-pressed studio team later in the week. But sadly this was not the case. After another marathon shift, Stubbs signed off with the promise that "Sue Rider and Steve Barker will be up the mountain later." We'll put it down to snow-blindness.

★16 / 2 / 98

Football Diary:

● If Richard Sneekes looks dishevelled on the pitch, his appearance off it is no better. Every morning Sneekes drags himself up to do the school-run, dropping off son Georgio at 8.30 before heading for training with West Bromwich.

One of the other dads took pity on the unkempt, unshaven, unrecognisable figure and, thinking the Dutchman was an unemployed lay-about, offered him a job as a labourer on a building site. It was not until the potential employer visited the club shop, and saw a team picture, that he realised his mistake.

● Darragh Ryan, 17, son of former Republic of Ireland international Gerry, suffered an horrific broken leg playing for Brighton against Peterborough last November. As part of his rehabilitation his parents took him for a holiday in the United States. Unfortunately, going though customs at Miami airport the metal pins holding his leg together set off the alarms. He was detained for five hours: the authorities didn't believe his explanation.

Sport Around The World:

● Olympic chiefs are running a campaign to attract more women into the Games, but images of sex on sledges are hindering the introduction of unisex luge. The International Luge Federation passed a rule before the 1994 Lillehammer Games allowing men and women to race together in the doubles event. But no women were in the doubles discipline at Nagano this year.

FIL officials say the Olympic future of the doubles event, in which both competitiors, clad in thin, tightly-fitting suits, lie on their backs on the luge, has even been in doubt in the past because the International Olympic Committee did not think it looked "nice". "There have been some pretty heated discussions about the sexual aspects of luge," FIL official Harro Esmarch said. "Some people's fantasies have no boundaries. In the past the media have focused on the sexual aspects and attacked us."

● Australian Terry Purcell and American Cindy Moll are the first winners of a new race in world sport - the Empire State Building run-up. Purcell, 27, won the 86-flight, 1,576-stair climb from the lobby of the Manhatten landmark to the observation deck, a verticle distance of two-tenths of a mile. His time was 10 min 49 sec, an average of 7.6 sec per floor. Moll, 29, needed 14 min 17 sec to win the women's division. She told USA Today: "My legs started to feel rubbery, but I got that burst of energy in the last floor."

Letters To The Sports Editor:

● SIR - Michael Parkinson's reference to Bomber Wells was indeed nostalgic. I was bowling for Gloucestershire at the opposite end to Brian and, having finished my over, walked back to my place at long leg. I heard shouting and, on turning round, just saw the ball going by me and finishing for four. He had bowled two balls in that time, and when he had finished his over someone calculated it had taken 57 seconds. I then had to commence my stint again. Some rest. - FRANK McHUGH, West Tarring, Sussex.

● Could it be that the failings of our cricketers over the past few years can be linked in any way to the growing fashion for sporting ridiculous-looking sunglasses? Is it possible that a ban on the wearing of such glasses may, in fact, contribute to an improvement in the team's performance? If nothing else, it may make it easier for the players to find their razors and have a shave. - DOMINIC JOHNSON, Horsham, Sussex.

Robert Hardman

Jumbo way to have a ball in Nepal

Beautiful people were not in abundance. There was no hum of idle banter between models and B-list celebrities at this polo match. But then, we were several thousand miles from Windsor Great Park on the edge of a Nepali swamp. The nearest thing to a jodhpured Argentinian beefcake was me in a pair of jeans. And the nimble-hooved polo pony in this case was a 25-year-old elephant called Bhrikuti.

In terms of pace, elephant polo is probably nearer to croquet than the sort of action Jilly Cooper turned into a novel. But I have played few sports as entertaining or as demanding as this peculiar game. The basics are the same as conventional polo but the kit is rather different. In elephant polo, every player also needs a driver (or panthit) since an elephant will only take commands from a familiar voice. Although the ball is the same size as a normal polo ball, the stick is 12-feet long with a tiny head on the end. Imagine trying to hit a golf ball one-handed from the upper deck of a slow-moving double-decker bus and you have some idea of the task in hand.

I had come to the Tiger Tops Lodge in Nepal's Royal Chitwan National Park to look for tigers and, by chance, found myself at the Wembley of elephant polo. Once played by Nepali kings, the sport had died out until a chance meeting in St Moritz between Jim Edwards, owner of Tiger Tops, and James Manclarke, a Scottish enthusiast for eccentric sports.

Manclarke knew that Edwards played polo and kept elephants at Tiger Tops. He suggested a game of elephant polo, promising to provide some elongated sticks if Edwards came up with the elephants. Edwards thought nothing more until April 1982 when a telegram arrived from Manclarke: "Have long sticks. Get elephants ready."

A one-off became an occasional tournament and word spread. Wealthy polo-lovers from all over the world wanted to get involved. Edwards decided that proper rules were needed and registered the "World Elephant Polo Association" with the Nepal Sports Council. Originally, the sport was played using a football until the elephants discovered that stamping on the ball was great fun. The field was also halved in size from conventional polo dimensions. Before then, much of the game was taken up simply getting from one end to the other. It is also a sport geared in favour of females. Some might call it chivalry, others sexism, but the rules are clear: women may hold their stick with both hands but men can only use one; handicapping in the true sense of the word.

No one seems to mind too much. The annual world championships now have a waiting list of those wanting to pay the £5,000 entry fee for a team. Recent competitors range from polo stalwarts like Stephanie Powers to an eccentric Florida bakery magnate who comes back year after year.

It is, of necessity, one of the most exclusive sports in the world. When Edwards applied for Olympic status, he was told that elephant polo might have a slim chance of exhibition status in the unlikely event that Nepal ever stages an Olympics. There are few places in the world with a ready supply of trained elephants, which can cost

When you are caught in a four-elephant scrum, it is hard enough to see the ground, let alone the ball

up to £20,000 each, and games are restricted in order to protect the animals. For them, it can be a tiring exercise. Hence the fact that matches are limited to 10 minutes each way and only played in the winter months. Twenty minutes in the "saddle" - which involves being roped on to the animal's shoulders - was quite enough for me, too.

Simply hitting the ball can involve several attempts since an inhaling elephant rises by two inches. A stick drawn back for an accurate hit can whizz clean over the ball when you swing through. And more than a few attempts soon start to wear on that solitary arm. Eventually, gasping for breath, I found it easier to drag the mallet along the ground like a rake. My team-mate, Louise, proved the crackshot in our blundering victory over rival members of the British press. With her two-handed advantage, she knocked in two goals and I managed to add a third with none in reply.

Much of the game was spent hitting blind. When you are caught in a four-elephant scrum, it is hard enough to see the ground, let alone the ball. At one point, the ball disappeared altogether. Bhrikuti, naughty girl, was standing on it. It required a referee armed with a penknife to dig it out of the turf. In football, it is usually the striker, in American football, the quarterback. But when it comes to elephant polo, the hero of the day is surely the groundsman. Having to run on to a pitch between 16 legs - each capable of grinding you to a pulp - in order to scoop up 20lb of freshly dumped elephant dung with your bare hands must be the grottiest job in world sport.

★18/2/98

Mark Nicholas

England's cricket captain ponders his future

Michael Atherton, captain of England since July 1993, is at the crossroads again. It is not the first time but this, irrevocably one suspects, is the crunch. If England lose the final Test, and with it the series against the West Indies, his position will become untenable. It is life on a knife-edge for Atherton, a man who is always under debate, a man often accused and too rarely applauded. It would get to anyone, let alone one so private. The exasperation on his face as he returned to the pavilion, having been caught on the boundary after a mis-hook, revealed, yet again, his ongoing desperation to outwit his critics.

Never can 15 months of international cricket have so crystallised the fraught public existence of an England captain or the wild inconsistency of his team. Humiliation in Zimbabwe, recovery in New Zealand, elation to begin with against Australia, depression and derision to follow, jubilation again to finish at the Oval. The will-he-won't-he-stay-in-the-job saga was followed by ironic success for England in Sharjah without him. Then came Jamaica and that dramatic hour before Trinidad twice in the most exhausting back-to-back Test matches of his time. And all through these past months there has been the thread of Hamlet's self-inquisition, to be captain or not to be captain, and the relentless media probing that accompanies the question. Talk about life in the goldfish bowl.

It was not known at the time but after the Trent Bridge Test, the fifth against Australia last summer, which England lost, Atherton had had enough and resigned. This was not the move of a martyr but the conclusion of an unselfish leader whose team had failed to regain the Ashes, and who decided that, after four largely unsuccessful years in the most personally demanding role in British sport, it was time for someone else to have a go.

Lord MacLaurin, chairman of the England and Wales Cricket Board, told him he was making a mistake. "I thought it was wrong and uncharacteristic for Michael to buckle under media pressure," said MacLaurin. "His being hounded out benefits no one, not the game, not the team and certainly not the man. It was a case of resisting emotional issues and letting the dust settle. Anyway, it was bad timing with only one Test of the summer left and such an assortment

of cricket to come in the winter. We needed a show of solidarity and I was very keen for him to see it through." Atherton told MacLaurin that he felt he had done all he could for the team and had nothing left to give. MacLaurin urged him to think again and call him back. Atherton did and, surprisingly in the light of his comment that he was a stubborn Lancastrian who would not change his mind, he agreed to continue. Then, after the Oval Test which England won so thrillingly, Atherton again considered his future. On the journey back to London for the press conference he told David Graveney, the chairman of selectors, that he was unavailable to captain the side in the Caribbean. Graveney rang David Lloyd, the England coach and a close friend of Atherton, who urged him that their work together was only half done.

The call which swayed it, though, was from Alec Stewart, his likely successor if he resigned. "I thought it was fine for him to stand down if he felt his batting form was affected by the captaincy, but not if he bowed to pressure from outside. Really, that shouldn't get to him or to any of us. I felt we could win here and with his experience and toughness I thought our best chance was with him as captain," says Stewart now.

There is a relevance and poignancy to Stewart's advice that gave it further conviction. During Graham Gooch's tour to India in 1992-93, Atherton was cruelly excluded from any of the selectors' plans until the final Test in Bombay. In one of those silly run-out cock-ups, he and Stewart found themselves stranded at the same end with no one doubting that Atherton was out of his ground and should have gone. Instead he turned away from his batting partner and wandered back into the crease. The umpire wrongly gave Stewart out.

There was never a whisper from Stewart, and never has been through the various rumours that he was about to replace Atherton as captain. Indeed, their support for each other is a feature of the team and another convincing reason for them to open the batting. On the two occasions they have found some momentum at the crease during this tour, England won once and should have won the other. They put on 91 in the second innings of the first of the Trinidad Tests and then in the second, chasing a record 225 to win in the

DAY BY DAY REVIEW

1: Jonathan Edwards claims Britain's second triple-jump gold at the European Indoor Athletics Championships and John Mayock claims a surprise gold in the 3,000 metres.

2: The West Indies win the fourth Test by 242 runs.

3: Nigel Spackman resigns as manager of Sheffield United.

7: Wales recover from 13-3 down to beat Scotland 19-13 at Wembley in the Five Nations' Championship, while Ireland lose 18-16 to France in Paris.

8: McLaren score a one-two in the opening Grand Prix of the season, the Australian, but David Coulthard is condemned for moving over and letting Mika Hakkinen win the race after a pre-race agreement.

10: Rangers agree a £3 million deal with Crystal Palace for Paul Gascoigne.

11: Ieuan Evans, the Welsh captain, announces his retirement from international rugby.

15: Greg Rusedski is beaten by Marcelo Rios in the final of the Newsweek Champions' Cup in Indian Wells.

16: England's hopes of winning the fifth Test are washed away by rain.

17: Istabraq, ridden by Charlie Swan, wins the Champion Hurdle for Ireland at the Cheltenham Festival. Aston Villa are knocked out of the UEFA Cup, in the quarter-final, beaten on the away-goals rule after beating Athletico Madrid 2-1 at Villa Park.

19: Cool Dawn, with Andrew Thornton aboard, wins the Cheltenham Gold Cup at 25-1. Middlesbrough agree a £3 million fee with Rangers for Paul Gascoigne.

21: Wales win their second Five Nations' game of the season, beating Ireland 30-21 in Dublin.

22: In the Calcutta Cup, England beat Scotland 34-20 at Murrayfield, Paul Grayson scoring a try and kicking four conversions, a penalty goal and a dropped goal.

24: Mike Atherton resigns as England captain after West Indies complete a 3-1 series win, by winning the sixth Test by an innings and 52 runs. Paul Gascoigne joins Middlesbrough for £3.5 million. Tony McCoy rides a double at Chepstow to draw level with Peter Scudamore's record of 221 jump winners in a season.

25: England are held 1-1 by Switzerland in a friendly in Berne with Paul Merson scoring a late equaliser. In other friendlies, Scotland lose 1-0 at home against Denmark, Wales are held scoreless by Jamaica, the Republic of Ireland are beaten in the Czech Republic, and Northern Ireland beat Slovakia. Petite Risk is Tony McCoy's record-breaking 222nd winner of the season, at Ludlow.

28: Barnsley have three players - Barnard, Morgan and Sheridan-sent off amid dreadful scenes at Oakwell during their 3-2 defeat by Liverpool. Cambridge win the University Boat Race by three lengths, their sixth successive victory. Lennox Lewis comes from behind to win his defence of the World Boxing Council heavyweight title against Shannon Briggs in Atlantic City.

29: Extra-time goals by Frank Sinclair and Roberto di Matteo give Chelsea a 2-0 win against Middlesbrough in the Coca-Cola Cup final. Nick Knight's 122 helps England to a 16-run victory over the West Indies in the first one-day international in Barbados.

30: The Leeds United team, returning from a 3-0 defeat at West Ham, survive an emergency landing at Stansted airport.

last innings, they put on 129 for the first wicket, which set up the memorable victory.

Defeat in that first Test at Port of Spain drained Atherton. "It was a key game, what with them having lost their three previous Tests in Pakistan, and losing again would have torn them apart. We were all desperately upset to lose," he said. "It was around 36 degrees most days and every session was as tense as the last. We were knackered and it was immediately obvious that we needed two days of rest to clear our minds." In the team meeting 72 hours later Atherton stressed that for the first three days of the previous game England had been the better side, had deserved to win and eight times out of 10 would have done so. Just about everything planned had worked, he added. The only mistake had been relaxing on the last day and expecting to win. The West Indies wicketkeeper, David Williams, played probably the freak innings of his life in support of Carl Hooper's masterly unbeaten 94 and England had umpiring decisions go against them.

But the "expecting to win" was the interesting

and public examination that go with being captain is tough. It got to Mark Taylor's play and look at the team he has got to get him out of jail. Athers has achieved great loyalty in the ranks and the candidates put forward to replace him - Stewart and Hussain - are his greatest supporters. I'm not surprised his teams keep coming back. That resilience is the reason he is chosen as captain."

On this tour Atherton has appeared relaxed. Uncommonly, on Test match mornings and at press conferences, he has smiled. In Guyana, on the first morning of the fourth Test, he casually asked Paul Allott about the pitch and therefore what his team should be. Imagine that issue still on a captain's mind an hour before play! He conducted his press conference at the end of the match through a realistic eye and in a pleasant manner.

His regret in Guyana was losing the toss; the dismay was the important catches which went to ground, particularly Shivnarine Chanderpaul, who was on nine when he was dropped at slip and went on to make a hundred. "I don't believe that our bowling is the problem people say it is - we've

good form," he said. "I am honest with my own game and admit I was in trouble last winter but I am in good shape now and I'll score plenty of runs. Poor pitches and good bowlers have got me out this tour, nothing more. I am not worried."

He has not, he adds, planned anything special to counter the 14 similar ways that Curtly Ambrose has got him out in Test cricket. He is kidding himself about his form - were he not captain he may not be playing.

And so to the Achilles heel of the man, or is it that this weakness is his strength: his extreme, unrelenting stubbornness? Once, when we were in a selection meeting on England's A tour to Zimbabwe in 1990, Atherton, who was vice-captain, disagreed with a point of principle so he picked up a newspaper and read it. That was rude. A week later in a team meeting he said that he was the best catcher in the team, so should field at backward point, the key position, in the one-day matches. That was cocky. In the first over of the first game he flew to his right and held a stunning catch. It was sensational money-where-your-mouth-is stuff, and typical.

He has never liked the press and has been obstinate in his refusal to charm them. He has a contempt which he does not disguise for certain types of newspapers and journalism, so if they judge him by his dealings with them he has got no chance. He will not compromise himself and if it costs him his job then so be it.

He talks of his time at Cambridge University as "my life at college," which characterises the unexplained self-deprecation that is his style. He is wary of the public school type but is fond of John Barclay, the effervescent Etonian who managed England's last two tours. He has captained England more times than any man, more than the Oxbridge set of May, Cowdrey, Dexter or Brearley and yet you feel his heart is with the Huttons, Greigs and Bothams, who led from the shop floor.

There has been the thread of Hamlet's self-inquisition, to be captain or not to be captain, and the relentless media probing that accompanies the question

thing. Before the tour Atherton had said that in 1994 England had come to the West Indies more in hope than expectation. This time his team were in expectation not hope, he said, and anybody around them, sensing their inner belief and for once genuine, not laddish, outward confidence, could understand this. Dean Headley, on the evening before the first Test, said: "If we don't win this series we will have only ourselves to blame."

Well, they did not win the first time in Trinidad and they were, ultimately, to blame, but the point was that unlike previous England tours abroad, which folded in front of Atherton's bemused eyes, the famous old fat lady was a long way from the end of her song. After an unpromising first day in the second Trinidad match, which the West Indies finished at 271 for three, England inched back, niggling away at the weaknesses and keeping the strengths - Lara, Chanderpaul, Ambrose and Walsh - in check. "To win, to come back as we did, showed great character," said Atherton, "which is why we should not be written off now after losing in Guyana."

"Mike is an incredibly strong person," said Graveney, "and is the main ingredient of the numerous fightbacks he has led. To open the batting at Test level and deal with all the hassles

looked like knocking the West Indies over twice in all three Tests - and I don't believe that Alec can open the batting and keep wicket in this heat," said Atherton. "I do know we must catch our catches and score more consistently in the first innings."

Which is where the captain's batting becomes an issue. He has had a rum time since his great defensive innings, the 185 in South Africa two years ago. Since then he has made just two hundreds and since the match-winner in Christchurch, New Zealand, a year ago last February, he has made only two fifties. He has worked hard this winter with Gooch and occasionally, the second innings of the second Trinidad Test for example, he has looked organised in his footwork and smooth in his strokes. Overall, though, he seems slower than usual, stuck in the crease and late with his hands in adjusting to the speed and movement of the new ball. He says he worked at basic things with Gooch and most specifically at being sideways on to the bowler. I believe his stance is a little too closed, too side-on exaggerated, which is a reason why he is not driving down the ground or through mid-on as often as he did. "I feel in

Bob Bennett, manager of this tour and until recently his chairman at Lancashire, said: "He can be abrupt but differences of opinion are instantly forgotten. I agree that his failure to appreciate the opposite view suggests a lack of flexibility. But I believe that his stubbornness is a strength and has seen him through a very difficult time for English cricket."

It was a difficult time indeed just over a year ago when the team were mauled in the media for their indifference on and off the field in Zimbabwe. I was there and whatever they say, whatever insular defence mechanism springs into action, they let English cricket down. "I don't agree," said Atherton, "it's as simple as that. I'm a sociable person and have loved every minute of every tour I've been on. We made friends in Zimbabwe, whatever people suggest. The press have got to write something, they never just say you played badly. In India in 92/93 it was because we dressed badly and didn't shave. In Zimbabwe it was because we didn't go out on the piss."

Over to Ian MacLaurin: "If Michael says that it is a shame. It's crass to put up a wall and hide behind it. If 15 cricketers fester in a room the siege mentality thing develops. Peter Chingoka, the president of the Zimbabwe Cricket Union, said to me: 'Ian, we were so looking forward to hosting the England team, frankly now I would be delighted to see them go tomorrow'. That's awful but it's all of our faults, not only the captain or the management. It's Tim Lamb, it's me, it's everyone. We're Team England and should all take the rap."

MacLaurin likes Atherton and says he has many of the qualities he looks for in business. "I admire his thorough preparation and his determination to make something of his team. He had a torrid time with Ray Illingworth and it set England back, but he came through that and has handled the huge pressure of being public property pretty well. I believe he could be more flexible, could open up a bit and take account of the wider perspective, and whatever his opinion, I am afraid that the little things such as shaving for public appearances do matter, to spectators and specifically these days to sponsors. Before meeting him I thought England needed a new captain but the first time we had dinner together I was prepared to think again. I asked him who had talked to him about the brief for the job and its responsibilities and who had guided him through it, and he said no one. It's ridiculous we appoint a 25-year-old as captain of England and there is

no back-up for him. It is vital to get the infrastructure right and to plan for the future. I think we are doing that now and if Michael does stand down after the tour then we must ensure that it happens with dignity and that he is properly appreciated."

If he did go it would be at a time when the tactical element of his captaincy is approaching its best. He may still not grab the main chance as sharply as, say, a Mike Brearley or an Ian Chappell, but he makes few mistakes now, is actually less cautious than he was and reads pitches and his players better than ever. Through the learning years he sought advice from Chappell more readily than from any former captain. He likes the whole Channel Nine commentary ethic, no flannel, just get stuck in and tell it as you see it.

So what is it with Atherton? Does he warrant acclaim as English cricket's most appointed general or is it simply that he is the man in power and in our faces so frequently that discussion of his merits is inevitable? Probably he is cut out to be a captain but not to be a public figure. He has done a tough job with dignity and purpose but, perversely, he may finish with his contribution to the stability of the team largely unknown.

Graveney points out that: "Some people are happy in the public domain, Michael defends his

privacy vehemently, which is why he retreats to the Lake District when the glare of publicity is at its most powerful - after his appointment as captain, for example, or after the ball-tampering affair against South Africa. He is a good captain and an outstanding player and will relish concentrating on his batting when one day he stands down as captain. He may not be the all-consuming person the media want but in a working relationship with me, for example, he is excellent." The last word is for Bennett, who has known him man and boy. "He could have portrayed his own warmth of character better because inside he is a genuine, kind person who has been reluctant to let the outside world know or begin to understand him. He is as honest as they come you know, and fiercely loyal."-for sure, he is that and more. To be England's captain of cricket is, in its way, to be as exposed to public opinion as a prime minister or a member of the Royal Family. The unavoidable intrusion into your life leaves scars. The Test Match here in Barbados will almost certainly decide whether Atherton relinquishes his title and escapes the intrusion. In his own words, taken from his biography of last year: "I am a sportsman, not a statesman." And were that an epitaph to his five years in charge, it would do nicely.

★14 / 3 / 98

Obstacle course... horses and jockeys set off into the Cheltenham countryside during the National Hunt Festival •**Russell Cheyne** ★17/3/98

Martin Johnson

Doncaster paupers running out of time

In the satirical magazine *Private Eye* there is a fictitious football team called Neasden FC, who play in the North Circular Relegation League, have never won a game, regularly lose 10-0 via a spate of own goals from their "midfield maestro" Baldy Pevsner, employ a one-legged goalkeeper named Wally Foot and have two remaining supporters, Sid and Doris Bonkers.

Currently, however, there is a real-life equivalent of Neasden, operating (albeit not for much longer) in Football League Division Three, and going by the name of Doncaster Rovers. Doncaster are propping up the duffers' division with a total of 16 points from 38 games, they have just let in seven at Cardiff and need to concede only three more at home to promotion-chasing Lincoln this (a racing

been nothing like as bizarre as those off it, largely revolving around the club's self-styled benefactor Ken Richardson, the manager Mark Weaver, and a small hard-core of remaining supporters who are deeply upset with Richardson.

Doncaster Council, whom Weaver suspects of wanting the club closed down, and a number of prospective buyers, some identifiable some not, who are apparently prepared to fork out nearly £4 million for a club which Weaver himself - only slightly tongue in cheek - values at 50p.

Richardson is currently bailed to appear before Sheffield Crown Court on a conspiracy charge following an arson attack on the club's main stand in 1995. When fans talk about how many more

Remarkably enough Richardson is asking £3.75 million to buy him out when £3.75 would appear to be nearer the mark, and even more remarkably an Essex nightclub owner, Anton Johnson, appears to be willing to pay it, and most remarkably of all, Richardson has so far found various reasons for not snapping Johnson's hand off over what appears to be a pinch-me-I-must-be dreaming deal. Driving into the car park, you get the impression that the only prospective bidder would be a local potholing club.Standing (if only just) directly opposite the well appointed Doncaster racecourse, home to England's oldest classic the St Leger, the football club's Belle Vue ground could not even be described as attractive to a woodworm colony.

The paint-flaked door underneath a 'Sponsors Lounge' sign looks as though it would attract the attention of the RSPCA if it was used as a dog kennel, and the club offices consist of two ramshackle temporary buildings. A couple of weeks ago the Scunthorpe firm who paid for them to be installed came to take them away because of "adverse publicity" and relented only after an impassioned plea from Weaver. He would happily risk a splintered posterior by sitting in what passes for a dugout, but he is wary of incurring more serious bodily damage if he watches from anywhere other than "a little alcove" beneath the

"We've got a big advert for a tile depot on the back of the main stand," he said, "and we get more visits from people wanting to refurbish their bathrooms than inquiring about tickets"

certainty on current form) to clock up a century in the goals against column with nine matches still to play.

With such a daunting task in prospect, the minute they left Cardiff the Rovers' management team swung straight into their tactical planning for Lincoln with an attention to detail that has probably never occurred to Alex Ferguson or Arsene Wenger. "Er, see you next week, lads, and don't forget it's a three o'clock kick-off." No further information was required, for the simple reason that Rovers no longer have any coaching staff with which to conduct training sessions. The players can train if they want to, but they have to pay their own expenses.

There are seven full-time professionals, a residue that would struggle to hold down places in the Vauxhall Conference, and a manager who joined the club as a commercial employee, has never played professional football, and who has pruned his staff so severely that he recently registered himself as a player. However, events on the field have

matches it will take for the Rovers to catch fire, they are actually referring to a box of Swan Vestas. At the moment Richardson has vacated what, in more senses than one, can be described as the hot seat in the stand. He says he has had enough of watching a team who are terminally hopeless, while the supporters say that he has been driven away by their choruses of abuse. Richardson retains control of the club, despite having no official title. The board of directors comprise a friend, his daughter and his niece.

Doncaster occupies a prime development site, said to be much coveted by the Asda supermarket next door, if the council, who own it, decide to sell. There is a covenant attached to the lease stipulating that it cannot be sold for private development as long as football is played on it, but it appears that as soon as football ceases, the site will be turned into a supermarket. It is probably a moot point even now as to what the Rovers produce there on a Saturday afternoon can reasonably be described as football.

stand. Only his sense of humour appears to keep him going. "We've got a big advert for a tile depot on the back of the main stand," he said, "and we get more visits from people wanting to refurbish their bathrooms than inquiring about tickets." He produced a balance sheet from the recent home match against Barnet, showing a profit of £715.35. Among the items of expenditure was a bill for £675.64 from the police, who sent two men on horseback to control a seething crowd of 729. And the club is not even allowed to keep the manure.

Weaver is well aware that the supporters are unhappy with Richardson, but he points his finger at Doncaster Council as the major villains of the piece. He said: "The Council could certainly get the lease back if there was no more football here, and it's interesting to see just what they are doing as landlords in terms of keeping the club going. The facilities are a disgrace. I wouldn't blame supporters for not turning up whatever the results, because this is the most decrepit ground in football. You wouldn't take your kids along for fear they might catch something. "Then there is the council's annual safety check. To pass the ground safe for this season cost us £140,000, so if they really want a football club in this town, why do they put that sort of pressure on us? Most of the abuse is now directed at me, not Richardson, but I can only work with the tools that I've got. We had a crowd of 500 for Rochdale, including 100 complimentary tickets, and out of that we have to pay the stewards, car park attendants, you name it. It cost £100 to staff the snack bar for the Barnet game, and the takings came to £64."

Weaver took the full brunt of the fans' anger at a Save The Rovers supporters' meeting at the Earl Of Doncaster Hotel just down the road from the Odeon cinema. Interestingly, the Odeon was charging £2 for *The Titanic*, which is a good bit less than people are being asked to pay to see the Rovers go down. The meeting, better attended than most matches, was primarily concerned with hurling abuse at Weaver, who eventually left - for his own protection - by a side door. By contrast, Johnson departed to a chorus of "There's only one Anton Johnson." Well, there certainly cannot be two like him, and not every supporter was convinced by his reasons for wanting to pay £3.75 million for Richardson's controlling interest. "Because I'm football mad," said Johnson. In the opinion of many, the word 'football' was slightly superfluous. Bob Gilbert, who has launched a personal crusade against Richardson and Weaver on his Rovers' Internet site, said: "Personally, I don't think the Rovers will exist by the end of this year. This has been a depressed town since the miners' strike, and there's no enthusiasm left for the football club now. However, this is no longer just about Doncaster Rovers. The football authorities are the so-called custodians of the game, but in practice, they are simply custodians of the wealthy Premier League boys. When it comes to the Brightons and the Doncasters, they couldn't give a tuppenny damn."

★21 / 3 / 98

Neil Cowie powers on for Wigan Warriors during the semi-final of the Rugby League Challenge Cup against London Broncos •**Gary Prior** ★29/3/98

31

Sarah Sperry (centre) celebrates with her John Cleveland team-mates after winning the Girls' Tournament at the National Schools Sevens at Rosslyn Park

John Inverdale

There now follows an article for those of you who were about to despair. Those who just can't believe all the complete and utter nonsense that's been going on the past couple of weeks. Those who were beginning to fear that the values you held so dear had been cast to the four winds. It is a story of a match in the Buckinghamshire countryside last weekend, kicking off at 1pm so everyone could watch the TV in the afternoon.

It's the story of Olney RFC, of Southern Counties North, against Gloucester second XV. (Olney had been due to play Chipping Norton, a beautiful village adjacent to that home for abject golfers, Chipping Badly, but for reasons that needn't detain us, they cried off). On the wing for Olney . . . 28-year-old Jason Page, plumbing and heating engineer, reasonable rates charged, no job too small. On the wing for Gloucester, P Saint-Andre, last seen leading France to a cataclysmic defeat against South Africa before Christmas.

The vice-president of Olney, Duncan Rodgers, was particularly pleased about this change of opponents. He's got a French au pair you see, so she rang all her mates, and suddenly there were loads of mademoiselles on the touchline.

Back at the match, Page was in confident mood. "Lining up opposite him before the kick-off, he didn't look anything special. I thought, `I'll be all right here'." Page normally works on a Saturday morning and nips off for the game in the afternoon…"It can be pretty tiring if someone's rung you at one in the morning saying they've got a burst pipe."

Olney scored first, and then Gloucester scored lots, but the crucial thing is, at least as far as Page is concerned, Saint-Andre failed to score until he, Page, had been forced from the field with a hamstring pull less than 10 minutes from time. And they had a good laugh about it afterwards, watching France scramble past the unlucky Irish, with Saint-Andre shouting invective at the screen in the Olney clubhouse as humiliation loomed for his former team-mates.

"It wasn't till I saw him in the showers that I realised he had pretty good upper body strength," said Page. The crucial difference between a county player for Buckinghamshire and a First Division star was obvious, as Ireland made a crucial line-out error and Raphael Ibanez sneaked over for the winning score. "I was well into the lager, he was still on orange juice."

No matter. Gloucester have invited Olney back for some good old Kingsholm hospitality next season. They enjoyed the camaraderie, the friendship, the fun. The spirit of the game lives on, and even those at the top level haven't lost sight of it. It's not all about club against country, money and more money. As you read this, Gloucester are probably enjoying Richard Hill's final rallying call to arms before trying to topple the Premiership leaders, Saracens, tomorrow. Page is adjusting a ballcock. Then he's on his way to take it out on the winger for Oxford Harlequins. He'd better be good because, one Saturday in March, Jason ate Philippe Saint Andre for lunch.

★ 14 / 3 / 98

Football Diary:

● Nicky Hammond, the Reading goalkeeper, has his one-time manager Glenn Hoddle to thank for recommending faith healer Eileen Drewery, who accelerated his recovery from a stomach muscle strain through the laying-on of hands. "I feel a sort of warm sensation although on occasions her hands have been ice-cold," said Hammond. "There's a divine power that is channelled through her."

● Another in the series of primitive bartering between clubs for players: Salisbury offered Fareham Town a toilet block in part-exchange for striker Anton Romasz, scorer of 38 goals this season. Geoff Butler, the Salisbury manager, made the unusual offer to Chris Solen, chairman of Fareham. "We made it clear we were not in a position to offer the sort of money they wanted for Romasz," said Butler. "We did have a couple of Portakabins, but we'd sold them to Tamworth. So I told him about the portable toilets, and he said, 'That'll do'." Sadly the deal got stuck in the U-bend, and was not completed.

Sport Around The World:

● A New Zealand skier at the Paralympic Games in Nagano had to fend off a wild monkey in his hotel room near the slopes. "I was watching the television in my room alone when a large monkey opened a door and leapt in from the hotel's balcony," said Matthew Butson, 24, who has only one arm. "I picked up my artificial arm and threatened it. It was 4 ft tall and I thought it was going to attack. It was scary." The hotel manager confirmed that no one was hurt but said there were about 200 wild monkeys nearby, and they sometimes leapt through open windows and snatched bags from the rooms.

● When India A met Australia in Jamshedpur, their line-up featured newcomer K N Ananthapadmanabhan. Should he play a first-class match in Sri Lanka we could have the scoreboard compiler's dismissal from hell: K N Ananthapadmanabhan c Kaluwitharana b Wijegunawardene.

● Back in 1952, Ben Hogan decided to give a dinner for past winners of the Masters at Augusta. This year they will be having cheeseburgers, fries and milkshakes. The champion chooses the menu, and Tiger Woods, who won last year, said: "That's part of being young. Burgers are what I grew up eating, so that's what I'm eating. Sandy Lyle served haggis when he was champion."

● A top Italian basketball team finished a local derby game with only three players after an almighty 10-minute punch-up in a European Championship play-off. The referee dismissed two of the starting line-up and the entire bench of Teamsystem Bologna after a fight with city rivals Kinder Bologna, who won 64-52. Kinder had three men thrown out of the game but could call on replacements. Two from each side were banned, including Gregor Fucka, the Teamsystem man who started the trouble by throwing the ball into the face of an opponent.

Letters To The Sports Editor:

● SIR - As I watched David Beckham send his free-kick over the top of the Monaco goal, I wondered how many more such opportunities will be squandered by futile attempts to curl the ball into the top corner. The sequence is monotonously familiar. The ball is positioned - hopes raised, breath held - the ball sails harmlessly over the bar. Up and down the country the same routine is followed, week in, week out. Is not there a manager anywhere with the wit to plot something different. - T M HUGHES, Sawtry, Hunts.

Simon Hughes

Thames glory briefly borrowed

Surreal, isn't it? A ding-dong between two eights of super-trained hunks on a famous river watched by 200,000 spectators and 400 million on television, and none of the contestants earns a penny. A definition of true amateurism or outright masochism, take your pick.

"All rowers are peculiar people," the Olympic gold medallist Matthew Pinsent observed before the start. The participants are like human guinea pigs, relative unknowns testing their bodies to the limit during six months of total abstinence, in pursuit of a simple goal. To get to the winning post first. Hell, they will even indulge in gamesmanship if it helps. Then after their 15 minutes of glory (or misery) they are back to being anonymous again, a perfect Warhol fit. It is the purity of this ambition that gives the Boat Race its enduring appeal.

And yet there is an infuriating aspect to it too. Half of London descends on the Thames riverbank this one Saturday in March, then more or less desert the capital's greatest asset the other 364 days a year. A mini armada accompanied the crews under Hammersmith Bridge where the day before only two vessels passed in half-an-hour. Fifty yards away, the Great West Road, the busiest stretch of Tarmac in northern Europe, was, as usual, jammed. One of those vessels, Driftwood II, was a metaphor for Oxford and Cambridge universities. It chugged around clearing away any potential obstacles from the rowers' path as employers still tend to for Oxbridge graduates. Their rugby teams and cricketers still get privileged access to Twickenham and Lord's, which they have ceased to deserve.

The Boat Race is also regarded in some quarters as an anachronism, but it is not necessarily. A large proportion of the population may be ambivalent towards it ("I'm more interested in what happens between Brentford and Oldham this afternoon," said my cab driver), but there was no doubting the supreme skill or ultimate commitment of the competitors, eight of whom were international oarsmen.

After the months of arduous training - lifting weights most people could not even roll, rowing for hundreds of hours - the scientific tests, the brilliant technical advice, the monastic lifestyle, all for just one race, these are probably the best prepared sportsmen in the world. Cambridge's president David Cassidy said: "By Saturday morning, you feel you could pull up a tree."

And then they were off. Our boat throttled forwards and soon had to maintain a surprising speed to keep up with the crews. Cambridge's principal tree-pullers, the German Olympians Marc Weber and Stefan Forster, soon tried to break Oxford's resolve. In a display of awesome power, Weber, known as the Seve Ballesteros of rowing - for his versatility and natural talent rather than his appalling sense of direction - and the Herculean Forster, opened a gap on the Fayed bend (Fulham Football club on one side, Harrods depository opposite).

A tumultuous roar accompanied the move. The crowd were six deep at Hammersmith, augmented by several chefs from the River Cafe. There would have been quite a wait for the *linguine al granchio*. The Oxford cox tried desperate, disruptive tactics, to no avail. By Chiswick Mall, adjacent to Daley Thompson's

....

The scientific tests, the brilliant technical advice, the monastic lifestyle, all for just one race, these are probably the best prepared sportsmen in the world

....

house, they were spent. Cambridge, however, had found a beautiful rhythm and shot past the finish as the heaviest and fastest Boat Race crew of all time by some distance. A stunned Pinsent blurted out: "16-19, 25 seconds quicker than the record, that's unbelievable." He was clearly relieved he had not had to row against them. Nor will anyone else have to, the quirkiest element of the Boat Race. After the post-race reception with the 'bufties' (old Blues) and the Savoy Ball afterwards, the victorious Cambridge crew were to assemble only once more. To put the boat on its trailer the following morning. Then they headed off in an assortment of directions - in Weber's case to likely retirement - probably never to reunite.

At the muddy finish the Cambridge rowers conducted their interviews while their Oxford counterparts barely had enough strength to get their wellingtons on. The swift incoming tide forced the winners into the tent, the losers to their private grief. The Beefeater signs floated away, symbolising the end of their 12-year sponsorship. Who will the next benefactors be, Manpower"

★30 / 3 / 98

Early one morning... Suny Bay joins stable-mates on Charlie Brooks' gallops in Lambourn before the Grand National •**Russell Cheyne** ★31/3/98   35

1: West Indies overtake England's 266, Nick Knight top-scoring again with 90, with one wicket in hand in the second one-day international in Bridgetown.

2: Chelsea are beaten 1-0 in Vicenza in the first leg of their European Cup-Winners' Cup semi-final.

3: Greg Rusedski and Tim Henman give Britain a 2-0 lead in the Euro-African zone match against Ukraine in Newcastle. One Man, the most popular steeplechaser since Desert Orchid, is put down after a fall at Aintree.

4: Earth Summit, the 7-1 favourite, wins the Grand National at Aintree, followed home by Suny Bay and Samlee. England notch up their 21st Triple Crown by beating Ireland 35-17 at Twickenham. West Indies beat England by five wickets in St Vincent to win the third of the one-day internationals.

5: Arsenal beat Wolves 1-0 at Villa Park in one FA Cup semi-final, and meet Newcastle in the final after they beat Sheffield United by the same score in the other. France complete their fourth win out of four matches to take the Five Nations' title with a resounding 51-0 victory over Wales at Wembley. England flop again in the fourth one-day international in St Vincent, all out for 149 and beaten by four wickets. Lee Westwood wins the Freeport McDermott Classic in New Orleans. Britain complete a 5-0 whitewash of Ukraine in their Davis Cup tie in Newcastle.

7: Paul Edwards, the British shot putter, is banned for life by the British Athletic Federation after being found guilty of drugs abuse for the second time.

8: England end their tour of the Caribbean with a 4-1 defeat in the one-day series, losing game five by 57 runs in Port of Spain.

12: Mark O'Meara holes a 20 ft putt on the final green to win the US Masters by a shot at Augusta, his first major title. Michael Schumacher scores his first Grand Prix win of the season, pushing Mika Hakkinen into second place in the Argentinian race.

16: Chelsea fight back from 1-0 down on the night, 2-0 on aggregate, to beat Vicenza and reach the final of the European Cup-Winners' Cup.

18: Naseem Hamed successfully defends his WBO featherweight title for the 10th time, stopping Puerto Rico's Wilfredo Vazquez in the seventh round in Manchester. On the same bill Chris Eubank is beaten in a cruiserweight title fight by Carl Thompson. Arsenal take over at the top of the Premiership by beating Wimbledon 5-0, while Manchester United are held at home by Newcastle. Lord Howell, former Minister of Sport and Football League referee, dies aged 74.

21: Matthew Le Tissier scores a hat-trick for England B against Russia B at Loftus Road to enhance his hopes of a World Cup place.

22: Alan Shearer scores twice as England beat Portugal 3-0 in a friendly at Wembley. In other friendlies, Scotland are held at home by Finland, Argentina beat the Republic of Ireland and Northern Ireland beat Switzerland.

26: David Coulthard pushes Michael Schumacher into second place in the San Marino Grand Prix at Imola, though Mika Hakkinen is forced to retire. Catherina McKiernan, of Ireland, wins the women's London Marathon, with Liz McColgan second, while Spain's Abel Anton wins the men's race in a course-record 2 hr 7 min 57 sec.

29: Attilio Lombardo steps down as player-manager of Crystal Palace after five defeats in seven games. Michelle Smith, Ireland's Olympic swimming champion, announces she is determined to clear her name over fresh drug allegations.

Marcus Armytage

Suny Bay's grand plan

Monday morning was the start of Suny Bay's easy day this week. A stretch of the legs for five minutes on the treadmill in the equine gymnasium at 7.15. A long trot in the fresh air of an overcast day up on Neardown, one of the hills overlooking the 'Valley of the Racehorse' for a further warm-up. A canter up the grass, another long trot before a half-speed blow-out up a six furlong, steeply inclined all-weather gallop, part of the investment made by Andrew Cohen, Suny Bay''s owner, to Uplands, the Lambourn yard in which he employs Charlie Brooks to train his and other people's horses.

The dappled grey gelding then trots half a mile to warm down, walks another half-mile home, has a shower, spends half an hour on the horse-walker under infra-red lamps to dry off and the remaining daylight hours turned out in his paddock. So that is an easy day? Six or seven miles at varying paces? If that is the calm before today's storm there is going to be one hell of a gale blowing across the Melling Road at Aintree at 3.45 this afternoon.

"He's got to run four and a half miles on Saturday - there's no point in him staying in bed all week," says Brooks. Running four and a half miles is not all Suny Bay has to do today. There is the small question of 30 obstacles, as daunting as they are inviting. Becher's Brook; as synonymous with Aintree as Nelson's Column is with Trafalgar Square. The Chair, 5ft 2in high and preceded by a 6ft ditch that yawns at you like a grave impatient for a coffin. Foinavon's fence, the smallest on the course but responsible for bringing all but its namesake to an unscheduled halt in 1967. The Canal Turn, which requires a little extra left-hand down from horse and jockey. Valentine's. And that agonisingly long run-in which seems so short if you're on the winner, so far if you're on the second.

Then there are 37 other runners to avoid, and, in Suny Bay's case, nearly as many adverse statistics to overcome. Only two greys have won the Grand National, The Lamb (1868 and 1871) and Nicolaus Silver (1961). Only four of the last 20 winners have carried 11st or more to victory and Suny Bay is shouldering top weight of 12st today. The last horse to carry that weight successfully was Red Rum in 1974.

The weight should not bother him - provided the ground is not too heavy after overnight rain.

He is a big, strapping, strong horse, all power behind the saddle and a backside on which you could spread a picnic blanket. Each morning this week there has been a bounce in his step, a swagger in his stride. "He has definitely improved since Cheltenham," says Simon McNeill, Brooks's assistant and a jockey in his own right, who rides out Suny Bay daily.

Graham Bradley, Suny Bay's jockey today, says: "He is one of those horses for whom the ground is more important than the weight. A lot of horses don't win the National because the ground isn't right for them on the day. It was too fast for him last year when he finished second to Lord Gyllene."

Suny Bay's last run was in the Tote Gold Cup, in which he finished fifth. His season got off to a winning start at Haydock back in November and 10 days later he completely disregarded the widely held opinion that he was incapable of running two good races so close to each other by winning the Hennessy Gold Cup. After disappointing in the King George VI Chase at Kempton on Boxing Day he returned home with a muscle problem in those powerful hind quarters, hence the warm-ups on the treadmill, the regular, almost daily visits from the stable's chiropractor, Mel Gurdon. If, as Brooks and Bradley insist, he was two weeks off a peak in the Gold Cup when he finished fifth to Cool Dawn then we will find out today. That was a fortnight ago on Thursday. The two weeks since then can be divided into a week spent recovering but still being exercised and a week spent building up for today; yesterday on the lorry bound for an overnight stay at Haydock racecourse, this morning a canter, and, at 3.45, he will be ready to run for his life.

In the Gold Cup he dragged his hind legs through the fence between the ditches. The gorse prickles he picked up became infected and within 24 hours he was reluctant to let anyone, not even his lad Phil Sharp, nor head lad Brian Delaney, near to bathe them. A couple of shots of antibiotics put that right, and within three days he had turned the corner. Small hairless scars are now the only evidence of that mistake, but for a moment it put his visit to Aintree in doubt.

The memory of his sore hind legs surfaced on Tuesday this week when Bradley schooled him over nine fences on Mandown. To the ordinary observer (me), he jumped impeccably, to Brooks he didn't jump with his usual aggression and to Bradley it felt all wrong. It was one of those gorgeous Lambourn mornings, mist shrouding the valleys like dust-sheets over furniture, but the sun was shining above it on Mandown and we should have felt glad to be alive. After speaking to Bradley we all felt depressed. Eddie Fisher, the head gallop man, leaned on his fork and prodded back the divots kicked up by Suny Bay. He has been known to throw the fork at anyone poaching a bit of virgin turf on his gallops without asking. "I hope we win it," he says, speaking on behalf of Lambourn, looking forward to the weekend. "Less of the we," says Brooks, a self-confessed bad loser. "I hope I win it." "I don't care as long as it comes back to Lambourn," says Fisher. "We've had a rotten year. We've usually had 350-400 winners by now. We won't have had many more than 150 so far this time - and only one Cheltenham winner." Suny Bay screwed a little awkwardly over one of the ditches. Bradley is not satisfied. "He usually takes me there and eats them," he says. "He was just being careful today and I'm sure it is because of his hind legs."

Decisions, decisions. You have to be flexible, think on your feet as a trainer and Brooks alters his plans for Suny Bay's Tuesday morning. After schooling he was to have walked home. Instead he decides he will school him over fences again on Thursday when he had planned to gallop him. He doesn't want him schooling and galloping so close to Aintree. "Tell you what, Brad," he says, "work him up the back of the Hill this morning."

There are 60 others to be trained at Uplands, however, and Bradley must first school a younger, wilder, tenser horse who always wants to go two gears faster than the jockey. The novice schools twice under restraint, all the time fighting Bradley for his head. "You know what I'd like to do?" says Bradley. "I'd like to take him flat out over the three 'National' fences [fences dressed with green fir to make them look like Aintree's]. That'll sort him." Brooks agrees to Bradley's request. "That is not an old jockey," he says, referring to the 38-year-old and the fact that most jockeys are past their sell-by date at 36. "I don't think many young jockeys riding the favourite would volunteer to do that on the Tuesday of National week. There must be two more good years in Brad yet."

Back in the yard, Bradley was happier because of Suny Bay's subsequent gallop. He, Brooks and Delaney discuss the schooling outside the tack room. It was decided not to school Suny Bay again on Thursday. It just presents another opportunity for something to go wrong, and as if on cue, it was announced later in the day that Belmont King had sustained an over-reach schooling that morning and was out of the race. It is better, they convince themselves, to go to Aintree with a horse jumping carefully. With the adrenaline flowing and all the excitement he will soon forget about his hind legs, and after all, exuberant jumping is the most common reason for horses falling at the first.

Bradley is old enough to be the father of Thierry Doumen, Joe Tizzard and half a dozen others riding in the race today. There are, however, those who believe some jockeys are lucky

round Aintree and others are not. Having finished only twice in 11 attempts, Bradley comes into the latter category. You know your luck is out at Aintree when you get a last-minute spare ride on the previous year's winner - as Bradley did on Hallo Dandy in 1985 - and you fall at the first. In 1995 he fell at the third on Zeta's Lad and another runner clipped the side of his helmet. He had 11 stitches in his ear and has only 70 per cent hearing in his left ear as a result. "If there's a party on downstairs," he says, making light of it, "I go to sleep on my right ear. I don't remember a thing about it except that I thought I'd be fine to ride in the Irish National a week later. It was three months before I was well again."

A jockey with a broken leg can, apart from a limp, look healthy. Not so with head injuries. I remember seeing Bradley a month after the fall. He looked so ill and pale I thought he would be lucky to ride again.

He was disappointed to be jocked off Suny Bay last season in favour of the now injured Jamie Osborne, and as far as good chances in the National go, the opportunities for Bradley are running out

....

He is a big, strapping, strong horse, all power behind the saddle, and a backside on which you could spread a picnic blanket

....

like the last grains of sand through an egg-timer. If he wants to add to his famous victories in the Cheltenham Gold Cup on Bregawn and Champion Hurdle on Collier Bay, it is now or never.

After all his work on Tuesday, Wednesday was a genuinely easy day for Suny Bay , just a trot. He even had the luxury of a lie-in, but by second lot the early morning mist had turned to low cloud which spat drizzle over Lambourn and Suny Bay.

McNeill will be able to view his progress (to the first at any rate) from Greenhil Tare Away, whom he rides for another stable today. In racing that is not considered treason, although were he to bring down Suny Bay . . .Greenhil Tare Away has completed the course once in five outings this season, doesn't like ditches, and is a horse other jockeys will want to avoid. "If Suny Bay goes down the inside I suppose you'll be down the outside?" I ask. "I thought I'd chaperone him," says McNeill, older than Bradley but no less brave. "It would keep everyone else away."

Most of the horses at Uplands are still exercised in sheets bearing the initial 'W' for Winter. Brooks took over from the legendary Fred Winter when the former Grand National winning jockey and trainer suffered a stroke in 1986. There are only four people at Uplands now who were there during Winter's day: Brooks, Delaney and the Cullen brothers. In his first year as a trainer, 1965, Winter sent out Jay Trump to win the National. Delaney led him up. He knows what winning the National is like." We had Jay

Trump, then Anglo the following year, and of course, Crisp," he says, turning away at the mention of the latter, who was caught on the line by Red Rum in 1973 having led all the way. "We had the cough in the yard when Jay Trump won. In those days horses coughed and had mucus coming out of their noses like candle wax. You knew they were ill. You can't tell you've got the modern virus until you run a horse, they never cough and they can go to pieces within a week. We've had it since Christmas but Suny Bay seems to have stayed clear of it."

Delaney is responsible for feeding Suny Bay and in a head lad that is an art. "That's changed as well," he reflects. "We feed them naked oats [genetically engineered huskless oats]. Suny Bay's as good a doer as we've got and if he ever went off his grub you'd know something was wrong. They used to get 15-17lbs of oats a day, but naked oats are very potent, they're heavier and all protein. It's easy to overfeed. My father always said any old fool could overfeed a horse but it took a clever man to just underfeed them. He'd also get alfalfa, fibre and additives. You don't feed them a linseed mash these days but the training has all changed and we're feeding them to be interval trained. We don't do the long hours of road work that we used to do. He's in great order, the horse. I think we just need luck now. Did you see how close Lord Gyllene came to being run out at the water jump by a loose horse last year?"

On Wednesday afternoon, Suny Bay had his racing plates (running shoes) fitted, on Thursday his last canter at home, and after a trot to stretch his legs yesterday he travelled up to the theatre of battle with Sharp, his doting lad. Last year Sharp stayed with Suny Bay and the other horses when everyone else was evacuated. He became a national hero. One newspaper even made him their racing personality of the year. When he went with Brooks to collect the award, the trainer said he should say something a bit more than just thank you. "What should I say?" asked Sharp. "Tell them," said Brooks, "that it was a good job you didn't know there was a bomb scare until Monday."

At breakfast on Monday morning most of the calls to Brooks's office were made by journalists wanting an interview with Sharp, who apart from Suny Bay last year, also led up runner-up Garrison Savannah in 1991. "I won't have Suny Bay beaten," predicts Sharp loyally. "Rough Quest is probably the biggest danger." Training one of the favourites for the National has its own stresses. "Perspective goes out of the window," says Brooks. "The tiniest little thing, like Brad saying he didn't school perfectly, puts you in a spiral of depression. Equally when Simon [McNeill] said he'd worked well on Thursday and nearly run away with him I was on a high for the rest of the day." Today, Brooks, as he has done for nine years, will join John Inverdale on Radio 5 Live before and after the National. In 1990 when I won on Mr Frisk, Inverdale asked Brooks what winning would do for the riding career of an amateur like me. "That is his career," said Brooks. It was, sadly for me, the truest thing said all day. If Suny Bay wins today it won't do Brooks's training career too much harm, nor, one supposes, his broadcasting career with 5 Live.

★4 / 4 / 98

EW Swanton

Captains must counter unsporting behaviour

A week in the frenetic world of international cricket can be a long time. In the euphoria of the two one-day matches in Barbados we rejoiced in two performances of high quality in several respects, albeit one was narrowly lost;

···

"We have to ask ourselves what sort of a game we are to pass on to future generations"

···

superlative fielding and a splendid sense of mutual confidence carried over from Sharjah; in particular Nick Knight's batting was a revelation which must bring him back into the forefront of Test reckoning.

The colourful St Vincent weekend was a rude awakening because a greatly improved West Indian performance was so ineptly countered. England, of course, have no counterparts to Brian Lara and Carl Hooper. If both are on song over 50 overs their side will almost certainly win. What was so disappointing was the batting technique, especially against the slow bowling shrewdly managed by Lara, timid lack of footwork and the incessant "working" of the ball to leg rather than hitting straight. The series is lost but let us hope for a worthier epilogue at Port-of-Spain.

My intention is to write an appropriate valedictory piece on Michael Atherton's captaincy, and I will come to it. However, the Test series was so unsatisfactory in crucial ways that no one who knew the game in better times, and who saw one Test in person and much of the rest on TV, can withhold judgement.

Integral to all cricket and beyond all else is the pitch, and the undisputed truth is that the only good one from start to finish of the tour was in Barbados: one out of six, though Antigua played well enough after the first day. With so much depending on Test matches, all concerned, and not least the spectators, are entitled to a perfect surface and I trust the International Cricket Council will voice their disapproval and consider penalties in future cases. The best batsmen, and likewise the best bowlers, have always developed their skills on plum pitches.

The most serious indictment of the Test series, however, was the undue pressuring of the umpires by constant appealing, some of it quite ridiculous. Worst were cases, tantamount to cheating, of gestures calculated to deceive the umpire. Michael Holding, whose shrewd and fair-minded comment on television throughout the series was a model - he was one of what I took to be a generally well-balanced and impartial team of TV critics - wrote from the heart in a *Sunday Times* article entitled 'This Unsporting Life' giving chapter and verse and censuring both sides. On the same day Dominic Lawson, editor of *The Sunday Telegraph*, who watched the Barbados Test, was equally disparaging.

On my inquiry Lord MacLaurin, chairman of the ECB, tells me he went along completely with both these articles. "We have to ask ourselves what sort of a game we are to pass on to future generations, and especially to the young cricketers now growing up," he said. "There is to be another of the annual meetings of the captains of all Test countries at Lord's in May prior to the series against South Africa. The captains' responsibilities must be expressed clearly once more. Only the accepted standards of sportsmanship will be tolerated."

What sort of a game are we indeed passing on? Andrew Longmore's bitter denunciation of school cricket standards in the new *Wisden* underlies the depth and breadth of the problem. Ian MacLaurin added that David Graveney, chairman of selectors, and David Lloyd, the coach, hold equally firm views.

It may be remarked that despite the serious blemishes the two teams, and especially the two captains, remained on friendly terms - which, of course, was very much to the good. The conclusion, however, must be that each side's conduct was tacitly accepted by the other. Lastly, on this matter, my impression was that Barry Jarman, the referee, whose function was to fortify the umpires and do his best to preserve the spirit of the game, was too tolerant.

And so to Atherton: as I watched him announcing his resignation in Antigua after the last Test, even-tempered, managing a smile, unhistrionic, completely in character, my mind

went back to the Lord's Test of 1993 against Australia. His stock was at such a low ebb that when he went to the wicket against a massive score he must have felt this was probably his last chance. Such was the background to the two innings of 80 and 99 wherein he batted over six chanceless hours. But for the slip turning for the third run, which would have given him his hundred, England might even have saved the match.

Gooch had already said that he would resign if and when Australia retained the Ashes, Alec Stewart and Mike Gatting being the favoured contenders. Some people now began to think again. Three Tests later, with Australia three up and two to come, the selectors turned to Atherton, and in his second Test as captain England won a handsome if belated victory, the first in 19 Tests against the old enemy.

England proceeded that winter to West Indies and the usual pummelling by speed. Surviving much intimidation, the captain topped the averages with 56. England surrendered the Wisden Trophy series 3-1, the victory being the famous one at Bridgetown wherein Atherton and Stewart put on 171 for the first wicket. Such has been very much the pattern of things throughout Atherton's almost five years in the job.

When assessing England's prospects in the West Indies at this new year I ventured to say that the result of the series would depend upon the degree to which England's faster bowlers could match the West Indies' opening attack. In the event the disparity was depressingly wide and conclusive. A captain can only be as successful as the talent under him allows. The crucial encounter was that of the first of the Trinidad Tests played on the hastily prepared pitch following the fiasco in Jamaica. Angus Fraser, with 11 for 110 in the match, had to face the fact that he was on the losing side. Against the England team of Sharjah the West Indies could not have made 150. Atherton must have known in his heart that the real chance he had had of winning the rubber had then almost certainly disappeared.

Atherton is phlegmatic by nature but as the tour progressed he must have been weighed down by the ceaseless columns of conjecture surrounding the captaincy. Day after day *The Times* ventured into psychological introspection, measuring up Atherton's worth against several candidates for the succession. While England were fighting their long rearguard in Antigua, *Daily Mail* readers were told "the match is already so far out of England's reach that it has long since become an irrelevance. Its chief purpose now must be as the final exercise in sorting the men from the boys, of deciding which of a handful of candidates will succeed Atherton". I found myself sighing for the craft of cricket-writing other, of course, than as in the columns of *The Daily Telegraph*. In certain instances, apart from his regular under-use of the razor, the late captain has disappointed. He even declined, surprisingly and inexcusably, on his last day to apologise for a silly gesture on the field despite strong pressure to do so. Yet over most of his record span of 52 Tests he has been the bulwark of the side, an indomitable fighter giving them a courageous example to which they have responded with the utmost respect and much affection. From his two taxing years as Cambridge captain he has shown an admirable sense of fairness and sympathy, an instinctive leader of men. These have been sterling virtues in the service of English cricket: may he now enjoy his batting with the burden off his shoulders. ★7/4/98

All bar none...the entire Arsenal team, with the hindrance of Newcastle's Stuart Pearce, defend against an Alan Shearer free-kick •Frank Coppi ★12/4/98

Along way from home ...two Tellytubbies slog it out around The Tower of London during The London Marathon •**Russell Cheyne** ★26/4/98

Michael Parkinson

The pain of Jake's progress

The golf course at the Phoenician Hotel hugs Camelback Mountain where cacti stand like sentinels on the rim and the desert blooms in pink and yellow flowers. If I wax lyrical it is only because I share the course with hummingbirds and hawks, jack rabbits and lizards. At one hole, where you park your buggy and climb the steps to a tee cut into the mountain, a gang of chipmunks under contract to Disney observe your departure before invading the vehicle looking for food. There are signs warning of rattlesnakes which, I fancy, are more a talking point for tourists than a public safety announcement. None the less, my imitation of a rattlesnake delivered as my wife reaches the top of her back swing is the most effective way I have yet devised of beating Mary.

The only problem we have is that of being a two-ball in a four-ball society. Holiday golf is designed for four players which means a twosome like us being paired with strangers on the first tee. It is like an arranged marriage: sometimes it works, more often than not it is a complete disaster. Jake from New Jersey said he was a 24-handicapper. It proved to be a generous assessment of his ability to hit a golf ball. He was equipped with the latest technology, carbon shafts, titanium balls, plutonium woods. He would have been better served by a croquet mallet. He insisted on playing the championship tees and was only dissuaded from fulfilling his foolish ambition after nine interminable holes by the intervention of the course marshal, who pointed out we were holding up play so badly the golfers behind us were building shelters for the night and the management had set up soup kitchens and group counselling.

Top of Jake's problems as a golfer was his inability to hit the ball further than 50 yards no matter which club he chose. This was entirely due to his habit of playing the ball so far outside his left foot even a straight-faced club sliced under the ball created a high, spinning lob. After every shot, he would curse and pose the rhetorical question: "What am I doing wrong?" Answer there came none. We know a hopeless cause when we see one. Like all slob golfers, Jake possessed neither the sense nor the manners to give up when his situation became hopeless. He was undoubtedly the most awful putter I have ever seen. He was awesomely bad. I do not exaggerate when I say his judgement of line and length were such that a blindfold would only have improved matters.

On average, he took five putts to get within the shadow of the flag. He was a serial putter, the kind who pursues the ball to the hole with total disregard for putting in turn or trampling an opponent's lines. Like all players who do not understand the conviviality of the game, he had no concept of sharing a round with his partners. Only once did he remark on an opponent's shot. He was standing next to me as I played my second shot across a lake to the green on the last hole.

By this time, I was past caring. It was 210 yards to the pin and I hit a five-wood which landed on the water 10 feet from shore, hippety-hopped on the surface and skipped on to the green to finish four feet from the pin. "Jeez. What happened?" said Jake. "Did you not see the gloved hand of the Lady of the Lake catch the ball and lob it on to the green?" I asked. He was unimpressed. "You couldn't do that again if you played golf until you were 100," he said. What I wanted to say was that if ever I did repeat the shot, the only certainty was he wouldn't be in the same four-ball. But I didn't. Instead, I smiled at a flowering cactus and waved at a passing hummingbird. Who wants ructions in Paradise?

The good news is the Arizona Diamondbacks no longer have the worst record in the National Baseball League. They won a series against the Marlins to put the Florida team in bottom spot. None the less, no one is getting too optimistic. There is something not quite right about this Arizona team, a tendency towards eccentric behaviour which makes them play like champs one minute and clowns the next. Mind you, any team playing in a stadium with a swimming pool at long-on is unlikely to behave in conventional manner. Last week, a home run landed in the pool and the ball was removed by a girl in a bikini. Normally, balls hit into the stands are kept by spectators as souvenirs. On this occasion, the club asked for their ball to be returned so it could be mounted and placed in the Hall of Fame. In spite of improved form, comparisons with the New York Mets of 1962 continue.

It is still possible the Diamondbacks could lose 120 games in their first season and challenge Casey Stengel's legendary outfit for the title of worst team ever. There is a competition among local sport columnists about who can tell the best story about Stengel's collection of weirdos and misfits. They played such awful baseball, they became a cult and the fans lived in dread of them winning. It seems to be agreed that if there was one player who more than any other contributed to their losing streak it was Marvin Throneberry.

'Marvellous Marv' was a one-man disaster area, a player renowned for snatching defeat from the jaws of victory. In one game, he drove the ball to centrefield for a certain triple. As he stood at third hitching up his pants and basking in the crowd's acclaim, the umpire called him out for not touching first base. When Stengel made to confront the umpire, he was stopped by one of his coaches. "Don't waste your time boss, Marv missed second, too," he said.

Throneberry won a prize for his prowess as a slugger. He was presented with a boat. The nearest lake to where he lived was 150 miles away. The most water Marv had seen in his life was in the bath tub. Still, a boat is a boat. He put the cabin cruiser in his garage awaiting the flood. Then he was told he would have to pay tax on it because it was classified as earned income. Marv thought it was a gift. Concerned by such financial problems, he plucked up courage to ask Stengel for a rise. This took guts, considering he was the worst ball player in the worst team in America, and the man generally believed to be most responsible for Stengel's brittle disposition. Wearing his best suit, Marv opened the door to Stengel's office and stepped inside. As he slammed the door behind him, the knob came off in his hand. Stengel was not at his desk. He had gone to the races. Throneberry was rescued from an upstairs window by officers from the New York Fire Department.

....

After every shot, he would curse and pose the rhetorical question: "What am I doing wrong?"

....

At season's end, the Marvin Throneberry Fan Club, which by now included just about the entire population of New York, threw a dinner for their hero. When Marv arrived, the security guards wouldn't let him in because the joint was full. So he sat in a bar across the street watching the partygoers have a good time on his behalf.

There is something heroic about Throneberry, a majestic aspect to his innocence and incompetence no longer to be found in a game where agents and spin doctors iron out the wrinkles so what you get is as interesting as processed cheese. I have the feeling that if the Arizona Diamondbacks turn out to be as bad as the Mets, it will be classified as a disaster. In 1963, Stengel's team became a much loved institution.

Final thought from Stengel (we must never tire of quoting the Classics) upon being asked his opinion of an unpromising 19-year-old ball player: "If he lives for another 10 years he has a fair chance of becoming 29."

★27/4/98

April 1998

Sarah Edworthy

Antipodean racer takes on Murray's mantle

Football Diary

•Like most managers Graham Taylor preaches the philosophy of football being a team game, and therefore is not greatly enamoured with player-of-the-season awards. There is another reason. "I'm not a great lover of them since I was cheated out of winning one at Lincoln," he says. Apparently the mother of the only other contender went around one of the major department stores in Lincoln, and collected votes from customers for her son, who finished well ahead of Taylor. Did he not like that.

Sport Around The World

•There are times when Floyd Patterson cannot remember his wife's name, who he beat to win the world title, or how many rounds there are in a fight. The sorry state of Patterson's mind became apparent after a hearing to consider the legality of "extreme fighting" - a new concept in individual combat. Patterson was forced to resign as head of the New York State Athletic Commission, who held the hearing, when the promoters of "extreme fighting" made a videotape of his deliberations.

Patterson, 63, who was world champion in 1956-59, and again from 1960-62, has serious problems with short-term memory, and NYSAC had tried to shield him from public scrutiny. Under questioning from a lawyer, Patterson could not recall that he beat Archie Moore to win the title in a 1956 fight in Chicago. He also thought title fights were 15 rounds instead of the current 12. "It's hard for me to think when I'm tired," said Patterson. "Sometimes I can't even remember my wife's name."

•A squad of footballers are in training for a non-footballing display of talent to save their club from bankruptcy. The lads of Alfacar, near Granada in southern Spain, who play in the top division of the regional league, are planning to perform a Full Monty. They have taken over the main discotheque in the town of 5,000 for a 40-minute striptease. Thirteen of the players will take part, but eight others will remain on the bench on the orders of their girlfriends. Club president Jose Fernandez said: "We're in dire financial trouble. The idea came after some of the lads had seen the British film. I don't know if I've got the shape to join in the routine, but I will certainly be up there on the stage."

Letters To The Sports Editor

•SIR - English stew. Take a dozen mediocre cricketers. Remove hearts, guts and residual talent then marinade in a mixture of excess pay and self-importance. Stuff them with over-confidence, lack of effort and lethargy and stew them in their own fat for three days in a hot climate. Serve on a bed of lame excuses with a lip-gloss sauce and garnish liberally with sack cloth (but no ashes). - BOB WYDELL, Oswestry, Shropshire.

•SIR - Most people are aware of the old adage about lies, damned lies and statistics. We can now add a fourth element: the Duckworth/Lewis system of determining the results of one-day cricket matches. No computer in the world can predict human inspiration or fraility, but that is what this outrageous system purports to do. What is wrong with calling it quits in undecided league and international matches? As for rain-affected cup ties, is it beyond the nous and flexibility of the cricket authorities to arrange replays. It may be inconvenient, but so what? - KEN BLIGHTON, Pontefract, W Yorks.

You have to be brave, and protected with a reinforced carbon-fibre insouciance, to take over the mantle of Murray Walker so we should salute Charlie Cox - trademark one-liner: "That car's got as much grip as a dog on lino" - who has taken over the Voice of Motorsport's microphone in BBC *Grandstand's* coverage of the British Touring Car Championship. As he says himself, his new role is absolutely daunting.

"I got to be his sidekick last year so as I walked around the pits at Thruxton, everyone was asking how does it feel to be Murray? And the only response was (Australian drawl in crescendo): 'Great, great, great. It's maaaaarvellous to be Murray'. I've always been a fan of his. I was co-commentating with Murray Walker long before Murray ever knew about it."

Cox has impeccable credentials for the job. A part-time driver in this season's British GT Championship, his past honours include winning the British Saloon Car Championship (Class A) in 1993 and 1994, and the prestigious Willhire 24-hour race in 1993. In a BTCC event at Brands Hatch in 1995, he achieved what was then the highest placing for an independent driver, finishing fifth after starting 19th on the grid.

He is not a purist or a techno-bore. He loves the fun of it. In terms of action-packed experience he did not actively seek, he can also draw upon the sensation of suffering one of the BTCC's most spectacular crashes, rolling his Ford Mondeo 11 times. He had to be cut from the wreckage and was out of work for three months recovering from head injuries. "It was an expensive and very painful way of getting media coverage," he says.

His day job is managing director of DMG Radio Ltd. He started in radio journalism in 1975 in Sydney, moving to London in 1990 to run LBC and London Talkback, so he's been a talk guy, a producer and the boss. After a year of moonlighting alongside Walker's contagious outbursts, his broadcasting style is even more "seat of the pants" stuff.

"I just start waving my arms around and go for it. I look like I'm directing traffic. It was absolutely frantic with Murray. He would always stand up and I would sit down and he said: "I'll hit you when it's your turn". Every second response I made started with 'boof' as I was partially winded. The engineers would turn the sound of my own voice down in my headphones and turn Murray's up to make me yell more. If you turned the sound of us off we'd look like a pair of crazed baboons dancing around a glass cage."

A feature of motor-racing commentary pairs is that reluctance to relinquish the microphone. It is easy to envisage a brawl on the commentary booth floor as two ex-drivers fight for airtime like drivers fighting for their line into a corner. With former Formula One driver John Watson - a bit of a Michael Schumacher on that front - their introductory commentary was commendably bumper to bumper. Or Braille-driving, as Cox might have put it. If Walker's trademark is muddly talking amid hysterical excitement, Cox's distinction is to throw in wry one-liners. A car has had "more hits than Elvis", the 1994 Alfa Romeo driver Giampiero Simoni, who routinely collected bits of other cars during a race, is summed up as: "So many wing mirrors, so little time".

"You can't work them out or it sounds like you have a bursting one-liner you've been waiting to drop on people. They're just colourful antipodean expressions. If anyone compliments me on the commentary, they always say how funny it was. They never talk about the majesty of my descriptions."

> ## "If you turned the sound of us off we'd look like a pair of crazed baboons dancing around a glass cage"

It will take less than 52 seconds to read the following (and you do not have to pay £16.95 on top of an annual Sky subscription, or view it through a snowstorm). Herbie Hide's ridiculous embarrassing moment in the ring of the Nynex Arena, which was supposed to herald the "big fight" section of the programme, devalued both the nature of a sporting contest and the WBO heavyweight title. If pay-per-view television itself devalues the validity of sport by restricting witnesses to a particular encounter, the promoters and Sky Box Office have conspired to produce a farce. No wonder Hide wanted to live up to his name; not the Dancing Destroyer, he looked keen to run off and Hide.

★20/4/98

In... Robert Croft, of Glamorgan, just gets home before Keith Brown's throw during the Axa League game against Middlesex •**Philip Brown** ★3/5/98   43

May 1998

2: Barnsley's defeat at Leicester confirms their relegation from the Premiership. Doncaster's last game in the Football League, at home to Colchester, is delayed by two pitch invasions. Sheffield Eagles crush Wigan 17-8 in rugby league's Silk Cut Challenge Cup final. Spencer Oliver, the European super-bantamweight champion, requires emergency surgery to remove a blood clot in his brain after his fight against Ukraine's Sergei Devakov.

3: Arsenal's defeat of Everton confirms them as Premiership champions. Despite winning 5-2 at Stoke, Manchester City are relegated to the Second Division.

4: John Higgins wins the World Snooker Championship. Arsenal add the women's FA Cup to their list of trophies, beating Croydon 3-2 in the final.

5: Alec Stewart is named as England captain for the six-Test series against South Africa.

6: Inter Milan beat Lazio 3-0 to win the UEFA Cup final in Paris.

10: Mika Hakkinen and David Coulthard score a McLaren one-two in the Spanish Grand Prix. Chris Bartle wins Badminton's three-day event on Word Perfect II.

11: Wim Jansen resigns as manager just 48 hours after Celtic end Rangers' nine-year run as Scottish League champions.

12: The FA decide Alan Shearer is not guilty in the Neil Lennon Affair. England are beaten 44-11 in the semi-finals of the women's Rugby World Cup in Amsterdam. Brian Little takes over as manager of Stoke.

13: A goal by Gianfranco Zola lands Chelsea the European Cup-Winners' Cup with a 1-0 win.

16: Arsenal complete the Double by beating Newcastle 2-0 in the FA Cup final. Rangers are beaten 2-1 in the Scottish Cup final by Hearts.

17: Newcastle land rugby union's Premiership after beating Harlequins 44-20. Sheffield Wednesday part company with manager Ron Atkinson.

20: Real Madrid win the European Champions' Cup with a 1-0 win over Juventus in Amsterdam.

23: England's footballers are held 0-0 at Wembley in a World Cup warm-up game by Saudi Arabia. Scotland draw 2-2 with Colombia in New York. Llanelli beat Ebbw Vale 19-12 to win the Swalec Cup final.

24: England save some face by winning the last one-day international against South Africa by seven wickets at Headingley. The Paul Cayard-skippered EF Language wins the Whitbread round-the-world race.

25: Charlton reach the Premiership after beating Sunderland 7-6 in a penalty shootout, following a remarkable 4-4 draw in the First Division playoff at Wembley. Colin Montgomerie wins the Volvo PGA Championship by one stroke at Wentworth.

26: Scotland are beaten 51-26 by Fiji in the first match of their summer tour.

27: Michael Owen scores his first international goal in England's 1-0 win over Morocco in Casablanca.

29: England are held 0-0 by Belgium in Casablanca in their final World Cup warm-up game. Chelsea sign Pierluigi Casiraghi from Lazio for £5 million.

31: Glenn Hoddle leaves Paul Gascoigne out of his 22-man squad for the World Cup. Graeme Hick's 132 against Sussex at Worcester is the 100th hundred of his career.

Mudlark Shay Barry returns victorious on Wally Wallensky at Punchestown •**Ed Byrne** ★**1/5/98**

Paul Hayward

English warm to Johnny Foreigner

Beneath the twin towers at Wembley a group of Newcastle supporters sang the theme tune to *Dad's Army* with the words: "Who do you think you are kidding Mr Wenger, if you think the Double's done?" But that was before Arsenal beat Newcastle with goals from Marc Overmars (Dutch) and Nicolas Anelka (French) to complete the European conquest of English football.

The Premiership, the FA Cup, the Coca-Cola Cup, the European Cup-Winners' Cup: all have been won by non-British managers of teams led by Continental luminaries. The closest thing Arsenal's first Double-winning side had to a foreign player was Charlie George, who came from another galaxy. Eddie Kelly, who scored in that '71 final, recalled that on the night of the team's championship-winning celebration he managed to stay in the pub until eight o'clock the following morning. Some of the shaggy-haired heroes of that season look as if they have been carousing ever since.

The truth is that English football has been taught a series of resounding lessons by people who were drawn to the extravagant spending of another outsider: a certain R Murdoch. Who scored the winning goal for Chelsea in Stockholm? Gianfranco Zola. Who is footballer of the year? Dennis Bergkamp. Who broke Rangers' run of nine consecutive Scottish titles? Another Dutchman - Wim Jansen. And who fused on to Highbury's ploughman spirit the pace and sophistication of the mainstream European game? Arsene Wenger, *l'etranger* whose French flag is firmly planted in a few good old Anglo prejudices. Moved as he was by the generosity of Newcastle's fans in applauding Arsenal at the finish, Wenger even meditated on the virtues of "the English people" like an explorer who had found the natives up river surprisingly agreeable.

Wenger is walking proof that the English game has nothing to fear from the intelligent application of ideas that were once regarded as pure quackery in what is, at root, a deeply parochial and conservative realm. Sometimes even Wenger seems amazed at how quickly he was able to subjugate the English leagues. Wow - he makes his players eat rice and pasta instead of steak and kidney pies. Incredible - he applies stretching routines and discourages boozing on the grounds that games are often decided in the final third of the game when lager-legs are starting to lag. The Arsenal players even look different: more sinewy, leathery, lighter and quicker in reflex and thought.

The attention to detail is impressive. Before a poor final kicked off the Arsenal substitutes changed into light white T-shirts to help them stay cool. The Newcastle reserves wore cloying black tops that hugged the neckline. On the field Wenger could have laid a spirit level along his back four and got the bubble dead centre. Newcastle's defence lurched forward and back like a line of rioters taking on the police. It was Overmars and Anelka who punished them with batons.

English football is in a curiously schizoid state. The FA and leading clubs are knocking up centres of excellence in an attempt to improve skills and homogenise coaching programmes. Simon Clifford, a primary school teacher, has just formed a national association for the promotion of *futebol de salao*, a small-ball game that Clifford believes to be the secret of Brazil's success. In the meantime Manchester United have made a Dutchman (Jaap Stam) the world's most expensive defender and Wenger is looking to buy two new players, almost certainly from abroad. The newspapers offer a daily tickertape of overseas targets, many of whom are known only to wiseguy scouts and Euro-footie

....

Newcastle's defence lurched forward and back like a line of rioters taking on the police

....

trainspotters. Up go the English academies, and off go the raiding parties to all ports European.

It would require either a displaced native player or a seriously dim mind to think that Johnny Foreigner is undermining the English game. Hang around outside a Premier League ground and the evidence of conversion is scrawled on thousands of replica-shirted backs. The most popular names are Vialli, Zola, Bergkamp and Ginola (though Shearer still dominates Geordie shoulders). The polyglot Wenger is revered and

adored at Highbury, where the 1971 side are merely a honeyed memory for Arsenal fans under 35. At their best, the present team produce a wonderful synchronicity between defence, midfield and attack. For opponents a triple nightmare looms: first Petit and Vieira, then the Praetorian guard of possibly English football's most successful back four. Get through that lot and there is still David Seaman to deal with. That is assuming they have stopped the runaway train of Parlour and Overmars and smothered the scoring prowess of Bergkamp, Anelka, Wright or Wreh.

There are those who argue that Arsenal are merely the best of a bad bunch, who, Chelsea aside, were shown up in Europe as impostors. Though such caution acts as a useful corrective to the eulogies being heaped on a team still largely untested east of Ipswich, it is unreasonable to deny the magnitude of Wenger's achievement in reviving a team who were on the floor of their soul before Christmas. The Arsenal of '98 combine a ferocious collective spirit with occasional decorous flourishes and as such provide a template that most Premiership managers will be falling over their contacts books to copy. Tony Adams and Pat Rice are highly influential figures inside Highbury. Gwyn Williams and Graham Rix underpin Vialli's success. Foreign players and coaches are the catalysts rather than sole creators.

The FA Cup final was again a wonderfully clamorous and technicolour English ritual that generated heights of passion that the clubs in Wenger's own country can only fantasise about. Wenger, Ginola and Eric Cantona have all spoken admiringly about the furnace blast of British footballing ardour. But when the heart has had its say the head makes the important moves. From the nadir of November and December, when they lost four League games in six, Arsenal's season has turned into a pageant. At Christmas the sages were wondering whether the present Manchester United might be a match for Sir Matt Busby's great teams of the 1950s and Sixties. Now they are wondering whether the Arsenal has been so well stocked.

English football's gradually eroding parochialism is both its weakness and its strength. In the seething crater of Wembley it was possible to imagine that football's boundaries were drawn by the oval of the old stands. The FA Cup final, the Premiership season, were fine as far as they went. But still it is worth recording that Chelsea's European victory was only the third by English clubs this decade in all three competitions.

Up in Glasgow even the winning goalscorer in the Scottish Cup final (Stephane Adaam) was foreign and the match reports were peppered with surnames such as Porrini and Rousset. It is no different in Spain or Italy, as it happens, so English football might be said to be coming into line with European football's post-passport world. Newcastle, too, are bristling with foreign imports, but under duress their fans chanted for the injection of some native Geordie steel. "One Stevie Watson," they sang, "there's only one Stevie Watson." Their team wore black and white, but might as well have been playing in sepia.

★18/5/98

Simon Hughes

Home from the ends of the earth

Sea Breeze. To most people a pleasurable phenomenon that cools a stifling afternoon or adds a bracing edge to a dank winter walk. But to round-the-world yachtsmen the term has entirely different connotations. Hundreds of miles from land, the Roaring Forties whip waves into liquid Himalayas and spike daggers of freezing water through the thickest dry-suits. In the treacherous ocean between New Zealand and South America, to call the prevailing wind a sea breeze is to regard climbing Everest as a fell walk. These sailors have fought with the mother of all sea breezes.

Their return to Southampton all spick and span after 128 days at sea, the boats re-trimmed and fitted, sails newly sewn, logos freshly applied, belies the harrowing ordeal they have survived. Only their bleached, matted hair, rugged complexions and the slight wildness in their eyes hints at the daily calamity of participation in the Whitbread. Swedish sponsored, American skippered, EF Language had already scored enough points to clinch the 31,600-mile race before finishing the last leg in second place. The predominantly American crew stepped up to accept the Volvo Trophy looking calm and rested.

Yet some months before, an intrepid journalist boarded EF Language as they were lurching across the Indian Ocean. "Welcome," said the oil-skinned crewman helping him up, "though I can't imagine why you'd even want to come aboard. Everything's broken, everybody's hurt, we stink, the boat stinks, we haven't been out of our foul-weather gear for 16 days." None of them had had a wink of sleep either.

The British crew of Silk Cut, meanwhile, were recounting a near-death encounter with a huge vessel in the Atlantic fog. "We suddenly noticed another blip on our radar getting very close, and we thought it was a yacht," said trimmer Ado Stead. "Then our blip and their blip merged, and I saw the bow wave of this giant ship, ahead of us. We looked up and saw the side of the ship towering over and I shouted, 'Bear away!' Another 60 feet on and we'd have been history."

Such traumas are 10 a penny in the Whitbread which largely explains why once on terra firma crews replace rough days on the ocean wave with tough nights on the tiles. The wild bender is a turbulent sea substitute. In harbour, the Silk Cut boys usually play 'fizz-buzz', a drinking game in which by far the least unpleasant forfeit is downing a pint of sea water, before the inevitable skirt-pursuit begins. Naturally, the eight-month event takes its toll on domestic arrangements. Gordon Maguire, the handsome watch leader of Silk Cut, began the race married to Eileen. Now

they are getting a divorce and he is dating the model Jo Guest.

The night before the final leg from La Rochelle, the Silk Cut crew were appropriately restrained. They met early for dinner, sipped beers and picked glumly at plates of crustacea, having discovered to their dismay they'd been herded into a shellfish restaurant. "After weeks of living off salty mashed potato and porridge, all we want on shore is steak, something we can chew on," said helmsman Gerry Mitchell.

....

Only their bleached, matted hair, rugged complexions and the slight wildness in their eyes hints at the daily calamity of participation in the Whitbread

....

Having shaken several leathery hands, I sat between Mitchell and the engineer known only as Lightning, a gorilla of a man who beat Jonah Lomu in a speed-winding challenge during the Auckland stop-over. Neither crewman had a job after the Whitbread or knew what the future held. Why did they do it? "One night you're sitting down below feeling awful, cold, wet, hungry, at your lowest point," said Mitchell. "The next night you're on deck, the sea's smooth, you can see nothing but shining stars and you think, 'Ah, this is the life'." Sailing naked, which is apparently what they do crossing the Equator, must be a similar thrill.

The serious business of negotiating the final leg began at midnight. Vincent Geake, Silk Cut's navigator, the only crew member without a tan (he inhabits a gadget-laden cubby hole below deck), outlines the proposed route to the rest. There is a discrepancy in the wind reports from French and English weather stations, so they will have to play it by ear. "If flies suddenly buzz around the boat you can tell the breeze is about to change," Vincent informs me. It is reassuring that in this high-tech sport not everything is measured by instruments.

Smith, with his wiry mop, craggy features and spindly body, easily mistaken for an ageing rock star, listens attentively, then gives a quick pep talk: Silk Cut can still finish second overall. "Right, the deal is, it's going to be very close, the boats aren't

going to be separated by much. Sail changes are going to be crucial, if anyone gets too far ahead, it's going to be impossible to catch up. So we'll have to be ready for some quick action."

The gargantuan figure of Dennis Conner - plus wife about a third of his size and age - pops by to wish Smith all the best. "Good luck, Lawrie," he drawls, "looks like this last leg will be a real sailboat race. Makes a nice change." "There he goes, the world's only leading sportsman who can't see his own feet," comments one of Smith's colleagues as Conner climbs back on board Toshiba.

"That's the one thing we haven't had our fair share of - luck," observes Smith, reflecting on his £6 million campaign. "Our mast is the same as EF Language's. If theirs had broken instead of ours [off the South American coast] our final positions could probably have been reversed."

The purple sloop cruises slowly out of port to the cheers and waves of a thousand well-wishers, and makes its way to the race start. These are two yellow buoys not easy to spy among all the private yachts and spectator boats. Silk Cut sails up and down the approach, Geake shouting regular time checks. With five minutes to go all nine competitors are circling behind the start line, like the runners in the Grand National. "Ten seconds, nine, eight . . ," Geake shouts to the seven men on deck frenetically winding and winching.

Sitting at the stern, all I can see are the towering sails of the other boats converging on ours, jockeying for the best track. Somehow they all peel away and miss each other, and the race is on. "Gybe!" shouts Smith. "Reach and set." He wants the spinnaker up, but 50 feet away, the bowman can't hear him. Most seem to have a telepathic understanding with the skipper, tightening a winch or adjusting a sail without being told.

The chop from a veritable armada of spectator boats is proving more of a handicap than the other competitors, and Smith steers away on a different tack, but a large cruiser packed with EF Language supporters encroaches too close. "Oi, piss off," the Silk Cut crew yell repeatedly, gesticulating. The commotion dies down after half an hour and with the yacht bowling along at 12 knots, I wish them luck, and escape into a passing dinghy. Later, we fly over the fleet, six abreast heading into the sunset. From the air they look like one-winged moths crawling over a glass table.

It turns out Silk Cut have gone too wide and missed the best breeze. They zig-zag up the Solent trying to find eddies but finish fourth, half an hour behind the leg winner, Merit Cup. They get a tumultuous welcome from the throng cramming cruisers, ferries and shore vantage points, but are a disappointing overall fifth.

On the podium, Smith sprays his loyal men with champagne, but Paul Cayard, the Californian skipper of the victorious EF Language, tucks a bottle quietly under his arm. Herein lie their differences. Smith is a flamboyant leader, thriving on instinct, flying by the seat of his pants. Cayard, a brilliant businessman and tactician who turned down the job to manage Ferrari's Formula One team, is meticulous, leaving nothing to chance. "They [EF Language] did 100 things one per cent better rather than one thing 100 per cent better," compliments Grant Dalton, skipper of Merit Cup.

This was the Whitbread's 25-year watershed. Finding an international event increasingly difficult to support, the brewery have handed control over to Volvo for the next round-the-world in four years' time, making this the last finish in Britain. From now on it is likely to wind up in Gothenburg. Announcing that it will henceforth be known as the Volvo Ocean Race, the new sponsors emphasised their core values - "strength, leading edge technology and safety" - in building a new image for the event. Just as long as they don't insist the boats are installed with irritating warnings telling passengers to belt up . . . ★25/5/98

Tim Rice

Romantic veil tale brings new twist to Ashes saga

The shock news that England may not be travelling to Australia this winter to regain the Ashes of a burnt bail but the Ashes of Florence Rose Murphy's veil, will, all Englishmen hope, not dampen the sporting ardour of our team when they set out on what cynics already regard as mission all but impossible.

Miss Murphy, who presented the England captain, the Hon Ivo Bligh, with an urn of ashes after the England win at Sydney in January 1883, has recently been exposed by her daughter-in-law, the Dowager Countess of Darnley, as having burnt her veil, not a bail as claimed at the time. This story rings only too true, if only because setting fire to a bail in the SCG bleachers, even in those less safety-conscious times, would have been a lengthy process certain to attract the attention of the most sluggish of groundstaff. A quick flash with an F R Spofforth souvenir lighter, however, would have reduced a delicate veil to embers within seconds. But above all, Miss Murphy had romantic designs on the England captain, and the way to a cricketer's heart is via his sporting equipment.

It is unlikely that Bligh, later the Earl of Darnley, would have expressed more than a passing interest in a charred headscarf, but a roasted bail was the Full Murphy. Florence duly became Mrs Bligh (and later the Countess of Darnley), and she presented the urn to the Memorial Gallery at Lord's after her husband's death in 1927.

Extensive research by your correspondent (i.e. the *Sydney Morning Herald* found in Los Angeles airport) has revealed that there were further torrid displays of passion taking place behind the pavilion in those pioneer days of Test cricket. Five months before Florence's conflagration, Australia achieved an extraordinary seven-run win at the Oval, their first on English soil. This led to the *Sporting Times'* mock obituary stating that the body of English cricket would be cremated and the ashes taken to Australia, which in turn inspired Florence's pyre the following winter. The Australian captain at the Oval, W L Murdoch, removed a chunk of the ball that had secured victory and had it mounted in a gold and diamond brooch. This he gave to a bank manager's wife, Mrs Greenlaw, about whom little is publicly known, and about whose relationship with the leading Australian batsman of his day, even less.

The rest of the ball resides today at the Melbourne Cricket Ground and there is indeed a little piece missing. That segment is to be auctioned by Christie's down under and is expected to raise around $A315,000 (£125,000), mainly because the gold and diamond brooch is still attached to it. The intrinsic worth of the item is around $A32,500, but its historical importance raises the odds considerably.

A letter from Jack Blackham, the Australian wicketkeeper in that Oval match, written in 1924 to Mrs Greenlaw's daughter, states that "your mother . . . was a great lover of cricket and a personal friend of Mr Murdoch". However personal the friendship between Mrs Greenlaw and Billy Murdoch, we must assume that there was nothing doing by 1884, when on the boat home from Murdoch's fourth tour of England, the great player was captivated by the charms of Jemima Watson, an Australian gold-mining heiress from Bendigo and amateur actress. Jemima also caused Billy to forget about a Derbyshire lass of whom he had become fond during the tour. Possibly her distractions accounted for Murdoch's disappointing innings of six against Derbyshire in early June, though he ended the summer in a blaze of glory which included the first double century in Test cricket, 211 at his happy hunting ground, the Oval.

Murdoch married Ms Watson almost as soon as they were down the gangplank. He scored only five and seven in his first Test as a married man just a week later and then, along with the entire Australian side, was dropped after the authorities refused to pay their team 50 per cent of the gate money for the next match. Murdoch, a solicitor, resumed full-time legal practice and did not return to the Australian XI until he captained his country for his fifth (fourth as captain) and final tour of England in 1890.

Murdoch and his wife eventually settled in England. He even played for England, against South Africa at Cape Town in March 1892, under the captaincy of Walter Read. He captained Sussex from 1893 to 1899, and then played for London County for a few years with his friend and rival, W G Grace. In 1911, seven years after his last first-class match, by now 56 years old and with five children, he revisited Australia after the death of his brother and father-in-law, to attend to family matters, but was never to return to his adopted country alive. He died watching a Test between Australia and South Africa, collapsing in the Melbourne pavilion from a stroke.

His distraught widow arranged for his body to be embalmed and shipped to England. During his funeral at Kensal Green cemetery on May 18, 1911, all play on English county

Miss Murphy had romantic designs on the England captain, and the way to a cricketer's heart is via his sporting equipment

grounds was suspended, such was the esteem in which he was held, both as a man and as a cricketer.

Billy Murdoch's energy, charm and zest for life captivated all who came into contact with him, male or female. It will be surprising if this is not reflected a century after his greatest cricketing achievements by a hefty sum being paid for his romantic offering to Mrs Greenlaw, and disappointing if this does not cause MCC members to reflect further on the crucial contribution women have made to cricket. ★6/5/98

Henry Winter

Shearer on defensive over clash

The debate over the muscular style of Alan Shearer, the Newcastle United and England centre-forward, has intensified. Shearer spoke out in his defence, following an incident that left Neil Lennon, of Leicester City, with a cut and bruised face. Meanwhile, Christian Gross, the Tottenham Hotspur head coach, said that Shearer broke Ramon Vega's nose several days earlier. Kenny Dalglish, in turn, vociferously supported Shearer.

Both Lennon and Shearer looked at the videotape which showed the Newcastle player's left boot catch Lennon in the face. Lennon's version was that "it was a bit naughty". The Leicester manager, Martin O'Neill, refused to take the matter further, although in the heated aftermath of the match he had said: "You don't do that whether you are Alan Shearer or the Pope."

Shearer himself said: "I have now seen the television pictures of the incident and I am amazed how bad it looks by comparison to what actually happened. I was brought down by Neil Lennon over by the touchline and we both fell clumsily. As I tried to get to my feet I had to really tug my left foot free and the momentum of doing this looked on television like a kick. It certainly wasn't and the fact that Neil is virtually unmarked confirms this. If I did accidentally catch him, I certainly did not mean to. I would never try to deliberately hurt a fellow professional."

The Football Association said they were awaiting the report of the referee, Martin Bodenham, who did not speak to Shearer following the incident. "At this stage what course of action we take is totally dependent on that," a spokesman said. As any action is unlikely to be initiated immedicately, if at all, there is no possibility of Shearer being suspended for the FA Cup final on May 16. Leicester consider the case closed. "I'm not going to pursue the matter and there will be no official complaint," O'Neill said before adding: "the video evidence will prove it for itself."

Since returning from a horrific pre-season ankle injury, Shearer has been involved in various incidents, notably with Stevenage Borough's centre-halves, Leeds United's Jimmy Floyd

Robert Edwards

Britain's sports car ace who defied the odds

This week marks the 40th anniversary of the death of one of Britain's most remarkable sportsmen. On May 19 1958, Archie Scott-Brown succumbed to the burns he had received the previous day in a crash at Spa-Francorchamps, in Belgium. At the time, Scott-Brown was a popular media figure, and his partnership with Brian Lister, the Cambridge-based manufacturer, was a double act which caught the imagination of a generation of fans. At the time, Scott-Brown was one of the relatively few successful British drivers. He joined the first rank relatively early in his career with his entry to the 1956 British Grand Prix. Scott-Brown, though, was very different from his fellow competitors.

He was born with only one sound limb, his left arm. His right arm and both legs were severely truncated, and only after several dozen operations as a child was he able to walk. His racing cars were built to accommodate his height of five feet and he would change gear with his left hand, the stump of his right arm being jammed through the steering wheel to maintain control.His progress through the lists as a club racer was swift, though, and by 1954, he had teamed up with Lister, who persuaded his family firm to set aside a budget to produce a sports car bearing the Lister name. Powered by MG, Bristol, Maserati and Jaguar engines, the Lister marque romped home in domestic sports car races time after time, beating works teams and privateers alike. Initially, though, Scott-Brown's racing licence was revoked on medical grounds; it took him two months to recover it.

Outside sports cars, Scott-Brown drove in Formula One for Connaught, the Surrey-based firm owned by Ken McAlpine. In his first time out in a Formula One car, at Goodwood, he broke Mike Hawthorn's circuit record in testing and, if the car held together, he usually featured in the race. Foreign events were sometimes a problem, though. He was entered for the Italian Grand Prix at Monza in September 1956, but, even after taking provisional pole position, his entry was refused on medical grounds. Other organisers were less difficult and his entries were accepted at Sebring, Kristianstad and Nurburgring. Typically, though, if Scott-Brown was not allowed to drive the car, nobody else did.

It was the withdrawal of the works Jaguar effort at the end of 1956 which allowed the development of the Lister-Jaguar and out of 14 races entered during the 1957 season, Scott-Brown and the Lister won 11 of them. The withdrawal, for financial reasons, of the Connaught effort meant that Scott-Brown had no Formula One drive for 1957 so he was able to concentrate on sports cars. The sports car Grand Prix at Spa-Francorchamps in 1958 was a dangerous race, the circuit speed reaching up to 180 mph on the straights. The weather was unreliable, and the circuit was often wet in some areas, dry in others. Scott-Brown lost control while dicing for the lead with his team-mate Masten Gregory. The Lister-Jaguar skidded on a wet piece of track, slid off the circuit and flew over the verge into the infield where it tipped over and burst into flames. Two policemen pulled him out, but without fireproof clothing, he was too badly burned to survive. He died, aged 31, the next day.

★18/5/98

Rachel Yankee of Arsenal Ladies tangles with

Hasselbaink and Adrian Moses, of Barnsley. David Ginola has criticised Shearer, and Gross has followed suit regarding Vega.

"Shearer broke Vega's nose after just two minutes with his elbow and Ramon had to play the whole game with the injury," Gross insisted. "I cannot say if it was deliberate, but it was a heavy challenge. Shearer is a very physical player and a very clever player. He uses his body well and protects the ball very well. It must be difficult for him when he is under pressure for 90 minutes against a player like Sol Campbell or Martin Keown."

Dalglish rushed to Shearer's defence. "Alan is a fine ambassador for the game and people who make accusations against him do so because he is easy prey," the Newcastle manager said. "It happens to anybody who does well at football. They end up getting criticism which is difficult to justify and certainly doesn't carry much truth."

Of the Lennon incident, Dalglish said that it was momentum not malice that carried Shearer into the Leicester midfielder. "There was nothing malicious in it. I have never seen Alan do any-thing to deliberately hurt or injure anybody. He's competitive but not like that. Alan doesn't ask for any favours or give any favours. He only wants to be treated as an equal. He doesn't want preferential treatment. But he doesn't want to be punished because of who he is. It was not the first time he's been criticised or the first time the criticism has been wrong. The last time was against Barnsley. If you go through the videotape, you will see that every single challenge was a free-kick, every tackle a foul. The referee punished them and he was right every time."

The Newcastle manager was keen to address the issue of other fans' attitudes towards Shearer. "To be booed at an away game is a mark of respect," Dalglish said. "It is only a minority. It doesn't seem to have any affect on Alan. It's natural for good players to be given stick when they go to another ground."

The Leicester defender, Matt Elliott, played down the Filbert Street incident. "It was a foul by Shearer and something happened when the two players went down by the touchline, but I think people have highlighted it because it was Shearer and because there's been a bit of hype about him recently.

"If it had been one of the other players then such a meal would not have been made out of it. I'm not condoning it but these things do pop up from time to time. Shearer is getting a lot of attention at present but these things come in phases. I am sure it will go quiet for him soon - certainly on the disciplinary side if not on the goals front. Being England captain, he is always going to be under the spotlight, but I don't think it will bother someone like him. He gets criticism in the media for being too nice at other times. He can't win and all he can do is keep proving how good a player he is."

Lennon also introduced a welcome note of perspective into the whole hullabaloo. "I don't think there would have been such a fuss if it had been somebody else other than Alan Shearer involved," Lennon said. "If the ref didn't see it, you just have to get on with it."
★1/5/98

Croydon keeper Louise Cooper during their FA Cup final win over Croydon at the New Den •Philip Brown ★30/6/98

Sport Around The World:

- Boys and girls as young as 10 are taking drugs for body-building and to do better in sports, according to an American survey. Of 965 schoolchildren aged 10 and 11 were questioned by a Minnesota university, 26 were using anabolic steroids. The course of drugs would cost about $200, and a researcher says: "I don't know a lot of 10-year-olds who have $200. I think we have to look at brothers, sisters, parents and youth coaches."

- Allegations of witchcraft involving a pair of goalkeeping gloves sparked violence at an African Champions' League tie and an apology from Mozambique's government to their Zimbabwean counterparts. Mozambique's Ferroviario were eliminated by Dynamoes but 15 people, including a policeman, were injured following a dispute over the Zimbabwean goalkeeper's spare gloves, kept by his right-hand post, which Ferroviario's fans claimed contained magic charms after their team missed a penalty and other chances.

The match was stopped when a Ferroviario player was booked for snatching the gloves. Then, after a voice repeatedly announced through loudspeakers: "The Zimbabwean goalkeeper has witchcraft", Ferroviario fans invade the pitch and snatched the gloves again. Police used batons to restore order and dogs to trace the supporters with the gloves.

- Sport is not good for your sex life (or it is, depending on your point of view) - but it does increase alcohol consumption. Those are the conclusions of two studies reported in the Journal of American College Health. The first showed that 78 per cent more alcohol is consumed by college athletes than by students who are not active in sport. Another study, by the Women's Sports Foundation, concludes that girls who play high school sports delay becoming sexually active and are less likely to get pregnant than those who steer clear of games. A spokeswoman for the Foundation told the *Dallas Morning News* that: less than half as many female students are likely to get pregnant as girls who don't play sport; they are more likely to begin sex later in adolescence; they are more likely to have fewer partners and more likely to use contraceptives.

- Akebono, the 38-stone sumo wrestler, has become a father. His Japanese-American wife gave birth to a daughter who weighed a puny 7 lb 7 oz.

- Boris Becker was "very uncomfortable" when photographed nude in the company of 30 or 40 strangers. "Normally I undress only in front of my wife," Becker said. It took a couple of hours before he became comfortable enough with the photographer to pose for underwear advertisements "in a room full of strangers".

Cricket Diary:

- Michael Andrews may be a name to look out for if the 10-year-old Shropshire lad can produce more performances in the same vein as his unbeaten 241 in just 100 minutes. With a perfect schoolboy sense of priorities, he cited the main benefit of his innings for Birchfield School, Albrighton, against a touring team from Surrey as being let off homework for the night.

Giles Smith

All Wright on the night

When Arsenal's Ian Wright was carried off on a stretcher at Anfield, the first question television viewers asked was: "Will this render him doubtful for *Friday Night's All Wright?*" As any viewer will tell you, the last thing you need when you've got a crucial chat show pending, is for your host to be carrying a niggle.

But the worries proved needless. We knew this from the moment Wrighty came on stage pretending to limp. Wrighty is the first Arsenal player to be given his own show since Bob Wilson, but his style is a little noisier. "Wotchew fink?" he said, giving the pin-stripe suit an injury-defying twirl.

Television needs another chat show like it needs another series about vets. Still, you get something a little different from Wrighty, even if only in terms of chaos and competence. And despite the fact that the show has only appeared once before, stars are apparently falling over themselves to get near it.

"None of them are here plugging anything," Wrighty said, referring to his guests. "They're here because they want to be on." Stars such as the pop group Cleopatra, for instance. As their number gave way to deafening applause, Wrighty advised us to "look out for that record. Top five by Sunday." But he didn't mean it in a plugging sense, obviously.

Chris Eubank, too, was here first and foremost for the company - even if he did take time out during his interview to announce the date of his next fight. "I'm a conscious and gentle human being and I'm in a barbaric sport," said Eubank, the only thesaurus to have boxed. Later he would earn our congratulations by becoming the first person since 1754 to use the term 'besmirch'. (Wrighty gave him a puzzled look. "Slandered," explained Eubank. "Thanks Chris," said Wrighty). The grim battering which Eubank received last time he stepped into the ring seems to have completed a remarkable transition in the public perception of him from posturing dandy to have-a-go heart throb. "It's fantastic to be loved," he said. News of the rematch caused the audience to whoop wildly - though surely this was akin to someone agreeing to get run over by a truck again, simply because they got a lot of sympathy the first time.

When Wrighty introduced the actress Rosanna Arquette, he told us she was "all the way from Hollywood with nothing to plug," and we were impressed to think the magnetism of the Arsenal and England striker could exert itself at that distance. Our admiration faltered only temporarily when Arquette sat down and explained she was in London to start work on a film, but it had fallen apart, leaving her at a loose end until Sunday.

Whatever, she chose good company in Wrighty. True, he has a tendency to say "What can I say?" a lot, where some might argue that, as the show's presenter, it is his job not to be confused about this. But when he gets round to it, he has a crisp way with a question. ("You and Naz," he said to Eubank. "What's going on?") That said, an exchange took place during the Arquette interview which pointed up at least one of the problems faced by a chat show in which the host is himself a celebrity. Arquette mentioned that the British press could be cruel. "Tell me about it," said Wrighty. "Tell me about it," replied Arquette. "Tell me about it," insisted Wrighty. This threatened to go on all night. And for as long as the celebs were telling each other about it, no one was going to be telling us at home anything about anything.

More succint and a little calmer, Gary Lineker took us to Germany (*Gary Lineker's Golden Boots*, BBC1) and gave us a history lesson on that nation's football which was gripping and pointed. And this despite the worst link-line yet heard on television which wasn't in a local news report. (Entering a newsagent owned by a former German footballer Lineker said, "George Schwarzenbeck used to play matches for Germany. Now he flogs them.")

How delightful to see Gerd Muller again. 'Der Bomber' has grown a beard in a late attempt to look like Bill Oddie, but otherwise lacked none of his old ruthlessness. Charged with barging a member of his own side out of a scoring position, in order to score himself, Muller replied: "If he is too slow, that's his problem."

> # Wrighty is the first Arsenal player to be given his own show since Bob Wilson, but his style is a little noisier

Titled 'The German Machine', the programme bought entirely into stereotypical notions of German football as steely, efficient and coldly disciplined. But that's because they are all true. If you want to qualify as a coach in Germany, you study in a 40-hour week for six months. If you want to do it in England, you go to Lilleshall for a fortnight. As Lineker pointed out at the close, the German national side are sponsored by Mercedes-Benz, England by a breakdown company. Tell me about it.

★11/5/98

Steve Bunce

Oliver comes to terms with sense of loss

It started to go wrong for Spencer Oliver minutes after he was raised on a platform high above 100 members of the Highgate Choral Society at the Royal Albert Hall on May 2. It is the last moment as a prize fighter that he can remember before the black lights descended and his mind went blank. Oliver, 23, was knocked out in round 10 by Ukraine's Sergei Devakov. He lost his European super-bantamweight title and 90 minutes later needed emergency surgery to scrape a blood clot from the surface of his brain. He was just another boxing statistic and everybody involved in the sport retreated to the bunkers of their senses to wait out his sorry fate.

After 60 hours amazing news was circulated. Oliver was awake and he was fine. It was impossible, former victims were still coming to terms with their injuries weeks, even months after their final fights. But it was true. Oliver was talking, he was walking, he was due for release and the doctors had told him he was going to be fine.

Seven days after the fight Oliver was in the hospital's garden, glowing in the sunshine with 50 metal staples glistening in a terrifying arc on the right side of his head. Now, three weeks later, his condition is remarkable. "Something has been taken away from me and that will always hurt," said Oliver. "I know I'm lucky to be alive, I could have died in the ring or in the operating room. The surgeon told me how serious it was. I worked from the age of seven to get to the top in boxing. Days and years in gyms. I was just starting to get what I wanted: a car, a house that is paid for and there was a future, and then some bastard came along and ruined it. I'm sorry, but that is how I feel. I'm not depressed, just telling the truth."

Oliver and his manager, Jess Harding, who still looks haunted by the night and his six-day vigil at his boxer's bedside, plan to open a bar. They are friends, closer than most boxers and managers. Their friendship heightened Harding's suffering when Oliver went down and the medics performed the cheerless spectacle of saving a young fighter's life. Harding's face, as he stood in the ring, his hands behind his head, was a poignant reminder of boxing's cruel ability to ruin.

They remain inseparable. Each day since Oliver stirred from painful slumber and looked at Harding's unshaven face has been a celebration. They have been in demand and both look exhausted by their good fortune. Harding admitted: "I need a night in." They act like two lovers who are scared to say goodbye. It is touching but the hollow look in Harding's eyes conceals their grief over the bitter disruption of their plans.

Now the pair are standing on the outside waiting and remembering what they had. Oliver was unbeaten in 14 fights before the seemingly routine defence against Devakov, who was not a known puncher but was a thorough professional who studied Oliver's flaws. The fight, like so many that end in the operating theatre, was a desperate struggle. "I've not watched it yet. I'm not ready to sit down and look at the end of my career. That would be depressing," said Oliver. "I went to boxing the other night and I watched one fight - a mate of mine getting chinned - and I looked over at Jess and we both knew. We got up and went to the bar. I'm not ready yet.

"What makes the end even harder to accept is the fact that I was there. I was a star and I had a life to look forward to. I knew what I had to do to be a millionaire fighter and that is what I was going for. It is gone now and I don't think anybody, other than another fighter, can understand what I have lost," said Oliver.

I doubt Harding will ever watch the fight. He once fought for the British heavyweight title and was starting to attract attention as a promoter and manager. Now he is uncertain about his future in a sport that has so dramatically destroyed his hopes. Before the calamitous night was over Frank Maloney, the fight's co-promoter, told me Harding would have gladly walked in and swapped places with Oliver in the operating theatre. Any father would do the same.

Oliver's recovery from the night's brutal afflictions and a prognosis of no long-term damage is the best by a British boxer since records were kept of ring injuries. However, it is also a perverse conclusion to a tragic evening because stricken boxers are not meant to be as happy and well as Oliver. His redemption from the medical serenity of an intensive care unit to his present state intensifies the sense of loss. "I have seen fighters like Michael Watson in their wheelchairs and I used to think that will never happen to me. Then it did, but I'm lucky, I have walked away with everything. The only thing I have lost is my career," added Oliver.

Today he will be at Buckingham Palace - "She wants to give me an award for dedication to sport." Just four weeks ago he was in limbo. His life monitored by machines after he was saved by a neurosurgeon. Harding knew he would emerge from under the operating theatre's ring of intense lights during a night of non-stop tears. He knew he would win the final fight and survive. Oliver opened his eyes a few days later.

★ 1 / 6 / 98

DAY BY DAY REVIEW

1: Haile Gebrselassie shaves nearly five seconds off the world 10,000 metre record in Hengelo, Holland. Sir John Hall steps down as Newcastle chairman.

4: Monica Seles knocks out Martina Hingis in the semi-finals of the French Open. Terry Venables is appointed manager of Crystal Palace.

5: Shahtoush, ridden by Michael Kinane, wins the Oaks at Epsom.

6: England's rugby players suffer their worst defeat, 76-0, in the Test against Australia in Brisbane. Wales beat Zimbabwe 49-11, while Scotland beat New South Wales 34-10. High-Rise, the 20-1 chance, is steered to victory in the Derby by Olivier Pesiler. Arantxa Sanchez-Vicario wins the women's title at the French Open, beating Monica Seles in three sets.

7: Michael Schumacher stays calm in a crash-littered race to win the Canadian Grand Prix in Monteral. Carlos Moya lands his first Grand Slam title, beating Alex Corretja in the French Open final.

8: Rain washes out play on the final day of the first Test, between England and South Africa, which ends in a draw. Sepp Blatter wins the vote for FIFA presidency.

10: The World Cup starts in France (see separate section).

13: Haile Gebrselassie, the 10,000 metres record holder, adds the 5,000 metres world record in Helsinki.

16: England are taught a lesson by New Zealand Academy in Invercargill, losing 50-32. Kieron Fallon rides Dr Fong to victory in the St James's Palace Stakes at Royal Ascot.

17: Walter Swinburn rides Exclusive to victory in the Coronation Stakes at Royal Ascot.

18: Frankie Dettori lands the Gold Cup at Royal Ascot on Kayf Tara.

20: England suffer another heavy rugby Test defeat, losing 64-22 to New Zealand in Dunedin, while Scotland crash 33-11 to Australia in Brisbane.

21: South Africa win the second Test by 10 wickets after England, following on, set them just 15 to win. Mark Ramprakash is fined £850 and suspended for one game for showing dissent during the match. Lee Janzen hits a final-round 68 in the US Open.

22: Tim Henman kicks off Wimbledon fortnight with a five-set win over Jiri Novak, of the Czech Republic.

23: The New Zealand Maoris add to England's dispair with a 62-14 hammering in Rotorua.

24: Greg Rusedski limps out of Wimbledon, in his first-round tie against Mark Draper, while Tim Henman needs four sets to despatch David Nainkin.

26: Steffi Graf is beaten in straight sets at Wimbledon by Natasha Zvereva.

27: New Zealand win the second Test against England 40-10 in Auckland, while Wales go down 96-13 to South Africa in Pretoria.

28: Britain's athletes win the European Cup in St Petersburg with wins from Jonathan Edwards, Mark Richardson, David Walker, Colin Jackson and both relays. Michael Schumacher narrows the lead in the drivers' championship by winning the French Grand Prix.

29: Tim Henman sees off Pat Rafter to become the first Briton since Bunny Austin in 1939 to reach three successive Wimbledon quarter-finals. Sam Smith's run in the women's singles ends in the fourth round against Natalie Tauziat.

30: Walter Smith takes over a manager of Everton.

Paul Hayward

The breathless genius careers to a standstill

That Soho kebab was doused with symbolism as well as sauce. It was Greek food for a Greek tragedy. An eight-year cycle stretching back to Italia 90 began and ended with tears. England, in the language of counselling so common among its modern stars, have moved on. Yesterday was probably Gazza's last day at the centre of the footballing cosmos.

The English game has staggered out of denial. Glenn Hoddle, born-again Christian and proponent of faith-healing, has led his country into the light of an honest recognition of how far Gascoigne's athletic abilities have declined. It was the end of many things, not least Gascoigne's chance of winning a World Cup. Gone forever is the idea that English players can live like rock stars but still play like angels. History, like his younger and fitter midfield opponents, is passing Gascoigne by.

A World Cup squad is made up of 22 players and not 21 plus one breathless genius. There is no point villifying Gascoigne himself, though it was significant that Hoddle threw him out of the camp for abusing his body but let him stay in after he had abused his wife. Gazza errs not because he wants to but probably because the destructive forces in him leave him with no choice. One wonders how Chris Evans, Danny Baker and his other showbiz cronies are feeling now: like the friends who never took the car keys off the drunk driver; like men blinded by reflected glory until they themselves helped to kill the light.

The malaise in Gascoigne's physical state stretches all the way back to that instant tackle for Spurs in the 1991 FA Cup final. The current crisis has been rumbling since before Christmas when his precarious marriage to Sheryl began to snap. A large part of his self-destructive behaviour, say those close to him, stems from that estrangement. The pattern of his recent behaviour extends far beyond the recent Kebabgate saga to the winter when Gascoigne sought solace in the falsely warm embrace of bar and bottle.

An image keeps presenting itself of England's most naturally creative talent careering about wildly five minutes into his debut for Middlesbrough in the Coca-Cola Cup final in April, and the weird grins and facial ticks that overcame his countenance on an ominously demented afternoon. Here was a man unable to exercise rational control even with his last World Cup only weeks away, the doors of the last chance saloon closing behind him.

Hoddle has dispensed with the myth that Gascoigne is indispensable to England's campaign. He has also shown that Christian compassion and patience are not boundless. A

....

Gone forever is the idea that English players can live like rock stars but still play like angels

....

former team-mate of Hoddle's confided that he was always "cold on the ball". At the critical moment he was cold in control of his country's hopes. He had the air of one of those Victorian reformers who offered sinners the chance to repent, but then turned the key in the door when the chance was spurned. Those close to him say he has a hard, almost brutal streak. The culling of Gazza was carried out after only a "two or three minute chat" and with incontrovertible evidence that it was right.

The capacity to elevate football above a hurried trade of kick and chase has remained in Gascoigne's feet, though his increasing tendency to surrender possession of the object that has always given a purpose to his troubled life would have been exploited mercilessly in France by leaner and more agile Brazilians or Italians. The tippy-toed scurrying with which he has attempted to cover the turf is a sign that the strength in his legs has atrophied, and the fire in his lungs largely gone out. If this sounds like a case of kicking a fervent patriot when he is down, then so be it. Professor Anthony Clare is among those who have argued that one of Gascoigne's primary problems is the absence of anyone to confront him with painful but inescapable truths. He has been indulged on a scale that is reminiscent of George Best.

Amid the feeding frenzy that a brave and logical decision engendered, Hoddle looked cool on the ball in La Manga. He said just enough to reveal his true feelings (and regret) at the speed of Gascoigne's fall. "It's a great pity that Paul hasn't got himself fit," said a coach who would have been justified in feeling betrayed by Gazza's post-season binge, and was careful in that sentence to place responsibility where it really lay.

Almost without knowing it, Hoddle might function as a catalyst for another of the seismic changes affecting our previously cosy and parochial national game. The cult of fitness and sports science stirs up an ambivalent response but most of us know, such is the business of sport now, that the days of footballing playboys and party animals are over. The game is too fast, too physically demanding for a notorious carouser such as Gascoigne to get himself fit by sweating under an anorak in training for two weeks and purging his body of poisons.

There is hope for him, and closer than he may know. His Middlesbrough team-mate, Paul Merson, disappeared into a maelstrom of addictions to cocaine, alcohol and gambling but has emerged to become one of Hoddle's chosen 22. Gascoigne's career could conceivably be resurrected with the 2000 European Championship campaign which starts this autumn.

Now the debate moves beyond the chattering phone polls and internet surveys on whether Hoddle was right. Those players who were willing to make sacrifices that Gazza could not find it in himself to make have their own weighty reckonings to face. For them France will be an inferno. Other fires threaten to consume Paul Gascoigne.

★ 1 / 6 / 98

Australian Pat Rafter plays a stretched backhand volley during his victory over Magnus Gustafsson at Wimbledon •**Philip Brown** ★27/6/98

That winning feeling… Pete Sampras makes a close re-acquaintance with the men's singles trophy at Wimbledon •**Philip Brown** ★5/7/98

while Jana Novotna tries to come to terms with her first victory in the women's competition •**Mike King** ★4/7/98

Christopher Martin-Jenkins

Cricketing immortals welcome nearly man into their ranks

A man's reach should exceed his grasp, or what's a heaven for? Graeme Hick may never be a truly fulfilled talent unless he returns to the England side and enjoys an Indian summer, like Tom Graveney, one of the three who have now scored their hundredth hundred at Worcester. But his is a rare and wonderful achievement and this is a time to forget the frailty and congratulate a gentle man and glorious batsman.

Of course he has sometimes disappointed himself and others. The perfect talent, after all, has never existed. As Enoch Powell observed of politicians, so one might say of cricketers that every career is bound to end in failure; or, if not failure, at least not complete satisfaction. Don Bradman, as everyone knows, made nought in his last Test innings.

Along the way, Hick's performances have often demanded comparison with Bradman. His first century of any kind was recorded at the age of six. He was still a schoolboy of 18 when he represented his native Zimbabwe in the World Cup of 1983, and played a part in the sensational defeat of Australia at Trent Bridge. In 1988, three years before he could qualify for England as a Test cricketer, he made the highest score then made in England this century: 405 not out against Somerset at Taunton.

A few weeks later he joined Glenn Turner as one of only two post-War players to score 1,000 runs before the end of May, and in what was to prove a deceptive indication of his ability to dominate Test attacks, he reached the landmark at the last possible opportunity against a full West Indian Test attack. How could a man lacking mental steel have started an innings against some of the fiercest and finest fast bowlers in the world knowing that he had to make at least 153, with the eyes of the world upon him, and succeed as handsomely as Hick did then - he eventually scored 172 - yet prove fallible so often when the inevitable Test career did finally begin?

He has managed to conquer the best bowling under extreme pressure, but more often than not he has not. A natural shyness, the long wait to qualify for England and the huge, unreasonable expectations when he did all help to explain it. So did the fact that one or two loose technical habits became ingrained against relatively easy bowling. But that has never been the whole answer to the way in which a man who sees the ball so early by nature and sends it winging to all parts of the boundary with such grandeur so often, has been

••

But a hundred first-class hundreds puts each man who has done it on a pinnacle of cricketing accomplishment

••

prey to the yorker, the bouncer and even the googly at different times for England.

As rabbits and hedgehogs have learned, with time, not to become transfixed by the headlights of oncoming cars, Hick has improved but never managed to completely conquer this tendency. There is something, too, in John Bracewell's withering observation of the 'flat-track bully'. But a hundred first-class hundreds puts each man who has done it on a pinnacle of cricketing accomplishment. It does not make him a great player, but it does make him a cricketing immortal. It is a shame that the youngest man to score fifty hundreds, in 1990, could not also be, eight seasons later, the youngest to a hundred. Hick will not mind being second to Wally Hammond, one of the greatest all-round cricketers who pulled on a batting glove, nor being admitted forever to a club whose 23 other members include Bradman, W G and Jack Hobbs among the greatest names of the past and Viv Richards and Graham Gooch among his contemporaries.

It is delightful that he should have reached his milestone on his home ground, as Grace and Hammond, Hayward and Compton, Ames and Amiss, Graveney and Turner, John Edrich and Boycott all did, but several of the others did not. Gooch, the last man to do it - early in 1993 - reached his in Cuttack at the start of a tour which was to become something of a debacle; Phil Mead, though he had risen from the soil of Hampshire, was destined to reach his milestone at Kettering. Anywhere would have done, of course, for them all. It is a milestone possible only for someone blessed with rarefied talent and, do not doubt it, considerable character too. Hick has often seemed a shrinking violet; but disciplined living, a determination to keep himself fit, perseverance and immense powers of concentration have all gone into the career which reached what may not be its final peak at the age of 32.

An adopted Englishman he may be, but Worcester has long been his home and he has been happiest there, among his own admirers and supporters, rather than in the hostile atmosphere of Test cricket, or amid the restless atmosphere of an overseas tour, where reporters hover and cameras pry. He deserved his joy in the presence of his wife, Jackie, who has shared many a moment of depression as well as elation since his England career began seven years ago and ended, temporarily, with 13 innings which produced only one fifty, following his truly commanding century against South Africa at Centurion Park in November, 1995.

Vivien Saunders, author of *The Golfing Mind*, advises those who get tense on big occasions to envisage their favourite hole on their favourite course and mentally to drive off there rather than from the tee on which they actually are. That psychology applied to Hick might well have brought out the best in him more often in the Test arena, where so often he seems to have frozen.If only he could have transported himself to a sunny afternoon at New Road when Waqar or Wasim or Warne or Walsh was running in to him on some distant field, there would surely have been more than the four hundreds scored so far from his 80 Test innings which have brought an average of 36.Not a failure; but equally not the full extent of what might have been achieved by one of the hardest, straightest and sweetest drivers of a cricket ball who ever lived.

★1/6/98

Martin Johnson

Light showers delays play

There is always something special about the Lord's Test match, not least for the strange affect it has on people. We have had, in recent times, David Gower abandoning a press conference with the words: "That's it boys, I'm off to the theatre", David Steele taking guard in the gents' toilet, Ted Dexter speculating that England's performances may be connected to the alignment of the planets (come to think of it, astrology is just about the only job left that doesn't qualify for an ECB blazer) and, on South Africa's previous visit here, the curious sight of the England captain presenting his trousers to the match referee.

Rules are rules, of course, as a championship crowd at the Oval discovered some years ago when tea was taken with Surrey requiring two runs to win and Leicestershire one wicket

None of this, however, comes remotely close to cricket's most peculiar characteristic, namely, the bigger the crowd, the more important the occasion and the more expensive the seats, the bigger the effort to remain off the field of play for as long as is conceivably possible. Sixty-six overs were lost to the weather, which is roughly 66 overs more than would have been lost had the match been between Upton Snodsbury and Old Teacakians rather than England and South Africa.

Lord's is the only Test match venue in England that has yet to succumb to some degree of crowd yobbery, but the spectators' patience was tested as cricket's 11th commandment, Thou Shalt Not Play, was invoked with all its customary ritual. Whether or not it really was too wet to start proceedings until 1.30pm, it was not exactly brilliant PR for the players to be running around on the outfield without anyone remotely threatening to fall down in a muddy heap. Furthermore, why *Wisden* consistently fails to record Law 43: As Soon As Play Restarts, The Lunch/Tea Interval Shall Be Taken, is something that the editor should find room for in the 1999 Almanac.

The crowd were just settling back into the cricket following an afternoon interruption, when, after 55 minutes' play, the players became hungry and trooped off for their toasted teacakes and jam scones. Rules are rules, of course, as a championship crowd at the Oval discovered some years ago when tea was taken with Surrey requiring two runs to win and Leicestershire one wicket.

There is also a tradition involving the removal of the covers. Firstly, Pickford's could effect a house removal in half the time, and secondly, if it takes 20 minutes to take the covers off, then another 15 minutes is added while the outfield makes the crucial transition from ever so slightly damp, to ever so slightly less damp. After a light shower, the operation to remove the covers took from 2.40pm to 3pm, but play did not restart until 3.15pm. There is, of course, no provision for play to restart at quite so silly a time as 3.14pm, and 'as soon as possible' is clearly ridiculous.

There is another, no less important, tradition involved in halting play, which is known as bad light. Bad light, according to the regulations, is invoked when there is a risk of physical injury. In practice, however, it is invoked whenever one of the fielders removes his sunglasses. It is also invoked, as was the case here, at the precise moment that the batsmen appear to be seeing it like a football and creaming it to all parts of the ground. Ergo, as soon as Hansie Cronje and Jonty Rhodes began playing with joyous abandon, the umpires offered them the light. The batsmen, as etiquette demands, duly held a mid-pitch conference, and once they had established that they were both playing Dean Headley with a stick of rhubarb, they marched briskly back to the pavilion.
★ 19/6/98

JUNE

10: Scotland come within 17 minutes of holding Brazil, the world champions, in the opening game, before Tom Boyd chests the ball into his own net.

11: Roberto Baggio, who missed the crucial penalty in the shootout in the 1994 final, converts a penalty five minutes from time to prevent Chile springing a surprise against Italy.

13: Nigeria pull off the first surprise of the tournament, beating Spain. Patrick Kluivert is sent off for elbowing Belgium's Lorenzo Staelens.

15: England kick off with a comfortable 2-0 win over Tunisia, though the stay in Marseilles is spoilt by trouble in and around the city involving England fans.

16: Scotland's hopes are kept alive when Craig Burley equalises against Norway, while Brazil's victory over Morocco means they are the first team to qualify for the second round.

18: Zinedine Zidane is sent off for stamping on Amin Fuad Anwar, Saudi Arabia's captain, in France's 4-0 win.

21: Gabriel Batistuta hits a hat-trick in Argentina's 5-0 demolition of Jamaica, while Iran score a political point by beating the United States.

22: Michael Owen finally enters the World Cup, and scores England's equaliser against Romania before Chelsea's Dan Petrescu punishes an error by club-mate Graeme Le Saux for the winning goal.

23: Scotland, who have Craig Burley dismissed during the 3-0 defeat by Morocco, head for home.

24: Spain score six against Bulgaria but fail to move into the second round because Paraguay beat Nigeria.

26: A stunning free-kick by David Beckham helps England to a 2-0 win over Colombia and a place in the second round as group runners-up.

30: Michael Owen scores a memorable solo goal, but England go out in the second round on penalties against Argentina. David Batty misses the crucial kick after a 2-2 draw during which David Beckham is sent off for kicking out at Diego Simeone, Argentina's captain.

JULY

3: Italy, finalists in 1994, go out in the quarter-finals, beaten 4-3 on penalties by France.

4: Germany and Argentina, two of the pre-tournament favourites, are knocked out in the last eight, by Croatia and Holland respectively.

7: Brazil qualify for the final, but only after a penalty shootout which follows their 1-1 draw against Holland.

8: Defender Lilian Thuram scores twice as France beat Croatia 2-1 in the second semi-final, though their celebrations are dampened when captain Lauren Blanc is sent off after clashing with Slaven Bilic, and will miss the final.

11: Croatia take the bronze medals with a 2-1 win over Holland.

12: Paris erupts into an all-night party after France beat Brazil 3-0 to win the World Cup for the first time. Mystery, though, surrounds the appearance of Ronaldo, who is said to have suffered a fit before kick-off, who was anonymous during the game.

Giles Smith

Ron Atkinson coined the phrase "a stumble-job", which one hopes to see taken up widely next season

The Final may still be a way off, but it will take a committed performance indeed to prevent this column's special Glenn Hoddle Award for Party-Pooper of the Tournament from ending up on the mantelpiece of David Pleat.

Pleat, in his role as co-commentator for the BBC, has rocketed into a seemingly unassailable position by accusing the Cameroonians of "trying to impress individually", a remark so dour and dispiriting that it put one in mind of the great panel days of Don Howe and Denis Law.

It seems to be Pleat's opinion that football is a team game. I suppose he's right, but somehow it's not the kind of thing you want to hear during a World Cup. Sitting at home, you would trade as many hours as were available of Austria playing "as a team" for a flash of Cameroonian brilliance.

And the same applies to commentary and presentation. "I was reading a profile of the Brazilian team in one of the French papers today ..." said ITV's Clive Tyldesley, casually dropping his shoulder and revealing to us his fluency in a foreign language. Doubtless Pleat would mark this down as a needless attempt to impress individually, but here we welcome it as one of those gratuitous displays of skill which make the World Cup the compelling television spectacle it is.

The big story was the dumping of David Beckham, just days after he had told the BBC's Ray Stubbs that he wasn't thinking of filling the role vacated by Geri in the Spice Girls. Now he may have to think again. Clearly, in the mind of Glenn Hoddle, two sarongs do not make a right.

Still, this decision meant that for the first time one was able to use the words "clearly", "mind" and "Hoddle" in the same sentence. "What you see with your cameras sometimes isn't the real thing," England's media-savvy coach mysteriously told the BBC last week, during one of its many fruitless visits to Nantes. So confusing was Hoddle's furtiveness that Barry Davies went into the game with Tunisia believing that Tony Adams was England captain. I don't blame him: I went in believing it was Ray Clemence.

Meanwhile Hoddle, subject to a sudden attack of realism, was telling anyone who pointed a microphone at him that 1-0 would do him just fine. The team went one better than that, of course. Or they certainly seemed to. But if Glenn is right about cameras, how can any of us really be sure?

"Those of you with your World Cup wallcharts will doubtless have worked out..." began John Motson, before referring to the likelihood of England and Germany meeting in the quarter-finals. Moments of individual brilliance seem to be coming from Motty in unusual quantities.

"And we just caught a shot of Bert Millichip there," he informed us during the Germany v United States game. "Dangerous play has been decreed and a booking ensued," said Motty, apparently translating, as so often, from his own Latin. So much for Tyldesley's French.

But everyone's at it, seeking their opportunity to shine and, if necessary, inventing the language to do so. Referring to a fall which deceived the referee into awarding a free-kick, Ron Atkinson coined the phrase "a stumble-job", which one hopes to see taken up widely next season. And Brian Moore has spoken of his fear that "the dice might go the other way". He should get those dice inspected.
★18/6/98

Paul Hayward

The mourning after the night before

The heroic English, *L'Equipe*, the French sports daily, called them, before France 98 and the same old gang of quarter-finalists waved Glenn Hoddle's team goodbye. "*Quel Soiree*" - what an evening - the front page swooned. Nice to have been of service in laying on a night's theatre. Now comes the autopsy and an uncomfortably long list of why-oh-whys.

Take your pick from: England are out because David Beckham has a nasty temper; Hoddle picked the wrong team against Romania; England made defensive howlers in Toulouse; Alan Shearer has been in mysteriously limp form; the hand of God rose again in the Argentinian penalty area; Paul Scholes missed a shimmering chance at the end of the first half; England cannot take penalties and chose the wrong men anyway.

Or maybe it was because some bright spark

decided to ban baked beans.

Whatever, the bubble in the spirit level has settled, which for England was a place only in the last 16, a couple of converted penalties away from the quarter-finals. In that group of eight are the three diminutive European states of Holland, Denmark and Croatia.

Above those over-achievers loom world football's four usual suspects, who have taken out a time-share on the trophy since 1966. There they are again: Brazil, Germany, Italy and Argentina, threading their way towards the final as if following some celestial edict.

Late on Tuesday night, the first impulse was to acknowledge a performance of impossible bravery which had the people of France purring the next morning and offering the departing English pitying looks. The English warrior spirit is as robust as ever in its best and most debased forms. The two faces of English football on the pitch are Michael Owen's sublime goal and David Beckham's dismissal, which emasculated his team but ought to be remembered as a stupid rather than a malevolent act.

Kick out at an opponent under the referee's nose with the score 2-2? Are we entirely sure this is prudent?

Heaping more invective on Beckham is futile. "Beckham is a silly offender in this match and he will regret it for a long, long time," said Bobby Robson, who presided over the Italia 90 defeat. "Glenn will be devastated, sad. What does he say to Beckham? What does he say to his players? They defended magnificently, created so many great, great chances but it all ended in heartbreak. It has happened three times now with penalty shoot-outs. Three times and we have lost them."

Sporting history is so often a sequence of accidents and cock-ups. By the time the shoot-out started, Beckham, Anderton, Scholes and Le Saux had all left the field and Gareth Southgate (remember Euro 96?) and David Batty had come on. After Owen, Shearer and Paul Merson, England were down to defensive players, and one - Paul Ince - who had turned his back on the shoot-out with Germany at Wembley two years ago because he wanted no part of it. This time Ince took the second penalty and missed. It is as if England are stuck in some vicious historical loop in which only the names of the players change. Stuart Pearce and Chris Waddle; Southgate; now Ince and Batty - two new pizza adverts waiting to be made.

Hoddle is renowned as a meticulous organiser, a lateral thinker who set out to control every element of his team's preparation from diet to media-exposure to matters spiritual. He even instructed Paul Smith, the fashion designer, to disregard his preference for dark blue suits and go for beige. Penalties, though, remain an English blind-spot. The failure is not of nerve but of technique. Defenders, the theory goes, make poor penalty takers. Wrong: Roberto Ayala, the Argentine sweeper, scored the cheekiest penalty of the 10, prodding a slow shot into David Seaman's left-hand corner.

In England's eight-year Groundhog Day repetition, four defensively-oriented players - Pearce, Southgate, Batty and Ince - have all been called upon and failed. In the context of football's world hierarchy, the victories over Tunisia and Colombia were meaningless yet they did reveal flashes of destructive brilliance of the sort England had not shown in a tepid build-up.

One measure of England's strength was the way Daniel Passarella, Argentina's coach, and his cornermen celebrated their equaliser moments before half-time. Passarella was one of his country's greatest defenders, and can recognise when a team is on the rack. Off the Argentinian bench they poured like footballing Keystone Cops.

Above all, there is the terrible sense that, had England been able to scrape through this ordeal, they would have contributed to another epic confrontation with Holland on Saturday, and even a semi-final with Brazil.

As the anguish seeped away yesterday, a few hard facts rose up. Given the Romania result - which meant England faced Argentina rather than Croatia - Beckham's sending off and routine

....

In England's eight-year Groundhog Day repetition, four defensively-oriented players - Pearce, Southgate, Batty and

penalty fiasco, England were stacking up the odds against themselves going through.

They put themselves out. There was no malign fate sending them home. The fever of English participation has calmed and the edge of trepidation has gone. English malevolence has been flushed from the French system like a toxin. England fans sang the loudest, bought the most tickets, started the most fights, supported their team the most fervently and gave the most cause for thinking that the worst forms of nationalism are as virulently embedded at the end of the century as at the start.

On Tuesday night a large phalanx of England fans sang: "What's it like to lose a war?" and: "You'll never take the Falklands" and: "We're pissed and we're proud of it." Police were nowhere to be seen when a group of 40 Englishmen tried to re-enact the Malvinas conflict after Argentina's first goal and again at the game's sad end. Rotten losers, rotten winners, they put English football back five years just as Owen, Scholes and Beckham (before he became the fifth Englishman ever to be sent off) were driving it forward.

"But the English, what passion," said Passarella after the game. "England were very serious contenders. This was in many ways the most difficult of the second-round matches."

It was certainly the most intense, the most unwatchable, the most overwrought, the most unrelentingly dramatic of the 56 so far.
★2/7/98

Colin Calderwood

Hand of fate has ruled against me

My World Cup came to an end a few minutes into the second half against Norway in Bordeaux. The Norwegians were 1-0 up and there was a cross coming over which I had to deal with. There was one of their players behind me - Harvad Flo, I think - and I was trying to block him. Vidar Riseth was coming in fast with Craig Burley covering him and, as I went down, Riseth's knee caught me hard on my right hand.

I knew right away something was badly wrong because three fingers pointed one way and the other in a different direction, but it was numb rather than sore at first. Then I tried to grab Tore Andre Flo and the pain just took my hand away. I could feel bones clicking and there was pain every time I made contact, which taught me a lesson, because I had no idea until then that you use your hands so much in a game.

I was taken to hospital in Bordeaux where a specialist said that, if I wanted to continue to play football for three or four years, then I must have an operation. I had hoped it would be possible to play with plastic tubing or support but the doctors are afraid that I could make the injury even worse and do myself permanent damage.

So I'm out of the finals, but Craig Brown has invited me to rejoin the squad after I have my operation and I'll certainly be with them for the Morocco game. It hasn't really hit me that the finals are over for me, but when I was watching the Norway game again self-pity began to hit me.

It was a particularly strange feeling coming home because I passed my wife, Karen, at Gatwick Airport with our children, Abby and Alfie. They're off on holiday for a week to Portugal.

The atmosphere in the squad, meanwhile, is exceptional. We are frustrated at having only one point because we feel we should have drawn with Brazil and beaten Norway. When we've gone behind in both games we've gambled a wee bit. But when we did equalise, we went on to be the better side. When we've had to go for a win in the past - against Switzerland in Euro 96 and against Austria in the World Cup qualifiers - we've played our best football.

We fancy ourselves against Morocco yet this could be the trickiest game of the three because they play in little triangles and then quite often knock the ball long rather than run it into the other box. I think Scotland will do it this time. I'll just have to settle for leading the Mexican Wave - with one hand.
★18/6/98

Henry Winter

Penalty high for lack of practice

For a nation who helped introduce penalties to the world, England are not very good at taking them. Three times in the Nineties, England have bowed out of major tournaments through an inability to place a stationary ball from 12 yards past a goalkeeper as well as the Germans and Argentinians do.

It is difficult for those who have never addressed a penalty at this level to imagine the pressure, the noise, the myriad distractions from a gesticulating goalkeeper to provocative fans to a simple piece of paper fluttering into view. Glenn Hoddle yesterday talked about the mental side of penalty-taking. England's coach argued that English footballers have problems with penalties because, given recent history, they expect to lose. Yet the suggestion of a national character flaw does not sit well alongside the reality that his footballers had displayed unbelievable strength of mind in holding Argentina for 75 minutes with 10 men.

In the final analysis, England failed with two-fifths of their penalties, as at Euro 96 and Italia 90, because they did not practise enough. Paul Ince and David Batty had never taken a competitive penalty before.

"I'm not denying practice does help," Hoddle said. "A golfer can practise 1,000 putts on the putting green. But he can then go out on the last day of a tournament when there's 30,000 there and miss it. If it was all down to practice, practice and it always went in for you, then it would be a simple scenario. It isn't like that."

We practise them. David Seaman has practised saving them. But it is on that walk from the halfway line where a player knows whether he is going to miss it. You can't force someone to take one. David Batty and Paul Ince said they wanted to take a penalty. When you get a positive vibe from a player, you've got to go with it. The five who wanted to take them were up for it."

This indicates depth of character. No one could question the toughness of Alan Shearer, Ince, the new Paul Merson, an ice-cool Michael Owen and David Batty. Yet rather than accepting that England should simply have practised more, Hoddle believed that doubts must have been nagging at Ince and Batty, particularly the lessons of recent history

Too many things go through your mind if you keep losing at penalties. If you keep winning them, like the Germans, then psychologically they feel that it is going to go their way. The confidence is there." England, it seemed, were far too aware of their failings at penalties.

"That is why we sent everyone up we possibly could on set plays on the golden goal because ourrecord on penalties has not been fantastic. It's just a mental thing. Germans keep winning them."

So let us look at the successful teams' methods. As a matter of training-ground routine, Argentina, like Germany, work on their penalties, alleviating the staccato nature of the practice by staging it as a competition for all squad members. Argentina's coach, Daniel Passarella, an accomplished international penalty-taker himself,

also joins in. Passarella was clearly priming his line-up for penalties during extra time when he removed his captain, Diego Simeone, for Sergio Berti. The River Plate midfielder tucked away Argentina's first penalty low past David Seaman.

Even against a keeper of Seaman's class, only one Argentinian failed and that was Hernan Crespo, their second taker. The following three penalties, from Juan Veron, Marcelo Gallardo and Roberto Ayala were all expertly dispatched. You could almost smell the training-ground sweat, the accumulated hours of practice.

Even if the penalties had gone past the five, the smart money would have remained on Argentina. England had all their defenders coming up next with Gareth Southgate, who failed at Euro 96, next but one in line. Hoddle's options had been reduced by David Beckham's dismissal and the need to remove Darren Anderton so David Batty could stiffen midfield. "Anderton would have been on the sheet. David would have definitely been on the sheet," said Hoddle.

Having Seaman in goal gives a team a chance. Berti Vogts, Germany's coach, said yesterday he was surprised to see Seaman smiling as the penalties were sorted out. He misunderstands the England keeper's nature, some would say an English trait, that of exuding calm in the face of the storm.

Seaman walked out and stared at Argentina's bullish fans. He then lifted his arms, like an eagle spreading its wings, to intimidate Passarella's chosen five. "We were confident David would save one of the penalties," Hoddle said. This he did, from Crespo, but the moment England's own five revealed their identity by lining up in the centre circle, it was fairly clear that Seaman might need to save two.

So it proved. The sooner penalty-taking is included in the national curriculum, the sooner England will make the 12-yard step from gallant failures to assertive finalists. For all Hoddle's talk, it is practice that makes perfect.
★2/7/98

Donald Trelford

Hoddle pays for trusting to luck

All other explanations having failed, it must have been the lack of baked beans that accounted for England's early exit from the World Cup.

Just think of the surge of energy that even one serving of beans (655 kilo-joules and 158 calories, according to the tin in my kitchen cupboard) might have given to the tired feet of Paul Ince and David Batty at the penalty shoot-out.

Seriously, though, it must be nonsense for Glenn Hoddle and others to say that there is no point in practising penalties because nothing can prepare a player for the crippling emotional tension of such occasions. You might just as well say the same of place-kickers at rugby, yet they spend hours alone on the pitch perfecting their

craft. The whole point is to instil a technical routine into the mind of the kicker that shuts out the noise of the crowd.

At the very least, the Football Association's coaching experts could compile a video on penalty-taking, showing in slow motion the difference between good and bad technique. This is called professionalism and it is the opposite of kick and hope. Even Jack Charlton's rough-and-ready approach - "decide which way you're going to kick it and don't dither" - would have been more use than a soulful look and a nervous pat on the back.

The England coach obviously feels that despite the services of Eileen Drewery, the forces of Destiny and Lady Luck were ranged against him. I would say that the luck has been with Hoddle at

this World Cup. Left to himself, he didn't seem to have a clear tactical plan. It was only when Ince was injured that he brought on David Beckham against Romania. It was only through the pressure of the crowd and the media that he started Beckham and Michael Owen against Colombia.

It was only after Beckham was sent off against Argentina that the defence got themselves properly organised. Before then the Argentinian midfield had been cutting us to shreds. We (and Hoddle's reputation) were saved by Ince, Gary Neville, Tony Adams and Sol Campbell, who played out of their skin.

The whole world was astounded by the instant maturity shown by Owen at this level. But the one person who should not have been surprised was

Hoddle, who had talked of "nursing" the boy wonder into the World Cup. Owen needed a nurse like Ronaldo needs a haircut. The man who did need nursing was Beckham, as Alex Ferguson, his club manager, pointed out, clearly to Hoddle's annoyance. Yet Ferguson was right to rebuke Hoddle for his insensitive handling of the player, both before and after the red card incident.

After leaving Beckham out against Tunisia, he pointedly refused to say that Beckham would play any part in England's plans, even contradicting his deputy, John Gorman. He made the player bare his soul to the media in the depths of his disappointment and he was too quick to blame him in public for England's eventual defeat.

The spat between Hoddle and Ferguson is worrying, for the two men should be closely involved in developing the young talents of not only Beckham but also Paul Scholes, the Neville brothers and Nicky Butt. There was a suspicion of North-South prejudice by Hoddle (or maybe just pro-Spurs sympathy) in his preference for Darren Anderton over Beckham and his rejection of Butt and Phil Neville from the final squad.

Between tournaments the England coach has to rely on the clubs to look after his players, which makes good relations with the leading managers a key part of his job. Yet none of the clubs who supply the bulk of the England squad - Manchester United, Arsenal, Newcastle and Tottenham - has an English manager.

Hoddle's public comments often strike me as bewildering, defensive and self-serving. It is hard to tell if his obfuscation results from a wish to keep his thoughts to himself or because they are not clearly formed in the first place. It must be maddening to have to answer questions from people who know little about the game and whose motives can be dubious, to say the least, but he should regard these occasions as an opportunity to address the larger footballing public. It would be better still, of course, if the eloquence of England's performance on the pitch made all talking redundant.
★7 / 7 / 98

ALTERNATIVE WORLD CUP DIARY. As told to Alistair McGowan

Only an idiot couldn't take a penalty

•**Saturday, June 6:** *Flew to France. All the lads in good spirits. Teddy Sheringham got a bit cheeky with one of the air hostesses and went a bit too far, asking her if he could have a second meal. I sat by Darren Anderton on the flight. Initially he was by the window but we swapped so I was by the window and he had the aisle seat. I said: "Yeah, and that won't be the only time I'm after your place!" I laughed. Don't think he got it. Got to the hotel. I'm sharing with Graeme Le Saux. As we unpack, Graeme says: "I was thinking on the plane, if Martin Keown scores out here, it'll be a Ke-own goal; if young Michael scores, it'll be an O-wen goal and if David Batty ever scores it'll be an own goal." He laughed. I didn't get it.*

•**Sunday, June 7:** *Light training with Peter Taylor. Stretching and that. The Gaffer appears for a little while with one of them recorders that journalists are always putting under the lads' noses when they're doing interviews, though they never seem to ask me. He's very rude to David Beckham. First, he tells him Posh was the worst in Spice World and that the Gucci dress joke wore thin very early on. Then Glenn tells him he is not 'focused'. We all hear it - it's embarrassing, but we have to agree. We've all thought he was not properly focused for some time. It's like that bit in the new Woody Allen film, David is literally out of focus and it will be very difficult to play him as the TV people will think there is something wrong with their cameras. David is very upset. Well, we think he is; it's hard to tell with his face being so blurry. Then Glenn goes back inside. Hear faint tapping sounds coming from Glenn's room as we jog past later.*

We see Glenn again that night when we go out to eat. Some of the lads tease him by singing that Dexy's Midnight Runners song Come on Eileen. Glenn says we might scoff. I say: "That's lucky, 'cos we're in a restaurant." No one laughs. He says: "You might scoff, but Eileen Drewery used to 'help' Dexy's Midnight Runners." Apparently, she had a session with them which inspired them to write Geno. But then she wouldn't go on tour with them 'cos she didn't fancy the late nights and the drinking. Glenn says Come on Eileen was a plea to her - to try to get her to go on the tour. I laughed out loud. I don't think I was meant to.

•**Monday, June 8:** *Didn't sleep very well last night.*

First, Sol Campbell kept me awake with his music next door. He's really into Debussy, Satie and Faure and says that being in France is like a spiritual journey for him and he'd give anything to meet this Claire de Lune woman. On top of that there was a constant sound of tapping. Not just from Glenn's room, but from several others as well.

•**Tuesday, June 9:** *Glenn takes training. We do a bit of work on free-kicks. Incey says maybe we should practise penalities just in case. Glenn says there's no need. Only an idiot couldn't take a penalty. Incey laughs. After training, Glenn says that from tomorrow, due to popular demand, there's going to be an hour put aside every morning for creative writing. Says it's all to do with when Howard Wilkinson said: "There's a need for…players ter-ter-ter-to have some…some…some sort of…you know, vocational…wotsit."*

•**Wednesday, June 10:** *Training in the morning is interrupted by a phone call to Alan Shearer. Turns out that after all the adverts he's done, he was asked to audition for a sitcom about an obsessively clean man who lives on a train with a group of friends and a duck. And he's got the part! Everyone's pleased for him. Can't help wondering why I never get anything like that. In the afternoon, Scotland play Brazil, but no one watches except Paul Scholes. Instead, everyone decides to do their creative writing hour. Word has got around that Tony Adams is not happy that Alan is captain. Alan starts wearing his captain's armband everywhere just to wind him up. Kept awake again by the tapping sound. It never seems to end. Graeme says it's 'incessant'. Not quite sure what he means by this.*

•**Thursday, June 11:** *Seems everyone is writing books. At training, I suggest we should all try to think of the worst puns for the titles. Like: Ince-side Story, Blame it on Rio, A Room of My Ke-own. No one seems particularly keen. Alan suggests that instead we should try in future to fit the words from song lyrics into our interviews. Tony says: "What a stupid idea." But everyone else thinks it is a much better idea than mine. It's only because Alan's captain. Starting to sympathise with Tony. Perhaps I'll take him for a drink tomorrow. Oh no.*

•**Friday, June 12:** *No one seems into training today. Everyone is talking about their books. Rob Lee, Steve McManaman and Martin Keown are all*

writing for newspapers. Why don't I get asked to do anything like that? Martin says in future he's thinking of calling his column 'Ke-ownly Joking'. I say that's the pun of the week. We go out for a drink in the evening. Graeme is great with the French lingo, being from Jersey. I ask him if he ever met Bergerac. He says no, but we both agree the girl in it was very sexy - then realise we are both thinking of someone else - that blonde one from Lovejoy. Starting to miss the wives.

•**Saturday, June 13:** *We are all cheered by a postcard from Gazza. It says: "Having a great time in the States. I didn't know what state I'm in, like. Just that I am in a state. Ha! Haven't seen much of the sights as I am spending a lot of time writing a book about what it's like to be dropped by the Shredded Wheat man." I wonder if my writing is as good as Gazza's. That night, Michael Owen speaks for the first time. He tells us he is writing a thesis - whatever that is. It's called Inner city deprivation and its part in the Toxteth riots of 1980. Not much of a pun, that one.*

•**Sunday, June 14:** *First big game tomorrow. Everyone really fired up - writing like fury. Tim Flowers is writing poems. He writes one for Glenn. It goes like this:*
It's a difficult job for Glenn Hoddle. But if he uses his noddle
That and his firm faith in God'll
Mean winning in France is a doddle!
Everyone laughs. Graeme says it lacks a bit of imagery. Sol says he's going to try to set the lyrics to a piece of Faure and get Tony Adams to play it on the piano next time we have a sing-song. Alan looks jealous. Ha!

•**Monday, June 15 (8pm):** *Game goes well. 2-0 to us. Some of the lads get to do interviews afterwards - not me. Boo! On the coach journey home, everyone agrees they are itching to get back to the hotel and start writing about the game from their own angle.*

•**June 15 (a bit later):** *Very quiet here tonight except for the sound of keyboards. Graeme was right, it is incessant (I asked someone on the web what it meant). Everyone really into this writing thing except Paul Scholes, who has gone out collecting worms. Rest day tomorrow. More writing time. Hooray!*
★5 / 9 / 98

France 98

Russell Cheyne, The Daily Telegraph's chief sports photographer, covered the entire World Cup travelling the length and breadth of France. Given a

wide brief he photographed the games, the players and the fans. This is a selection of his favourite images •**Russell Cheyne** ★10/6/98 - 12/7/98   63

Henry Winter

France on top of the world

Like a bolt from the blue, France dethroned the world champions with two exceptional headed goals from Zinedine Zidane, his first of the tournament. France's first World Cup triumph was founded on the goals of Zidane and a late strike from Emmanuel Petit, and the masterful way these midfielders shook Brazil out of their measured stride.This was a marvellous moment for the hosts, a trigger for a lengthy party.

Stirred by a crowd who came to cheer throughout, the most precious 90 minutes in the history of French football showed the team at their best, capable of great creativity but allied to real guts. And strong hearts and legs were needed when Marcel Desailly was dismissed midway through the second half. "Victory is within us" screamed the posters around the ground. "*Le Jour de France*" said the headlines. And the players believed it, refusing to respect Brazil's status as favourites or their own as underdogs. France won because they had banished negativity from their minds. The French players had called on their Stade de France followers to behave like true fans, showing their colours and raising the elliptical roof. This they did, following the dressed-for-action example of Michel Platini, who had traded collar and tie for team shirt in the VIP box. How fitting, then, that France's current catalyst at No 10, Zidane, should serve up a first-half performance fit for the great man.

There was an optimistic note for the Blues with news that Ronaldo was out. According to the changing team-sheets, Ronaldo was in and out like a can-can dancer. But it emerged that Brazil's No 9 had been having a late X-ray on his injured ankle. Ronaldo, though, was anonymous, his lack of training showing as the French midfield took the firmest of grips. With their diligent full-backs, Bixente Lizarazu and Lilian Thuram, providing the width, France's midfielders cloaked the centre in a blanket of blue. Lined up in Christmas tree fashion, France had the numbers to keep the stranglehold tight.

Youri Djorkaeff, playing just behind Stephane Guivarc'h, was magnificent, swerving past yellow shirts like a breeze through fading daffodils. Petit was also at his best, pursuing every ball with relentless intent. And in the midst was the inspirational Zidane. Zidane was to provide the defining moments of the half, a brace of headed goals from corners. Before then, the game's currents changed twice. First the force was with France, seen with attempts on goal by Djorkaeff and Guivarc'h. Then came Brazil, having seemingly weathered the storm, going close through Roberto Carlos, Ronaldo and Rivaldo. Then the first-half tide turned. Just before the half-hour, the flaws in Brazil's defence were exposed. Pressurised by Christian Karembeu, Roberto Carlos misjudged his overhead clearance and conceded a corner. Brazil have tall central defenders in Junior Baiano and Aldair, who should be able to repel aerial attacks. Not here. Their concentration slipped. Their organisation crumbled. This was Sunday park defending. As Zidane made his run in to meet Petit's inswinging corner, the Brazilians should have been alive to the danger. Instead it was left to Leonardo, not the most imposing presence, to challenge Zidane, who comfortably placed his header past Taffarel.

Zidane saluted his first goal of France 98 before disappearing under a mound of jubilant team-mates. Confidence coursed through Aime Jacquet's players. France were in the driving seat, powering forward on all fronts, now going wide as well as repeating their precise passing patterns through the middle. Brazil were rattled, witnessed nastily when Dunga's studs burrowed into Deschamps' midriff.

Back came France, dismissing such indignities with the disdain of a team at full throttle. Petit,

•••••••••••••••••••••••••••••••••••••••

France won because they had banished negativity from their minds

•••••••••••••••••••••••••••••••••••••••

firing with his right boot, sent a shiver through the side-netting. Guivarc'h, released by Thuram's fabulous long-range pass, again should have scored but shot too close to Taffarel. No matter. Zidane simply added a second with another header, this time following a left-wing corner. Brazil should have learnt. Once shy, twice bitten, it seemed. Djorkaeff's corner bent in towards the near post where Zidane, now stooping, sent another firm header into the back of Taffarel's net. The crown was slipping. Mario Zagallo had to gamble. Denilson arrived for the ineffectual Leonardo. And so the siege began.

Within 10 minutes, Ronaldo had been presented with a glorious chance. Brazil's famous No 9, normally such a prolific finisher, turned Guivarc'h and thundered the ball goalwards. Fabien Barthez not only got in the way of the flying ball but clutched it firmly. France were living on the counter, welcome breaks from the yellow waves crashing towards them. Guivarc'h, freed by Frank Leboeuf's long ball and Cafu's doziness, should have given France a third but sliced his shot horribly and was quickly replaced by Christian Dugarry.

France were standing firm but after 66 minutes they lost a mainstay of their defence, Desailly, dismissed for a second bookable offence, this time a late challenge on Cafu. Petit, showing his versatility, went to Leboeuf's side, making an all-London central defence. Almost Petit's first action was to rob Ronaldo with a perfect tackle. Patrick Vieira soon arrived, replacing the outstanding Djorkaeff, to increase the Premiership presence as France continued to frustrate the Brazilians. Vieira's first contribution was a stirring through Brazil's midfield, so relieving the pressure on his defence. Vieira's club-mate, Petit, then completed the triumph by finishing off Dugarry's through ball.

Brazil: *Taffarel; Cafu, Junior Baiano, Aldair, Roberto Carlos; Dunga; Leonardo (Denilson 46), Cesar Sampaio (Edmundo 74), Rivaldo; Bebeto, Ronaldo.*

France: *Barthez; Thuram, Leboeuf, Desailly, Lizarazu; Karembeu (Boghossian 56), Deschamps, Petit; Zidane, Djorkaeff (Vieira 75); Guivarc'h (Dugarry 66).Referee: S Belqola (Morocco).*
★13/7/98

The crowning moment... the French players show off the World Cup •Russell Cheyne ★12/7/98

David Miller

Mystery deepens over Ronaldo's lacklustre performance

The mystery of Ronaldo's initial omission from Brazil's line-up for the World Cup final, in which inexplicably they capitulated to France, and his strange, late reinstatement before kick-off, deepened amid many conflicting statements and rumours. The one clear deduction to be made is that the decision was not taken by Mario Zagallo, the coach. In other words, his hand was forced. By whom and why?

The refusal by Zagallo to explain Ronaldo's absence inevitably reeks of a cover-up. Amid a disastrous performance by the rest of the team, Ronaldo himself was clearly unfit, giving an abject display. Why was he put back into the team in place of Edmundo? Why was he not substituted, at half-time or even in the second half? Brazil's 165 million population, and a few others, would like to know.

With the rumours flying, the news agencies published a claim by Ronaldo that he had suffered a nervous fit. The earlier stories were that he had been sick. While this might explain the poverty of his performance, it makes it even harder to understand why he should have been put back into the team, which was bound to be counterproductive. The explanations by both Zagallo and Ronaldo do not ring true.

The first suggestions were that his troublesome knee - or ankle - was not responding to pain-killing injections. Another was that, at only 21 he lost his nerve and felt unable to play. All that seems certain is that feeling nauseous after lunch - the initial medical claim - or having had a fit during his sleep the previous night, Ronaldo arrived at Stade de France with Lidio Toledo, the team doctor, well after the team, apparently having been to hospital. In his absence, Zagallo had held a team talk, and Edmundo was included in the formation handed to FIFA.

The more complex rumours involve Nike, the team's sponsors, and Ronaldo's fianceé, Susannah Werner. The former, emanating from Globo Television in Brazil, is the more serious. It is that Nike, who have a contract with CBF, the Brazilian football federation, for £73 million over 10 years, called Ricardo Teixeira, the CBF president, demanding that Ronaldo, their prime advertising vehicle, be included. Globo claimed that Teixeira persuaded Zagallo, who wanted to omit Ronaldo, to reverse the selection, Teixeira guaranteeing that he would take "personal responsibility" for the player's fitness and performance. The supposedly reluctant Zagallo was allowed to revise the team sheet - already handed to 4,000 journalists and TV stations - as regulations allow.

Nike have rejected Globo's claim, a spokesperson saying: "This is absurd. We have no input into the selection of the team. The coach decides the line-up. It was up to the CBF, their medical people, Zagallo and Ronaldo himself as to whether or not he played."

The alternative allegation, carried in agency stories, is that the players forced Zagallo's hand. I find that hard to believe, and whatever Ronaldo's sickness, the justification for leaving him out was powerful.

What makes the explanation questionable is the conflicting evidence from Toledo on whether Ronaldo was ill during the night or, according to

another statement by Toledo, sick after lunch on the day of the match. Furthermore, if the fit was during the night, why the hospital visit late afternoon?

A further unsubstantiated rumour is that Ronaldo discovered shortly before the final that Miss Werner had been socialising, during his time in the training camp, with a Globo employee and that this was the cause of his physical and emotional distress.

Talking to Globo about the alleged "fit" in his sleep, Ronaldo said: "When I woke up I couldn't remember anything but I felt terrible all over. I have never felt so ill and I hope I'll never feel it again." Toledo said the illness was due to stress, but why had he said previously that it happened after lunch?

....

The refusal by Zagallo to explain Ronaldo's absence inevitably reeks of a cover-up

....

Comments by Roberto Carlos, the left-back and Ronaldo's room-mate, strongly hint at the element of emotional upset, which could indicate Ronaldo's concern about private matters. "He's stressed out," Roberto Carlos said. "I have a family, my wife and kids to support me, but he doesn't. We need to give this boy a break."

Bebeto, Ronaldo's attacking partner, said: "Before the game, we were worried about his condition and the way he was thinking." Dunga, the captain, said that the uncertainty had got to the players. This claim seems unrealistic for a group of the most experienced professionals, many with major European clubs.

The evidence of some major disruption, however, within the dressing-room was evident from the team's failure to appear on the pitch for their warm-up period. There is, I suspect, much explanation still to come.

★14 / 7 / 98

Back on the wall... the most famous No. 9 shirt in the world on duty for Nike •**Russell Cheyne** ★18/6/98

Slaven Bilic

I don't deserve to be blamed

Croatia's defender offers his perspective on the Laurent Blanc sending-off

The sending-off of Laurent Blanc for hitting me in the face has turned into a big issue because he will now miss the World Cup final. If it had happened in an earlier game - like the red cards for Patrick Kluivert and David Beckham - it would not be such a talking point.

As a fellow professional I feel very sad for Blanc. He was on a coach outside the stadium after the game and I looked at him and raised my hand to say I'm sorry for what happened. But the bottom line is that I don't feel blame and I don't deserve to be blamed for his

I fell on the floor when I saw the referee coming because I had one booking from the previous game and didn't want to miss a possible final appearance

predicament. He hit me intentionally in the face - he has admitted he lost control - and technically that is a sending-off. He made a mistake and he got punished for it. The sad thing is that so many players in this tournament have made bigger and nastier challenges but got away with it.

We have just watched the incident again on television. The French commentators are all agreed that there was "reason enough" for Blanc to be sent off. None of them is slaughtering me as friends in England say Alex Ferguson and Alan Hansen are. To call me a cheat is ridiculous. I don't care a lot for Hansen's opinion. He has not had a good word

for Croatia from the start of the tournament. His prediction was that France were going to murder us. Even after the game against Germany he said we were lucky. Well, why wasn't he ever lucky with Scotland?

What happened is this: The referee awarded a free-kick. I was marking Blanc so I tried to stop him from jumping. I put my hand on his stomach and tugged his shirt. He reacted by hitting me across the chin with his hand. He didn't hit me that hard, but I fell on the floor when I saw the referee coming because I had one booking from the previous game and didn't

want to miss a possible final appearance. I stayed down on the floor because I didn't want the referee to give us both yellow cards.

It was not an isolated case. The French players were doing it all game. Between Thuram, Desailly and Petit there was a lot of elbowing going on. The fact is the referee can't see it because there are always so many people in the box.

I don't like players using elbows. People may say I was sent off three times in the Premiership last season but it was never for dirty play. They were for mistimed tackles. You have to mark a player close and sometimes hold him by his shirt. This World Cup you have seen it all the time. If you can't tackle from behind, you have to do something else. Players try to do it cleverly, to conceal it.

I think the World Cup refereeing started very well in the first round. Then FIFA put pressure on the referees to use the rules more and we saw some strange decisions. The quarter-finals and semi-finals were good again. I thought the referee on Wednesday night [Spain's Garcia-Aranda] was brilliant. He was under enormous pressure because everyone wanted France to meet Brazil in the final even before the tournament started. But he was completely neutral. I went to him after the game and told him he really impressed me. He said he appreciated that.

★10 / 7 / 98

Off...Laurent Blanc receives the "red card" from referee Garcia-Aranda in the semi-final against Croatia •**Russell Cheyne** ★3/5/98

Giles Smith

Barnes retains for four more years this column's commemorative Frank Bough pullover and restraining helmet

So farewell, then, Brian Moore, ITV's Voice of Football. O'Sullevan, Moore...the trouble when these big guys step down is that they leave holes too wide to fill. Did we see Moore's heir apparent during France 98? I don't think so.

But we did witness the new, improved Clive Tyldesley, and this was some consolation. Tyldesley's commentaries were once famous principally for the volume at which he could shout "Oh". For France, he reinvented himself as a smooth-talking sophisticate, equal to any challenge. The French producers loved close-ups of players receiving treatment almost as much as they loved close-ups of Ronaldo's girlfriend. Confronted one afternoon with a full-screen close-up of Fabien Barthez's naked left buttock and a spray-can, Tyldesley quietly remarked, "After nine o'clock, please." He seemed to be in control.

Not everyone was. Official statisticians have already declared that more hot air was generated during this tournament than during any televised sports event of modern times - and most of it by Ron Atkinson. Ron was supposed to be one of ITV's match summarisers, but there was nothing summary about anything he did, and he receives this column's special Top Guffer award: a glass bowl in the shape of the Dounreay Reactor.

Meanwhile, the Trevor Brooking Award for an Individual Mispronunciation (sponsored by Linguaphone) goes, in a crowded field, to Kevin Keegan for his version of "Lizarazu" which, during France's quarter-final with Italy, came out "Lizza-razza-zoo". Had Kev been reading Dr Seuss? It was quite a tournament all in all for Keegan, who, as well as picking up a Mystic Meg Home Magic Set for his uncannily prescient match-readings, also nabs the Leonardo da Vinci Scholarship for Applied Physics, thanks to this analysis of the importance to Romania of Gheorghe Hagi: "He's got to be the fulcrum on which everything starts and, almost, finishes." If Keegan ever offers to put up a see-saw in the garden for your kids, just quietly say no.

We pass on to awards in the fashion categories, and it should be said straight away that this World Cup did not turn out to be quite the clothing jamboree that many had hoped for. True, Ally McCoist put in some sterling work early on by dressing up as Rupert the Bear. He also pre-empted by an entire fortnight the Romanian vogue for cheap hair dye (Jimmy Hill would probably argue that this was a tactical move, enabling Ally to be more rapidly identified in a crowded studio). In addition Barry Venison's impeccable impression of a young Clark Kent certainly attracted the judges.

Above all, though, France 98 will go down as the tournament in which John Barnes appeared, on more than one occasion, in an entirely conventional jacket. Barnes's wardrobe for France seemed to be under new sober rules. But, like the trouper he is, he had merely saved the best until last. He turned up for Saturday afternoon's preview programme on ITV in an all-in-one body-stocking apparently fashioned entirely from sea urchins, and redeemed himself at a stroke. Barnes retains for four more years, then, this column's commemorative Frank Bough Pull-over and Restraining Helmet.

And Champion Broadcaster overall? You've got to hand it to the BBC - but without at the same time sticking it to ITV. Chiefly, the things one might not have enjoyed about the ITV coverage were the things beyond their control. You can't exactly blame ITV for its tragic lack of Lynam. Nor can you blame it for the commercial breaks, which add to the already panicked business of live outside broadcasting a whole new level of adrenal mayhem.

The fact Bob Wilson managed some 20-odd games' worth of this without once turning to the camera, cramming all his fingers in his mouth and emitting a long and ear-piercing scream of terror, means that all of us should be out of our seats at this point and applauding.

And we probably can't even blame ITV entirely for those Vauxhall sponsorship flashes, though wouldn't it be nice to know exactly who we can blame, along with their home addresses? Oh, those funny foreign accents! About as witty as a whoopee cushion, these ads seemed to be engaged in a valiant mission to make the unmissable unwatchable. It is, I think, the moral responsibility of anyone who suffered five weeks of this pain to take a personal vow, as I have done, never again to travel in a Vauxhall-built vehicle, even as a passenger.

ITV made one major tactical slip and were punished for it. They decided to follow the circus. Like Mahomet, they went to the mountain, in other words; whereas the BBC rented an apartment and let the mountain come to Des Lynam. Out of the windows we could watch the Paris evening settle down, and do much the same ourselves. ITV went for immediacy: and immediacy turned out more often than not to mean a narrow hardboard cabin behind Row Z, with standing room only. Even in Jim Rosenthal's Paris-based operations centre, ITV's computer-generated backdrop might as well have shown Venice for all the local colour it imported into your living room.

Still, only four years until everyone gets to try again.

★13 / 7 / 98

1: Tim Henman wins his quarter-final at Wimbledon, beating Petr Korda in straight sets.

2: The first day of the third Test at Old Trafford attracts a crowd of just 11,200, causing concern within the game, and they see South Africa rattle up 237 for one.

3: Pete Sampras ends Tim Henman's Wimbledon with a four-set win in the semi-finals.

4: Jana Novotna wins the Wimbledon women's title for the first time. England's ill-fated rugby tour of the southern hemisphere ends with an 18-0 defeat by South Africa in Cape Town.

5: Pete Sampras is taken to five sets by Goran Ivanisevic but still lands his fifth Wimbledon singles title. Simon Crafar, of New Zealand, wins the British Motorcycling Grand Prix at Donington Park.

6: England keep the Test series alive by holding out for a draw at Old Trafford. Sheffield Wednesday appoint Danny Wilson as manager.

9: Mark Richardson inflicts only the second defeat in nine years on Michael Johnson in the 400m in Oslo.

11: Essex dismiss Leicestershire for 76 to win the Benson and Hedges Cup by 192 runs. The Tour de France starts under a cloud when it emerges that the Festina maseurs car was stopped by police and found to contain steroids and other banned substances.

12: Michael Schumacher wins his third grand prix.

13: Chris Boardman, who was leading, suffers serious head injuries as he crashes on the second stage of the Tour de France.

14: Hicham El Guerrouj shatters the world 1500m record in Rome, clocking 3min 26sec.

17: Festina are expelled from the Tour de France over drug allegations.

18: Chris Eubank is stopped for the first time in his career, in a WBO cruiserweight fight in Sheffield against holder Carl Thompson.

19: Mark O'Meara wins The Open after a four-hole playoff with Brian Watts, while Justin Rose's last-round 69 lifts him to within two shots of the title. Brian Baister is voted in as chairman of the RFU, ousting Cliff Brittle.

23: Bristol rugby club call in the receivers.

24: Riders delay the start of the 12th stage of the Tour de France in protest at their treatment by organisers, police and journalists over the drug scandal dogging the race.

25: Swain, ridden by Frankie Dettori, wins the King George VI Stakes at Ascot.

26: Mika Hakkinen and David Coulthard score a McLaren 1-2 in the Austrian GP, relegating Michael Schumacher to third.

27: Alec Stewart achieves his first win as England captain as England level the series with an eight-wicket victory over South Africa thanks to Mike Atherton's unbeaten 98.

28: Coventry, with debts of £2.5 million, are the latest rugby club to call in the receivers.

29: Mike Tyson loses his cool and swears at the commission investigating his attempt to regain his boxing licence.

30: Roger Black retires from athletics after failing to win a place in Britain's European Cup team.

Mick Cleary

England's backs to the wall as disaster follows disaster

The England squad flew out of Cape Town with not a backward glance. What remained behind them was not nice at all. The last five weeks have been a salutary experience: in turn traumatic, soul-destroying, tedious, frustrating, irritating and utterly predictable. What was true when the tour hitched its wagons back at the end of May was still true when the trimmed-down squad unbuckled its cargo at Heathrow.

England never had the personnel to compete. Their forwards were always going to give an account of themselves but the back line was so callow that it ought to have been sponsored by Farley's Rusks. No matter how resilient, how stroppy, how crafty the pack managed to be, they knew, and the opposition knew, that there was nothing threatening beyond Matt Dawson. So are England a shambolic ruin? The team, no. The infrastructure with all its political in-fighting, yes. That sour, chaotic backdrop brought about this tour in the first place.

There is no doubt that a full-strength England would be highly competitive. They showed that last autumn. The southern hemisphere has got its nose in front at the moment, but then it was always so in amateur days of old. Professionalism, Super 12, the slick marketing Thatcherite approach of the game down there has not fundamentally altered that balance as far as England are concerned. It is true that England need to overhaul their fitness programmes. The southern hemisphere backs are huge creatures.

So, was it all worth it? Was it worth the couple of million pounds it cost to send the show on the road? Was it worth the humiliation, the constant ridicule, the morale-sapping accumulation of defeats? This is the worst tour party to have left these shores. Their record reads like a casualty list from a war zone. Well over three hundred points conceded. It is a disastrous return. And for what? So that a learning curve could be plotted heading off to a point somewhere into the stratosphere?

Clive Woodward will argue that this is precisely why it was worth it. That young players like Josh Lewsey, Pat Sanderson and Phil Vickery had several years' worth of nurturing crammed into a few short weeks. They have emerged as better, more rounded, more street-wise players as a result of being exposed to the brutal realities of rugby south of the equator. On the flip side there are those like Matt Moore, Alex King and Jonny Wilkinson who, at various times, were grievously wounded in the cross-fire. They, and several others, will take many months to recover. Wilkinson, 19, was held back by Rob Andrew at Newcastle so that he could mature slowly. Woodward thought he was ready.

Their forwards were always going to give an account of themselves but the back line was so callow that it ought to have been sponsored by Farley's Rusks

At least Woodward should now know who can cut it and who can't. But does he? Were the guys who fell by the wayside given a fair crack of the whip? There were only seven matches, four of them Tests. That is no time at all to truly mount a case. The schedule was so fierce and unrelenting that seasoned internationals would have been scalded by the experience.

The tour was a pitiful slog round the globe. It was badly planned and poorly realised. There was a sense of desperation in the air from start to finish. It seemed that the only way to cope was to throw resources at everything. The 37-man playing party was the biggest taken. The 15-man back-up squad - from motivators to kicking coaches to defence specialists - was the biggest any side anywhere has assembled. Yet the kicking, the tackling, the mental toughness and even the logistical detail were all lacking. Quite why the team flew to places in New Zealand where they weren't even playing to then have to hit the road (or the skies) on the very day of the match was a mystery. The size of the party meant that keen focus was lost. Far better to have worked more intensely with fewer people.

What does it all mean? Already you can hear the wolves gathering. Pretty soon they will be howling that the Premiership clubs have brought disgrace on the English game. Certainly that was the perception in Australia and New Zealand. It is a false, seditious, simplistic line. The clubs did not withhold their players from this tour.

The issue is far more complex than that. Some players were actually injured, others needed treatment for chronic ailments. In half-a-dozen cases, though, Woodward chose to leave the player behind. It was his call on the likes of Lawrence Dallaglio, Jason Leonard and Martin Johnson. It was Woodward's sympathy vote

which excused Paul Grayson, Phil de Glanville and Jeremy Guscott.

The clubs must not become the convenient whipping boys in all this. Sure, they need to get their house in order on certain fronts, notably overseas players. There are too many second-string foreigners being picked up cheaply. It is the one issue in this current debate on which I agree with the Fran Cotton camp. The clubs simply have to work out a viable self-regulatory quota.

Woodward's objective was to unearth half a dozen players for next year's World Cup. The Gloucester contingent at Newlands - locks Dave Sims and Rob Fidler and tighthead Phil Vickery - all advanced their cases. Graham Rowntree found himself again after a year in the wilderness, while Ben Clarke looked perfectly at ease back in the international environment. The two Matts, Dawson and Perry, also gave a good account of themselves.

Woodward gambled on leaving top names behind in order to prepare them for the World

Cup. He has many points to raise about the experience. However, such is the mess at Twickenham, he is not sure that anyone wants to hear what he has to say. "I don't know who the boss is," he said. "It's frustrating being a professional in an amateur set-up. I'm not sure anyone there fully thought it through. The players have to take more responsibility to make sure they're in shape. I'll tell them to get on their bike if they're not prepared to front-up to their responsibilities. I'm sick of them saying they're stuck in the middle. They have to make up their own minds about when they play."

Let's hope that the experience really has been chastening for everyone. Let's hope that a tour like this will never be allowed to happen again. Let's hope that political differences will be buried once and for all. Any more time wasted bickering about who is right and who is wrong will only bring about this same sorry state of affairs once again. And that is a truly awful thought.
★6/7/98

The final furlong… Sweden's Jasper Parnevik measures a putt at the British Open Golf Tournament at Royal Birkdale •Gary Prior ★19/7/98

Martin Johnson

Sampras exploits faults in Croat's split personality

What with all this talk of laying ghosts and slaying demons, Wimbledon finals weekend felt more like a medieval exorcism than a couple of games of tennis. However, while Jana Novotna finally managed to shed her reputation as a mental marshmallow ("Miss Novotna to choke, new bawls please"), Goran Ivanisevic failed to get rid of his own as a player who would have won many more tournaments had he lost fewer of his marbles.

Ivanisevic was born in Split, and while he now lives in Monte Carlo, where it is well nigh impossible to have a next-door neighbour who neither plays tennis nor drives a racing car, he has always retained his Split personality. Moody, witty, a delightful touch player who is occasionally delightfully touched. You never know with Goran from one day to the next.

He had more than his fair share of chances against Pete Sampras, who had obviously paid too much attention to the Sunday morning newspapers. Described as being "from a different planet", Sampras duly took out residence on the Planet Zod during the first set, and had Ivanisevic taken either of two chances for a two-set lead, Croatia might still be on course for a tennis-football double.

What basically cost Ivanisevic the match, however, was his unreturnable service. Often, Sampras was unable to return it because he couldn't see it, but almost as often, he was unable to return it because it failed to cross his side of the net. It was like watching a left-handed Devon Malcolm bowling in a Test match: One ball exploding into the stumps, and the next five disappearing off the radar. Ivanisevic sent down 32 aces, a figure all the more remarkable for the fact that all those serves which just clip the opponent's racket en route to turning the centre line judge from a tenor into a soprano, are not even counted as aces. However, he also dished up 20 double faults, and Sampras is not the sort of player to take that kind of liberty with.

The first set provided plenty of high velocity ammunition, yet just as much ammo, perhaps, for the girls, who constantly complain about the disparity in prize money. The men certainly play more sets, yet whether they actually play more tennis is decidedly arguable. The list of first-set rallies adding up to more than four strokes ran to three - two five shotters and one lung-bursting marathon of six.

It would be marginally easier to get through

Novotna-like mountains of Kleenex at this pay discrepancy were it not for the fact that Jana pocketed a cheque for £391,500, although she clearly doesn't earn enough to buy herself a

decent set of curlers. Sampras, by the way, added a further £435,000 to his career earnings of $32,422,649, while Ivanisevic remains hovering around the breadline with a paltry

Goran Ivanisevic crashes down another ace •AP ★8/9/98

£217,500 to hand over to his Monte Carlo bank manager. It would be surprising if either of them bothered doing the weekend Lottery.

However, heaven knows how much more tennis the men would have to play were it not for the tie-break, introduced the year before the Borg-McEnroe epic in 1980. Wimbledon would probably have to be extended from the traditional fortnight to a month.

The first set began with the umpire warning the crowd to switch off their mobile phones, an instruction that was re-issued when a loud ringing noise erupted in mid-rally. However, this was actually the stewards' wall phone at the bottom of the press box stairs, and the beeping noise that mostly bothered the players was the one coming from the service line machine. Cyclops was clearly not working properly, and early in the second set, Ivanisevic, with Sampras's approval, successfully petitioned for it to be switched off.

Sampras's supporters, meantime, were silently petitioning their man to get himself switched on, which he proceeded to do by breaking for a 2-0 lead. However, the Croat came back to force a tie-break, and when he missed two set points - both on Sampras second serves - and then lost the third set as well, experienced Goran watchers waited for the towel to come in. This looked even more on the cards when Ivanisevic started muttering to himself in Croatian, but he then woke himself up with a remarkable half-volleyed return through his own legs - a dangerous shot to practise at home - followed by a series of more orthodox, but nonetheless brilliant, returns for a set-clinching break at 4-2.

If it was tough to follow the ball at times, it was a whole lot tougher for those watching the final on the giant TV screen at the back of No 1 Court. It is remarkable how many people turn up without Centre Court tickets to watch something they could see on their own TV at home, but Wimbledon has always been as much of a social outing as a sporting event. People turn up for all sorts of reasons. A picnic, celebrity-spotting, or merely to have their pictures taken against a backcloth of all those signs so evocative of Wimbledon itself - such as 'Ticket Re-Sale' 'Cushion Hire' 'Binocular Loan' and the 'Dutchee' stall. Only at Wimbledon could a hot-dog be called a dutchee, or a bag of sweets 'bon bons'.

The final set turned out to be just too much for an exhausted Ivanisevic, but it nonetheless went down as a remarkable final. And when a Wimbledon final goes the distance, and takes place without England losing a single Test match wicket during the entire five sets, what else can you call it but remarkable?
★6/7/98

Paul Hayward

Stop the violence now

Chris Eubank will probably end his violent decade throwing punches all the way to the vanishing point of his powers. Boxing's king of pain will just not walk away.

The most salient appraisal of his fifth consecutive defeat in a championship fight came from Steve Collins, one of his many recent conquerors: "Chris Eubank needs to be protected from himself." Collins, not a noted dispenser of compassion between the ropes, was having a job suppressing his sadness at seeing a fellow warrior beaten to a halt at the end of a fight that should never have taken place − certainly not just 91 days after Eubank was dispatched to the local infirmary by Carl Thompson with an eye that looked as if it had been hit by a truck.

It is a disgrace that Eubank was allowed to march into a rematch only three months after one of the most brutal encounters in British boxing history, and with his wounded left eye still showing signs of the damage inflicted on a raging night in Manchester.

Legally there was nothing to stop Eubank imperilling himself again against a bigger and equally determined foe. But morally he should have been told to take a minimum of six months off; or better yet be told by those who know (i.e. all the old fighters now cringing at his refusal to stop) to retreat to the family home in Hove and confine gloves to the attic.

Christopher Livingston Eubank is one of the finest fighters this country has produced and his bravery and gallantry are not in doubt. He is simply reasserting those virtues with pointless repetition and ought to be hauled out of the combat zone while he still has the presence of mind to make his own decisions. The needle is gouging chasms in Tina Turner's *Simply the Best* and the lumps and welts on his face are taking longer to recede.

By any objective analysis his continuing pursuit of money/glory/redemption/whatever else it is that keeps him going is riddled with anomalies and dangers. This was his 51st fight in 13 years and brings the number of rounds he has boxed to an alarming 392. The glamorous training locations of old have given way to the austerity of Bodmin Moor. Even in his latest incarnation as plucky loser (or possibly freak show fighter) he is unable to post the house − full notices without a Naseem Hamed above him to carry the card.

Christopher Livingston Eubank is one of the finest fighters this country has produced and his bravery and gallantry are not in doubt

Boxing folk have a term for the kind of ordeal Eubank again endured on a windy night in Sheffield. They call them 'wars'. Looking through those 51 bouts stretching back to a debut in Atlantic City in October 1985, the eye halts on at least eight battlegrounds. Two with Nigel Benn (the first eight years ago), two against Michael Watson, two with Collins in the Irish Republic and now another couple against Thompson, a fighter of limited finesse but immense strength and courage.

Eubank boxed cleverly for the first five rounds but gradually Thompson began to wear him down. The eruption of his eye injury in the sixth was entirely predictable given the amount of time he had given it to heal. "People say he had 12 weeks' rest, but it wouldn't have been that long," said Collins at ringside. "He went back into

training long before that and he would have been receiving punches on that eye after 10 weeks."

Thakur Sukdeo Singh, the ring doctor, returned to his seat after advising the referee to call a halt and muttered: "That's it. Completely blind. He can't see through that eye." A measure of the chaos enveloping this peacock of a man is that both he and his corner argued that he could have "survived another two rounds", when in fact there were still three to go. Certainly he was ahead on two of the three judges' scorecards, but Thompson was steadily asserting his greater might as a contest described by Hamed's trainer, Brendan Ingle, as "another great scrap" ground towards its denouement.

Another unavoidable issue is the dramatic oscillations in his fighting weight. As recently as October last year he fought Joe Calzaghe at the 12st limit for a world super-middleweight title. Before this cruiser-weight bout he struggled to make the 13st 8lb maximum. There was something not right about the proportions of his body, as if most of the weight has been loaded on across his shoulders. But the doomsday scenario keeps drawing Eubank in. At the end of the eighth round he slapped away an ice bag that was being applied to his hideously disfigured eye. It was a chillingly self–destructive act.

The risks of boxing are immense, but they are containable. It is a peculiar irony of Eubank's condition that he has always attempted to parade a bookish intelligence while being unable to make the smartest and simplest move of them all: to find the exit, as Barry McGuigan did, while the mind is still clear enough to read the signs; or, at the very least, to allow the body a decent period of recuperation before the violence starts up again. Watching him now, a strange, illogical, indefinable wave of admiration sweeps in. But that soon subsides. To say he should stop now is not the same as saying he should never have started. It is a good night for Chris Eubank these days when he doesn't end up in hospital.
★20/7/1998

Frankie Dettori

I knew Swain would never let me down

Winning the King George VI and Queen Elizabeth Diamond Stakes for the second time gave me a very, very big thrill. In fact, I will probably look back on it as one of my best days. You may think I'm getting over-excited but I can assure you it meant a great deal. Firstly, because it is the middle-distance championship of Europe and secondly because it was at Ascot, which I regard as my lucky racecourse. What a place to be lucky at. It was also, as it always is, a man's race and there was the added bonus of meeting the Queen again, which is always a thrill.

I had been under enormous pressure. Many people, including most of the Godolphin team and Sheikh Mohammed, thought I had picked the wrong one and that Swain was an old man incapable of beating horses half his age in such a race. My judgment was proved right though and, as you probably saw as I pulled up on Saturday, that doubled the enjoyment of winning. To win the Eclipse on one horse and then the King George on another three weeks later, well, life is great.

I made my mind up to ride Swain about 10 days ago and everyone in the yard was asking me if I was sure I had made the right decision. And I had to keep telling them I was, although they were sowing doubts in my mind. One of the main reasons I picked Swain is that he has 'done me' so many times. In last year's King George I rejected him, the rain came and he beat me on Singspiel. It was one of those things. But it happened again in the Dubai World Cup. Everyone told me to ride Predappio, which I did because he was working so well at home. Swain then ran one of the races of his life to finish second to Silver Charm and I finished last on Predappio. I didn't want it to happen again.

It was easy to forgive him for not winning the Hardwicke Stakes at Royal Ascot because it was a slowly-run race, he had a 5lb penalty and was outsprinted. People say he's old but time after time he keeps coming back to beat the best. In the race, I thought Daragh O'Donohoe did a fantastic job of pacemaking on Happy Valentine. It is an art to set the perfect pace; if you go too fast you are ignored, too slow and you are not making it enough of a test of stamina. I tracked Royal Anthem until about a furlong and a half out then I asked Swain to really lengthen and put a bit of daylight between himself and the others, which he did. I knew when he hit the front that he wouldn't let me down and that it would take something very special to peg him back.

When I crossed the line it was just the sheer excitement that took over. The reception was unbelievable and I think that British racing now appreciates that Swain is a brilliant horse. Last year everyone said he only won because it was soft but he has come back on good to firm and beaten the best again.
★27/7/98

WHAT THEY SAID

Hell, there are drunks all over the world
John Daly, who plans to attend an Alcoholics Anonymous meeting in Southport for the Open golf

....

I am envious when I look across at Chelsea. They pay some of their top players £40,000 a week. We pay some of ours £40,000 a year
Wimbledon manager Joe Kinnear resigns himself to another season of financial prudence

....

Wakefield is a bit like Wollogong except there aren't any beaches
Australian rugby league player John Bostock on the delights of his adoopted Yorkshire home

....

This is the most special in the whole of the world and I can't tell you how proud I am to have won it
Open champion Mark O'Meara

....

Do you need a manager?
A voice from the crowd to Justin Rose after his announcement that he will now turn professional. The role will soon be filled by his management consultant father Ken

....

It's down to the players - who else can you blame? We only had to win one game at the end of the season against London Scottish, and they couldn't even do that
Arthur Holmes, chairman of Bristol, after his relegated club went into receivership this week

....

The riders are disgusted by everything that has gone on. We will not be treated like cattle. Today we will not take to our bikes. It's finished
Laurent Jalabert, the French champion leads the riders protests at the 12th stage of the Tour de France

....

We know some aspects of that episode will be very difficult to shake off, but I'm here whether people like it or not
Freddy Shepherd, who was forced to resign as chairman of Newcastle United in March after making derogatory remarks about fans, on his return to the club

Severe temptation… Marco Pantani, the eventual winner, is urged on by a fan during a mountain stage of the Tour de France •(AP Photo)★22/7/98

Phil Liggett

The spectacle of an epic event being torn to pieces

For 26 years I have followed every day of the Tour de France. I have seen cyclists die, as in the case of Italy's Fabio Casartelli, I have seen my car reduced to a spade-load of debris after Basque Separatists blew it up near San Sebastian in 1992. And, above all, I have seen brave riders crawl across the finish, so that they can go through the same pain the next day. So the events of the past three weeks will be remembered by me and many others as one of the great sadnesses in sport this decade. The Tour's history, as colourful as the riders themselves, is full of stories of human endurance as man has persuaded his body to achieve feats which most

But if some are cheats, they must be weeded out and severely punished

would believe could never even be attempted.

Since the Tour started in 1903, and the early years of marathon stages, when riders would sleep on the roadside and secret controls were set up to stop cheats missing out the mountains, the event has entered the folklore of not just France, but the world. During July, Tour fever is an epidemic. A million spectators a day is quite normal, and 1,000 media men are seen bizarrely charging around back roads in an attempt to beat the riders to the line. Television is live to 100 countries and all they want to see and talk about is the race's *maillot jaune*.

The Tour is no longer just a sporting event, it is part of the fabric of French culture. Yet the doping scandals, and the way they have been handled these past few days has made many ask if the French themselves are trying to destroy their own heritage. Make no mistake, some cyclists – but not all – take drugs and so do athletes, swimmers, footballers and any other sportsmen who are chasing a big cash reward. Just now, the race is throwing up a clutch of young riders, like the Australians Robbie McEwen and Stuart O'Grady and the rider who is currently second,

Bobby Julich. I know these guys well, and I believe they are clean, living through hateful times which, as McEwen hopes, "will change soon".

Jean-Marie Leblanc is a sad looking race director walking around this week with a frown on his face and the drooping eyes of a bloodhound. Despite friends in high places - after all, he is the only man to get the Champs-Elysees closed for anything accept the Bastille Day parade - he sees his race as being under threat from the scandals which, so far, have had nothing directly to do with this event.

When the riders went on strike, after the TVM team had been taken to a hospital in police custody to give compulsory blood, urine and DNA tests, he launched an impassioned appeal to the riders "as friends" and to the 20 team managers not to stop but continue in the race whatever happens. More arrests are likely when the race returns to France, but at what stage will the police or examining judges admit why they are subjecting the riders and the race to a series of high-profile raids without apparent result? The public continue to watch the event in massive numbers and they mainly support the riders, but if some are cheats, they must be weeded out and severely punished. In modern times, when a medical knowledge seems as important as riding ability, there are always the suspicions which surround teams or riders who pay doctors a lot of money to be with them.

It is a fact that these teams or individuals who have private doctors, tend also to be the best performers. With the arrest of Dr Erik Reykaert from Festina, and with the confessions which followed, these doctors have to fight now to regain credibility. The International Cycling Union, the sport's governing body, have become transparent during this race, and have yet to face the biggest scandal to the hit the sport for many, many years. UCI president Hein Verbruggen did appear briefly to say: "We don't know how many take dope. It could be as many as 40 per cent."

When the latest round of arrests came, Verbruggen was on holiday in India. It is a week since the Festina riders admitted taking dope, yet there has been no announcement of long-term suspensions from the headquarters in Lausanne. In fact, some of the team are already planning their next races. The pain continues.

★31/7/98

Wimbledon Diary

● Boris Becker's admirers continue to grow even after his retirement from Wimbledon's grass courts. He turned up for his semi-final BBC commentary stint in a smart suit, sweating in his anxiety to acquit himself well. When the subject of payment for his guest summary was broached he didn't want one. He wanted to give something back to the championships that had given such a lot to him.

Rumours that Olga Barabanschikova removed her skirt after an honorary steward, clearly with aspirations to transferring to Henley Royal Regatta, reprimanded her for revealing a navel ring are unfounded. "She had to come back and change her skirt one day because it was blue and white, but we haven't heard anything else," said a WTA representative sternly.

Cricket Diary

● Andy Caddick chose an interview in an AXA League programme to outline his starkly competitive philosophy: "I'm all for sledging. It's part of the game and I do it myself." The Somerset bowler also responded bluntly when asked who he had been most pleased to meet in the game. Answer: "Nobody in particular."

Letters To The Sports Editor

● SIR - I really must take issue with David Miller's comments concerning the dismissal of David Beckham in the England v Argentina game. I have long suspected that sports writers, and the media in general, have no detailed knowledge of the Laws of the game, and now my suspicions have been confirmed. Beckham perpetrated a clear act of violent conduct, as described in Law 12. The player does not even have to make contact with his opponent to be dismissed, as in the eyes of Law 12 attempting to strike or kick an opponent is an offence punishable by dismissal. Perhaps the Editor could arrange for David Miller to attend a referee's training course, or at least to read a copy of the Laws every once in a while. Perhaps I could therefore express my view that referee Nielsen's decision to dismiss Beckham was wholly justified. - TIM CROMPTON, Class 1 Referee, Bury.

● SIR - I was amazed to hear Glenn Hoddle in an interview say that he did not blame Maradona for the goal in the 'hand of God' incident but rather he blamed the officials, for presumably not seeing it and/or not disallowing the 'goal'. This is like saying it is not the fault of a criminal that a crime is committed, but the fault of the police in not detecting it. Television coverage of this World Cup has yet again highlighted the cheating antics of professional footballers. In particular I refer to the theatrical dives when tackled, even when they have not been touched by an opponent, in an effort to convince the officials to award a foul or a penalty. It is too easy to blame the officials when they are deceived by professionals. When players stop cheating, football may well deserve the label of 'the beautiful game'. - IAN KNEE, Stoke Gabriel, Devon.

● SIR - I would like to express my heartfelt appreciation to tennis fans at Wimbledon for their encouragement and enthusiasm each year and most importantly during The Championships this year. They supported me as if I were British. I could hear and feel their presence during each match. They helped me play my best tennis and were truly part of my success. Thank you for helping me become your champion. I will always be grateful for what you helped me to accomplish and I look forward to returning next summer to what has become a very special place for me. - JANA NOVOTNA, 1998 Women's Champion.

2: Mika Hakkinen and David Coulthard record another McLaren 1-2 in the German GP at Hockenheim. Marco Pantani, of Italy, wins the ill-fated Tour de France.

5: Manchester United and Arsenal admit they are involved in secret talks aimed at setting up a European Super League.

6: Mark Butcher scores his maiden century for England.Michelle de Bruin is banned for four years after being found guilty of tampering with a urine sample.

7: Angus Fraser takes five wickets as South Africa are dismissed for 252 at Headingley.

9: Arsenal beat Manchester United 3-0 in the Charity Shield at Wembley.

10: England win the fifth Test and the series, 2-1, when they collect the last two South African wickets in front of a crowd of 10,000 who see 29 minutes' cricket.

13: The FA decide not to charge Brian Clough with misconduct after the 'bungs' inquiry because of his failing health. Mike Tyson drops his plea to regain his boxing licence hours before the commission in New Jersey were due to give their verdict.

14: Sri Lanka win the first game of the Emirates triangular one-day tournament against South Africa.

16: England defeat of Sri Lanka in the Emirates one-day tournament. Michael Schumacher wins the Hungarian GP. Vijay Singh wins the US PGA Championship by two shots in Seattle.

18: South Africa beat England by 14 runs in the one-day series, but fail to reach the final on net run rate.

19: Darren Campbell wins the 100 metres at the European Championships in Budapest in 10.04sec, the second fastest time by a Briton.

20: Sri Lanka beat England by five wickets to win the Emirates one-day tournament at Lord's. Dwight Yorke moves from Aston Villa to Manchester United for À12.6 million.

21: Britain enjoy a fabulous 15 minutes at the European Championships as Iwan Thomas wins the 400m, and Dougie Walker leads a clean sweep in the 200m.

22: Britain collect three more gold medals at the European Championships through heptathlete Denise Lewis, Colin Jackson in the high hurdles and the men's sprint relay team.

23: Britain finish the European Championships with nine gold medals, the latest from Jonathan Edwards, in the triple jump, Steve Backley, in the javelin, and the men's 4x400m team.

26: Mark James is named as Europe's new Ryder Cup captain.

27: Kenny Dalglish is replaced as Newcastle manager by Ruud Gullit.

28: John Crawley adds a century to that of Graeme Hick as England reach 445, to which Sri Lanka reply with 79 for one. Gustavo Poyet scores to land Chelsea the European Super Cup with a 1-0 win over Real Madrid in Monaco.

30: Sri Lanka's marathon innings ends on 591. Damon Hill stands on top of a podium lacking all the championship contenders after a crash-strewn grand prix in Belgium.

31: Sri Lanka are set just 36 to win the Oval Test, which they do in five overs. Spinner Muttiah Muralitharan taking match figures of 16 for 220.

Giles Smith

Golf zone would suit the dome to a tee

Details regarding what will eventually fill the Millennium Dome are fairly hard to come by. The topic is a tender and controversial one. We know there will be various "zones"; we hear much about the Dome "focusing the attention of the nation" at the century's end; and it seems highly likely that we will be able to celebrate the dawn of a new era by riding a moving stairway through the hollowed-out insides of a giant human figure which has no genitals. But that's about it. And, as yet, golf has not been mentioned once.

So when the New Millennium Experience invited me to participate in a Longest Drive competition, compered by Peter Alliss, actually inside the Dome, I counted myself among the blessed. After all, people in their thousands have been crying out for the opportunity to take a golf club to the Millennium Dome since the project's inception. Now I was going to do so on their behalf.

Ostensibly, the driving competition was a corporate event for constructors, engineers and contractors working on the site - McAlpine/Laing, O'Rourke Civil Engineering, Ellmer Construction, among many others. No one seemed too surprised when the pair representing London Underground turned up late. Yet I can't have been the only one who quietly wondered if he wasn't part of a surrogate trial relating to the potential future use of the Dome. If it didn't work out with the sponsors and the sexless giant, London could always boast the world's largest tented driving range. Which would be something to be really proud of.

Access to the Dome at the moment is via service roads which lead across acres of flat, stoney scrub, broken by ranks of blue Portakabins and the occasional dumper truck, and through a cordon of manned security gates. The challenge was to wind down the car window and not sound stupid while saying to a uniformed guard: "I'm here for the golf." At the site office, beyond the car park, one was issued with a hard hat, a pair of wellies and a fluorescent yellow tabard, or 'high vis jacket' as we prefer to call them in the construction trade. One was, if one wished, free to discard these potentially swing-impeding items during one's time at the tee (the teeing mats were in a rubble-proof net enclosure of their own) but in the meantime, worn over a suit, they were invaluable props for anyone wishing to pretend to be a member of the government on a visit.

In an undersized hat and oversized boots - a one-man Laurel & Hardy routine - I lumbered over the rubble and into the Dome. As one of the privileged few to have stood beneath that already notorious canopy (and one of even fewer to have stood there holding a three-wood), I can report at least one thing with confidence: the Dome is very large. It's 400 yards from one side to the other. That's even larger than the marquee at Barbra Streisand's wedding. We would have seen its like before if Billy Smart had only had the guts to think big. If you are going to spend £200 million on a tent, this is certainly the kind of tent you would want to see for your money.

....

"If Giles Smith happens to be one of your partners," wrote Bruce, "you may find it more entertaining to stay in the clubhouse and read the paper."

....

At the same time, for the Dome really to come together as a national focus for golfing excellence, some alterations would be necessary. You would have to change the colour of the roof for one thing. No disrespect to the architect Richard Rogers, but I'm not sure his mind was fully on golf when he designed this building. The white underside of the canopy swallowed golf balls whole. Indeed, unless, like me, you were used to flying the ball at cement-mixer height, where its short but sensationally dangerous path could still be picked out against the rubble and cement, you never got to see your ball again after striking it. Only thanks to the judicious deployment of a team of helmeted ball-spotters, distributed between the 175-yard and 250-yard markers and connected to the organisers by walkie-talkies could the tournament feasibly go ahead.

Going in, I can't say my confidence was high. Golf has not been good to me over the last year. I've written here before about the pivotal moment which tipped me into decline: a spectacularly incompetent charity golf performance at Wentworth in a fourball with Bruce Forsyth, in the wake of which I confronted a lot of demons and was forced to reassess radically my chances of turning pro in time for the next Ryder Cup. Nevertheless, I was mildly heartened to learn the other week that Forsyth had commemorated our encounter in the printed programme for the Fourth Bruce Forsyth Oxfordshire Golf Classic, which took place in June, and for which my invitation must have gone astray in the post. Under a smiling picture of himself, and beside the headline "Message From Your Host", Forsyth referred enthusiastically to his meeting with me as "one of the most frustrating golf days of my entire life." He also advised his guests to check their team-lists carefully for my name. "If Giles Smith happens to be one of your partners," wrote Bruce, "you may find it more entertaining to stay in the clubhouse and read the paper."

Still, there isn't a player on the circuit who doesn't take a certain amount of personal baggage around with him. And if my baggage happens to contain the former host of *The Generation Game*, then so be it.

At the Dome, the safety gear only increased my feeling of precariousness: all this incompleted building work; all these opportunities for major damage. It occurred to me that I would only need to lift my head during my down swing and I could offset the completion of the adjacent Jubilee Line extension by another six months.

Alliss, spurning the hard-hat and wellies in favour of a blue blazer with gold buttons and a pair of tassled loafers, was standing on a wooden pallet to one side of the traps. He was holding a microphone, plugged into a miniature PA system at his feet. I may be sticking my neck out here, but I got the impression he had done this kind of work before. "The prize must be good," he said, as someone moved crisply to the tee. "I haven't seen anyone move so fast since the old King died."

My arrival on the tee was greeted by Alliss with a generous remark to the effect that I could always be relied upon to produce "something unexpected". "I've been watching him for years," he added. This was not strictly true. Alliss has seen me play golf just once. But I can understand if it felt like that.

The first of my three balls, mysteriously underpowered, barely cleared the teeing mat. The second sprang alarmingly sideways off a nearby fence. There was a kind of awed silence from the onlookers behind me. But he who stays cool prospers. At the last moment, I changed my swing-thought. Previously I had been thinking "Spirit Level", which doubled as a personal calmative and a tribute to the surroundings. Now, abandoning that, I imagined that the ball was the window of Bruce Forsyth's living room. Down came the club, crack went the clubface and away the ball flew. Lengths were calculated according to where the ball first hit the ground/ n obstruction/a helmeted ball-spotter. Mine went 215 yards.

OK, so it wasn't Tiger Woods. It wasn't even Stuart Fenton, a sales director from Baco Contracts, whose ball was reported to be still rising when it hit a pylon around the 275-yard marker and who walked off with the trophy. But 215 yards. At first bounce. Eat that, Forsyth. Personally, I have always thought the Millennium Dome was a very good idea.

★1/8/98

Timothy Collings

Hill brings order to the chaos

Eddie Jordan danced an Irish jig, Damon Hill jumped high on the podium like Michael Schumacher does, commercial director Ian Phillips lifted a glass of champagne and the whole of Formula One joined the team in yellow in celebrating their moment of triumph. Never before can a maiden victory, after 127 outings over nearly eight years, have brought such delight as that of the Silverstone-based Jordan team in a rainswept Belgian Grand Prix.

To break the ice with a one-two, from Hill and his young team-mate Ralf Schumacher, was beyond even Dubliner Jordan's wildest dreams after their desultory start to the season. Yet,

cruelly and unfairly, it is a win that will be overshadowed in many people's eyes by an extraordinary chain of events in the most incident-filled and acrimonious race of the season, if not the entire history of Formula One.

If the 22nd win of his career left Hill almost lost for words, the 44 laps which kept spectators on their seat edges for nearly three hours had the opposite effect on everyone else. This was a race to remember - for reasons good and bad.

Not only did it end with a happy rostrum, Jean Alesi climbing alongside the two Jordan men for the first time since he joined Sauber, it also contained the biggest opening-ap multiple

shunt on record (with at least 15 of the 22 original starters suffering damage); a restart which triggered the use of the safety car after half a lap; the loss of the championship leader Mika Hakkinen at the first corner; enough additional shunts for a video compilation and, after a volatile collision on lap 25, an unplesant confrontation between Michael Schumacher and David Coulthard in the McLaren garage.

After the accidents involving Jacques Villeneuve on Friday and Mika Salo on Saturday, the thick cloud which hung over the Spa-Francorchamps circuit signalled another afternoon of crashes, long before the race began,

Carnage at Spa… race officials mix with drivers to sift through the debris after one of the worst crashes in Formula One history, on the opening lap

unwisely, without the safety car or a rolling start. Instead there was a standing start and, predictably, chaos. The repair bills the teams now face run into millions of pounds, not to mention the dangers faced by the drivers in such atrocious and treacherous conditions. What would their insurers say?

Schumacher's demise was the most spectacular. The man who was seeking to mark Ferrari's 600th grand prix with his fourth win in succession on this track instead marched away stone-faced and speechless. He accused Coulthard of trying to kill him in their crash (a theory denied by the Scot and all sensible witnesses) and used foul language to make his point as the pair were pulled apart.

Schumacher, who was consoled in the Ferrari motor home by Bernie Ecclestone, clearly believed that Coulthard, in his McLaren, had deliberately slowed up in front of him to cause an accident and so wreck his chances of taking the championship lead as he led the race by 30 seconds. The 10 points for winning would have lifted him three clear of Hakkinen. "I am very, very annoyed about what has happened here," he said. "It was clear we were ready to take the championship lead. We were by far the fastest cars out there. What I don't understand is that Coulthard was doing laps in 2.12 and then did 2.17 when I got close to him. It's not right to lift off like that. Obviously doing that on the straight is very dangerous. He has the experience to know that

you do not slow down on a straight like that without giving any warning. So one could think he did it deliberately."

Asked what he screamed at Coulthard, Schumacher said: "Yes, I asked him if he had tried to kill me."

The repair bills the teams now face run into millions of pounds

Coulthard said: "I find his behaviour totally unacceptable. If he wanted to discuss it, man to man, there wouldn't have been a problem. If he wants to accuse me of things like that then I have no interest in talking to him. The allegations that he made were untrue." Both drivers and Ferrari's second driver, Eddie Irvine, were called before race stewards, but no action was taken and the provisional result - showing that only eight of the 22 starters finished - was made official.

Coulthard was jeered by German fans, who blamed him for the accident. The Scot said: "I am 100 per cent certain that I did nothing wrong. I could see him coming from the previous corner. In those conditions you are not looking in your mirrors all the time. The team asked me to move across and tuck in on the right to keep out of his way. I did that and then he just drove straight into the back of my car."

Schumacher's reaction was hasty and unexpected, but demonstrated how pumped up he was in contemplation of recording another Spa victory. But, instead of winning, he suffered his first retirement in the race since he made his debut in the sport in 1991. The mass pile-up at the original start was caused by Coulthard's lurid spin, after a nudge by Irvine's Ferrari, into the barriers on the downhill rush towards Eau Rouge. Once the spray had settled, it took rescue crews 50 minutes to clear the track in preparation for a restart.

But Hill survived that and all that followed as he recorded one of the most satisfying wins of his career, his first with any team other than Williams and his first since winning the title in Japan in 1996. "This is a really great day for Jordan and it is a wonderful feeling. To win our first race and to get a one-two result is a fantastic result for everyone. We deserved it. We were strong all weekend, we qualified well and it was a very exciting race," said Hill. "I am delighted - in fact, I feel a little lost for words. I just got really lucky today."
★31/8/98

of the Belgian Grand Prix •**EPA Photo** ★**30/8/98**

79

Christopher Martin-Jenkins

England's triumph wins back the doubters

Two things were not in doubt when the dust had settled at Headingley: the fact of England's victory by 23 runs and the public longing for an overdue triumph.

Given free admission, more than 10,000 streamed into Headingley on a warm, misty morning, all of them knowing that two balls and the post-match interviews might be the limit of the entertainment. In the event they saw 29 minutes of cricket and the two wickets which sealed England's first win in a five-Test series since December 28, 1986.

Angus Fraser, who bowled three overs without conceding a run, and Darren Gough, whose six for 42 were his best Test figures, in his 25th match, were the bowlers to finish the job. But Alec Stewart, who had captained ably and batted and kept wicket to the highest standard throughout the series, was the first to stress that it was a team performance and the £200,000 winning bonus offered by Cornhill, Vodafone and the England and Wales Cricket Board will be shared by 18 players, not all of whom will be on the major part of the tour to Australia.

The issue was in doubt for six overs as South Africa, needing 34 more runs, inched towards their target in singles and leg byes. Moments of profound silence as Gough and Fraser ran in to bowl - Yorkshire's folk hero from the Rugby Stand End, Fraser down the hill from Kirkstall Lane - were followed by bursts of applause whenever a ball passed without a run being scored.

Shaun Pollock played straight and with confidence and it was not until the second ball of the sixth over that Allan Donald played with an angled bat at Fraser outside the off stump and got an almost indiscernible outside edge to give Stewart his 23rd catch of the series. Makhaya Ntini survived the rest of the over without trouble but, plunging forward to a ball which nipped back from the off stump after Pollock had taken a single in the next, he saw Javed Akhtar's bony finger lift for the ninth and last time in the match.

In a just world this would have been a drawn series. England had more than their fair share of luck in both of the Tests they won, not least in umpiring decisions. Far too many of the eight lbws which went against South Africa (two against England) were dubious and one of their national selectors was seething with anger at the inequity of it all, though the captain, Hansie Cronje, remained diplomatic.

But England were overdue a change of luck and they deserved it after the heroic recovery at Old Trafford. It is frightening how narrow was the line between the national apathy and media-led gloom which would have followed had England gone two down in Manchester; and the euphoria now being felt by all connected with England cricket, the professionals, the media and amateur cricketers of all ages included. South Africa might have won the series had Lance Klusener been fit to bowl on the last day at Old Trafford and in the last two Tests, but, equally, rain on the last day at Edgbaston might have saved them from defeat and England have been without Graham Thorpe for the last two

games. The search continues for at least one more bowler of the pace of Gough or Donald - Jimmy Ormond, Alex Tudor and Stephen Harmison are all capable of breaking through - and for a Test-class wrist-spinner. Whether to give Ian Salisbury one more chance or wait for Chris Schofield is one of several ticklish decisions the selectors have to make.

But winning can become a habit because of the confidence and team spirit which a success like this engenders. England actually won three Tests in a row last year - at Wellington, Christchurch and Edgbaston - but if they can defeat Sri Lanka at the Oval at the end of August and Shane Warne really is in doubt for the series in Australia, the corner may finally have been turned. Successful Test sides need good opening pairs, both batsmen and bowlers.

It is no coincidence that England have been able to make effective use at last of their three

Winning can become a habit because of the confidence and team spirit which a success like this engenders

leading fast and fast-medium bowlers, Fraser, Gough and Cork, while Mike Atherton called Mark Butcher "the find of the series". Butcher is left-handed, he plays straight and he scores at a decent pace. His emergence, coupled with the return of Atherton's form and fluency after diligent net practice to make himself stand taller and stiller in the crease, enabled England to get a sufficient number of good starts against the formidable Donald and Pollock.

Therein lay the basis of a close and constantly interesting series. Pollock did not find the right length for English pitches until the final game, but he will be a champion by the time he returns. Donald was officially South Africa's man of the series with 33 wickets, Atherton was England's and Butcher was Paul Allott's selection as the man of the fifth Test. In the long sequence of defeats under Mike Gatting, David Gower, Graham Gooch and Atherton - briefly also John Emburey and Chris Cowdrey - the rub of the green tended to go against England as it has against South Africa in the last few weeks.

That is sport and that is life. If Stewart turns out to be a consistent winner it will not be the first example of the right man in the right place at the right time.
★11/8/98

Game, set and series... Darren Gough celebrates the wicket of Makhaya Ntini to seal the series at Headingly •**Russell Cheyne** ★**10/8/98**

Where did that go?... Angus Fraser, England's leading strike bowler, in contemplative mood as South Africa chase quick runs •**Russell Cheyne** ★**10/8/98**

Michael Parkinson

Sifting fact from fiction in the pre-video age

You don't have to be a season ticket holder at Old Trafford to watch legends. They are available in any town, in any division to the child with imagination.

The real pleasure of the Football League's list of its 100 greatest players is in compiling another list of those who didn't make it. I cannot for the life of me understand why Steve Griffiths, George Spruce, Cec McCormack and Johnny Kelly are not included, never mind the omission of the immortal Skinner Normanton. Similarly, had I been born in Rotherham and not Barnsley I would have objected to the absence of Wally Ardron, Gladstone Quest and Horace Williams. And if Chesterfield had been my team I would have been upset by the exclusion of Ray Middleton, Tommy Capel and those notorious full-backs, Milburn and Kidd.

Anyone who grew up in Bolton when Hartle and Banks were in action would have no doubt of their right to a place in any all-time list. If one didn't get you the other one did. Banks used to favour dumping the winger on the cinder track around Burnden Park early on. "Gi'ing his arse a reight good gritting" was how he described it. This would be followed by Hartle shouting: "When tha's finished wi 'im, Tommy, chip him over to me," just in case the winger might be having any funny ideas about switching wings.

Even though the Premier League seems all-embracing, there are still children throughout the land who in their anecdotage will reminisce about a mythical centre-half for Peterborough or an eccentric goalkeeper at Walsall. You don't have to be a season ticket holder at Old Trafford to watch legends. They are available in any town, in any division to the child with imagination. What is different is that the oral tradition has become a technological one. In other words video evidence makes it increasingly difficult for today's nostalgic to adorn the facts as he once could. For instance, when my father told me that Pongo Waring (or was it Frank Barson) ran the length of the field heading the ball before deliberately nodding it over the opposition's bar because he was in dispute with the Barnsley manager over pay, I could only listen open-mouthed.

Similarly, my children have had to take my word that the finest exponent of the sliding tackle I ever saw was a centre half called Jack Kitchen, who made Tony Adams look like a Teletubbie. Kitchen used to cart the winger into the low cement wall at Oakwell with such force that to guard our eyes from flying concrete chips we took to wearing protective goggles. Nor can they dispute my statement that Bob Shotton was the best penalty taker that ever drew breath. He always used to hit the iron stanchion at the back of the net and the ball had rebounded to the halfway line while the goalkeeper was still diving. That's what I tell them.

A lot of the fun went out of the game when they got rid of iron goal-frames. The only time Shotton missed a penalty was when he hit the bar with such force that it made a noise like Big Ben chiming and set dogs barking in Huddersfield. I'm not pretending my children believe me, but they have no way of checking unless they ask their Uncle Jim, and he is a bigger storyteller than I am.

The point is, when it comes to the time my children start telling their children about Liam Brady, Gary Lineker and Alan Hansen they will have to be careful. Technology has restricted the boundaries of their nostalgia. Put it another way: they won't be able to tell tales like I did. Or my father before me.

For instance, my father used to love telling stories about the gigantic Willie Foulke who played in goal for Sheffield United, Chelsea, Bradford City and England. He claimed he once saw Steve Bloomer, of Middlesbrough, score a most remarkable goal against Foulke. It took place on a quagmire when Bloomer, who was renowned for the ferocity of his shooting, took a penalty and aimed for Foulke's ample belly. According to my old man, Foulke gathered the ball but such was the power of the shot he was propelled backwards over his line and into the net as if on rails. Ho hum, said I.

Years later I read an essay by Donny Davies about goalkeepers in which he recalled a goal scored by Shepherd, of Bolton Wanderers, against Elisha Scott, the famous Liverpool goalkeeper. Davies writes: "The Burnden ground was like a quagmire and the ball a ton weight. Shepherd let fly straight at Scott as it happened and Scott, without flinching, stooped and hugged the ball to his bosom, and still hugging it, felt himself slip back helplessly over his own goal line. Catching that ball must have felt like trying to catch one of the cannonballs used in the Napoleonic wars." Ho double hum, thought I.

Willie Foulke always intrigued me. For years I thought he had been imagined by my old man. I was delighted to see him included in the list of the 100 best. My father said he filled the goal. He was 6ft 3in tall and weighed 22st 3lbs. When he was injured it took six men to carry him from the field. He wouldn't fit on a stretcher. This, and much more, is confirmed in a fascinating new book called *He Always Puts It To The Right* by Clark Miller. It's a history of the penalty kick. Sadly, Mr Miller died before his book was published. His legacy is a joy. He points out that being a goalkeeper in the late 1890s and early 1900s was a job for a big man as well as a brave one. A tactic of those days was to deliberately take the keeper out of play. "Disposing" of the custodian was part of the game. Opponents thought twice about taking on 'Little Willie' or 'Fatty Foulke'.

The first Chelsea programme, in 1905, describes Foulke: "As fine a specimen of manhood as ever stepped on the field... In spite of his bulk he possesses all the activity of a cat combined with the playfulness of a kitten."

His eating habits would have dismayed today's dieticians. When he played for Chelsea his teammates came down for dinner at their hotel and found 11 empty plates. Foulke had arrived in the dining room early and scoffed the lot. He was one of the first superstars of the game. He promenaded the Fulham Road and King's Road in the latest fashions. He always wore a silk scarf with a gold pin stating 'King Custodian'. He was as feared by opponents as he was adored by the fans. He once picked up a centre forward and stood him on his head in the mud. He regularly threw opponents bodily into the back of his net. If he gave away a penalty he didn't bother. In those days keepers were not rooted to the goal line and the sight of Foulke, all 311 lbs of him, hurtling towards the penalty taker screaming and shouting meant a goal from the spot was far from a foregone conclusion. Foulke came to a sad end. He finished up in Blackpool saving penalties for pennies by inviting holidaymakers to "Beat Little Willie". He died from pneumonia at the age of 40.

The point about Foulke is you couldn't invent him. If someone wrote a novel with Little Willie as a football superstar, with his own place in the Pantheon, people would scoff and suggest the author was drunk in charge of a typewriter. So my father wasn't romancing after all and maybe Skinner Normanton was really as ferocious as I remember. Perhaps they really did build a gate at Barnsley which they would open for our flying winger Gavin Smith to run through so that he didn't collide with the wall. It was just that bit about fitting him with an arresting parachute that I made up.

In the end it doesn't matter. Sport's benison is a library of memories. I don't need a video. I've got the original movie in my mind. It might be black and white, but so is *Casablanca*. They can make all the lists they like, but it doesn't change a thing. Fact is they weren't there when Johnny Kelly made a mug of Alf Ramsey: when Cec McCormack put five past Luton; when Arthur Kayo broke off one of his thrilling runs down the right wing to pinch a chip from a fan leaning over the wall. Lists are for trainspotters. Real fans wear goggles.

★17/8/98

Marcus Armytage

Bollinger series champion-elect used bogus identity after failing drugs test in US

Angel Jacobs, the leading Flat amateur rider in the Bollinger series who is virtually assured of this season's title, was yesterday exposed as an impostor with two other identities. He has admitted to the Jockey Club that he is Angel Monserrate, 29, a Puerto Rican-born former professional jockey and work-rider in the United States, who was banned for failing a drugs test in 1995. The following year he rode posing as an amateur, which led to him being charged with criminal trespass, tampering with a sporting event and forgery. Under the name of 'Carlos Castro', he was led away in handcuffs by the track detective after winning a race in the US.

A month ago Sandy Murphy, secretary of the British Amateur Jockeys' Association, asked Jockey Club security to look into the persistent rumours. They handed the case over to the Licensing Department. However, with very close links to the Amateur Riders' Club of America, the Amateur Jockeys' Association of Great Britain decided to carry out their own investigations with the co-operation of the Licensing Department. Confronted last night by Jockey Club security, acting on evidence gathered by the Amateur Jockeys' Association and their counterparts in the US, Jacobs admitted being Angel Monserrate. It is inevitable that he will have his permit withdrawn by the Jockey Club and he will not be allowed to ride at Goodwood on later in the week.

Dick Milburn, the secretary of the Amateur Riders' Club of America, said that after his ban, Monserrate had applied to resume his career in 1996 by joining the club under the assumed name of Carlos Castro. Castro and Jacobs, his wife Lisa's maiden name, share the same birth date of Oct 26, 1968 and it was the discovery of that coincidence on his licence applications which ultimately led to his downfall. As Castro, he finished eighth on his first ride on July 5 and immediately attracted press interest, much like Jacobs has done in England this summer, for being so polished, effective and so much better than his 'flapping' amateur opposition.

On Aug 23, 1996, Monserrate had what was supposedly his second ride. The Amateur Club were reluctant to let him take part because he had not fully paid his subscription but the trainer and owner of the horse in question said they knew him and, on their word, he was allowed to ride. His mount, a 35-1 outsider, was narrowly beaten by the odds-on favourite and Castro again attracted favourable press. Suspicions were forming, though, because he tended to arrive late before a race and leave immediately afterwards. On his fifth ride, on Nov 23, an anonymous telephone call was received by the stewards at Aqueduct, in New York, saying that the jockey riding as Carlos Castro was not who he said he was. The stewards let him ride, he won the race but was arrested in the winner's enclosure. He was charged with forgery, criminal trespass (because he was banned from all New York racetracks) and tampering with a sports event. The anonymous tip-off was from a former employer of Monserrate, a well-known trainer, who had recognised him in the paddock before a race.

This season, riding in England, Angel Jacobs made an immediate impact. He arrived here in September and had his first ride at Wolverhampton in January. He stands out in his races because he is so stylish and streamlined compared with his opposition. Claiming a full 7lb allowance for his 'inexperience', he rode his first winner on Bold Faith for Willie Musson in the Bollinger Champagne Series Gentlemen's Handicap at Newbury on June 11. Raceform, the official form book, said: "Bold Faith was given a fine ride."

On July 3 he won another Bollinger race on Broughton's Lure, also for Musson, for whom he has been riding out this summer. At Newmarket, where he is based, he won another Bollinger race, on Indium. Raceform said the horse had "finally lost his maiden tag under a very capable amateur". He has a virtually unassailable lead in the Bollinger Series but now faces disqualification. His last winner came at Beverley on Aug 13 when he partnered Gymcrak Flyer for Gordon Holmes. Racecourse rumour has suggested for some time that there was more to Jacobs and his mysterious Puerto Rican background than met the eye. As several well-respected commentators have pointed out, he is a class apart from his part-time amateur rivals. I rode against him at Bath in June and was extremely impressed with his style. He was too good to be true.

This is another in a series of embarrassing incidents to hit British racing this year. Three jockeys were arrested at the start of the year by police investigating alleged race-fixing. More recently, a Starting Price compiler was also arrested. 'Ringers' - horses substituted for a lookalike - have littered racing's colourful past. Occasions when a jockey has masqueraded as another are much rarer, though an experienced Scottish-born jockey was recently deported from Canada for allegedly riding as an apprentice under a false name.

★27/8/98

1: Peter Such, the Essex spinner, is the surprise choice in England's party for the winter tour to Australia.

5: Paul Ince is sent off as England start their European Championship qualifying campaign with a 2-1 defeat by Sweden in Stockholm. Christian Gross is sacked by Tottenham. It is revealed that Rupert Murdoch's BSkyB have bid £575 million for ownership of Manchester United.

6: Lancashire reach their target of 109 for the loss of one wicket to win the NatWest Trophy at Lord's. Blyth Tait wins Burghley's three-day horse event.

7: Lancashire's defeat of Hampshire lands them the AXA League, their second title in two days.

12: Nedawi, the only Godolphin runner, wins the St Leger at Doncaster. Iwan Thomas wins the 400m gold medal at the World Cup in Johannesburg, followed by a first place for the sprint relay team.

13: Pat Rafter defends his US Open title by beating Mark Philippoussis in four sets in New York; Lindsay Davenport wins the women's title. Michael Schumacher wins the Italian Grand Prix at Monza.

16: Nicky Butt is sent off as Manchester United are held 3-3 at home by Barcelona in the European Champions' League, despite leading 2-0 and 3-2. In another group, Arsenal draw 1-1 in Lens.

17: Newcastle beat Partizan Belgrade 2-1 in the first leg of their European Cup-Winners' Cip tie, while Chelsea beat Helsingborgs 1-0.

19: Leicestershire collect the bonus point they need against Surrey to land the County Championship. The United States increase their Solheim Cup lead to 10-5.

20: Europe win the singles, but the United States still take the Solheim Cup 16-12 in Dublin, Ohio. Tim Henman retains the President's Cup in Tashkent.

21: Florence Griffith Joyner, the former Olympic sprint champion, dies after an apparent heart attack, aged 38. England complete the Commwealth Games in Kuala Lumpur in second place, behind Australia, in the medals table with 36 golds, Scotland and Wales manage three each, Ireland two.

22: Nick Faldo sacks his long-time coach David Leadbetter after a run of poor results.

26: Paolo di Canio faces a long ban after pushing over referee Paul Alcock. Lennox Lewis retains his WBC heavyweight title in a poor fight in Connecticut against Zeljko Mavrovic, while in Norwich, Herbie Hide takes just over four minutes to retain his WBO heavyweight crown against Willi Fischer.

27: Mika Hakkinen's victory in the Luxembourg GP opens a four-point lead over Michael Schumacher in the drivers' championship, with one race to go. Tim Henman records the decisive victory to give Britain a 3-2 win over India and gain promotion to the world group of the Davis Cup. Mark McGwire completes the American baseball season with an unprecdented 70 home runs.

28: MCC members vote to end their 211-year ban on admitting women.

29: Stan Collymore hits a hat-trick in Aston Villa's 3-0 away win against Stromsgodset to move into the second round of the UEFA Cup; Liverpool also go through 8-0 on aggregate against Kosice, while Leeds need penalties to beat Maritimo, but Blackburn go out against Lyons.

30: Gordon Richards, one of the most successful National Hunt trainers, dies, aged 68.

Andrew Baker

Smiling in perfect harmony

These are, we are constantly reminded, the Friendly Games, yet in the heat of competition, the mash of civility and good fellowship can often slip. In one discipline, however, happiness is compulsory: synchronised swimming, sport with a smile. But the cheery grin worn by all competitors at all times in and around the pool is not necessarily a sincere expression of how delighted they are to be here. It is an essential part of the synchronised swimmer's art, for it is crucial to convey grace and ease, and nothing impresses the judges so much as a full set of pearly whites on constant display.

Competitors must be possessed of the cardio-vascular capacity of a medium-sized whale allied to the speed and strength of a dolphin

Tuesday brought the final of the solo event, which may at first seem a contradiction in terms. What, one might ask, are the swimmers supposed to be synchronised with if they are on their own in the vast blue depth of the pool? The answer, impatiently supplied by experts who have grown bored with the question, is "the music, you nincompoop".

This is trickier than it is, in, say, ice dance, for one of the first things you notice when you dive into a swimming pool is that the sounds present on the surface are absent under water. So it is that synchronised swimmers often cannot hear the music which accompanies their performance. The solution, apparently, is to count along with the beat and time your movements accordingly. It should be becoming clear that this is a challenging pastime. Competitors must be possessed of the cardio-vascular capacity of a medium-sized whale allied to the speed and strength of a dolphin. They must also - and here they are ahead of other aquatic mammals - be able to smile and count at the same time.

All this before any account is taken of artistic ability. Half the points in synchronised swimming are awarded for technical ability - angle of leg with surface of water and so on - while the other half reward the artistic impression of the contestant's routine. The gold medal performance, for example, by Valerie Hould-Marshand of Canada, was an interpretation of the story of Shakespeare's Juliet. No mean achievement, this. Most stage actresses attempting the same role have the advantage of language, and in only the most avant garde productions are they likely to stand a considerable length of time under water. Hould-Marshand, 18, a team silver medallist at the Olympics, was delighted to have gone one better at the Commonwealth Games, ascribing her success to her work with an actor friend in researching the character. "I can't say that I have lived through Juliet's experience," she conceded. "I'm still alive, for one thing. But I tried to imagine what it would be like to have your heart broken into a million pieces."

One distraction for the gold medallist was a concern about her hair-do. In common with her competitors, Hould-Marshand was plastered with make-up and wore her hair heavily flicked back. At one point during her routine, though, the heat and water combined to threaten her coiffure. "I had a bit of a meltdown situation out there," she said. "But it all held together." Phew.
★15/9/98

Reaching out… Jamie Quarry, of Scotland, competes in the long-jump section of the decathlon at the Commonwealth Games •**PA** ★**17/3/98**

September 1998

Andrew Baker

Rhythmic gymnastics

Malaysians fail to repeat medal-winning efforts in sport with huge potential for errors

The notion of people scrambling desperately for tickets to a rhythmic gymnastics event may strike many British sports fans as somewhat strange, but at these weird and sometimes wonderful Commonweath Games what makes a sport compelling to the local audience is not drama, athletic prowess or speed, but Malaysia's chances of winning a medal. So the crowd outside the Putra Stadium yesterday afternoon was 10 deep, long after the rhythmic gymnastics competition had begun. The previous day the Malaysian girls had upset the form book by winning the team competition, and suddenly the individual contest had become the hottest ticket in town.

The stadium announcer went out of his way to make everyone feel welcome, addressing his opening remarks to "ladies and gentlemen, boys and girls, and you wonderful, wonderful, people out there." His voice oozed the kind of sincerity that could be seen on the faces of the performers -

sorry, competitors - who wore vivacious grins even when everything was going horribly wrong.

This is a sport where disaster is the competitor's constant companion. Purer pursuits have fewer potential hazards: short of falling flat on her face, not much can ruin the 100 metre runner's afternoon. But the rhythmic gymnast is bedevilled by compulsory props, any of which can wreck her routine at any moment. She must cavort with four in succession: rope, hoop, clubs and ribbon. And while one of the sport's few attractions is the unusual and often improbable things that the competitor can get these otherwise inanimate objects to do, one of its key appeals to even mildly malicious spectators is the range of ways in which the aforementioned objects can bite back.

The hoop is particularly dangerous, which is why wise competitors have a back-up lying just outside the edge of the square in which they compete. The point of the hoop routine is to roll

the thing around in as many ways as the gymnast can conceive. But this should not include rolling it off the stage and into the floral arrangements while its erstwhile owner looks on with the dismay of someone who has just missed an important bus.

One or two competitors needed no assistance from recalcitrant props to muck up their routines, having failed to take on board the rather essential element of rhythm. We shall not name names, but merely suggest charitably that the field from which Namibia selected their representatives cannot have been too large. Choice of music, too, is an area with considerable potential for self-sabotage. Where do these girls find the shocking soundtracks that accompany their routines? Is there an unscrupulous mail order firm specialising in albums with titles like *Now That's What I Call Music For Rhythmic Gymnastics IV*? Sad to relate, each dropped club, errant rope or knotted ribbon was greeted with warm applause by the Malaysians in the audience, while high marks awarded to foreign competitors were roundly booed. Having had little time to get used to having their own good sportsmen, the Malaysians have yet to embrace good sportsmanship.

The routines of their own competitors - particularly Carolyn Au-Yong - were greeted with something approaching hysteria. Each accomplishment met with gasps of awe and waves of applause, while Au-Yong presented throughout the happy smile and joyful countenance that spoke of imminent contracts for toothpaste endorsement. But despite her winning smile, Au-Yong could not secure the gold medal, which went instead to the Canadian competitor Erika Stirton. The way the arena magically emptied as Malaysia's medal chances slipped away suggested that the national obsession with rhythmic gymnastics may be short-lived.
★21/9/98

Simon Hughes

Dissatisfaction is spreading fast in clapped-out game

The denouement ended tamely and Leicestershire have carried the spoils back to Grace Road. Last weekend's top-of-the-table clash was billed in the sponsors' literature as the thrilling climax of the season. The destination of the County Championship was at stake and with it £100,000, enough to warrant live coverage on (satellite) television. The public were anything but thrilled. "What you going to the Oval for guv?" my taxi driver inquired, "nothing going on there mate."

His assumption was shared by 99.99 per cent of the metropolis. After an hour's play on the first day only 674 paying spectators had filed into the ground. With the considerable help of Surrey and Leicestershire members, this number had swelled to around 3,000 by mid-afternoon, the sort of attendance Third Division Halifax or Darlington might expect on an average day. The hospitality boxes were empty. Next year's competition is without a sponsor.

This is not, however, another attempt to

sound county cricket's death knell. It will survive just as neglected churches do. The word 'crowd' has not been used in association with the County Championship since the late Fifties. Post-war support dwindled with the emergence of television and lower unemployment, and has remained paltry ever since. I played for Middlesex in five title deciders during the last decade and none was watched by anything other than a smattering of diehards. The "ground full" signs rotted long ago.

Leap for victory... Helen Don Duncan, of England, bursts off the blocks in the 200 meters backstroke at the Commonwealth Games •**Reuters** ★17/3/98

In spite of large subsidies from the governing body, now running into millions per club, few counties ever manage much of a profit and most will make a loss this year. But significantly, players drawn from this unique professional system to represent England have won just one major Test series in 12 years, and that by the skin of their teeth.

The first-class forum meet next month to plot the path of the professional game. Radical change for the year 2000 is on the agenda. Will it happen? Is Rupert Murdoch the tooth fairy? Still, what is county cricket's role and how can it be enhanced? You can draw an analogy with a local branch railway line. It exists to get people from A to B and as a service to the community. The fact that, say, the Peterborough to Norwich line does not make money is irrelevant - it is a crucial regional link. Professional cricket's purpose is not only to move players from A (county) to B (country) but also to nurture the game in outlying districts, servicing interest among players and spectators.

But the county train is not running properly. Firstly, not everyone is able to board. Only cricketers who are contracted employees of the England and Wales Cricket Board are allowed on the platform, excluding a huge number of talented amateurs. Secondly, the climb from A to B is too arduous and many 'passengers' fall off along the way (witness all the one-Test wonders.) The track up-country is too steep. That is why the England locomotive is not so much a sleek express as a piece of unreliable rolling stock constantly in need of repairs. County cricket is clapped out.

Don't believe me? OK, here is a body of evidence gleaned from players, umpires, coaches, administrators and spectators in the last two weeks. Perhaps the most damning is from a 21-year-old with a double first from Cambridge currently playing for Kent. Ed Smith is in his third season of county cricket and has built up a vivid impression of what is wrong with it. "I think there's a crisis of confidence in the game, we don't respect ourselves. Players like Steve

James or Andrew Caddick perform consistently well for their counties yet aren't picked for England, because what they achieve at county level is regarded as almost worthless. That communicates a depressing message. "When young players come into the game they're usually keen and hard working, but initially they struggle. The more ambitious you are, the more people tend to try and knock you down. More experienced players don't work as hard but they've learnt to do certain little things to get by and avoid the pitfalls. Gradually the younger player learns that these short cuts are the best way to survive."

The height of ambition becomes getting a benefit. Instead of counties being centres of excellence they are dispensers of mediocrity. Why? "Too much cricket," says the esteemed Australian coach John Buchanan, whose experience with Middlesex this season he will largely want to forget. "Players are hardly ever physically, mentally, technically or tactically fresh, proper preparation just isn't in the culture and the journeymen become role models. And I've rarely seen a decent pitch all summer, even at Lord's." Umpire Bob White, who first played for Middlesex in 1955, would concur with the latter. "The pitches have been generally poor for a while, and subtlety in the game seems to have largely disappeared," he says. "There are very few flair players around - Paul Johnson, of Notts, is about the only one that comes to mind."

You have to go back a dozen years or so to find the source of this. With the departure of artful, imaginative leaders such as Brearley, Barclay and Fletcher, the game entered a more regimented era, directed by the likes of Gatting, Gooch and Micky Stewart. It was blow-the-whistle-and-out-of-the-trench command. They were hard working and disciplined and they meant well, but the general approach - batting and bowling styles, field settings - was stereotyped. Demand for success outweighed scope for self-expression and teams sought the safest route, sticking inflexibly to the middle lane rather than trying a bit of chicanery. Line and length was believed to be the only way forward through the corridor of uncertainty. Uniformity resulted and has largely remained.

A series of overseas coaches have tried to buck this trend, and failed. Attitudes are too deeply rooted. Buchanan, the strategist who guided Queensland to their first Sheffield Shield title in 1994/95 and followed it with a second two years later, tried to bring his scientific methods to Middlesex, but became powerless to stop them going into freefall. "What I wanted to do and what was already in place were never going to merge," he says. He was appalled by the concept of 'Naughty Boy Nets' - the familiar "punishment" to a heavily defeated team. I'd never heard that term before, it's a negative image of nets. In Australia, players look forward to practice, use it constructively." Buchanan is "disappointed" with his performance but was prepared to return in 1999. However, after a fabulous playing career, Gatting is likely to be announced as Middlesex's new director of coaching.

Buchanan's outline for progress includes reducing the number of championship games to 12, probably using a two-conference system, allowing more time for recovery and preparation. "But this time must be utilised properly." He was also adamant that pitches should improve. (Few matches have lasted the full four days this year and Gloucestershire's strips are so tailored to their seam bowlers, their coach congratulates a home batsman if he makes 25.)

Elsewhere among officials and observers, there is growing support for a regional tournament superimposed on the County Championship in May and June. This has much to recommend it. While leaving the existing framework untouched, it would provide a crucial ledge between the plateau of county cricket and the pinnacle of the Test arena. The 18 counties divide neatly into six regions, and though some of their names - Home Counties South (Sussex, Hants, Kent), East Midlands Trent (Northants, Leics, Notts) - sound more synonymous with *Come Dancing*, matches between them would provide a stiffer challenge for Test aspirants.

Followers of the first-class game could not really complain about it. The 125,000 county members would still see their beloved team as often as now, getting astonishing value for their £60 subs, and pay-on-the-day spectators do not have a voice. Only 21 dipped into their pockets to watch the third day of Northants v Sussex last week, two of whom declared they "didn't like the noise" at one-day matches. They had come to the right place. You would not blame Mal Loye, voted Cricketer of the Year, if he accepted a lucrative offer from a more popular county, in spite of Northants' spanking new indoor school.

While Loye jets off to Western Australia for some specialist tuition with the old South African batsman Peter Carlstein, domestic dissatisfaction rumbles on. The incessant dismissal of county coaches (12 departures in two years) and captains (Paul Prichard, appointed in 1995, is the longest serving) only deflects attention from the fact that it is the system that needs shaking up, and soon. If you can't get better engines to improve the service, try modernising the track.
★22/9/98

Mihir Bose

World's greatest female sprinter dies at the age of 38

The autopsy on the body of Florence Griffith Joyner, who died in her sleep on Monday aged 38, may conclude that her premature death was the result of drug abuse. However, authorities in California, where the post-mortem investigations have begun, warned that "it could take a few days or a few weeks" to reach a conclusion on the cause of death. Griffith Joyner's death is thought to have been caused by heart failure but the autopsy, undertaken by a police coroner, is to include a toxicology test, which is done when the cause of death is unknown. It is this which may reveal evidence of drug misuse.

Suspicions that Griffith Joyner, known worldwide as Flo-Jo, took drugs have been around since 1989 when the US sprinter Darrell Robinson claimed he had sold her human growth hormones. But Griffith Joyner vigorously denied it and never failed a drug test during a career that culminated with her breaking two world records and winning gold medals in the 100 metres, 200m and 4 x 100m relay at the 1988 Olympic Games in Seoul. Her world records for the 100 and 200m still stand. However, in the last 24 hours a chorus of statements from around the world have raised the spectre that the athlete's death was due to the use of anabolic drugs.

Jacques Piasento, coach of the European 100m champion Christine Arron, watched her train at the University of California in Los Angeles from 1984 to 1987 and said: "For me, she was then just a good sprinter, nothing more. Her genetic potential was less than that of Marie-Jo Perec or Marion Jones, for example. Then as time passed, I saw her build change at an astonishing rate. With her times, she could almost get into the men's 4 x 100m team. That's surprising for sure. I was evidently suspicious, but I didn't have any formal proof of doping. And then who's to say that her death was due to doping?"

Comments in Europe suggest that Flo-Jo was on drugs. The Swedish commentator, Torbjorn Petersson, said that Griffith Joyner's death reminded him of the death of Swedish discus throwers Goran Svensson and Stefan Fernholm, who died aged 36 and 37 respectively. "Both the Swedish discus throwers became entrenched in pill abuse and a dependence which took their lives," said Petersson. Werner Franke, a German expert on drugs in sport, told the public television station ZDF that he was certain Griffith Joyner had died through drug abuse. And Jeanne-Pierre de Mondenard, a French expert on drugs in sport, told France Inter radio station: "For the specialist there is no doubt. Her incredible physical transformation was not natural. Even if you trained eight, 10 or even 15 hours a day, it is humanly impossible to transform yourself in that way. By the drug use, she lost some of her cardio-vascular immunity. The process is known." But even as these voices raised a cloud of drugs suspicion over Griffith Joyner, there were others, including the International Olympic Committee, urging caution and describing her as a "very great champion".

The IOC director general, Francois Carrard, was keener to emphasise the sadness at the premature death of a great champion. When asked on the possibility of Griffith Joyner having used drugs, Carrard said: "We don't have an opinion because nothing is known about the matter."

Griffith Joyner is said to have had a similar heart seizure in April 1996 while on a plane bound for St Louis, but the IOC are unlikely to demand an inquiry. Carrard said: "At this stage we are not going to undertake proceedings. We will see. I am sure it's a matter we will talk about again." The talk will undoubtedly centre on the physical changes to Griffith Joyner in the latter part of her career.

Her incredible physical transformation was not natural. Even if you trained eight, 10 or even 15 hours a day, it is humanly impossible to transform yourself in that way

Griffith Joyner defended her honour, calling Robinson, who had started the allegations, "a compulsive, crazy, lying lunatic" - Robinson is now under psychiatric care in Seattle, having twice attempted suicide - but she did not help her cause by mysteriously retiring after the Seoul Olympics even though she was at the height of her powers. She also refused to respond to comments by Senator Joseph Biden, who used "before" and "after" photographs of Flo-Jo as evidence while warning about the proliferation of drugs in sport.

The argument may never be resolved but it may cause athletes who take drugs to pause. That is the hope of Zavier Sturbois, deputy chairman of the Belgian Olympic Committee and chairman of their medical commission, who said: "Athletes as well as coaches and sports leaders will certainly draw lessons from this death and they will cease to manipulate substances to the detriment of their athletes' health."

★23/9/98

In her pomp... Florence Griffith Joyner at the Seoul olympics, in 1988, where she won three gold medals •Tony Duffy (Allsport) ★9/88   89

Michael Parkinson

Good companions

My mother - 87 not out - the one who spent her honeymoon watching a Test match, has been clearing her drawers. As befitting a tea lady of many years' experience she has a large collection of cricketing memorabilia, particularly photographs. She sent me the one reprinted on this page and it didn't half uncork the memories. It is the Cudworth Cricket Club team circa the early Fifties. The man in jacket and tie with the fly-away hairstyle in the centre of the back row is my father, John William Parkinson, who had temporarily given up the game to watch me play at Barnsley. Very proud he was.

I grew up with my father playing in the Cudworth team. At first we played in a farmer's field in a hollow with rustling, ripened corn on one side and a view of Grimethorpe slagheaps over long on. Our best player was Jack Berry. He is sitting in the picture, second from the left. He bowled leg-breaks at medium pace and now and again fizzed a googly. He was the best bowler I ever saw in club cricket and in different circumstances would certainly have played at a much higher level. He had a lovely high action and would bowl until opening time if required. He was always giving employment to slips and gully, particularly our best fielder, Bob Bone. He is second from the left in the back row. You can't see his hands, which is a pity because seeing is believing. They were as big as dinner plates. He didn't catch a ball, he enveloped it. His other virtue was that he owned a lorry which took us to away games. Sometimes, when it had been used to deliver a ton of coal in the week, we would arrive at our destination looking like we had just done a shift underground.

I was 13 when they put me in the gully next to Bob Bone. Jack Berry got one to hit the top of the bat and it flew to my right hand and stuck. Fifty years on and I can still manage a slow-mo action replay. I can also remember when I threw the ball back to Mr Berry he nodded his approval. I had arrived. They didn't say much. Except my father. He never stopped talking throughout a game. Eric Smallman, front left sitting down, never said a word. He was an opening bat of immense concentration and total silence. He would have made a marvellous Trappist monk.

In those days there was a lot of chit-chat on the field, particularly during local derbies, some of it rude and personal. Smallman's silence and unchanging demeanour enraged his would-be tormentors. In one game the opposition's fast bowler ran out of insults, turned to my father who was batting with Smallman, and said: "What's up wi' yon bloke, John Willie. Is he bloody deaf or something?" My dad replied: "No, he's not deaf. He's Polish." Where he got that from I don't know, but it added to Smallman's mystique. He was sometimes referred to in the local press as "Cudworth's Polish opening bat" or "the cricketer from behind the Iron Curtain", which was news to his family who thought he came from Grimethorpe.

Norman Stewardson, he's the one on the extreme left of the back row, was a vision in cream. His flannels were pressed to knife-edge perfection. He didn't hang them up, he stood them in a corner of the dressing room. For all he was immaculate and precise in his dress he was a whirlwind at the crease. He had no time for blocking or nudging the odd single while waiting for the bad ball. He treated every ball he faced with utter disdain. The only challenge was how far he could hit it. He had a bat covered in what looked like a vellum sheath. Whenever he was asked what it was he would say: "Kangaroo skin. That's why t'ball goes as far as it does when I hit it."

Our other big hitter was George Roberts. He's the one sitting second from the right in the front row. His bat was the colour of a cello and was signed by Herbert Sutcliffe. Herbert would have had a fit if he batted with Mr Roberts, whose unchanging technique was to block one ball and then hit the next out of the ground. He had an eye like a sparrowhawk and one leg. When he was hit on the gammy limb the ball would make a noise like Big Ben chiming. "Owz that," the bowler would cry. "One o'clock and all's well," George would say before the umpire could put his finger up.

Remembering Herbert Sutcliffe, I was saddened to read of the death of Billy Sutcliffe, "Herbert's lad" as he was called. He bore the burden of a famous father with great good humour and was a much better player than he was given credit for by those who believed he captained Yorkshire because of his name. I remember fielding at cover point for nearly three hours at Headingley one Saturday afternoon long ago when Billy and the Aussie rugby legend Arthur Clues put on more than two hundred runs, a high percentage of them past me. I spent the entire afternoon trotting to the boundary to retrieve the ball from the feet of the one spectator who risked frostbite to watch us. At one point I asked him why he didn't co-operate by throwing me the ball. He replied: "Nay, lad, I've come here to see thee work, not do it missen."

That would have been about the same time the photograph was taken. If you look carefully you will see the ground underfoot looks rough. It was. Lethal, in fact. We left our home in the farmer's back yard and moved up the hill to a brand new sports complex. When we played our first season it was far from finished and so dangerous the local St John Ambulance Brigade brought their students to our games knowing they would get plenty of practice, particularly with splints.

At the time we had one of the quickest bowlers in the district, a strapping professional boxer called Terry MacDonald. He is not in the picture. If he was there wouldn't be room for the rest. He was a heavyweight good enough to get into the British top 10. Then he fought Nuttall (Archie? Albert?) from Stockport. Goodnight Terry. He ended up with a pub. Terry only played a season or two with us but long enough to create terror among the opposition. My father was captain at the time, and being a fast bowler himself, was Terry's greatest advocate. When he first came into the side, no one knew how quick he was. We soon found out. In his initial spell he persuaded everyone to stand a respectful distance from the wicket, including the men holding the bat. "By God, John Willie, but yon lad's quick," the opposing captain said to my dad. "He is that. But tha' should have seen him before he were gassed," said my old man. Thus another lie became legend, another invention became propaganda to booby trap the opposition.

Instead of keeping my old man in the pits during the war Winston Churchill should have made him director of psychological warfare. The year before I joined Barnsley they sent their second team to play us. These were the silvertails of local cricket. Their captain was Albert White, who was singled out for special treatment because he didn't work at the pit. He was a hairdresser. More than that he was a crimper

....

Instead of keeping my old man in the pits during the war Winston Churchill should have made him director of psychological warfare

....

with attitude. At Barnsley he played on a perfect batting strip. When he came to Cudworth he saw how the other half lived. He escaped with his life, but only just. The more he complained about the state of the pitch the faster MacDonald bowled. Albert departed saying our ground was only fit for cattle. Prophetic words.

Rebuked by the league for having a dangerous pitch, we instructed Old Cheyney, our groundsman, to do something about it. His solution was to make a mixture of manure, straw and grass cuttings which he stirred into a paste and spread on the wicket. When it dried and was rolled out it was as dead as a pudding. When it rained it became a foul smelling mire of such pungency it attracted flies from as far away as Sheffield. In fact, if you look at the picture you will notice that most of the team look slightly stunned, which is not surprising considering they are standing on a dung heap.

The picture might be slightly faded but my memories are not. I was happy, growing up with agreeable men. Most of them are dead now. Jack Shepherd is still alive. He is on my father's left hand. He was his favourite and my mate. A good cricketer but a better footballer with lovely skills. There are a couple of others apart from Jack who are still around, but the rest are gone. When I first looked at the photograph the other day I ached with sadness. Then I remembered the good times we had and felt better. Cricket is the most companionable of games, and the best natured. That is its genius and why it matters.

★ 28/9/98

Lewine Mair

Faldo sacks coach Leadbetter after poor run of results

Nick Faldo has sacked David Leadbetter, his coach of 13 years. He is now attached to Chip Koehlke, the head professional at his own Nick Faldo academy in Florida.

The two were working together at the Lancome Trophy in Paris. Leadbetter received the news by letter with Faldo telling him that the changed arrangements were down to his disappointing performances over the last couple of seasons: "The swing thoughts on which we have been working have so far not physically helped…" Leadbetter feels hurt that his premier pupil should have phoned rather than written. "You put in a lot of time and effort out there with someone like Faldo and it's a bit upsetting to get a cursory note to finish it all. It wasn't very classy," said Leadbetter from his base at Lake Nona, Florida.

In spite of the rejection, Leadbetter has written back and wished him well. "I still have the utmost respect for Nick," he said. "He hasn't always endeared himself to me from a personal standpoint but he has been a great pupil. He has, of course, been fabulous for my career but I would like to think that I have been good for his."

Faldo, in most eyes the best British golfer since Harry Vardon, was originally coached by Ian Connelly at Welwyn Garden City but in 1985 he left him and asked Leadbetter if he would help to revamp his action. "I don't care how long it takes but I want you to throw the book at me," said the then 27-year-old Faldo. As it transpired, it took two years to develop the beautifully grooved and athletic action which would win him three Open Championships and three Masters.

Leadbetter felt that he never did more for his player than before the 1996 Masters. Faldo had been playing poorly in the weeks leading up to Augusta and his frustration on the early practice days was apparent. When Leadbetter arrived on the Monday, he sorted out a simple mental routine which would turn the Englishman from a player set to miss the cut to one who would win. He told him to forget technique and to concentrate on nothing more than playing the course. Even on the practice ground, he had Faldo pretending he was playing Augusta hole by hole. As Faldo took out a driver for one shot and a seven iron for his next, so people in the stands started to ask what was going on. Undeterred, coach and pupil worked along the same lines on the Tuesday and the Wednesday and again before Faldo set out for his first round on the Thursday. "He began to feel comfortable

and his demeanour changed right round," recalled Leadbetter. Faldo said his closing 67 that year added up to the kind of performance for which he would want to be remembered.

Since that Masters victory, Faldo has won just the once - namely, last year's Nissan Open. Not too long after the Nissan, his putting went into decline and that has put pressure on the rest of his game. For the last 12 months, Leadbetter has kept reiterating that there is not too much wrong with his swing and that a couple of good rounds could put him back on track. The pair were still working on small points, largely because Faldo prefers to have a technical thought or thoughts on the go. However, his ever-more-pernickety adherence to the technical had people blaming Leadbetter for making him too theoretical. Others, including Nick Price, have always had it that Faldo has never used Leadbetter correctly. The Price way has been to take the occasional lesson and to take time to assimilate what he feels will work for him.

Leadbetter suspects Faldo's downturn has less to do with a couple of swing keys not working than the fact that he is no longer the focused player he was. Faldo said in an interview in these pages prior to the '97 Open: "I'm maybe too mellow at the moment . . . you've got to get the intensity right if you're going to win." Some believe that Brenna Cepelak, the college golfer he has had at his side for three years, has contributed to this by making him "a happier person". Happier he may be but, now that he is based largely in the States, he has to cross the Atlantic to see his children.

Leadbetter approves Faldo's intention to play more in Europe, less in the States. In fact, he suggested it earlier this year, his feeling being that he had lost the aura of invincibility that he had when he made just the occasional foray to the States.

Leadbetter acknowledges that "nothing is forever" and that a change of coach might help get Faldo back to where he was. However there have been too many cases of players splitting from their coaches, only to think better of it, for anyone to be convinced that Leadbetter and Faldo will never work together again. For the moment at least, Faldo will be convinced he has done the right thing. He goes into this week's Linde German Masters having finished sixth last week in France, with his final round a 65 plucked from his past.

★ 23/9/98

Big hitter… Sanath Jayasuriya, the Sri Lankan batsman, hits a six during the Test against England at the Oval •**Russell Cheyne** ★**31/8/98**

Matthew Fleming

If the art of entertainment is to leave the spectators keen for more, then the Sri Lankans have mastered it

On the attack... Marvin Atapattu hooks for Sri Lanka at the Oval •**Russell Cheyne** ★**31/8/98**

Many people thought the calypso cricket of the Seventies and early Eighties could never be matched for sheer enjoyment and brilliance, but this Sri Lankan team, though more subtle in certain aspects, play a similar brand of utterly instinctive cricket. It is rare indeed that when England are beaten in a Test, we do not immediately turn on our team to highlight supposed shortcomings as reasons for defeat. Rightly, people have appreciated the Sri Lankans' wonderful performance. We were beaten, we did not lose.

My first real experience of Sri Lankan cricket, or rather cricketers, was in the spring of 1995. Kent, boldly, and according to some, unwisely, signed Aravinda de Silva as their overseas professional. He arrived in Canterbury for our pre-season training complete with an absurdly inadequate selection of flimsy shirts, several bats and a companion. We assumed that Aravinda's friend was with him to act as his `Man Friday'.

It was on about their third day that Aravinda quietly asked if his friend could bowl in the nets. Of course, was the obvious reply, as batsmen are always keen for more cannon fodder at that stage of the season. Murali, as we had been told to call him, though as we hadn't quite grasped Aravinda's accent at that stage we were not entirely sure that we had got it right, failed to pitch his first delivery on the cut bit. This isn't that uncommon, as anyone who has tried to bowl their first ball of the season in early April wearing enough clothes to embarrass an Eskimo will tell you. What happened when it landed, however, was marginally unusual. It turned a prodigious distance and utterly bamboozled the batsman. So it was that the Kent players were privileged enough to face Muttiah Muralitharan during most of those pre-season preparations.

It was immediately obvious that he was something extraordinary. Just how extraordinary I had no real idea until the Oval Test. Over the last couple of years he has been Sri Lanka's leading wicket-taker but I naively assumed he would find the English wickets less suitable than the more 'spin-friendly' wickets of the subcontinent. How wrong I was. I had not appreciated the full extent of his skill. He bowls marathon spells and maintains incredible levels of concentration. He bowls very few bad balls, yet has great variation of pace and manages to keep attacking fields without ever giving the batsman an easy scoring area. Most importantly, he spins the ball amazing distances

and, what's more, he can do it both ways.

I actually faced the last balls bowled by the Sri Lankans on this tour while playing for Sir Paul Getty's XI. Having seen a lot of the Test, I thought I had worked out the best way to play Murali. I took an off-stump guard and was going to sweep if it was full and push him into the midwicket gap if it was short of a length. The first ball was short of a length so I went back, as planned, to nudge it into the on side for an easy

single. The ball had as much top-spin as off-spin, zipped off the wicket and defeated my frenzied jab to hit me mid-shin in front of off stump. Fortunately for me, the Sri Lankans do play with a smile and the wicketkeeper, slip and bowler were laughing so much they couldn't appeal. It wouldn't have done them any good, anyway, as Dickie Bird was umpiring! Tea and the ensuing rain saved any further humiliation. ★15/9/98

Mark Nicholas

Farewell Gatt, and thanks for the memories

That's it then for Gatt. After 25 years in county cricket, a monumental 551 matches and more than 36,000 first-class runs which have included 94 hundreds, Mike Gatting has taken his final curtain call. Probably.

I say probably, because he is an ever-optimistic never-say-die sort of good egg who may yet pop up somewhere, see his beloved Middlesex a man short, slip on the whites and cream another hundred. And then, with five to go, he will talk his way into a game against Oxbridge, plead a knock against New Zealand and earn a stay of execution on a day that we thought was done.

He says not though, says that he has enjoyed it all hugely and that he is ready now to concentrate on selecting England teams and sorting out the young players at Middlesex. He whispers that he might play the odd second XI game but only in a paternal role, absolutely not for his own ends.

We shall assume then that a cracking, if at times controversial career is over and we will remember it well. This is a man who has given his soul for cricket, whose extraordinary enthusiasm and irresistible spirit helped bring glory upon his county, and, all too briefly, upon his country too. The Middlesex team will miss him more than they know - are missing him already in truth - much as England did when he was dumped as captain 10 years ago last June. What a botch of a thing that was, sacking a man for having a party. He should, of course, have been dismissed for the unseemly business with Shakoor Rana a few months earlier - even he would tell you that now - but instead the hypocrites at headquarters gave him and each of his team a bonus of £1,000 for something or other, though no one knew what; for silence perhaps.

After that, and the trivia in Nottingham which followed, two attempts to reinstate him as captain were overruled and by the end of the 1980s a previously uncomplicated, much admired and fun-filled sportsman had become so suspicious, so bitter about all things England that he fell foul of seduction by the South African rand and its consequences. It was a desperate tour, unfinished, yet one which should not have begun, though Gatting will tell you good came from it, that it hastened South Africa's process of unification.

Which is Gatt really - a man who sees the best of things and people in life, a man of simple tastes and honest values, a streetwise and straight-talking bloke with a lion's heart? This is the man who retained the Ashes with a team that "couldn't bat, bowl, or field" and went on to win both one-day tournaments of that tour too. The man who made a brilliant, signature hundred in the MCC bicentenary match at Lord's and shone in the company of Greenidge and Gavaskar, Marshall and Hadlee. The man who tumbled at mid-on to catch Dennis Lillee in the final heart-stopping moments of Headingley 1981; the man who gorged himself on the Indian bowling of 1984 and catalysed that amazing against-the-odds series win under David Gower; the man who led Middlesex to title after title by uniting the most diverse characters in the most combative dressing room in the land. For ever it seems there has been Gatt, never quite a superstar but always his footprint solidly made in the cause of his team.

"I can't imagine being without cricket, it's pretty addictive you know," he says - and, as with all forms of addiction, it has not always served him well, for it has been spiked by the tendency to self-destruct. The pad-ups, two of them to Malcolm Marshall at Lord's in 1984 which questioned his quality as an international batsman; the reverse-sweep in the 1987 World Cup final in India which cast aspersion on his sanity; and then, fancy it being him to receive that ball from Shane Warne.

Because of the various dramas it is possible that memories of Gatting will linger as much for a row with an umpire and a supposed, but utterly unproved, romp with a barmaid, as for his deep-rooted patriotism, his commitment to all things cricket and his bagful of trophies. The vast majority, however, will understand his addiction and applaud it, knowing that if a man doesn't care he may as well not bother. Gatting cared all right, indeed he cared so much that he almost burst with his high-octane levels of emotion and devotion. For that, in an age of increasing indifference to cricket, we should thank him. Thank him for wearing his heart on his sleeve and for allowing us to share all he had got. Thank you, Gatt, and farewell. For now.
★21/9/98

the Pot of Gold Colin Montgomerie drives at the Eighteenth during the Dunhill Cup at St Andrews •**Russell Cheyne** ★9/10/98

Bumbling along with Captain Controversy

Dead flash!" said David Lloyd, the England cricket coach, on his choice of luncheon venue in Wilmslow. "Greasy spoon!" said the taxi driver on his way there. That is the story of his life. Few characters in sport, or life for that matter, find themselves in such fierce possession of opinions which are at incontrovertible odds with virtually every other sane being on the planet. He has a higher regard for the England cricket team, for example, than anyone else on earth including, one suspects, every member of the England cricket team. He is a short-fused, high-energy enthusiast, an incorrigible Tigger, frequently finding himself - aghast and bemused - in terrible, accidental trouble.

He is just emerging from the latest bout. "I've just about coom out me bunker this week. Oooh, gosh," he said, over his broccoli and cheese something (which was dead, if not flash), yelling rather to be heard above Kate Bush's *Wuthering Heights* on the juke box. "I've had two slight misdemeanours." You could say that. He has, in fact, had two socking great public roastings. One, for saying "we murdered 'em" of the Zimbabwean opposition (whom England had just failed to beat) in Bulawayo, 1996. Two, for questioning the bowling action of Muttiah Muralitharan of Sri Lanka (to whom England had just lost) in the latest one-off Test match.

But how you square this seething, tempestuous, Heathcliffian reputation with the evidently sweet, tousled-haired, twinkle-eyed figure sitting across the table is anyone's guess. Especially when you are talking about, believe me, Long Drop Tippling Toilets. "Ah, the Long Drop Tippler," he was saying, as we discussed the days of his rather eccentric formation in Accrington 51 years ago. "We lived in a terraced 'ouse. I remember like it were yesterday. It 'ad an outside toilet and it wasn't an automatic either. You 'ad to wait until enough water 'ad coom through to floosh it. You did. But me uncle and auntie - they lived up on a farm - and they just 'ad a dustbin. The council emptied it every week. Oh God!" So, I were 'ell bent on saying, 'right, I'm going to better meself'."

His chosen route was sport. Or rather, it chose him. "At football, I were David Beckham without the trimmins." At cricket, he showed such promise as a slow left-arm bowler/opening-middle order batsman, he was signed by Lancashire at 15. There would not have been many backward glances at his old technical college. "I did art, metalwork, woodwork, geometrical drawing - which I were absolutely useless at. I was frightened to death. I didn't want all that messing about in fires and furnaces, and banging about with chisels and that. I always had the thought that if I 'urt me 'ands, I couldn't play cricket." So, after 19,269 first-class runs, 237 wickets and 334 catches for Lancashire, nine England Tests (1974-5), a spell as an umpire, the acquisition of the hugely suitable nickname 'Bumble', the coaching job at Lancashire, promotion to

England, several Big Bang controversies, regular convulsions of mirth and innumerable bad golf shots, he only messes about with metaphorical fires and furnaces."

"I were desperate not to say anything that would offend anybody," he said of the latest seismic upheaval over Muralitharan, who will, ironically, play a few games for Lancashire next season. "But I 'ad a belief…" A short demonstration is mounted of arms straight, arms bent at the elbow, arms partially bent at the elbow, etc. Not surprisingly, the waitress came over and said: "Is everything all right?" It is now. After his reprimand by the England and Wales Cricket Board, apology and genuine contrition, Lloyd rightly remains in his post where he is genuinely prized by the players. The phone rang incessantly during his recent dark hour. Michael Atherton: "Just ringing. You all right?" Angus Fraser: "You silly old sod!" And so it went on. "Fraser just killed 'imself laffing. Nass phoned. Stewie …"

He sent one during the triangular tournament between England, Sri Lanka and South Africa demanding that national anthems be sung, signed "Gerupta Singh" of the Gurkhas Regimental Band

The affection is understandable. "I'm a passionate believer in England," he said, meaning the country in a patriotic capacity as well as the team he is paid to inspire. "I don't see anything wrong in that." In the dressing room before matches, he used to play tapes that mixed *Land of Hope and Glory*, with Laurence Olivier's Henry V, *Jerusalem*, and eight minutes' worth of Winston Churchill. "We will never surrender, never surrender, never surrender, never surrender," said the tape to a team who sometimes went out and surrendered. Lloyd's gaskets probably blew on such occasions.

But his loyalty is profound and paramount. The players know that, none more so than Atherton. "I think Athers is an 'ero," said Lloyd. "I've got great admiration for 'im and what 'e's done.

Anyone that knows 'im would pick 'is star qualities as resilience, strength, bloodymindedness, cussedness, determination, class and 'e's one of the best players in the world. 'E's often in pain from 'is back but you'd never know it. 'E reminds me of Brian Close. I once saw Brian 'it in the mouth and all 'is teeth were broken. Aaargh, 'e was a hell of a mess but 'e carried on batting and the next day one of 'is team couldn't take the field because he 'ad toothache! Athers is brave like that. 'E'll never show it.

"On the other side, 'e's a lad who cultivates this scruffy image. D'you know 'e's still got the same shoes 'e 'ad at Cambridge University." And, Lloyd might add, shocking taste in racehorse flesh. For reasons that surpass all understanding, Atherton, Lloyd and Lloyd's son, Graham, who plays for Lancashire, are united in some kind of Bumble syndicate that owns a fetlock under training with Venetia Williams. Has it won? "It 'asn't run yet," he said, revealing such depths of ignorance of the scheme that the jockey could probably drag a tin of Kennomeat round Cheltenham and convince Lloyd this was his horse. "It's just an 'arebrained idea," he said proudly. "All I know is, it's grey."

Unlike his life. Mischief and mirth are never far away. "I loove *Test Match Special* and I am the phantom fax sender." "Y'what?" I said, struggling hard with the notion that this is cricket's equivalent of Glenn Hoddle the International Introvert, whose sense of humour is as zipped up as his tracksuit. Yes, Lloyd gains vast gleeful pleasure sending faxes to be read out on the air from cricket-mad, fictitious characters with dubious-sounding names. He sent one during the triangular tournament between England, Sri Lanka and South Africa demanding that national anthems be sung, signed "Gerupta Singh" of the Gurkhas Regimental Band.

In the West Indies last winter, the sonorous voice of the public address announcer innocently declared: "Would Mr Branston Pickle on tour with Gullibles Travels kindly report to the car park where his vehicle is sandwiched in." We have only had half a bottle of Chardonnay each, but now we're both giggling helplessly. Any minute now that waitress will be back saying "everything all right?" with the slight chill timbre of Joyce Grenfell in her voice. "It's joost fun," said Lloyd, mindful he could be accused of frivolity. Far from it, this is light relief in a dark business. "It's deadly serious but it's good fun."

Fortunately, he is sufficiently well-adjusted to have a life beyond cricket, where the buffets of his outrageous (and often self-inflicted) misfortune can glance past his wiry frame harmlessly. "The focal point of me social life is Bramhall Golf Club where we've formed ourselves, about a dozen of us, into a regiment. I'm

the Commander and we've got a Brigadier, an Air Vice Marshal, Major 'Shadow' Davidson - because we never know what he's up to - a Rear Admiral and Squadron Leader E J Pimlott - 'e's the local butcher. It's like a little society of men be'avin' badly. "I'm not saying I'm cocooned but I rarely move out of me circle when I'm not with the cricket. I mean, nobody ever, ever recognises me in the street. But, I must say, with all the proceedings of the last couple of weeks people have been slappin' me on the back. I'm only the coach but it were gratifying. They're saying things like, 'you've got a really good team there, keep it going'."

Whether England can keep it going, or even start it up for that matter, in Australia this winter is a point worth mulling with the coach. He, as you might expect, is game. "I want Shane Warne to play," he said of the Aussies' large, potent, beaneating spinner. "I 'ate the Australians the way they 'ate us," he said. "It's a love 'ate relationship. Our game is terrific for forging friendships all around the world. I've no illusions that they're the best team in the world by a long way. We are complete underdogs and we will brace ourselves for the usual 'this is the worst England team ever' stories once we arrive. But never under-estimate us. We're 'arder, tougher, more ruthless than we ever were. This team doesn't lie down."

Lloyd rates Alec Stewart's captaincy as similar to Atherton's. "Brilliant," he said. " 'E's got the same openness, the same honesty. The only perceivable difference is that Alec will always, always state the bleeding obvious. It's 'is way of making sure. A double insurance. " 'E's done very well. We 'ad to wean 'im off opening but it was important for the team. It allowed Butcher to coom in as the opener and you've seen the growth in the rest of 'em. We keep saying to Ramprakash, 'yer in the team, yer in, yer in', and there's lots more to coom from 'im."

Whether there is lots more to come from Lloyd, gaffe-wise, you would have seriously to doubt. One more and he is out. Had he not thought of consulting with the team's psychologist, Stephen Bull, to find a means of dispersing his famous red mist. "No, but I will, because it detracts from the team. If I'm in the papers for the wrong reasons, it detracts from the team." He said this with such gentle contrition and consideration for the lads he regards as friends, only the hardest heart would pursue his banishment from the England set-up. He'd be all right: golf, fishing, faxes but one can imagine how much exile from the game he so loves would hurt him. On the other hand, the golf does need some work. "I've got a set of them Callaway clubs. I play off 15. I think I've got potential. I hit the ball a fair way but..." - he looked crestfallen - "at times I can't find it."

★ 12/9/98

From the Normandy Beaches to wine tasting at the Vatican

Reg Gutteridge may be the only one-legged TV commentator on the planet; he may even be the only one-legged commentator for whom Muhammad Ali would kneel and pray at his hospital bedside; he is almost certainly the only one-legged commentator whose grandfather taught Rudyard Kipling to box; but he is, and I defy anyone to contradict me, the only one-legged commentator ever to attend a wine-tasting party with Pope John Paul.

"My rendezvous with the Pope came about during the world amateur championships in Rome in '67," recalls Gutteridge . "Me and George Whiting - one of our finest boxing writers - had an afternoon off and feeling in the need of a bit of R & R, we scanned the 'What To Do In Rome' noticeboard in search of inspiration. 'Brilliant,' says I, 'English team - wine tasting: bus departs 2.30 pm'. Anyway, being journalists we miss the first bus but hop on the second one, which, as it turns out, is carrying the Irish team. Whoosh! Straight into the Vatican."

George and I look at one another in horror. You what?!? Twelve of us in this little room and in walks John Paul. Down the line he goes shaking hands and welcoming us in English. George mutters something like, 'Where's the bleedin' wine tasting then?' and all I can think of saying is, 'Forgive us our press passes'. I felt really guilty afterwards. Millions of people would have loved to have met the Pope and there I am, an east London Protestant - and a non-practising one at that - chatting away with him in the Vatican."

We are taking wine and our daily bread at West Lodge Park hotel in Cockfosters, where Sir Alf Ramsey plotted the downfall of West Germany over breakfast in 1966 and where, 32 years on, Gutteridge is snatching a brief respite from penning his autobiography with the assistance of Fleet Street legend and former EastEnders scriptwriter, Peter Batt. "Things like meeting the Pope always seem to happen to me so I'm hoping the book will be a bit different."

A bit different did he say through a mouthful of pork? Born into an Islington boxing family in 1924 (his father, Dick, and twin brother Jack were known as 'trainers of champions'), one of Gutteridge's earliest memories is of seeing Italian colossus Primo Carnera's prodigious jock-strap drying on a clothes-horse in front of the fire. "Carnera trained at my dad's gym whenever he was in London. He was known as 'The Ambling Alp' - 19 stone and six foot six he was -

so the sight of his equipment left an indelible impression. Although his cousin, Jack jnr, decided against joining the family business - "Uncle Jack's son was Jackie Pallo the wrestler; they made him change his name before he was allowed to wrestle..." - young Reg was inexorably drawn into the fight game. "My grandfather, Arthur, was the first pro on the bill at the opening of the National Sporting Club in 1891 and apparently gave boxing lessons to Kipling. When I was 10 my dad used to let me hold the boxers' dressing gowns at ringside in Bethnal Green which made me feel really important. So I grew up around boxing people and reeking of wintergreen."

He made a few appearances in the ring as an amateur, but by his own admission "was never going to be a champion; girl's hands, you see..." ; and any lingering hopes he might have cherished were brutally destroyed in Normandy on August Bank Holiday 1944 when the 20-year-old Gutteridge leapt out of a Sherman tank ("the Germans called them 'Tommy Cookers' because they were so easily blown up") and came down on a land mine, blowing away the bottom half of his right leg. "I wasn't lucky, but it could have been a hell of a lot worse. When I woke up in hospital I thought my balls had gone as well but after they took the dressings off I discovered I had taken a small blast burn in the groin."

....

He grabbed a small ice pick from the bar-top and stuck it into his leg where it quivered like a tuning fork. Liston backed off and the leg was returned to Roehampton hospital for repairs

....

"I'm not bitter about it; it happened during wartime and war is a terrible, terrible thing. My father and his brother both died young - dad was only 46 - through heart trouble brought on by being gassed at the Somme. They were gassed on the same day because as twins they went everywhere together. Some people like to glorify war but it's not like that. Everyone at the front was as white as wax with fear - shells bursting all round you. Great camaraderie, but incessant fear…" Though his voice trails off as he is briefly transported back to the hell of Normandy and the memory of exploding shells, Gutteridge is quickly up off the canvas. "I went back long after the war for ITV and this French radio commentator comes up and says, 'Monsieur, I hear you lose a foot in Normandy?' And I said, 'You haven't found it, have you?' "

Reg digresses from the narrative to share a couple of anecdotes concerning his wooden leg: like the time he cleared the Mediterranean of boisterous German tourists by turning upside down in the sea, thrusting his stump into the air and screaming "SHAARK!!!"; and the occasion he silenced the forbidding Sonny Liston during a friendly argument in a cocktail bar during which the self-styled 'most dangerous man in the world' was making fun of 'horizontal British heavyweights'. "You want to see courage?" demanded Reg, "well let me see you flippin' well do this…" So saying, he grabbed a small ice pick from the bar-top and stuck it into his leg where it quivered like a tuning fork. Liston backed off and the leg was returned to Roehampton hospital for repairs where they "thought I was suffering from woodworm".

Having been invalided out of the Army in 1944, Gutteridge returned to the London *Evening News*, which he had originally joined as an office boy at the age of 14 and swiftly moved up through the ranks to become boxing correspondent, a position he retained even after being signed up by Dickie Davies's *World of Sport*.

Thereafter, his life became a dizzying whirl of commentaries: Sugar Ray Robinson, Floyd Patterson, Ken Buchanan, Archie Moore, Henry Cooper, Sonny Liston, and the golden era of Muhammad Ali. "The three Ali-Frazier fights have to be the highlights. Ali transcended sport and I'm proud to say he's written the foreword for my book. He says, 'I should have whupped Reg Gutteridge because he thought George Foreman could beat me. So I once forced him to interview me between rounds because I was fighting some bum in the Far East and I was bored'.

"Which is true. I think I'm right in saying it's the only occasion in broadcasting history that a boxer has given an interview on TV during the 30-second interval. Ali was boxing Rudi Lubbers of Holland in Jakarta and he calls down to me at ringside where I'm doing a live commentary for *World of Sport* saying, 'Get up here, Reg'. I tell London what's happening and this plummy voice of the producer - a real bloody luvvie - comes down the line: 'Sorry, no can do old boy. We're doing a jockey at Catterick at the moment'. So now I've got to shout up at Ali, 'next round, next round' and he holds the guy up for another three minutes. Anyway, Ali comes back to his corner, leans over the ropes and starts, 'Hello ma

Philip Brown

friends in London. Ah'm gettin' old, ah coulda taken this bum out in the first round in the old days'."

Like many ring experts, Gutteridge thought the brash young Cassius Clay might have been a flash in the pan in his early days. "Everyone knew he was handsome and good with words but we all underestimated his sheer bravery. I remember his third fight with Frazier - the Thriller in Manilla - and he's on the ropes right above me when Joe gets him on the chin with a fearsome left. I looked up and Ali's legs had turned to jelly. 'Uh-oh, he's gone' I thought. Then as clear as anything through the bedlam I hear Ali say, 'Shit, Joe, they told me you were finished' and Joe, who's still pounding, away replies, 'Well they lied'."

Any talk of Ali must include the 'Rumble in the Jungle' with George Foreman when Gutteridge, like most of mankind, believed the old champ was in genuine physical danger. "He came into the ring and because of the bright lights the only people he could see at ringside who he recognised were me, David Frost and Harry Carpenter. 'Hey, Reg,' he hollers, 'they tell me you think this ol' man can beat me.' And I put my head on the work-table in front of me because in that instant I knew I'd tipped the wrong fella. 'Bloody hell,' I said, 'he's going to do it'. No fear, you see."

There is more, much more: receiving the OBE for "services to boxing broadcasting and journalism" from the Queen; being befriended by Glenn Miller in London three weeks before the band-leader's death while he was in the uniform of an invalid soldier; being asked to lure Ali on to *This Is Your Life* (not to mention his own date with Michael Aspel's red book); pretending to be at ringside in sun-drenched Bermuda for Ali's final bout against Trevor Berbick when he was actually sitting in the snow at Harringey dogs ("it rather gave the game away when I'm describing the action and this voice comes over the Tannoy: 'The hare's running, the hare's running'); all which should make his autobiography - entitled *Uppercuts And Daisies* - a sporting best-seller.

But we will take our leave of Reg talking - as he so often does - of Ali. "A wonderful man, just wonderful. He's made millions and given it away. He tries to hide it, but I've seen him stuff bundles of hundred dollar notes into the hand of a man in a wheelchair in Las Vegas. In 1989 I was taken into Hammersmith Hospital with blood poisoning and Connie, my wife, reckoned I was too ill to have any visitors. It was quite serious at the time and it looked like I was going. Anyway, I wake up this day and there's Ali standing at the foot of my bed. He sat there and held my hand then knelt and said a prayer. When he went out I didn't half cry."
★16/3/98

Walker warms up for another year of verbal mayhem at the microphone

The motor-mouth of Formula One displays consuming passion for anything powered by an engine

There are wheelnuts and there are wheel nuts. Murray Walker is one of the latter. "Yes, I think it is an obsession," said the man, and more specifically THE VOICE of Formula One, broadcasting all around the car-crazy world. "Elizabeth says if it hasn't got an engine in it, I'm not interested."

Elizabeth is Mrs Walker, who has been going to bed with a pile of *Autocars* for probably more years than she would care to remember. Her husband is 74 (receding rapidly to 12 at the mere mention of brake fluid) and for 50 of those years, he has been commentating on motor racing in a manner that can best be described as excitable. As excitable as a man with a colony of ferrets down his trousers. Squeals on wheels.

"AND NOW TAMBAY'S HOPES WHICH WERE PREVIOUSLY NIL ARE ABSOLUTELY ZERO," he is yelling at me now in those bubonically strident tones, demonstrating (a) his commentating voice and (b) the type of on-the-spot gaffe that can happen to anyone in the full pelt of race reporting. Well, not just anyone.

Patrick Tambay in a Lola Ford in 1986 •**Fotosports International**

Be clear. Walker is not just anyone. He is peerless. In a sport as ridiculous as Formula One, he is the corresponding voice of insanity. But he does more than merely match the madness around him. He is its equal and opposite force. If there is one person on this earth whose pure enthusiasm allows him to believe that Michael Schumacher is a nice man who oversteers from time to

time, Mika Hakkinen won on competitive merit in Jerez and Nigel Mansell isn't boring, it is Murray Walker.

Here he goes. "The chap that Britain regards as the evil Hun, Michael Schumacher, is actually an extremely nice bloke. He's friendly, cheerful, helpful, enormously professional, stupifyingly eloquent in what is to him a foreign language and I think he's a bloody nice bloke. I'm naive enough, idealistic enough, to think that what happened in Jerez was most certainly not a premeditated foul but an instinctive reaction." Hmm. "Yes, that's what most people say."

You could not, in a million years or even for Bernie Ecclestone's take-home, find a more glowing passion for grand prix racing than the one delivered in all sincerity and decibels by Walker year on year. He is the antidote to cynicism and the irony is that he was plucked from the realm of advertising, where he was apparently the proud author of the line: "Trill Makes Budgies Bounce With Health". Of course he was.

When you meet him, far from being a high-octane 'luvvie', he is steeped in old-world courtesies that went out with the Morris Minor. Her wears woolly jumpers at home, drives his BMW carefully and, when you enter his office to chat (every square inch dedicated to the sport he so patently loves), he pulls up a stool to sit close and pay attention. You may not believe this, but every sentence was measured and grammatical. "I had arty aunts," he explained. His uncle was a professor of South African history at Cape Town and Cambridge Universities. And his father rode bikes.

When Walker Jnr tried to follow in his father's exhaust fumes, he discovered he was merely adequate. So he decided to talk about it instead. "I got an audition with the BBC after doing the public address at a car and motorcycle hill climb in Shelsley Walsh, Worcestershire. There was a BBC producer there and I was determined I would impress him with my mastery of the subject and delivered a non-stop barrage of commentary." It worked.

When Baron Toulo de Graffenreid won the British Grand Prix in 1948, Walker was the BBC commentator, sharing the pleasure with Max Robertson, who was utterly uninterested in the wretched, noisy business. So this is his 50th year. Then it was a bit different. "There were no safety features at all. There was just a piece of rope between the cars and the crowd, no helmets, no goggles, no seat belts, no crash protection, no gravel traps, no barriers, the marshalling was rudimentary and the medical facilities were laughable.

"There was a major crash right in front of me. A chap called John Bolster was thrown out of his car and I thought he was dead, lying on the ground in front of me. I thought: 'God, they didn't tell me what to say about this.' So I just said 'Bolster's gone off'." Which covered all eventualities, when you think about it.

Now, the whole procedure is slightly more sophisticated. He has a full-time job and a commentary box. He also has a co-commentator with more than a passing interest in the sport. Former driver Martin Brundle is remarkable for the cogency of his thoughts, but more than that he works in rhythmic tandem to a man on 17,000 revs.

"Well, it's a fast-moving, colourful, exciting, dangerous sport. If you can't get excited about that..." explained Walker, getting excited. He refuses to sit down while he works: ferrets on the rampage. "I didn't realise it till I saw a television documentary but the whole time I'm commentating, I'm swaying from side to side. In order for Martin to stand close to me, he has to do it as well. He says we're like a couple of windscreen wipers."

The result of all this is fame and affection, the like of which only Elton John and the Queen Mother can match. "Where am I famous? Here, yes. Canada, yes. South Africa, yes. Australia, yes. Oh, I'm big-time in Australia. I once went into this specialist bookshop in Sydney. I'd been looking for a wonderful book called *Auto Course* for the 1978 season. I was collecting the series. It was the only one I hadn't got. I thought: 'These colonial dumbos won't realise how important the book is.' So I go into the shop incognito and the chap comes up and says 'Can I help you', and I said: 'Oh, I'm just looking actually. Er, just as a matter of interest, I wonder if you have a copy of, um, 1978 *Auto Course*?' 'Nice try, Murray,' he said."

Walker's fame is a mystery to his mother, 100 last October, who cannot work out why all these strangers say 'Hullo, Murray' round the shops in Southampton. "But you must know him,

Philip Brown

dear, he knows your name," she is apt to say. "I'll explain later, mother," he replies. He is marvellously tolerant of the attention; only once in a while does it all go horribly wrong.

"I was opening a racing-car show at the NEC and this chap from the *Sunday Mercury* came up and said: 'What about this, then?' He meant an innocuous interview Walker had done for *Autocar* in which our hero declared he would drive at 80 mph on an empty motorway in clear weather. "But as I've never seen an empty motorway in clear weather, the question was entirely hypothetical."

The canny reporter then escorted Walker to an on-show McLaren, seated him in it and said: 'Smile!' Anyone over about six would scent a set-up and, sure enough, the next day he was front-page news. "I drive at 80, says Mr Motorsport."

"The report contained virulent condemnation from the chief constable of Warwickshire - 'We've got enough problems without hooligans like him on our roads' - and some more vilification from the chief executive of the Royal Society for the Prevention of Accidents. So I hasten to say, I never do more than 70 mph and if you suggest otherwise, I shall sue."

Does Martin Brundle ever collapse with uncontrollable mirth on the floor of the commentary box, I had to ask. "Sometimes," he admitted. For instance, we were talking about his noble attempt to speak in the native tongue of some of the countries he visits. Swedish? French? German? He couldn't quite decide which one to learn. "So to cut a long story short, I convinced myself that because I went to so many countries, there was no point in trying to learn any of their languages." You have to think about that for a while and then you realise it is a fledgeling Walkerism hatching. Not as magnificent as "THERE'S NOTHING WRONG WITH THE CAR EXCEPT THAT IT'S ON FIRE!" but evidently from the same racing stable. Later on, he was to say: "That's what's coming out of my mouth at the time I'm talking," which is another fine example of the genre. But, and I don't know what this says about me, I knew exactly what he meant.

Anyway, his predictions for the 1998 season: "I think McLaren will have the edge in the constructors' championship and Schumacher will have the edge in the drivers'. Damon Hill and Jordan: "Sadly and reluctantly, I have to say that Damon will be lucky to win a race and he hasn't a snowball's chance in hell of the championship." Heinz-Harald Frentzen with Williams: "He was seen as the young Messiah who was going to blow everybody off but he was a lot bigger in people's perceptions than he may be in fact. Suddenly he gets thrown into Williams in place of England's darling, with a car that's difficult to drive and a team-mate who's the master of mind games. Jacques Villeneuve is as tough as old boots and doesn't give a stuff what everybody thinks of him. Frentzen is a thin-skinned, sensitive chap who does give a stuff what people think. This year, for him, it's now or never." Eddie Irvine at Ferrari: "He's a very good driver. He's also a very difficult bloke. He's - and I'm always conscious of the fact I've got to live with these people - moody and unpredictable. But he can be tremendous fun." David Coulthard with McLaren: "He hasn't been able to grip the public imagination by doing well. He's won three races but Damon has won 21. Anyway, he's - not dour - but he's not a jump-up-and-down type. Not like Nigel Mansell. You'd have thought he was having an orgasm when he was racing, the way he pandered to the public and played to the crowd. David just isn't like that. He's very quiet and constrained. When I'm interviewing him on television, I hiss at him 'David, give us a smile'." Walker demonstrates a hugely unsettling grin, which must account for Coulthard's sometimes startled expression on camera.

All in all, I cannot think of a finer man to make bearable, even loveable, the whole ridiculously expensive business. The wonderful news is he has no intention of giving up. "Elizabeth says, 'You'll bloody well live to 100 like your mother and go on doing it then'." We do hope so, Murray.

★ 7/3/98

Noades enjoys his role as the three Ronnies

This week, Ron Noades was named Division Three's manager of the month for August, for services rendered at Brentford. He thus became the first chairman to win an award for management - though by no means the first chairman to consider he deserved one - and also the first club-owner to do so. For such is the 61-year-old property tycoon's extraordinary position at Griffin Park - an all-powerful trinity: Ron the owner, Ron the chairman, Ron the manager.

The problems at so many football clubs can be sourced to fallings out between manager and chairman. Lucky old Brentford, then, who are guaranteed against such disruption by all but the onset of schizophrenia. Which is unlikely, single-mindedness being one of Noades's most immediately evident characteristics. At Wimbledon, and then in an 18-year reign at Crystal Palace, Noades built himself something of a reputation as the archetypal football chairman: rich, opinionated, disputatious and with a name *Private Eye* could not have invented. At the end of last season, however, after agonisingly protracted negotiations, Noades sold Palace to Mark Goldberg, the managing director of a computer services group, for £22.85 million. Noades, who must have seriously contemplated retirement from football for at least two minutes, then bought David Webb's 51 per cent share in Brentford. The two deals left Noades with roughly £20 million in change. Brentford opened their arms and their safe and got ready for the Ron Noades Show. And so far so good: seven level-headed new signings (three from non-League clubs), a jump-start in the League, and a managerial trophy handed out at a three-hour lunch in Victoria. Though as Noades remarked, with the pragmatism which is not unusual to him, "three consecutive defeats is all I need to turn this around".

We met at the offices of Noades's business (leisure facilities, golf courses, property). The offices are situated just south of the M25 in an elegantly crumbling mansion which has known more recent use as a school: noise bounces off the bare floorboards and down the corridors, in particular the noise of Ron Noades on the phone. The grounds continue to be leased to Crystal Palace for training and from the windows of his own unfussy room, Noades can look down on the players that were once his. I asked him how he felt about that. "A bit envious: that I've built it and I haven't got it to use." Noades's final season at Palace was almost comically unfortunate - the absence of a home win before April and the appointment of a manager who did not speak English were two of the highlights - and there was some clamour for his removal.

Noades's by-word at Palace was careful housekeeping, which did not sit well alongside the contemporary Premiership season-ticket holder's desire to see new Italians arriving every hour, on the hour. Noades also estimated that, had he stayed at Palace, who were relegated, the club would have been £9.5 million overdrawn by the end of this season - an overdraft for which he was liable. "I didn't want to spend another year being the butt of the supporters for selling players," he said. It's the case, though, that Noades introduced a degree of financial stability at Palace which the club had never known, and at the end of his time there he got his share of warm letters. "But if you saw the local paper just before the deal went through," Noades said, "the whole of the back page was letters hoping that Goldberg would take over because they wanted big-name players to come in. That was disappointing." Thus far at Brentford, no cause for insurrection, though the voice of dissent has been heard. Noades dipped into the mountain of papers and open files on his capacious desk and prised loose a photocopy of a letter published recently in the *Hounslow Chronicle*. The letter took personally a recent suggestion by Noades that it was not helpful of Brentford fans to boo their own players. Noades read the letter aloud in its entirety, pausing only to add his own commentary - "… absolute crap… libellous… I never said that…".

The letter ended with a bold reminder to Noades that the fans who stumped up for tickets were the people "who pay your wages". It was clear from the expression on the multi-millionaire's face that, as the personal guarantor of Brentford's wage bill, he considered this last allegation to be, as it were, a bit rich. "Fans think that turnstile money pays for everything," Noades said. "But of course it doesn't, not any more. In a way, you're subsidising the sport so that the supporters can watch it - you could argue that."

You could, indeed - if you were prepared to be unpopular. And Noades doesn't seem to mind. However, he did want me to know that the writer of this letter was "as a matter of fact, totally isolated". Noades said he had checked on the Internet, where the response to his regime was reassuringly "positive". There appears to be nothing cosmetic about Noades's new managerial role - no simple sense in which he is a rich man mucking about in a tracksuit, as other rich men might tinker with yachts. He goes to training. He watches the reserves. He may rely on a three-man coaching staff (Ray Lewington, Brian Sparrow and Terry Bullivant) but Noades picks the team. Then again, many said he always did. "I got a reputation right through for interfering with the manager, which I've never ever done. I've never gone in the dressing room - apart from at Wembley and at the beginning of the season to wish the players well. But it suited managers to let people think that: if things weren't going well, they had an excuse. It's like when managers talk about not being given any money to spend. Most of the time managers aren't given any money to spend because the board don't have any confidence that they'll spend it properly."

One was somehow grateful this was now a conversation Noades only needed to have with himself. Noades put it unsentimentally when he said, of his switch from Palace to Brentford: "We're a leisure business. And as a leisure business we've replaced one football subsidiary with another one."

What baffles him is why the City, of all places, should have got interested in football. "We were going to go public with the leisure company, but the city said it wasn't interested in that, it was interested in the football club. In other words, the city was only interested in the one business we had that wasn't making money - because soccer was sexy. I could never understand it. And I could never understand people who invested in clubs that went public because I have never known a club pay a dividend."

It did not seem to concern Noades that other recent attempts to combine the roles of owner and manager had not brought happiness. "Barry Fry found out at Peterborough, didn't he? Put his house at the bank, took over the club, couldn't handle the debts, realised he'd mortgaged his life and very luckily got someone to take him out of it. He was lucky. Dave Bassett did the same thing at Wimbledon. He signed the guarantee for the overdraft. One night, he couldn't sleep and he drove to Sam Hammam's house and sat outside. Got taken off it the next day." Given the anxiety and the grief, why bother? "I suppose it's an ego trip," Noades said. "And I'm a soccer nut. I could easily have sold Palace and got out of football. But they're all supporters - all the chairmen and directors. You'd have to be. You only get hold of a football club when it's in a bad way." Asked if he missed the social life which went with being a Premiership chairman - his ticket into the directors' lounges at Old Trafford and Highbury - something a little like longing appeared in his voice. "Yeah," he said. "Well, my family more than me. My wife didn't want it to happen. But now she comes to Brentford and she enjoys it because if we lose we haven't got to worry about the bank manager on Monday. Then again," he said, "you go round the Brentford boardroom now you find it full of people who used to come to Palace. But, you see, lots of people would want to come to Palace. Not so many people want to come to Brentford. It's not such a big game for them, is it? Brentford v Rochdale? Whereas Palace v Bolton - that's different."
★5/9/98

Clown prince of snooker abdicates

Only an announcement that the Queen Mum had decided to resign her job could have inspired a greater sense of stunned disbelief. Dennis Taylor, the oldest and most beloved of snooker's royal family, is to hang up his chalk-topped sceptre. At the age of 50, the little Ulsterman with the big glasses and even bigger smile will continue making public appearances via the BBC microphone, after-dinner speeches and exhibition matches but, worn out after 23 years of public duty, he will grant himself one final tilt at the ultimate crown before leaving the game's young princes to squabble among themselves. "I have set my heart on bowing out at the Crucible," says Taylor, his soft County Tyrone brogue undiluted by 35 years spent living in Blackburn. "I haven't qualified for the World Championship since 1995 so I'll give it one more shot then get on with the rest of my life."

Now a lowly 52nd in the rankings, Taylor is spending the best part of a month sequestered in Plymouth where he is embroiled in a frantic series of first-to-five frame dog-fights to qualify for next season's major events; defeat by Stephen O'Conner - his eighth successive loss this year - in the fifth preliminary round of the European Open represented the final indignity. No TV cameras, no spectators, no atmosphere, Taylor gazed through the windows of the tournament office into the glorious afternoon sunshine beyond as he explained the reasons for his looming departure. "You try to psyche yourself up but, really, when you've been used to playing on television it's very difficult to motivate yourself in this environment. It doesn't seem natural having to play snooker in August. For 20-odd years I've been used to having the summer off and, to be honest, I'd rather be out there on the golf course (where he had just taken £55 off Willie Thorne) than be stuck in here practising. Here I am among all these youngsters who're desperate

to play in Bangkok or Beijing and it suddenly all comes home to me: 'What am I doing putting myself through this sort of thing?' I've had enough."

The nation, of course, will never have enough of Dennis Taylor who inspired an outpouring of affection in 1985 when he beat Steve Davis 18-17 in a heart-stopping World Championship final which he won on the final black at 12.19am - having caused a massive rescheduling of programmes on BBC2 after trailing 8-0 in the first session. For 13 years the image of the triumphant Taylor hoisting his mighty cue above his head like a weight-lifter whilst grinning fit to burst has been engraved on the memory of all 18.5 million viewers who stayed up to witness the climactic shoot-out to the most exciting match in snooker history. "They say it was 18 million or so but it was actually far more," smiles Taylor at the memory.

You try to psyche yourself up but, really, when you've been used to playing on television it's very difficult to motivate yourself in this environment

"Millions more were watching in clubs and pubs. There were even tales of lorry drivers being stuck on cross-Channel ferries because people were so engrossed in the match that they refused to give up their seats in front of the telly to move their cars." "A bit of a match" was all Taylor could find to say to the vanquished Davis, regarded as all but unbeatable at the time, as they shook hands at the end. (Frank Keating did rather better when he wrote: "It was like Sergeant Bilko beating Muhammad Ali over the full 15"). "I suppose everyone wanted me to win because I was such an underdog. Also, everyone knew I'd lost my mother, who was only 62, to a massive heart-attack a few weeks earlier, so there was this huge wave of sympathy. I received thousands of letters and telegrams and although Steve and I have never discussed the match - especially that black he missed when I thought the game was well and truly up - I can honestly say there's never a day goes by without someone mentioning it to me. Do I get bored talking about it? Like hell I do. It was my moment of moments."

Financially secure from that day forth, Taylor's fascination with snooker had begun some three decades earlier as an eight-

year-old in Jim Joe Girvan's tiny two-table snooker club in Northern Ireland where he was allowed to sit on the sidelines and hold the rest for the players "because I was always a good little boy". Blessed with a natural aptitude for the game, he moved to Lancashire where he took on a variety of jobs - "office worker, 12-hour shifts in a papermill seven-days-a-week, selling electrical appliances, managing a snooker club" - all the while trying to carve out a niche in the professional game then dominated by the likes of Ray Reardon, John Spencer and John Pulman. "My big break - if you'll pardon the expression - came in the early Seventies when I packed in my day job and, with two kids and only £200 in the bank, paid my own way to Canada where I made the final of the Canadian Open after beating Alex Higgins in the semis. More importantly, I also made a continuous 'break'of 349 - 349 points without missing a ball - which got me invited on to *Pot Black* in '74. My first opponent was John Pulman, who'd been world champion seven times and was a legend, so I was absolutely petrified. Although I knew I should try to make some sort of impression because it was my debut on TV I couldn't force a smile. Fortunately, he left a ball over the pocket for me and I actually went on to reach the final. Thanks entirely to *Pot Black*, suddenly I was 'a name'.

It was during the 1985 World Championship that Taylor also became 'a celebrity'; left without an evening game to show due to the early finish of two matches, the BBC asked Taylor to stage an exhibition of the trick-shot routine he had perfected during his many years of apprenticeship on the club circuit. "The thing that had always bothered me about trick shots was that whenever you missed one, it was always deathly quiet while you set up the next one. And so I became the first professional to tell a stand-up gag at the table, the worst gag you can ever imagine, I have to say." Man to doctor: I keep losing my memory... Doctor: How long's this been going on? Man: How long's what been going on?

Although the knack of winning has deserted him, Taylor has never lost the ability to 'work' an audience and won the World Trick-Shot Championship in Belgium earlier this year by dint of his expertise in making snooker balls disappear into the pockets in the most unlikely fashion whilst keeping up a string of running jokes. "I cheated a bit really, because all I did was change my Irish gags into Dutch gags

and the Belgians loved it." One non-Irish example of the Taylor wit: Man to doctor: Every morning when I get up I start singing *The Green, Green Grass of Home*. Doctor: Oh, dear. Any other symptoms? Man: Yes, at night, I can't stop singing *Delilah*. Doctor: I'm afraid you're suffering from Tom Jones Syndrome. Man: Is it serious? Doctor: Well, it's not unusual...

As Taylor prepares to abdicate his title as 'the man who put the smile on the face of snooker,' precious few of the young maestros who now populate the game appear to appreciate they are engaged in an entertainment industry. "There's some great lads out there but it's all so, so serious now because the money's so huge. It's unfair to expect them to turn round and start cracking jokes but it would be nice if one or two of them did. Having said that, it's not an easy thing to do - to come up with a funny quip in front of millions - and it's a long process learning how to handle an audience. I remember playing Bill Werbeniuk in the quarter-finals at the Crucible one night after the big fella had drunk about 27 pints of lager. Anyway, he had just climbed up on to the very edge of the table to reach an awkward cue ball when he let out the loudest fart you've ever heard. I'm chewing my cue to prevent myself laughing, the spectators are gnawing their fingers to do the same, and the match on the other side of the wall has come to a complete stop. So big Bill - all 22 stones of him and red in the face with effort - gets back down, stares at this little old couple in the audience challengingly and demands: 'Right. Which one of you did that?'"

As a fiercesomely proud son of the province with four sisters still living in the area, the laughter dries up abruptly when Taylor steels himself to address the tragedy of Omagh. "Horrendous, absolutely horrendous. The wife of a lad I used to knock about with when I was young had a shop there and they dug her out the day after. She'd been buried underneath the rubble. When you see the things that happen so close to you, especially when so many of them were so young, it puts my silly wee difficulties on the snooker table into perspective. I'll never understand what happened in Omagh." For once, the clown prince of snooker had nothing left to say.

★24/8/98

Superpower pushed to the limits

It was while he was throwing up over a crash barrier on the M4 that the revolutionary thought came to Steve Redgrave. "Why?" said his brain, in neon-inflamed flashing lights. "Why am I doing this to myself?" It was Christmas 1997. A time for family, frivolity and the Bacchanalian abandonment of the work ethic. Or in Redgrave's case, a time to get diabetes, colitis and a tube up his back passage to collect 12 biopsies of his colon at Charing Cross Hospital. "I suppose that whole period is the closest I've ever been to chucking it all in," he said in retrospect. How close is close? "Out of ten?" he said. "Nine and three-quarters."

We nearly lost him. The world's greatest living Olympian, the possessor of four gold medals and the ferocious quest for a fifth at Sydney 2000, almost decided that the toll on his wife and children, sanity and strength, mind and body (despite its freakishly efficient anaerobic capacities), was now too much to bear. As a man, a rower and an icon, he'd had enough. But then...

He can't stop, basically. That's why he was sitting at the back of a boathouse on the lapping fringes of Lake Varese spreading vast dollops of strawberry jam on fistfuls of rough Italian bread as a prelude to a quick 16km on the water. These were the fine-tuning preparations for the World Championships, the stepping stone towards his one true goal: the next Olympic gold.

Is it possible? Can a diabetic who will be 38 in the year 2000 reasonably expect to be part of a victorious coxless heavyweight four, crossing the threshold to Olympic history as the formidable Romanians, Germans and Australians are left swishing about in their wake? He can actually. The 'Fab Four', as they are known - Redgrave, Matthew Pinsent, Tim Foster and James Cracknell - are not just a boatful of broad shoulders, they're a superpower, and

Redgrave's iconic status is no small key to their invincibility. A Romanian rower once nudged Cracknell at a regatta. "How heavy is he?" whispered Redgrave's admirer, beholding the shapely 16 $^1/_2$ st bulk. Cracknell wisely added a few pounds for effect. The Romanian rolled his eyes in despair. "Oh, he's so strong. I am very weak." "They're a phenomenal outfit," said the British team manager, David Tanner. "I've never seen a crew as exciting or as exhilarating. It's quite staggering. But if they don't win in Sydney, then they haven't been successful. That's the chilling fact."

....

"I've never seen a crew as exciting or as exhilarating. It's quite staggering. But if they don't win in Sydney, then they haven't been successful. That's the chilling fact"

....

Chilling. That's axe murderer talk, and in terms of single-minded, off-the-wall devoutness, that would be a reasonable comparison. In 20 years, Redgrave's body has been routinely and masochistically exerted, exhausted, exacted and (only occasionally) exalted. No wonder it felt like an ex-body.

It's not all fluffy *Tales from The Riverbank*, not by any stretch of the Thames, and in the last year all hell has broken loose. The traumas have run as thick, fast and murky as the Amazon. In the last 12 months Redgrave has been seriously incapacitated by illness, the crew dismembered by a bizarre accident, their coach, Jurgen Grobler, implicated by the Stasi in an old East German drugs scandal and Cracknell dyed his hair green in South Africa. Rowing until your lungs scorch and your muscles scream is the least of it. It began with the appendicitis. "I'm in agony," said Redgrave to his wife one night in April 1997, on the eve of their supposed departure for a few blissful days in Spain. Being a GP as well as the British rowing team's doctor, Ann Redgrave was in a good position to make the diagnosis. Her first thought was: "He's got appendicitis." Her second thought was: "This is going to ruin my holiday." So she said: "Oh, you'll be all right", and sent him to bed. But she was right on both counts. It was appendicitis and it did ruin her holiday. There followed in swift succession: ambulance, hospital, operation, comeback. The doctors told Redgrave to take it easy for three weeks. He was back in training after 10 days.

For a while, long enough to win the World Championships, his body's rebellion was quashed. But the militant forces were merely regrouping for another attack. October 1997: "I felt really thirsty one Monday afternoon. I drank a pint of water and still felt thirsty. I drank another pint of water and still felt thirsty. After three or four pints of fluid and still having this tremendous thirst, I thought: hmmm, I know what this is, I've had it before." There followed another swift progression: urine dipsticks, GP, hospital, blood tests. Redgrave was diabetic. "It was a big shock actually. My immediate reaction was, 'All these years of training, I've finally pushed my body over the edge. Well, it's been a pretty good innings. Time to stop'." This he thought for the length of the drive between the GP practice in Marlow and Wickham Hospital. In other words: not long.

He was back in training. But it was agonisingly difficult training, physically and, above all, mentally. He could feel himself falling short of superhumanity. "It was awful. I'd suffered a recurrence of my colitis because that's stress-related and it was the stress of being diagnosed diabetic. And then we went to a training camp in South Africa, and I was just totally out of it. It was very upsetting."

"I remember phoning Ann and saying, 'I'm not enjoying this.' It's well documented that she didn't want me to carry on after the last Olympics. I expected her to say, 'You got yourself into this. Sod you.' That type of thing, but what she said on the phone was, 'We're in this together. We decided we'd go on and try and achieve this together.' That gave me the spirit to carry on." They went on a skiing holiday with friends just before Christmas. He felt ill and dejected, and preying on his mind was the knowledge that the doctors had taken as many biopsies as they had because they feared the onset of Crohn's disease. "It's more serious than colitis," said Redgrave. "If it takes a grip you start losing parts of your colon. I think it can even turn cancerous." As it is colitis is a pre-cancerous condition. Redgrave has to take his medication all the time, even when the symptoms are not flaring. "And all the time, I'm not sure whether it's all the training I've done that's brought this on. Pushing my body through its paces

over the years may have something to do with it. I don't know. It's just a feeling I have. You basically think, 'What the hell am I doing to myself?' " And to others, in fact.

Multiplication, you can hardly call it cloning, has been going on. Redgrave began as a single sculler, won the coxed fours at the 1984 Los Angeles Olympics, the coxless pairs with Andy Holmes at Seoul in 1988, the next two (Barcelona and Atlanta) with Pinsent and is now prospecting for gold in Sydney as part of this multi-faceted 'Fab Four'. Just how different they are from one another is demonstrated by Foster's suggestion that they should shave their heads and call themselves 'The Four Skins'. Where Redgrave and Pinsent exude

serious professionalism, pinstripes on their rowing vests, Foster (long blond hair, earrings, plays in a band) and Cracknell (more earrings, two tattoos, bleached hair) are conspicuous lads.

A little too conspicuously conspicuous as it turns out. No sooner had Redgrave recovered from his ailments and Pinsent been restored following a cracked rib than Foster caused the most serious fall-out of their year-long collaboration. He was dancing in a boathouse and punched his hand through a window. "In the shock of it, you don't actually realise what you've done. Then I saw the girl opposite me was actually being sprayed with my blood." He collapsed soon afterwards and so did the Union flag-swathed myth that Superman could never be beaten. Redgrave comes from Amersham, not Krypton after all.

With Foster absent, the Redgrave crew were defeated at the Munich regatta this summer. It was his first loss since 1992, after 72 unbeaten races, and Cracknell, above all, was incensed. "My whole life, my funding, everything was tied up in rowing," he said. He viewed Foster's accident as a traitorous episode of rank irresponsibility. "It pissed us off a lot. We didn't phone him at all while he was out injured. And he didn't phone us at all." "Yeah, I was ignored," said Foster. "Sent to Coventry," which is an appropriately land-locked city for his grounding in disapproval. He would cycle into Henley to train, see the lads, be spurned by them, train and cycle home. In the end, it required all the skilful wiles of Grobler to reintroduce him into the four.

A meeting was held in the gym of the Leander Club. Views were aired. Foster apologised. "At the time, James didn't want him back in the boat," said Grobler, "but I started with Matthew. I did a little bit of shifting around. And finally..." Now you can barely see the scars. On Foster's hand, or in the crew. Before their swan-scattering training session in the long shadows of the Italian evening, Pinsent was getting Foster and Cracknell to pitch him stones to hit baseball-style into the water with an oar. (He missed most of them.) Redgrave was benignly busy with his bread and jam, and subsequent insulin jab to the stomach. There was only peace, harmony and redoubtable belief apparent. "Maybe," said Foster, looking on the bright side, "it gave us something to achieve. Maybe you can run out of goals. But with me being out of the boat for a while, it gave us something real and current to aim at."

Certainly, Pinsent's delight when the reunited four hunted down and defeated the Olympic champion Australians by a length at Henley this year was demonstrated by his punch in the air just before they crossed the finish line. He was thoroughly dressed down for that. "Oh, dearie me," said Foster, in mock-matron outrage. "It's like jeering at the goalkeeper before you shoot," explained Cracknell. But the gesture spoke volumes, of relief as much as celebration. Then they won Lucerne. Dream back on track. For all Redgrave's talismanic qualities, the other three are equally remarkable in their way. Pinsent, a double Olympic gold medallist, has to live with Redgrave's inevitable overshadowing. The new boys will ever be hod-carriers to Olympic history or the men who made Redgrave lose. Their chalice is emblazoned with the skull and crossbones.

Redgrave and Pinsent earn £1 million over four years from their sponsors, Lombard. Foster and Cracknell get £16,000 each from the Lottery, modelled the spring collection for Marks and Spencer, and Foster was once recognised in his local opticians. If the boat was as lopsided in reality as it is financially, it would ship gallons of water and sink. "It can become an issue in the boat if you're jealous," said Foster, who isn't. "A couple of times at press conferences, all the journalists want to do is talk to Steve and we're left twiddling our thumbs. And don't forget Matthew is going for his third Olympic gold. Imagine if it was Linford Christie. Yet he just gets forgotten. He's the second-most successful Olympian in God knows how long. It's a bit unfortunate for him." But there is no bitterness in the air. If anything, the two-man influx is proud of its lightening influence on the legendary intensity of Redgrave. "He still has the same ability to be focused but my impression now is that he's enjoying himself," said Foster. "He's late for things now, because he knows I'll be even later. He's more of a laugh. He's a bit like a naughty schoolboy now."

Even so, he is not Gazza. Foster and Cracknell had to think hard to remember whether they had seen Redgrave drunk. "We haven't," they concluded. "Because whenever he is, so are we."

So the crew, for all its creative, diverse, Beatlemaniacal tensions, is essentially a study in togetherness. Twenty-two years ago a young Cracknell asked Redgrave for his autograph at the World Rowing Championships in Nottingham. Redgrave said No. Now he is trusting his destiny to the boy. "Do I love them? Yes and no. Strange answer," said Redgrave. "With Tim's injury, it's been proved to us - and me as an individual - that this is the unit that

works. It's the four people who make the boat go as well as it does." Five, if you include Grobler, and they do. The revelations, garnered from old Stasi files and mysteriously released into the ether, that their coach had been involved in the systematic steroid-enhancing of East German rowers in the late 1970s and 80s was a desperate blow to the team. "I wasn't surprised. I was surprised. And I was disappointed in some respects," said Redgrave, fluxed with conflicting emotions, even six months on. "I'm close to Jurgen. There's a special bond there. Obviously when he first came to Britain, we asked him about drugs. He said there had been a lot of experiments but they found out it wasn't beneficial in rowing and so he didn't do it."

Redgrave, in the light of the new allegations, had felt misled. "But Jurgen didn't have any choice. They wouldn't have given him the job. And seeing how he reacted to what came out, the stress and strain he was under, the hurt and the shame of what happened..." He lapsed into a silence heavily pregnant with forgiveness. "Based on the system he was involved with, he had no choice, no choices at all."

....

"You think I'm fanatical, don't you? Well, if I am fanatical, I won't be able to stop. But I don't think I am"

....

Redgrave accepts he is now tainted by association. "Yeah, oh yeah, I'm sure I have been. And there's also the diabetes. Diabetes can be one of the side-effects of anabolic steroid abuse. What can you do? I know I'm clean. I've always been clean, but if you made a very big issue about it you could be a target. Someone could easily spike your drink, especially at a World Championships." Grobler himself is straightforward. "OK, I have to live with my past," he said simply. "But I think I can still look in the mirror. I have given no drugs to no athlete here, ever."

In this statement he has the unequivocal support of the entire Amateur Rowing Association. "His ethics are unimpeachable," said Tanner. "One day someone on the fringes of rowing might be caught taking something they shouldn't, but it absolutely won't be Redgrave and Pinsent." But that is not the only absolute Ann Redgrave wants. After years and years of living with indomitable ambition, borderline fanaticism and a bad patient - "you know what men are like; he moans like mad when he's ill" - she hopes that absolutely, positively, this is Redgrave's last Olympics. He will be over 40 in 2004 and, surely, the motivation and the engine will have started to flag by then. Won't it? "You think I'm fanatical, don't you?" said Redgrave. "Well, if I am fanatical, I won't be able to stop. But I don't think I am." But 42 would really be past it, wouldn't it? There ensued a long, marital bliss-endangering pause. "Well, there was this guy of 42 who won the Olympic gold before," he said ominously. "In the eight..."

★ 29/8/98

Phil Shephard-Lewis

Cricket's chance to captivate a new audience

The 1999 cricket season will be unique. There have been World Cups in the United Kingdom before, but none so grandiose as this year's is going to be, and none with so much at stake. When England set the ball rolling in 1975 it was a bold experiment, but it would not have been the end of the world had the Prudential Cup not been the great success it was. Now the game in this country cannot afford expectations to be disappointed. World Cup 99 is expected to make big money, to promote the game worldwide and re-invigorate it in the country where batsmen first took on bowlers in rustic fields with no middle stump, no pavilions, no sight screens, no press, no radio, no television, no slow-motion replays, no advertising, no purpose at all really except to play a game which came naturally and have a wonderful time doing it.

The stimulus which the tournament should give to the game in the United Kingdom is only part of the cricketing, as opposed to the monetary, reward which would accrue if all goes well. The thrust of the International Cricket Council has been towards 'globalisation' since the MCC in effect gave the world body independence during the enlightened chairmanship of Colin (now Lord) Cowdrey. The hope is that the ICC will take a goodly share of an overall profit which should at worst be measured in hundreds of thousands of pounds. Most of it will go towards developing cricket in areas of the world like the United States, Europe and Africa, where at present the game has only a toehold on public awareness.

Television holds the key to these riches, and to the hope that the 42 matches will be seen by a bigger audience even than the one hundred million who watched the last World Cup in India, Pakistan and Sri Lanka. Gate money on the relatively tiny grounds of the UK will be small by comparison, so the great majority who watch will do so on small screen pictures transmitted by the BBC and BSkyB. The television deals done by the host organisers, the England and Wales Cricket Board, were even more important than those with various 'global sponsors' who have supported the event, albeit not quite to the ambitious extent for which the ECB had been hoping.

Commerce aside, what matters is that the cricket itself lives up to expectations, capturing the imagination in particular of the young. There is a healthier position at the base of the cricket pyramid in the UK than there was, and a need for many more of the development officers now at work in the 38 counties if children keen to play the game are to get the chance to do so. But football has so dominated the sporting scene in recent years and to such an increasing extent that cricket is perceived by some, including the ECB's marketing director Terry Blake, to have lost what he calls "street cred". Blake's hope is that from May 14, when England play the first match of the tournament against Sri Lanka, the holders, at Lord's, to the final at the same expensively modernised ground on Sunday, June 20, cricket will captivate a new audience in its coat of many colours.

The World Cup, happily, has managed to transcend all other one-day tournaments. For players and followers of the game alike it is the tournament that counts and a prize fund of $1 million will do nothing to dampen the ambition of those truly outstanding performers who invariably come to the fore when the stakes are so high. No one who saw the 1975 final will forget Clive Lloyd's joyous, irresistible hundred from 94 balls, or the fielding of Viv Richards which followed. Four years later at Lord's it was Richards himself who made the match-winning hundred, Collis King who murdered England's medium pacers and Joel Garner, with toe-crunching yorkers, who vanquished a fine array of English batsmen after Geoff Boycott and Mike Brearley spent too long laying a base.

India upset the West Indies in the 1983 final, and Australia and England spoiled the party for the hosts by winning their semi-finals in Pakistan and India before the Calcutta final of 1987. After that the lights came on, the coloured clothes appeared and the World Cup became the plaything of the countries from the sub-Continent. Wasim Akram and Mushtaq Ahmed were too good for England in their third final appearance at Melbourne; Aravinda de Silva to good for Australia in their triumph at Lahore last time.

There has not, therefore, been a home winner of the World Cup yet. England's dream is to change that this time, and at their very best they are capable of fulfilling it, especially if weather conditions favour the sort of seam and swing bowling which is still the strength of English cricket. If Alec Stewart and Darren Gough are the toast of the land by the middle of June, the 'Cricket in Crisis' headlines of last summer will finally be exposed for the exaggerated nonsense they were.

There is an extensive warm-up programme against county sides for the 12 countries, comprising the nine Test-playing nations plus Bangladesh, Kenya and Scotland, who came through to the finals from the ICC qualifying tournament in Malaysia in 1997. The overseas teams arrive in early May and they will base themselves at county grounds for 10 days or so before the serious cricket starts. England, gambling that the weather will be better in the south-eastern corner of the island, will prepare at Canterbury.

World Cup matches will all be 50 overs a side unless, of course, the weather interferes. Rain (or even snow which fell at Buxton in June shortly before the first World Cup in 1975) is the one serious threat to the tournament's success. In the first phase of the competition each team will play the others in their group of six, eliminating three from each group and leaving six sides to compete in the so-called Super Six, taking with them only the points scored against other successful teams in their group. There are two points for a win, one, heaven forbid, for an abandoned game.

In the second round the three counties who have qualified from Group A will play the three qualifiers from Group B, gaining two points for a win again plus any carried though from round one. The top four then go through to the semi-finals at Old Trafford and Edgbaston on June 16 and 17.

All this excitement, and hype, which will undoubtedly accompany the World Cup, will leave the second half of the season dangerously vulnerable to anti-climax. If England have won in Australia, or Alec Stewart has lifted the expensive World Cup silver trophy towards an adoring home crowd at Lord's, success against New Zealand in the four Cornhill Tests which follow at Edgbaston, Lord's, Old Trafford and the Oval would be initially assured. If not they will be seen as matches between two of the weaklings of Test cricket.

That would be a bad thing for county cricket, from which the main body of the England team will be absent for a large chunk of the summer. Last year's investigation into whether England players should be centrally contracted in future produced a compromise which will keep them nominally tied to their counties but loaned to the ECB. For county cricket 1999 is a transitional year anyway before a reshaped programme comes into place in 2000, underwritten by a new television contract.

Sponsorship of the Championship, discontinued by Britannic Assurance after 15 years, and of the new 50-over National League, which has replaced the 40-over Sunday League, was heavily dependent on the contract. The mid-season Super Cup, an extra one-day knockout tournament formed as an experiment this year to give an extra incentive to the top eight counties in the 1998 Britannic, is being anticipated rather more keenly by the successful eight than by the cynical press, and naturally, the ten who did not make it.

They include two of the heavyweights of county cricket in the last 25 years, Middlesex and Essex, a fact which underlined the extraordinary volatility of the county game in its present state of fascinating, unpredictable, but rather alarming flux. Don't ask me who will win the Championship itself this year, but if a gamble is essential it would be unwise not to put Lancashire on the shortlist. Increasingly they are the richest and most powerful club in the land. What is it about Old Trafford?

Time to fund the home-grown stars of the future

If two-legged life-form is ever found on Mars, it is a short-odds bet that Premiership managers will be there on the runway, waiting for the Shuttle's re-entry with open arms and chequebooks. As we hurtle towards the Millennium with all the control of Mr Bean on a runaway train, English football's obsession with foreigners shows no signs of slowing, with new worlds relentlessly explored for any Tomas, Dirk or Harald who can control a ball.

Elite clubs form affiliations with smaller Continental clubs, a clever plan designed to import low-cost youngsters as well as the finished articles. Free transfers, cheap unknowns and expensive has-beens fill our arrivals lounges without thought to the impact on the eco-structure outside.

Blinded by ambition and avarice, English football patently fails to realise it risks its very Englishness. The flirtation with foreigners having become a full-blown love affair, the old English partner having been abandoned at the altar, clubs are in danger of losing all links with the communities who sustain them. And the England national team cannot benefit from having so many possibles languishing on the benches or reserve sides of the Premiership. Or simply not being developed at all.

A warm welcome will always be on offer for the Bergkamps, Cantonas and Zolas, for such esteemed Footballers of the Year whose myriad qualities will rub off on domestic products. Their abstemious ways, their warm-down routines, the way they train longer and, in the case of managers like Arsene Wenger, the way they coach is an example to all born on this sceptred isle.

Listen to the young Manchester United players. They all talk in awe of Eric Cantona, of the way he would practise so diligently and then stop and talk to them, advising them, helping them mature into the internationals of such rich promise.

Listen to Ryan Giggs. "We just learnt from Eric's actions, the way he played and trained. Players like the Nevilles, Butt, Scholes and Beckham stay behind and just practise, free-kicks and shooting. These are things they've inherited because that was what Eric always used to do."

But for every constructive Cantona there is a selfish visitor to these shores, travellers more mercenary than missionary. The antics of Pierre Van Hooijdonk, a goalscoring Dutchman with a penchant for own goals over contracts, hardly endeared him to Nottingham Forest. Other trouble-makers included Fabrizio Ravanelli, of Italy, and the Brazilian Emerson. At least, Emerson's compatriot, Juninho, sounded sorry to leave Middlesbrough. Paolo di Canio, the Italian with long side-burns and short fuses, even had the nerve to accuse an English referee of diving - after pushing him over. Bizarre.

To rail against foreigners is not zenophobia, simply a desire for English football to breathe, to finance our own youth systems not those of Italy, France or Scandinavia. Take last year. Take the internationals against Switzerland, Romania and Sweden where England conceded goals to players like Ramon Vega, Dan Petrescu and Andreas Andersson who earned their fields of corn in the Premiership, painfully biting the hand that fed them daily.

Imagine the England team 10 years hence, when the full effect of the foreign invasion has been understood, when the Premiership has become simply a finishing school for Scandinavians and Slovaks, Austrians and Australians. Whoever chooses the England team, probably Michael Owen given the pace of his current development, will have fewer names from which to build a team.

Take goalkeepers. Even now, the Premiership is predominantly made up of foreigners between the sticks. Ray Clemence, England's goalkeeping coach, is deeply worried about the shortage of talent emerging. As he searches the country, Clemence also knows that those stars who do emerge can be stifled by the obsession with imports.

In an ideal world, a quota system would be introduced that stipulated every team must field at least two home-grown players, not bought-in Englishmen but those nurtured in-house. This would not be a problem for enlightened clubs like Manchester United, who regularly field players like Beckham, Scholes, Butt and the Nevilles, or Liverpool, who call on Owen, Fowler, McManaman and Carragher. It would provide a timely incentive to those clubs, like Chelsea, whose first-team reads like a world XI.

Unfortunately, the boys from Brussels would throw their law-books at anything that restricted freedom of movement within Europe. Protecting local species is not in the EC's pan-European interests. Borders are for gardeners not for the self-styled governors of a continent moving towards federalism. The way things are going clubs will be soon to be able to apply for EC set-aside grants to miss out on home-grown crops.

If such a limit remains a legal non-starter, as it surely is in this post-Bosman world, then English football must consider a self-imposed levy on transfer deals involving foreign clubs, a sort of human import duty. Brussels would probably become prickly over this but there are enough examples of import duties, such as cars and drinks.

The levy would be simple, a five per cent slice of the fee taken by the Football Association, not the Premier League, to be used to fund all 92 clubs' youth systems. Nothing else, just youth. Call it seed money for future harvests. An argument could be made for the monies going just to the 72 Nationwide clubs, although the Premiership bullies would stamp their well-pedicured feet. The money would have to be divided among all the professional ranks.

It is difficult to see who could disagree with such a move. To put the figure into perspective, this cut would be less than the agent's fee. Which is more worthy? Underwriting Eric Hall's cigar-bill or funding the stars of the future?

At a conservative estimate, a five per cent levy would generate £5 million a year. The impact would be three-fold. First, the revenue would help all 92 clubs produce young talents, to encourage clubs like Peterborough United to keep on fostering callow contenders like Matthew Etherington, Matthew Gill and Simon Davies.

Many have successful schemes but extra cash is always welcome. Even if every one of the 92 clubs applied for a cut it would mean at the very least one new coach (perhaps an ex-pro recommended by the PFA and trained by the FA) on a £50,000 salary. Or better facilities and equipment. Some clubs run good youth systems on £150,000 a year; the new cash would make them be able to take the next step up.

Secondly, a levy would serve to make imports less attractive. As foreign clubs are unlikely to be too enamoured at handing over a slice of their action, the fee would have to come from the English buyer, obviously on top of the sum agreed with the Continental seller. This might end some deals but if an English club is put off by finding an extra five per cent to cement the deal then, clearly, the player is not worth bringing over in the first place.

With foreigners less financially appealing, English clubs will be more tempted to shop local. Clubs might see Nationwide players, currently over-priced by chairmen slavering at the Premiership's riches, as more realistic propositions. The Premiership would become more Anglicised, more local heroes would rise up and the tide could be turned.

Thirdly, the money would stay within English football. By benefiting all clubs, it would also help the elite by bringing on talents rather than looking for ready-made professionals overseas. There are countless examples of leading clubs who released youngsters who, having dropped down, then rose to the heights. As a teenager, David Platt was freed by Manchester United to Crewe Alexandra; his subsequent CV was pretty impressive.

The levy contains problems. One obvious disadvantage is that clubs would simply restructure payments, perhaps by agreeing to exhibition matches with the gate receipts going to the seller. Another loophole is that a player could buy out his contract with a foreign club and sell himself to an English one, pocketing a huge signing-on fee which would compensate him for his payment to his original employers. The absence of a transfer fee would preclude a levy being implemented.

Free transfers would also circumvent the levy system. But at least this prevents English clubs fuelling the prosperity of their Continental counterparts. It is time the English looked after their own.

Rugby World Cup will expose the gulf between rich and poor

It would be wonderful to declare rugby union a stress-free zone for the forthcoming year. Never mind the odd back-row forward who comes reeling out of a scrum clutching a nibbled ear, the assault on the sensibilities of every rugby follower these past couple of years has been just as grievous. The sport which used to patronisingly present itself as 'the ruffians' game played by gentlemen' has come crashing down from the moral high ground almost from the day on which it turned professional three-and-a-half years ago. This ethical vacuum has little to do with players being paid for performance and everything to do with the lust for power.

I have seen some ill-tempered brawling on the field in my time and, I have to admit, even enjoyed a vicarious kick, so to speak, from it. Yet there has been nothing to remotely match the venom, spite, rancour, viciousness, duplicity and underhandedness of rugby's political dealings. So, from us all, a plea to administrator in club and union alike - leave your ego and your prejudice in the dressing-room for the next 12 months. Give us back our sport, with its honesty, grace, thunder and drama. We don't mind the occasional scrap there. But no more off-field snarling and posturing. If so, it will ruin what ought to be a terrific year for the sport.

The centrepiece will be the World Cup, which kicks-off on Oct 1 at the new Millennium Stadium in Cardiff and ends there five weeks later on Nov 6, having sidestepped around different grounds in the five nations en route. Twickenham will host both semi-finals with Lansdowne Road, Murrayfield and the Stade de France getting their share of the knock-out action at the quarter-final stage. RWC'99 sees twenty teams competing in five initial groups of four teams, an increase of four teams from last time. South Africa as holders, Wales as hosts, New Zealand and France as runners-up and third-placed respectively in 1995, are the only teams who will not have had to qualify.

This is only the fourth such tournament. The first was held in New Zealand and Australia in 1987, and such has been the acclaim for each successive World Cup that it is difficult to understand now quite what the initial apathy to such an event was all about. Until that is, you consider the present-day mess. That is, men in suits sitting round tables, arguing the toss about who gets what, who has the rights to this and so on. The concept was simple and appealing. It has worked every time.

The last (and only) tournament in these parts in 1991 delivered the sport to a whole new audience. Previously only those with cauliflower-ears or a liking for ten pints and a curry with a game of rugby as the main course in-between, had a notion of loose rucks, rolling mauls and crooked feeds. It was likely, moreover, that few of these more basic rugger-buggers had actually heard of Jeremy Guscott, Rob Andrew and Will Carling. Rugby forwards are an introverted breeds and rarely pop up their heads to look further afield. These fancy three-quarters were strangers within their own England team at the time. They finally made acquaintance in the 1991 final itself and it cost them dear. Their packs, having ground their way past France in magnificent style in the quarter-final, and slogged their way past Scotland in not so magnificent style in the semi-final, then had a complete identity crisis against Australia in the final. England threw the ball wide, their own forwards spread their arms in protest, the Aussies and the crowd opened their eyes in amazement and the trophy headed down under yet again.

Still, the sport had new heroes and new status. It was to gain on both fronts next time around in South Africa in 1985. Who can forget the sight of the giant black-shirted menace by the name of Jonah Lomu? Certainly not Tony Underwood and Mike Catt, just two of the England players flattened by the formidable All Black winger on his way to the try line. He was a visitor there four times that afternoon in Cape Town, a day of humiliation for England and a day of joy for rugby followers. It was that occasion which prompted Rupert Murdoch to reportedly turn to one of his aides and say: "Who is that guy? We must have him."

Rupert got his man. And who will we get this time around? New faces will grace our playing fields and fill our screens (ITV are the host broadcaster). Relish the resurgent Australians with Matt Burke, Ben Tune and Joe Roff creating panic and opportunity in equal measure in their strong-running from the back prompted by the guile of Stephen Larkham at fly-half.

Admire, too, the Springboks who will not give up their crown easily. They have been through a fair amount of trauma since they won the title in such emotional circumstances, President Mandela articulating his approval for the traditional sport of the Afrikaner by donning the Springbok No 6 shirt, the number worn by the captain, Francois Pienaar. The streets of Johannesburg saw incredible scenes that night as black and white embraced. My own

fared little better against Australia in Brisbane. England have the resources to do well. However, the All Blacks are in their group. If England should lose that match then they face a play-off to reach the quarter-final. That game would be at Twickenham so England should go through to the quarter-final proper. And there, in Paris, await the Springboks.

Ireland are in the same group as Australia, Scotland make early acquaintance with South Africa, while Wales have the easier ride with only Argentina officially qualified at the time of writing.

Even though there will be great feats to fire the imagination during the tournament, one lurking anxiety refuses to go away. With more teams involved than before (20 compared to the usual 16) then the risk of mismatch is all the greater. It was bad enough last time around with the All Blacks flattening Japan 145-17. If the scores do become seriously lop-sided then the tournament will be discredited. Far from encouraging the smaller nations a thumping defeat might have the opposite effect.

There is concern, too, that pitting amateur players, from the likes of Morocco (were they to eventually qualify), against one of the super-powers would run the risk of a serious injury. The intention may have been noble three years ago in extending the invitation to the lesser lights. Since then, though, the gap between rich and poor has widened as a direct consequence of professionalism. The full-time players are fitter and stronger. In rugby that still counts for a lot.

car was swamped on the way back to the hotel by hordes of youths. Only hours earlier we would have been terrified. Suddenly it didn't seem to matter. Since that day the 'Boks have clung on to the roller-coaster and have come up the other side again. Pienaar left in bitter circumstances, then coach Andre Markgraaf was dismissed for racial comments, and the 'Boks were beaten on their own soil 18 months ago by the British Lions.

South Africa will begin favourites having dominated the southern hemisphere's tri-nations series last summer. We witnessed the once unthinkable of seeing the All Blacks slide to five defeats in succession, their worst run post-war. Are they on the wane? Whisper it quietly for they would like nothing better, come the autumn, than to confront the person who wrote them off. They will be back. Their tradition demands it.

France will be pushing for honours, particularly on their own turf. What of the home unions? All four countries suffered during the summer, none more starkly than Wales and England. Wales shipped over 90 points to South Africa, while a depleted England

The World Cup will be the principal point of focus. There are no summer tours of real note with the respective countries limbering up in various fashions. The Five Nations' Championship, the traditional centrepiece of the winter calendar, will be an historic event no matter what the standard of rugby. It will be the last to include just five countries. Italy will join the feast from 2000. The furious lobbying from the media for their inclusion was due entirely to the strength of their rugby and nothing whatsoever to do with the prospect of wild weekends in Rome, sumptuous backdrops, beautiful women, vast quantities of fine wine and the odd plateful of decent food. No, nothing at all. After all the Five Nations is a serious affair, is it not? On the field, yes. Off the field, no. Let's hope, in this ever-changing sporting landscape, that certain rituals will be preserved intact.

Money in sport soars through the ozone layer into the stratosphere

In 1931 Sir Stanley Matthews earnt a pound a week at Stoke. Those were the days when footballers employed two feet, no accountants and expected women to lay hot hands on them, but not necessarily for the purposes of faith healing. Sixty years on, Alan Shearer earns £38,000 a week.

These are the days when footballers are more likely to employ two footmen than two feet. They inhabit the realm of celebrity-royalty and their courts are resplendent with accountants, agents, dressers, shoppers, barbers, chauffeurs, publicists, publishers, physios, doctors, specialists, consultants, dieticians, clairvoyants, colonic irrigators, probation officers, security guards and addiction counsellors to wean them off gambling, nicotine, alcohol, and compulsively seeking the advice of addiction counsellors.

Footballers are rich. They are rich beyond the dreams of Geoff Hurst, who was earning £90 a week when his hat-trick won the World Cup, or Johnny Haynes, of Fulham and England, who became the first £100-a-week player. The sport has hyper-inflated like a hot air balloon, swollen by the cavalcade of Croesuses from abroad whose multiple vowels match the multiple noughts on their paychecks.

Dennis Bergkamp, £7.5 millions-worth of non-flying Dutchman, costs Arsenal around £40,000 a week. Jaap Stam, so visually reminiscent of a recently-released Middle Eastern hostage, may owe the wild stare in his eyes to his price tag to Manchester United of £10.75 million. Ryan Giggs was paid £1 million in 1996 to appear in a Fuji Film advertisement in Japan. That is some measure of how much the football world has changed. Frank Worthington would have appeared in all the *Emmanuelle* films for nothing.

In three seasons, the Premiership's wage bill has more than doubled. So much so that when the Dutch international, Pierre Van Hooijdonk, returned from the 1998 World Cup having spent many a profitable (he wished) hour with the likes of Bergkamp and Marc Overmars in the dressing-room, he demanded a £400,000 hike in his wages per year before he would countenance returning to Nottingham Forest. Amsterdam being famous for its bikes, Forest told him to get on one.

But other less dispensable players and profligate clubs have come to mutual accommodations, and Manchester United will certainly not be the only club who has to hire ex-SAS-trained bodyguards to escort their young millionaires from work to home in future.

Or Manchester Sky Box Office United as they will no doubt be hailed by the Millennium. The fact that Rupert Murdoch suddenly discovered a life-long interest in football, interest enough to bid nearly £700 million for the purchase of Britain's most lucrative club, was a signal that the sport is very big business indeed. He looked at the club shop at Old Trafford and thought: there's gold in them there tills.

Given Murdoch's first experience of football in Australia was as a run-down poor relation to rugby and Aussie Rules, this was a monstrous giveaway of his real motive: profit. Where Murdoch came from, football was the sport of cissies and pansies ruthlessly mocked by the boulder-shoulders taking part in more macho activities. Then suddenly, he could not wait to own his replica shirt. Roy Keane's probably, given their mutually ruthless reputation.

And yet Premiership footballers are still tackling from behind sport's most extravagant earners. In the Forbes list of the top 40 money men in sport, published in 1997, Mike Tyson earnt, they reckon, about US$75 million. By 1998, of course, he was pleading poverty which would easily have been explained if he had spent it on Manchester United replica shirts. It is still quite a lot of money.

> **The fact that Rupert Murdoch suddenly discovered a life-long interest in football, interest enough to bid nearly £700 million for the purchase of Britain's most lucrative club, was a signal that the sport is very big business indeed**

Michael Jordon hung in the air in second place having earned around $52 million. He may have invested it more wisely than Tyson. There is evidence he still has some left. Michael Schumacher's earnings and endorsements brought him $33 million (with a little knocked off for car repairs, presumably).

Sport has gone platinum. For the elite in boxing, motor racing, golf, tennis and football money has gone through the roof and proceeded through the ozone-layer (holed, among other things, by Giggs's three sports cars including an Aston Martin DB7) to stratospheric proportions.Cause was television (hence sponsorship, fame and the likes of Posh Spice consenting to consort with a ball kicker), effect is yet unknown.

You can guess though. The Bible had a good deal to say about money and not all of it complimentary. "The love of money is the root of all evil," said Timothy, for instance. Evil may be weighing the evidence a little too heavily but when footballers earn twice as much as their managers, drive flashier cars, import finer wine and employ better lawyers, the asylum is in danger of being run by the inmates.

Discipline was certainly notable by its absence at the start of the 1998-99 football season with three Arsenal players being sent off in the first month, Nicky Butt of Manchester United being similarly evicted two games running, and Paolo di Canio of Sheffield Wednesday committing the ultimate sin of pushing a referee to the ground.You could argue this had far more to do with ungovernable tempers than unlimited bank balances but arrogance is often the corollary of acquisition. Sportsmen have been made Somebody by their sport, somebody with the potential to be skewered by the sychophants and lapel brushers at their beck-and-call. Not everyone of them is Gary Lineker. Some aren't as bright as their highlights.

Will Carling, the former English rugby captain, uttered his most cogent sentence when he said: "Every penny I make is down to who I am and what I have achieved in the game." From his vantage point in the back row he was able to springboard to a wealthy existence unimaginable to the cauliflower-earred denizens gone before. In the immediate aftermath of his international retirement, he drove an £80,000 Mercedes 500SL, became managing director of his own company, gave after-dinner speeches at £3,000 per time, posed topless for a Sunday supplement and embarked on private life only barely less public than President Clinton's. Amateur rugby players used to be able to count on shredded ears and a limp in perpetuity. Money has created a few fate (You could argue about which one is worse).

But while the leading sportsmen (and in a gnat's portion of cases, sportswomen too) are getting richer, the sports themselves may not exactly follow suit. Football, for one, appears to have financial dysentery. For all the pouring in of television's multi-millions, it pours right out again in player transfers and wages, barely touching the sides.

The trickle down effect to the grass roots, from the Premiership to the rest of the Football League, is just that: a trickle. In fact, in the close season of 1998, Premiership clubs

bought just five Nationwide League players. The total amount of money paid by the Premiership to Division One was just over £8 million - two-thirds of Manchester United's Dwight Yorke. Rather like Marks and Spencers, the Premiership managers are just seeking comparatively cheaper supplies from abroad. For the time being, the leading vessels in the sport will stay well afloat whatever shipwrecked spectacle the odd little rubber dinghy in the Third Division may make of itself. Digital technology will represent a gushing oil well to those clubs with a vast potential audience.

While nobody, probably not even Bernie Ecclestone who has been carting eight superwagon loads of it round the Formula One circuit, could explain the physical components of digital, it has become the shorthand for a future where Arsenal, for instance, could beam all 19 home matches into, say, 500,000 fervent households at, perhaps, £20 a time. Total: £190 million per season. Double it to one million fervent households. Multiply it by 10 or 20 for Manchester United's worldwide fan base... The day will inevitably dawn when crowds are recruited from the ranks of resting actors and paid a few pounds to make a noise.

You can see why rancour and churlishness of the genuine fan has matched the Halleluja choruses among the television moguls. They see their sport being reinvented as a series. Prequel: the Charity Shield. Sequel: The FA Cup final. Perhaps this is daft and Diplodocan of them. If an actress can earn four Dennis Bergkamps for jutting cheek bones and learning her lines eventually, perhaps it is only right that fitter, blonder and global entertainers like David Beckham should have their share of the spoils. The ratings of the 1998 World Cup, rising to a zenith of 17 million viewers, was enough to suggest that footballers are the new Valentinos. Or perhaps Valentino was just an old Ronaldo.

If the product improves and corruption is limited to Eric Hall's monstrous use of the English language, then the influx and influence of money may be bearable. But can all sports say that? Andre Agassi earned over £3,000 a minute for defeating Cedric Pioline 6-0, 6-0 in the 1998 Grand Slam Cup, and then complained vociferously that he had been unable to play in the Davis Cup because it had been inconveniently sited in Milwaukee, which is miles away from where he lives. Are these two facts in any way related?

Perhaps the proof is in the miraculous humility of Pete Goss, the man who sold his family house to finance a yachting dream and risked his life to save a fellow competitor in the Southern Ocean. He worked on the tugboats once, until the unions called a strike, demanding more money for less work. "I couldn't understand that attitude at all," he said. "So I joined the Royal Marines."

Martin Johnson

Why silence is not always golden

Anyone who has watched sport on American television will know just how fortunate we are with the standard of our commentators. It is rare to tune into a broadcast on CBS or NBC without being left with the impression that the major qualification needed by US commentators is an ability to talk at a decibel level capable of breaking double glazed windows at ten paces. Or indeed that our friends from across the water have ever realised that it is occasionally permissible, and indeed sometimes preferable, to remain silent for a couple of seconds now and then.

It is also a fact that were we to share the Americans' total incomprehension that a single sporting contest can take place over five consecutive days, with every possibility of neither side actually winning, then there would be no such thing as one of the greatest commentating institutions: *Test Match Special.* Even people who wouldn't know a silly mid-off from a light meter tune in on a regular basis to a broadcast, which is arguably more interesting when rain has stopped play.

And after a word from Christopher Martin-Jenkins, it will be Fred Trueman.' Well, er, if you ask me, er, er, I mean, if, er, I can tell you, er, I, er, in, er, in my day, er, I mean, er, Alec Stewart, er, nice man, er, you know, don't get me wrong, er, lovely man, but, er, if you can tell me Christopher, er, what's going off out there, er, frankly, I just don't know. Simple as that.' 'Well, thanks Fred, and now we welcome World Service listeners...'

Many people choose to listen to *TMS* while watching television with the sound off, but while that at least keeps them up to date with Henry Blofeld's pigeon count, or the number of red buses Blowers has spotted since lunch, it also means missing out on the eloquent tones of Richie Benaud. Richie has an unrivalled knack of getting across, in a single word, the same message that takes his erstwhile Geoffrey Boycott half an hour.

Thus, when the slow motion replay reveals that a slip fielder has clearly cheated when claiming a catch, Richie might come up with something like: Mmmmmm'. Just occasionally he might feel inclined to expand with a: 'verrrry interesting, that', which, for Richie, almost constitutes an attack of verbal diarrhoea.

Test cricket can be a complex game, in which the spectator is heavily dependent on expert analysis. An example of this would be the final Test against South Africa at Headingley, during which the Pakistani umpire, Javed Akhtar, unilaterally decided to change the lbw law, with the effect that you can now only be given out leg before wicket if the ball has hit the bat first. It is important,

therefore, for Richie and his colleagues to convey this information to the viewer, along with the fact that catches are now only valid if the ball has missed the bat entirely.

Nowadays, however, Test cricket has hit upon a way of making commentators almost redundant. With the advent of the stump microphone, you no longer need a Benaud or a Boycott to tell you what's happening, you just listen to Alec Stewart behind the stumps. In days gone by, when Robert Croft had just bowled one a foot wide of off stump, without the remotest hint of spin, a ball which the batsman had studiously ignored, you would have had to rely on the commentator to tell you that this was a seriously unplayable delivery. Now, though, you get all the information you need from Alec. 'Bowwwwled Crofteeeee!'

"The defence," said Mark, with piercing insight that only a former player can truly possess, "is conspicuous by its lack of absence"

The players have also taken over from the commentators in letting the viewer know whether or not they are on the end of a poor umpiring decision - a trail first blazed by Chris Broad in the 1980s when he either required the assistance of a forklift truck to leave the field, or reduced the stumps to sawdust before bidding the umpire farewell.

Broad, a charming bloke as it happens, has now joined those who used to sit in judgment upon him, in the BBC TV commentary box. What's more, he has quickly discovered that batting in a Test match is a piece of Brian Johnston's chocolate cake next to commentating on one. Marvelling, as we all were last summer, at yet another breathtaking piece of fielding from the South African Jonty Rhodes, Chris told viewers that he had 'simply run out of expletives to describe this man'.

Mark Lawrenson is another professional sportsman to make the switch to the microphone, and he too managed to puzzle viewers during an early season football match. "The defence," said Mark, with piercing insight that only a former player can truly posses, "is conspicuous by its lack of absence." These gaffes - less of a hazard for the newspaper hack who has both time to correct himself, or has his bacon saved by a sub-editor - are known in the trade as 'Colemanballs', after David Coleman the pioneer and ultimately master of this delightful broadcasting art.

Coleman, who must have tonsils made of tungsten, is still going strong in his 70s, which means that he has had more time than most to drop himself in it. Just about every gaffe going has been attributed to Coleman, but I think it may have been Frank Bough who once informed *Sportsnight* viewers that it was 'time to go ringside, where Harry Commentator is your carpenter'.

Harry was a brilliant carpenter, as it happens, although his one Achilles heel - if you can call it that - was in letting you know where his emotions lay. Whenever Muhammad Ali fought, Harry was firmly in his corner, and when the ageing Ali downed George Foreman in Zaire, Harry screamed: "Oh my God, he's done it! He's won back the title at 32!" Nowadays, of course, as big George has demonstrated better than anyone, heavyweight boxers only reach their prime when they turn 60.

Given the odds stacked against Ali, this was a far more allowable wearing of the blinkers than we saw and heard from ITV's men during the World Cup. Brian Moore was almost up there alongside that Norwegian commentator ("Maggie Thatcher, Winston Churchill... your boys took a hell of a beating!"), while Kevin Keegan followed England's equaliser against Romania with "there's only one side gonna win this now, Brian". And in fact, in that Keegan didn't actually name which side, he may have been unfairly ridiculed.

Mind you, Kevin's patriotic prediction pales into insignificance next to Brian Clough during England's World Cup qualifier against Poland at Wembley in 1972. Poland, somewhat unsportingly it seemed to me at the time, appeared to be playing an octopus in goal, but Brian did not share the viewers' increasing nervousness. "Sit back, relax," said Cloughy. "The goalie's a clown." Later, after England had been eliminated by an octopus with a red nose, Cloughy yelled: "Don't blame England, don't blame Alf, I'm to blame, and [pointing his finger at the camera] you're to blame. We're all to blame." It was never quite clear what exactly he was ranting on about. A friend of mine recalled watching the game while his mother was doing the ironing at the back of the room. "Bloody silly man," she said. "What's it got to do with me?"

One of the most obvious things about commentating is that there are different decibel levels for different sports. Hence, if you adjusted the volume for Whispering Ted Lowe on one channel, then flicked over to the Grand Prix and Murray Walker on another, you'd be lucky to survive the experience without perforating an eardrum. Even in his quieter moments, Murray sounds like a man with his trousers on fire, and my favourite Murrayism (we all have our own) was when he yelled: "For once in my life, I am at a loss for words!"

Murray, of course, has become the all time doyen of Colemanballs, even more so than the great man himself. As a result of his combined decibel/gaffe count, Murray has been supplied with a string of James Hunt-type co-commentators,

who are charged with whispering quietly into the microphone, shortly after Murray has shrieked: "And nothing! I repeat nothing! Can stop Michael Schumacher now!" "...Er, actually Murray, I think if you look closely you'll find that heap of twisted metal embedded in the tyre wall used to be a nice red Ferrari."

Another commentator who relies on sheer volume to overpower the viewer is Sid Waddell, for whom the sight of some enormous, pint-swilling beer belly propelling what are known in the game as 'arrows', somehow - for reasons known only to Sid - conjures up vivid images of Agincourt. Sid's similes are also so bizarre that he must sit up all night preparing carefully scripted off-the-cuff remarks.

At the opposite end of the Waddell scale is golf's Peter Alliss, who has a feel for his art developed following an apprenticeship with the late Henry Longhurst, and a dry wit which seldom fails to enchant. A holed 50-yard putt which would have Murray yelling: "For once in my life I am lost for words!" might well be described by Alliss something like this: "Well, he'll be happy to get down in two here... it's looking pretty good, mind you... will it?...no it can't... can it?... surely not... it is you know. Cor blimey o'riley, it's almost cheating. That could be worth a bob or two come five o'clock tonight."

Sometimes a commentator will come out with a phrase that earns him immortality, as Kenneth Wolstenhome did in 1966 with "They think it's all over". Which made me think, listening to Fred on *Test Match Special* at Headingley, what it might be like if commentators swapped sports occasionally. "Now, then, er, that, er, Russian linesman, er, I mean, er, over the line? er, I don't know what's going off out there, Christopher, er, and, er, the boy wearing 10, er, whatisname, er, 'Urst, that's it, er, decent player, er, nice fellah, er, but, er, you know, in my day, er, that Nat Lofthouse, er, now 'ee could score ruddy 'at-tricks."

of the Year, on one of his most arduous assignments. •**Phil Shephard-Lewis**

1999
Day-by-Day
Fixture Planner

★28 Dec - 3 Jan	Darts	PDC World Championships. *Purfleet*
★2 Jan - 6 Jan	Cricket	Fifth Ansett Australia Test - **Australia V England.** *SCG Sydney, Australia*
★2 Jan - 10 Jan	Darts	Embassy World Darts Championship. *Lakeside Country Club, Frimley Green*
★8 Jan - 20 Jan	Football	FIFA Confederations Cup 1999. *Various, Mexico*
★10 Jan	Cricket	Opening Match Of The Carlton & United Series - **Australia V England.** *Gabba, Brisbane, Australia*
★14 Jan - 18 Jan	Games	1999 ESPN X Winter Games. *Crested Butte, USA*
★18 Jan - 31 Jan	Lawn Tennis	Australian Open Championships. *Melbourne Park Australia*
★23 Jan	Football	118th AXA Sponsored FA Cup Fourth Round. *Various*
★27 Jan	Football	Worthington Cup Semi Finals 1st Leg. *Various*
★31 Jan	American Football	Superbowl XXXIII. *Miami, USA*

English gymnast Andrew Atherton vaults during the XVI Commonwealth Games in Kuala Lumpur •**AFP** ★14/9/98

January **1999**

	Sport	Event	Location	Broadcast
Monday **4th**	Cricket	Fifth Ansett Australia Test, Australia V England - (Day 3)	*SCG, Sydney, Australia*	(BSkyB)
Tuesday **5th**	Cricket	Fifth Ansett Australia Test, Australia V England - (Day 4)	*SCG, Sydney, Australia*	(BSkyB)
Wednesday **6th**	Cricket Rugby Union	Fifth Ansett Australia Test, Australia V England - (Day 5) Allied Dunbar Premiership 1 - Wasps V Saracens	*SCG, Sydney, Australia* *London*	(BSkyB) (BSkyB)
Thursday **7th**	Table Tennis	ITTF Pro Tour Finals Begin	*Paris, France*	
Friday **8th**	Football	FIFA Confederations Cup - Brazil V France	*Guadalajara, Mexico*	
Saturday **9th**	American Football Football Football Lawn Tennis Football	AFC & NFC Divisional Play-off Games FIFA Confederations Cup - Bolivia V Egypt FIFA Confederations Cup - Mexico V Saudi Arabia Hyundai Hopman Cup Finishes Arsenal V Liverpool	*tbc, USA* *Mexico City, Mexico* *Mexico City, Mexico* *Perth, Australia* *Highbury, London*	(BSkyB/Ch5) (BSkyB) (BSkyB)
Sunday **10th**	American Football Basketball Cricket Darts Football Table Tennis	AFC & NFC Divisional Play-off Games Sainsbury's Classic Cola National Cup Finals Carlton & United Series - Australia V England Embassy World Championships Finish FIFA Confederations Cup - New Zealand V USA ITTF Pro Tour Finals Finish	*tbc, USA* *Sheffield Arena* *Gabba, Brisbane, Australia* *Lakeside Country Club* *Mexico City, Mexico* *Paris, France*	(BSkyB/Ch5) (BSkyB) (BSkyB) (BBC)

Notes

January **1999**

	Sport	Event	Location	Broadcast
Monday **11th**	**Cricket**	Carlton & United Series - England V Sri Lanka	*Gabba, Brisbane, Australia*	(BSkyB)
Tuesday **12th**	**Bobsleigh** **Football** **Football**	European Championships Begin FIFA Confederations Cup - Mexico V Egypt FIFA Confederations Cup - Saudi Arabia V Bolivia	*Winterberg, Germany* *Mexico City, Mexico* *Mexico City, Mexico*	(Eurosport)
Wednesday **13th**	**Football** **Football**	FIFA Confederations Cup - Brazil V USA FIFA Confederations Cup - France V New Zealand	*Guadalajara, Mexico* *Guadalajara, Mexico*	
Thursday **14th**	**Football** **Football** **Games** **Golf**	FIFA Confederations Cup - Mexico V Bolivia FIFA Confederations Cup - Saudi Arabia V Egypt 1999 ESPN Winter X Games Begin Alfred Dunhill South African PGA Championship Begins	*Mexico City, Mexico* *Mexico City, Mexico* *Crested Butte, USA* *Johannesburg, South Africa*	(BSkyB)
Friday **15th**	**Cricket** **Football** **Football** **Table Tennis**	Carlton & United Series - England V Australia FIFA Confederations Cup - Brazil V New Zealand FIFA Confederations Cup - France V USA English National Championships Begin	*MCG, Melbourne, Australia* *Guadalajara, Mexico* *Guadalajara, Mexico* *Bath*	(BSkyB)
Saturday **16th**	**Horse Racing** **Snooker** **Football**	The Victor Chandler Chase Nations Cup Begins Leeds United V Middlesbrough	*Ascot* *Telewest Arena, Newcastle* *Elland Rd, Leeds*	(BBC) (ITV) (BSkyB)
Sunday **17th**	**American Football** **Bobsleigh** **Cricket** **Football** **Football** **Golf** **Rallying** **Table Tennis**	AFC & NFC Championship Games European Championships Finish Carlton & United Series - England V Australia FIFA Confederations Cup - Semi Final FIFA Confederations Cup - Semi Final Alfred Dunhill South African PGA Championship Finishes Rallye Automobile Monte Carlo Begins English National Championships Finish	*tbc, USA* *Winterberg, Germany* *SCG, Sydney, Australia* *Guadalajara, Mexico* *Mexico City, Mexico* *Johannesburg, South Africa* *Monte Carlo, Monaco* *Bath*	(BSkyB/Ch5) (Eurosport) (BSkyB) (BSkyB)

Notes

	Sport	Event	Location	Broadcast
Monday 18th	**Games**	1999 ESPN Winter X Games Finish	*Crested Butte, USA*	
	Lawn Tennis	Australian Open Championships - (Day 1)	*Melbourne Park, Australia*	(BBC/BSkyB)
Tuesday 19th	**Cricket**	Carlton & United Series - England V Sri Lanka	*MCG, Melbourne, Australia*	(BSkyB)
	Football	FIFA Confederations Cup - Third Place Game	*Guadalajara, Mexico*	
	Lawn Tennis	Australian Open Championships - (Day 2)	*Melbourne Park, Australia*	(BBC/BSkyB)
Wednesday 20th	**Football**	FIFA Confederations Cup - Final	*Mexico City, Mexico*	
	Lawn Tennis	Australian Open Championships - (Day 3)	*Melbourne Park, Australia*	(BBC/BSkyB)
	Rallying	Rallye Automobile Monte Carlo Finishes	*Monte Carlo, Monaco*	
Thursday 21st	**Golf**	South African Open Begins	*Cape Town, South Africa*	(BSkyB)
	Lawn Tennis	Australian Open Championships - (Day 4)	*Melbourne Park, Australia*	(BBC/BSkyB)
	Snooker	Qualifying Tournament For Embassy World Championship Finishes	*Blackpool*	
Friday 22nd	**Ice Hockey**	49th NHL All Star Weekend Begins	*Tampa Bay, USA*	(BSkyB)
	Lawn Tennis	Australian Open Championships - (Day 5)	*Melbourne Park, Australia*	(BBC/BSkyB)
Saturday 23rd	**Cricket**	Carlton & United Series - England V Sri Lanka	*Adelaide Oval, Australia*	(BSkyB)
	Football	118th AXA Sponsored FA Cup Fourth Round	*Various*	(ITV/BSkyB)
	Lawn Tennis	Australian Open Championships - (Day 6)	*Melbourne Park, Australia*	(BBC/BSkyB)
	Golf	South African Open Finishes	*Cape Town, South Africa*	(BSkyB)
Sunday 24th	**Ice Hockey**	49th NHL All Star Weekend Finishes	*Tampa Bay, USA*	(BSkyB)
	Ice Skating	European Championships Begin	*Prague, Czech Republic*	(Eurosport)
	Lawn Tennis	Australian Open Championships - (Day 7)	*Melbourne Park, Australia*	(BBC/BSkyB)
	Snooker	Nations Cup Finishes	*Telewest Arena, Newcastle*	(ITV)

Notes

January **1999**

	Sport	Event	Location	Broadcast
Monday 25th	**Lawn Tennis** **Snooker** **Cricket**	Australian Open Championships - (Day 8) Regal Welsh Begins Carlton & United Series - England V Australia	*Melbourne Park, Australia* *Cardiff International Arena* *Adelaide Oval, Australia*	(BBC/BSkyB) (BSkyB) (BSkyB)
Tuesday 26th	**Lawn Tennis** **Yachting**	Australian Open Championships - (Day 9) 1999 World Sailing Championship Finish	*Melbourne Park, Australia* *Melbourne, Australia*	(BBC/BSkyB)
Wednesday 27th	**Football** **Lawn Tennis**	Worthington Cup Semi Finals 1st Leg Australian Open Championships - (Day 10)	*Various* *Melbourne Park, Australia*	(BSkyB/ITV) (BBC/BSkyB)
Thursday 28th	**Golf** **Lawn Tennis**	Heineken Classic Perth Begins Australian Open Championships - (Women's Singles Semi-finals)	*Perth, Australia* *Melbourne Park, Australia*	(BSkyB) (BBC/BSkyB)
Friday 29th	**Cricket** **Lawn Tennis**	Carlton & United Series - England V Sri Lanka Australian Open Championships - (Men's Singles Semi-finals)	*Waca, Perth, Australia* *Melbourne Park, Australia*	(BSkyB) (BBC/BSkyB)
Saturday 30th	**Cyclo-cross** **Lawn Tennis** **Football**	World Championships Begin Australian Open Championships - (Women's Singles Final) Arsenal V Chelsea	*Poprad, Slovakia* *Melbourne Park, Australia* *Highbury, London*	(BBC/BSkyB) (BSkyB)
Sunday 31st	**American Football** **Cyclo-cross** **Golf** **Ice Skating** **Lawn Tennis** **Snooker**	Superbowl XXXIII World Championships Finish Heineken Classic Perth Finishes European Championships Finishes Australian Open Championships - (Men's Singles Final) Regal Welsh Finishes	*Miami, USA* *Poprad, Slovakia* *Perth, Australia* *Prague, Czech Republic* *Melbourne Park, Australia* *Cardiff International Arena*	(BSkyB/Ch5) (BSkyB) (Eurosport) (BBC/BSkyB) (BSkyB)

Notes

125

Saga World Indoor Bowls Championship at the Guildhall in Preston •**Russell Cheyne** ★23/1/98

★1 Feb - 14 Feb	**Skiing - Alpine**	World Championships. *Vail, USA*
★2 Feb - 14 Feb	**Bobsleigh**	World Championships. *Cortina D'Ampezzo, Italy*
★6 Feb	**Rugby Union**	Ireland V France. *Lansdowne Rd, Dublin, Ireland*
★6 Feb	**Rugby Union**	Scotland V Wales. *Murrayfield, Edinburgh*
★7 Feb - 14 Feb	**Snooker**	Benson & Hedges Masters. *Wembley Conference Centre*
★10 Feb	**Cricket**	Carlton & United Series First Final. *SCG, Sydney, Australia*
★11 Feb - 14 Feb	**Basketball**	NBA All Star Weekend. *Philadelphia, USA*
★12 Feb	**Cricket**	Carlton & United Series Second Final. *MCG, Melbourne, Australia*
★13 Feb	**Football**	118th AXA Sponsored FA Cup Fifth Round. *Various*
★14 Feb	**Cricket**	Carlton & United Series Third Final. *MCG, Melbourne, Australia*
★17 Feb	**Football**	Worthington Cup Semi Finals 2nd Leg. *Various*
★20 Feb	**Rugby Union**	England V Scotland. *Twickenham, London*
★20 Feb	**Rugby Union**	Wales V Ireland. *Wembley, London*
★22 Feb - 28 Feb	**Lawn Tennis**	Guardian Direct Cup. *Battersea Park, London*
★24 Feb - 28 Feb	**Golf**	World Golf Championships- The Anderson Consulting World Golf Matchplay. *Carlsbad, USA*

February 1999

	Sport	Event	Location	Broadcast
Monday 1st	Skiing - Alpine	World Championships Begin	*Vail, Usa*	(Eurosport)
Tuesday 2nd	Bobsleigh	World Championships Begin	*Cortina D'ampezzo, Italy*	(Eurosport)
Wednesday 3rd	Cricket	Carlton & United Series - England V Sri Lanka	*SCG, Sydney, Australia*	(BSkyB)
Thursday 4th	Golf	Malaysian Open Begins	*Kuala Lumpur, Malaysia*	(BSkyB)
Friday 5th	Badminton	Liverpool Victoria National Championships Begin	*Burgess Hill*	
	Cricket	Carlton & United Series - England V Australia	*SCG, Sydney, Australia*	(BSkyB)
Saturday 6th	Rugby Union	Allied Dunbar Premiership 1 - NEC Harlequins V Leicester Tigers	*Twickenham, London*	(BSkyB)
	Rugby Union	Lloyds TSB Five Nations - Ireland V France	*Lansdowne Rd., Dublin, Ireland*	(BBC)
	Rugby Union	Lloyds TSB Five Nations - Scotland V Wales	*Murrayfield, Edinburgh*	(BBC)
	Football	Aston Villa V Blackburn Rovers	*Villa Park, Birmingham*	(BSkyB)
Sunday 7th	American Football	AFC/NFC Pro Bowl	*Honolulu, USA*	(BSkyB/Ch5)
	Badminton	Liverpool Victoria National Championships Finish	*Burgess Hill*	
	Golf	Malaysian Open Finishes	*Kuala Lumpur, Malaysia*	(BSkyB)
	Rugby Union	Allied Dunbar Premiership 1 - Wasps V Bath	*London*	(BSkyB)
	Snooker	Benson & Hedges Masters Begin	*Wembley Conference Centre*	(BBC)

Notes

	Sport	Event	Location	Broadcast
Monday 8th	**Lawn Tennis**	Sybase Open Begins	*San Jose, USA*	(Eurosport)
Tuesday 9th				
Wednesday 10th	**Cricket**	Carlton & United Series First Final	*SCG, Sydney, Australia*	(BSkyB)
Thursday 11th	**Basketball**	NBA All Star Weekend Begins	*Philadelphia, USA*	(BSkyB)
	Golf	Dubai Desert Classic Begins	*Dubai, United Arab Emirates*	(BSkyB)
Friday 12th	**Cricket**	Carlton & United Series Second Final	*MCG, Melbourne, Australia*	(BSkyB)
	Rallying	International Swedish Rally Begins	*Karlstad, Sweden*	
Saturday 13th	**Football**	118th AXA Sponsored FA Cup Fifth Round	*Various*	(BSkyB/ITV)
	Football	Manchester United V Arsenal	*Old Trafford, Manchester*	(BSkyB)
	Swimming	FINA Swimming World Cup Begins	*Glasgow*	
Sunday 14th	**Athletics**	Bupa Indoor Grand Prix - Ricoh Tour	*NIA, Birmingham*	(Ch4)
	Basketball	NBA All Star Weekend Finishes	*Philadelphia, USA*	(BSkyB)
	Bobsleigh	World Championships Finish	*Cortina D'ampezzo, Italy*	(Eurosport)
	Cricket	Carlton & United Series Third Final	*MCG, Melbourne, Australia*	(BSkyB)
	Golf	Dubai Desert Classic Finishes	*Dubai, United Arab Emirates*	(BSkyB)
	Lawn Tennis	Sybase Open Finishes	*San Jose, USA*	(Eurosport)
	Motor Racing	1999 NASCAR Winston Cup Series - Daytona 500	*Daytona International Speedway, USA*	(BSkyB)
	Rallying	International Swedish Rally Finishes	*Karlstad, Sweden*	
	Skiing - Alpine	World Championships Finish	*Vail, USA*	(Eurosport)
	Snooker	Benson & Hedges Masters Finish	*Wembley Conference Centre*	(BBC)
	Swimming	FINA Swimming World Cup Finishes	*Glasgow*	

February **1999**

Sport	Event	Location	Broadcast

Monday 15th

Sport	Event	Location	Broadcast
Snooker	Regal Scottish Open Begins	*Aberdeen Exhibition & Conference Centre*	(BSkyB)

Tuesday 16th

Wednesday 17th

Sport	Event	Location	Broadcast
Football	Worthington Cup Semi Finals 2nd Leg	*Various*	(BSkyB/ITV)
Golf	Qatar Masters Begins	*Doha, Qatar*	(BSkyB)

Thursday 18th

Sport	Event	Location	Broadcast
Badminton	1998 World Grand Prix Finals Begin	*Jakarta, Indonesia*	

Friday 19th

Saturday 20th

Sport	Event	Location	Broadcast
Golf	Qatar Masters Finishes	*Doha, Qatar*	(BSkyB)
Rugby Union	Lloyds TSB Five Nations - England V Scotland	*Twickenham, London*	(BSkyB)
Rugby Union	Lloyds TSB Five Nations - Wales V Ireland	*Wembley Stadium*	(BBC)
Football	Coventry City V Manchester United	*Highfield Rd, Coventry*	(BSkyB)

Sunday 21st

Sport	Event	Location	Broadcast
Badminton	1998 World Grand Prix Finals Finish	*Jakarta, Indonesia*	
Snooker	Regal Scottish Open Finishes	*Aberdeen Exhibition & Conference Centre*	(BSkyB)

Notes

February 1999

	Sport	Event	Location	Broadcast
Monday **22nd**	**Lawn Tennis**	Guardian Direct Cup - (Day 1)	*Battersea Park, London*	(BBC/Eurosport)
Tuesday **23rd**	**Lawn Tennis**	Guardian Direct Cup - (Day 2)	*Battersea Park, London*	(BBC/Eurosport)
Wednesday **24th**	**Basketball** **Golf** **Lawn Tennis**	England V Belarus The Anderson Consulting World Golf Matchplay - (Day 1) Guardian Direct Cup - (Day 3)	*Sheffield Arena* *Carlsbad, USA* *Battersea Park, London*	(BSkyB) (BBC/Eurosport)
Thursday **25th**	**Golf** **Lawn Tennis** **Snooker**	The Anderson Consulting World Golf Matchplay - (Day 2) Guardian Direct Cup - (Day 4) Liverpool Victoria Charity Challenge Begins	*Carlsbad, USA* *Battersea Park, London* *Assembly Rooms, Derby*	(BSkyB) (BBC/Eurosport) (ITV)
Friday **26th**	**Golf** **Lawn Tennis** **Rallying**	The Anderson Consulting World Golf Matchplay - (Day 3) Guardian Direct Cup - (Day 5) Safari Rally Kenya Begins	*Carlsbad, USA* *Battersea Park, London* *Nairobi, Kenya*	(BSkyB) (BBC/Eurosport)
Saturday **27th**	**Basketball** **Golf** **Lawn Tennis** **Football**	Dairylea Dunkers All Star Game The Anderson Consulting World Golf Matchplay - (Day 4) Guardian Direct Cup - (Day 6) Chelsea V Liverpool	*Newcastle* *Carlsbad, USA* *Battersea Park, London* *Stamford Bridge, London*	(BSkyB) (BSkyB) (BBC/Eurosport) (BSkyB)
Sunday **28th**	**Golf** **Lawn Tennis** **Rallying** **Snooker**	The Anderson Consulting World Golf Matchplay - (Final) Guardian Direct Cup - (Final) Safari Rally Kenya Finishes Liverpool Victoria Charity Challenge Finishes	*Carlsbad, USA* *Battersea Park, London* *Nairobi, Kenya* *Assembly Rooms, Derby*	(BSkyB) (BBC/Eurosport) (ITV)

Notes

Gareth Thomas tackles Gary Armstrong in the Five Nations clash between Wales and Scotland at Wembley Stadium •**Russell Cheyne** ★8/3/98

★3 Mar	**Football**	UEFA Champions League Quarter Finals 1st Leg. *TBC*
★5 Mar - 7 Mar	**Athletics**	World Indoor Championships. *Maebashi, Japan*
★5 Mar	**Rugby League**	Start Of JJB Super League. *Various*
★6 Mar	**Football**	118th AXA Sponsored FA Cup Sixth Round. *Various*
★6 Mar	**Rugby Union**	France V Wales. *Parc De Princes, Paris, France*
★6 Mar	**Rugby Union**	Ireland V England. *Lansdowne Rd, Dublin, Ireland*
★9 Mar - 14 Mar	**Badminton**	Yonex All England Championships. *NIA, Birmingham*
★16 Mar - 18 Mar	**Horse Racing**	Cheltenham Festival. *Cheltenham*
★17 Mar	**Football**	UEFA Champions League Quarter Finals 2nd Leg. *TBC*
★20 Mar	**Rugby Union**	England V France. *Twickenham, London*
★20 Mar	**Rugby Union**	Scotland V Ireland. *Murrayfield, Edinburgh*
★21 Mar	**Football**	Worthington Cup Final. *Wembley, London*
★21 Mar - 28 Mar	**Ice Skating**	World Championships. *Helsinki, Finland*
★26 Mar - 28 Mar	**Rugby Union**	Credit Suisse First Boston Hong Kong Rugby Sevens. *Hong Kong*
★27 Mar - 28 Mar	**Athletics**	IAAF 27th World Cross Country Championships. *Belfast*
★27 Mar	**Football**	England V Poland *Wembley London*
★27 Mar	**Football**	Northern Ireland V Germany. *Windsor Park, Belfast*
★27 Mar	**Football**	Scotland V Bosnia & Herzegovina. *TBC*
★31 Mar	**Football**	Moldova V Northern Ireland . *Kishinev, Moldova*
★31 Mar	**Football**	Scotland V Czech Republic. *TBC*
★31 Mar	**Football**	Switzerland V Wales. *TBC, Switzerland*

March 1999

Sport	Event	Location	Broadcast
Monday 1st			
Lawn Tennis	Evert Cup Begins	*Indian Wells, USA*	(Eurosport)
Tuesday 2nd			
Football	UEFA Cup Quarter Finals 1st Leg	*Various, tbc*	(BBC/Ch5)
Wednesday 3rd			
Football	UEFA Champions League Quarter Finals 1st Leg	*Various, tbc*	(ITV)
Thursday 4th			
Football	European Cup Winners Cup Quarter Finals 1st Leg	*Various, tbc*	(Ch5)
Golf	Portuguese Algarve Open Begins	*tbc, Portugal*	(BSkyB)
Friday 5th			
Athletics	World Indoor Championships Begin	*Maebashi, Japan*	(BBC/Eurosport)
Rugby League	JJB Super League Begins	*Various*	(BSkyB)
Saturday 6th			
Football	118th AXA Sponsored FA Cup Sixth Round	*Various*	(ITV/BSkyB)
Rugby Union	Lloyds TSB Five Nations - France V Wales	*Parc De Princes, Paris, France*	(BBC)
Rugby Union	Lloyds TSB Five Nations - Ireland V England	*Lansdowne Road, Dublin, Ireland*	(BBC)
Rugby Union	Scotland V Italy	*Murrayfield, Edinburgh*	(BBC)
Football	Liverpool V Manchester United	*Anfield, Liverpool*	(BSkyB)
Sunday 7th			
Athletics	World Indoor Championships Finish	*Maebashi, Japan*	(BBC/Eurosport)
Golf	Portuguese Algarve Open Finishes	*tbc, Portugal*	(BSkyB)
Motor Racing	Qantas Australian Grand Prix	*Albert Park, Melbourne, Australia*	(ITV)

Notes

March **1999**

	Sport	Event	Location	Broadcast
Monday 8th	**Bowls(lawn/green)**	British Isles Indoor Bowls Championship Begins	*Bournemouth*	
	Lawn Tennis	Mercedes Super 9 - Newsweek Champions Cup Begins	*Indian Wells, USA*	(Eurosport)
	Snooker	China International Begins	*tbc, PR China*	
Tuesday 9th	**Badminton**	Yonex All England Championships Begin	*NIA, Birmingham*	(BSkyB)
Wednesday 10th	**Skiing - Alpine**	Cafe De Colombia Alpine World Cup Finals Begin	*Sierra Nevada, Spain*	(Eurosport)
Thursday 11th	**Golf**	Turespana Masters Begins	*tbc, Spain*	(BSkyB)
	Table Tennis	ITTF Pro Tour - English Open Begins	*Hopton-On-Sea*	
Friday 12th	**Bowls(lawn/green)**	British Isles Indoor Bowls Championship Finishes	*Bournemouth*	
Saturday 13th	**Basketball**	Uni-ball Trophy Final	*NEC, Birmingham*	(BSkyB)
	Rugby Union	Allied Dunbar Premiership 1 - Northampton Saints V Leicester Tigers	*Northampton*	(BSkyB)
	Football	Everton V Arsenal	*Goodison Park, Liverpool*	(BSkyB)
Sunday 14th	**Badminton**	Yonex All England Championships Finals	*NIA, Birmingham*	(BSkyB)
	Golf	Turespana Masters Begins	*tbc, Spain*	(BSkyB)
	Lawn Tennis	Evert Cup Finishes	*Indian Wells, USA*	(Eurosport)
	Lawn Tennis	Mercedes Super 9 - Newsweek Champions Cup Finishes	*Indian Wells, USA*	(Eurosport)
	Skiing - Alpine	Cafe De Colombia Alpine World Cup Finals Finish	*Sierra Nevada, Spain*	(Eurosport)
	Snooker	China International Finishes	*tbc, Pr China*	
	Table Tennis	ITTF Pro Tour - English Open Finishes	*Hopton-On-Sea*	

Notes

March 1999

Sport	Event	Location	Broadcast

Monday

15th

Tuesday

16th

| **Football** | UEFA Cup Quarter Finals 2nd Leg | *Various, tbc* | (BBC/Ch5) |
| **Horse Racing** | The Smurfit Champion Hurdle Challenge Trophy | *Cheltenham* | (Ch4) |

Wednesday

17th

Football	UEFA Champions League Quarter Finals 2nd Leg	*Various, tbc*	(ITV)
Horse Racing	The Queen Mother Champion Steeple Chase	*Cheltenham*	(Ch4)
Squash	British Open Begins	*Birmingham*	

Thursday

18th

Football	European Cup Winners Cup Quarter Finals 2nd Leg	*Various, tbc*	(Ch5)
Golf	Moroccan Open Begins	*Agadir, Morocco*	(BSkyB)
Horse Racing	The Tote Cheltenham Gold Cup Steeple Chase	*Cheltenham*	(Ch4)
Lawn Tennis	Mercedes Super 9 - The Lipton Championships Begin	*Key Biscayne, USA*	(Eurosport)

Friday

19th

| **Speed Skating** | Short Track World Championships Begin | *Sofia, Bulgaria* | |

Saturday

20th

Rugby Union	Italy V Wales	*tbc, Italy*	(BBC)
Rugby Union	Lloyds TSB Five Nations - England V France	*Twickenham, London*	(BSkyB)
Rugby Union	Lloyds TSB Five Nations - Scotland V Ireland	*Murrayfield, Edinburgh*	(BBC)
Football	Aston Villa V Chelsea	*Villa Park, Birmingham*	(BSkyB)

Sunday

21st

Football	Worthington Cup Final	*Wembley Stadium*	(ITV/BSkyB)
Golf	Moroccan Open Finishes	*Agadir, Morocco*	(BSkyB)
Motor Racing	China Grand Prix	*Zhuhai, PR China*	(ITV)
Rallying	Rallye Du Portugal Begins	*Oporto, Portugal*	
Speed Skating	Short Track World Championship Finishes	*Sofia, Bulgaria*	
Ice Skating	World Championships Begin	*Helsinki, Finland*	(BBC/Eurosport)

Notes

	Sport	Event	Location	Broadcast
Monday 22nd				
Tuesday 23rd	Snooker	Benson and Hedges Irish Masters Begins	*County Kildare, Ireland*	(BSkyB)
Wednesday 24th	**Rallying**	Rallye Du Portugal Finishes	*Oporto, Portugal*	
Thursday 25th	Golf	Madeira Island Open Begins	*Madeira, Portugal*	(BSkyB)
	Golf	The Players Championship Begins	*Ponte Vedra Beach, USA*	(BSkyB)
Friday 26th	**Rugby Union**	Credit Suisse First Boston Hong Kong Rugby Sevens Begin	*Hong Kong, Hong Kong*	(BSkyB)
Saturday 27th	Athletics	World Cross Country Championships Begin	*Belfast*	(BBC/Eurosport)
	Football	England V Poland	*Wembley Stadium*	(BSkyB)
	Football	Northern Ireland V Germany	*Windsor Park, Belfast*	(BBC)
	Football	Scotland V Bosnia & Herzegovina	*tbc*	(BSkyB)
	Rowing	Head Of The River	*London*	
	Rugby Union	Allied Dunbar Premiership 1 - Leicester Tigers V Wasps	*Leicester*	(BSkyB)
Sunday 28th	Athletics	World Cross Country Championships Finish	*Belfast*	(BBC/Eurosport)
	Golf	Madeira Island Open Finishes	*Madeira, Portugal*	(BSkyB)
	Golf	The Players Championship Finishes	*Ponte Vedra Beach, USA*	(BSkyB)
	Ice Skating	World Championships Finish	*Helsinki, Finland*	(BBC/Eurosport)
	Lawn Tennis	Mercedes Super 9 - The Lipton Championships Finish	*Key Biscayne, USA*	(Eurosport)
	Rugby Union	Credit Suisse First Boston Hong Kong Rugby Sevens Finish	*Hong Kong, Hong Kong*	(BSkyB)
	Skiing - Alpine	English Championships Begin	*tbc*	
	Snooker	Benson and Hedges Irish Masters Finishes	*County Kildare, Ireland*	(BSkyB)
	Squash	British Open Finishes	*Birmingham*	

	Sport	Event	Location	Broadcast
Monday 29th	**Snooker**	Embassy World Championships Final Qualifying Round Begins	*Telford International Centre*	
Tuesday 30th				
Wednesday 31st	**Football** **Football** **Football**	Moldova V Northern Ireland Scotland V Czech Republic Switzerland V Wales	*Kishinev, Moldova* *tbc* *Zurich, Switzerland*	(BBC) (BSkyB) (BBC)
Thursday 1st	**Swimming**	World Short Course Championships Begin	*Hong Kong, Hong Kong*	(BBC/Eurosport)
Friday 2nd	**Curling** **Lawn Tennis** **Skiing - Alpine** **Snooker**	Ford World Curling Championships Begin Davis Cup By NEC Round 1 - Great Britain V USA (First Day Singles) English Championships Finish Embassy World Championships Final Qualifying Round Finishes	*New Brunswick, Canada* *tbc* *tbc* *Telford International Centre*	 (BBC)
Saturday 3rd	**Football** **Greyhound Racing** **Ice Hockey** **Lawn Tennis** **Rowing** **Rugby Union** **Football**	FIFA World Youth Championships Begin Grand National Sekonda Superleague Play-off Championships - Semi Finals Davis Cup By NEC Round 1 - Great Britain V USA (Middle Day Doubles) Oxford V Cambridge Boat Race Allied Dunbar Premiership 1 - Bath V Leicester Tigers Liverpool V Everton	*Various, Nigeria* *Wimbledon, London* *Manchester* *tbc* *River Thames* *Bath* *Anfield, Liverpool*	 (BSkyB) (BBC) (BBC) (BSkyB) (BSkyB)
Sunday 4th	**Ice Hockey** **Lawn Tennis** **Rugby Union** **Snooker** **Swimming**	Sekonda Superleague Play-off Championships - Final Davis Cup By NEC Round 1 - Great Britain V USA (Last Day Singles) Allied Dunbar Premiership 1 - Newcastle Falcons V NEC Harlequins British Open Begins World Short Course Championships Finish	*Manchester* *tbc* *Newcastle* *Plymouth Pavilions* *Hong Kong, Hong Kong*	(BSkyB) (BBC) (BSkyB) (BSkyB) (BBC/Eurosport)
Notes				

The London Marathon •**Russell Cheyne** ★26/4/98

★2 Apr - 4 Apr	**Lawn Tennis**	Davis Cup World Group Round 1 - Great Britain V USA. *TBC*
★3 Apr	**Rowing**	Oxford V Cambridge Boat Race. *River Thames, London*
★7 Apr	**Football**	UEFA Champions League Semi Finals 1st Leg. *TBC*.
★8 Apr - 11 Apr	**Golf**	The Masters. *Augusta, USA*
★10 Apr	**Football**	118th AXA Sponsored FA Cup Semi Finals. *Various*
★10 Apr	**Horse Racing**	The Martell Grand National Steeple Chase. *Aintree*
★10 Apr	**Rugby Union**	France V Scotland. *Parc De Princes, Paris, France*
★11 Apr	**Rugby Union**	Wales V England. *Wembley, London*
★13 Apr	**Cricket**	County Championship Begins. *Various*
★17 Apr - 3 May	**Snooker**	Embassy World Championships. *Crucible Theatre, Sheffield*
★18 Apr	**Athletics**	Flora London Marathon. *London*
★21 Apr	**Football**	UEFA Champions League Semi Finals 2nd Leg. *TBC*
★26 Apr - 9 May	**Table Tennis**	45th World Championships. *Belgrade, Yugoslavia*

April 1999

	Sport	Event	Location	Broadcast
Monday **5th**	Football	Newcastle United V Tottenham Hotspur	*St James' Park, Newcastle*	(BSkyB)
Tuesday **6th**	Football Greyhound Racing	UEFA Cup Semi Finals 1st Leg Blue Riband(Final)	*tbc* *Wembley Stadium*	(BBC/Ch5)
Wednesday **7th**	Football	UEFA Champions League Semi Finals 1st Leg	*tbc*	(ITV)
Thursday **8th**	Football Golf	European Cup Winners Cup Semi Finals 1st Leg The Masters (Round 1)	*tbc* *Augusta National, USA*	(Ch5) (BBC)
Friday **9th**	Golf	The Masters (Round 2)	*Augusta National, USA*	(BBC)
Saturday **10th**	Football Golf Horse Racing Rugby Union Rugby Union Football	118th AXA Sponsored FA Cup Semi Finals The Masters (Round 3) The Martell Grand National Steeple Chase Ireland V Italy Lloyds TSB Five Nations - France V Scotland Tottenham Hotspur V Arsenal	*Various* *Augusta National, USA* *Aintree* *Lansdowne Rd., Dublin, Ireland* *Parc De Princes, Paris, France* *White Hart Lane, London*	(ITV/BSkyB) (BBC) (BBC) (BBC) (BBC) (BSkyB)
Sunday **11th**	Curling Golf Motor Racing Rugby Union Snooker	Ford World Curling Championships Finish The Masters (Round 4) Brazilian Grand Prix Lloyds TSB Five Nations - Wales V England British Open Finishes	*New Brunswick, Canada* *Augusta National, USA* *Interlagos, Sao Paulo, Brazil* *Wembley Stadium* *Plymouth Pavilions*	 (BBC) (ITV) (BBC) (BSkyB)

Notes

April **1999**

Sport	Event	Location	Broadcast

Monday 12th

Tuesday 13th

Cricket	County Championship Begins	*Various*	(BSkyB)

Wednesday 14th

Thursday 15th

Friday 16th

Saturday 17th

American Football	Start Of 1999 NFL Europe League Season	*Various, tbc*	(BSkyB)
Cricket	National One-day League Begins	*Various*	(BSkyB)
Horse Racing	The Stakis Casinos Scottish Grand National	*Ayr*	(Ch4)
Lawn Tennis	KB Fed Cup - 1st Round Begins	*tbc*	
Snooker	Embassy World Championships Begin	*Crucible Theatre, Sheffield*	(BBC)
Football	West Ham United V Derby County	*Upton Park, London*	(BSkyB)

Sunday 18th

Athletics	Flora London Marathon	*London*	(BBC)
Lawn Tennis	KB Fed Cup - 1st Round Finishes	*tbc*	
Rallying	Rallye De Espana Begins	*Lloret De Mar, Spain*	
Motor Cycling	Malaysian Grand Prix	*Sepang*	(Eurosport)

Notes

139

April 1999

Sport	Event	Location	Broadcast

Monday 19th

Sport	Event	Location	Broadcast
Athletics	Boston Marathon	*Hopkinton To Boston, USA*	(BSkyB)
Lawn Tennis	Mercedes Super 9 - Monte Carlo Open Begins	*Monte Carlo, Monaco*	(Eurosport)

Tuesday 20th

Sport	Event	Location	Broadcast
Football	European Championships For Under 16's Begin	*Various, Czech Republic*	
Football	UEFA Cup Semi Finals 2nd Leg	*tbc*	(BBC/Ch5)

Wednesday 21st

Sport	Event	Location	Broadcast
Football	UEFA Champions League Semi Finals 2nd Leg	*tbc*	(ITV)
Ice Hockey	Start Of Stanley Cup Play-offs	*tbc, USA*	(BSkyB)
Rallying	Rallye De Espana Finishes	*Lloret De Mar, Spain*	

Thursday 22nd

Sport	Event	Location	Broadcast
Football	European Cup Winners Cup Semi Finals 2nd Leg	*tbc*	(Ch5)
Golf	Peugeot Spanish Open Begins	*tbc, Spain*	(BSkyB)

Friday 23rd

Sport	Event	Location	Broadcast
Boxing	ABA Senior Championships - Finals	*Barnsley Metrodome*	

Saturday 24th

Sport	Event	Location	Broadcast
Equestrian	World Cup Show Jumping Final Begins	*Gothenburg, Sweden*	(Eurosport)
Football	FIFA World Youth Championships Finish	*Various, Nigeria*	
Horse Racing	The 43rd Whitbread Gold Cup Handicap Steeple Chase	*Sandown Park*	(Ch4)
Judo	British Open Championships Begin	*NIA, Birmingham*	
Football	Leeds United V Manchester United	*Elland Rd, Leeds*	(BSkyB)

Sunday 25th

Sport	Event	Location	Broadcast
Equestrian	World Cup Show Jumping Final Finishes	*Gothenburg, Sweden*	(Eurosport)
Golf	Peugeot Spanish Open Finishes	*tbc, Spain*	(BSkyB)
Judo	British Open Championships Finish	*NIA, Birmingham*	
Lawn Tennis	Mercedes Super 9 - Monte Carlo Open Finishes	*Monte Carlo, Monaco*	(Eurosport)
Rugby Union	Allied Dunbar Premiership 1 - Saracens V NEC Harlequins	*Watford*	(BSkyB)
Motor Cycling	Japanese Grand Prix	*Twin Ring Motegi*	(Eurosport)

Notes

April/May **1999**

Sport	Event	Location	Broadcast

Monday 26th

Sport	Event	Location	Broadcast
Table Tennis	45th World Championships Begin	*Belgrade, Yugoslavia*	

Tuesday 27th

Lawn Tennis	BMW Open 1999 Begins	*Munich, Germany*	

Wednesday 28th

Games	The Womens Global Challenge Begins	*Various, USA*	

Thursday 29th

Golf	The 56th FIAT And FILA Italian Open Begins	*Turin, Italy*	(BSkyB)

Friday 30th

Basketball	Budweiser Championship Finals Begin	*Wembley Arena*	(BSkyB)

Saturday 1st

Horse Racing	The Sagitta 2000 Guineas Stakes	*Newmarket*	(Ch4)
Horse Racing	VISA Triple Crown Challenge - Kentucky Derby	*Louisville, USA*	
Ice Hockey	World Championships Begin	*Oslo, Hamar, Lillehammer, Norway*	(Eurosport)
Rugby League	Silk Cut Challenge Cup Final	*Wembley, London*	(BBC)
Rugby Union	Allied Dunbar Premiership 1 - Newcastle Falcons V Leicester Tigers	*Newcastle*	(BSkyB)
Football	Manchester United V Aston Villa	*Old Trafford, Manchester*	(BSkyB)

Sunday 2nd

Basketball	Budweiser Championship Finals Finish	*Wembley Arena*	(BSkyB)
Games	The Womens Global Challenge Finishes	*Various, USA*	
Golf	The 56th FIAT And FILA Italian Open Finishes	*Turin, Italy*	(BSkyB)
Horse Racing	The Sagitta 1000 Guineas Stakes	*Newmarket*	(Ch4)
Motor Racing	San Marino Grand Prix	*Imola, Italy*	(ITV)

Notes

Helen Duncan competes in the 200m backstroke at the Commonwealth Games •AP ★31/7/98

★1 May	**Horse Racing**	The Sagitta 2000 Guineas Stakes. *Newmarket*
★1 May	**Rugby League**	Silk Cut Challenge Cup Final. *Wembley, London*
★2 May	**Horse Racing**	The Sagitta 1000 Guineas Stakes. *Newmarket*
★12 May	**Football**	UEFA Cup Final. *Moscow, Russia*
★13 May - 16 May	**Golf**	Benson & Hedges International. *The Oxfordshire, Thame*
★14 May	**Cricket**	Cricket World Cup - England V Sri Lanka. *Lords, London*
★15 May	**Rugby Union**	Tetley's Bitter Cup Final. *Twickenham, London*
★16 May	**Football**	End Of The 1998/1999 Premiership Season. *Various*
★18 May	**Cricket**	Cricket World Cup - England V Kenya. *Canterbury*
★19 May	**Football**	European Cup Winners Cup Final. *Villa Park, Birmingham*
★22 May	**Football**	118th AXA Sponsored FA Cup Final. *Wembley, London*
★23 May - 29 May	**Cycling**	The Prutour. *Various*
★25 May	**Cricket**	Cricket World Cup - England V Zimbabwe. *Trent Bridge, Nottingham*
★26 May	**Football**	UEFA Champions League Final. *Nou Camp, Barcelona, Spain*
★28 May - 31 May	**Golf**	Volvo PGA Championship. *Wentworth*
★29 May	**Rugby Union**	Middlesex Sevens. *Twickenham, London*

May **1999**

Sport	Event	Location	Broadcast

Monday 3rd

Lawn Tennis	BMW Open 1999 Finishes	*Munich, Germany*	
Lawn Tennis	Mercedes Super 9 - Licher German Open Begins	*Hamburg, Germany*	(Eurosport)
Snooker	Embassy World Championships Finish	*Crucible Theatre, Sheffield*	(BBC)

Tuesday 4th

Cricket	Natwest Trophy 1st Round - Gloucestershire V Yorkshire	*Bristol*	(Ch4)

Wednesday 5th

Thursday 6th

Equestrian	Mitsubishi Motors Badminton Horse Trials Begin	*Badminton*	(BBC)

Friday 7th

Football	European Championships For Under 16's Finish	*Various, Czech Republic*	

Saturday 8th

Boxing	ABA Junior Championships	*Aston Villa Leisure Centre*	
Horse Racing	VISA Triple Crown Challenge - Preakness Stakes	*White Hart Lane, London*	(BSkyB)

Sunday 9th

Equestrian	Mitsubishi Motors Badminton Horse Trials Finish	*Badminton*	(BBC)
Lawn Tennis	Mercedes Super 9 - Licher German Open Finishes	*Hamburg, Germany*	(Eurosport)
Rallying	Rallye De France - Tour De Corse Begins	*Ajaccio, France*	
Table Tennis	45th World Championships Finish	*Belgrade, Yugoslavia*	
Motor Cycling	Spanish Grand Prix	*Jerez de la Frontera*	(Eurosport)

Notes

May 1999

	Sport	Event	Location	Broadcast
Monday 10th	Badminton	6th Sudirman Cup Begins	*Copenhagen, Denmark*	
	Lawn Tennis	Mercedes Super 9 - TTIMCup Begins	*Rome, Italy*	(Eurosport)
Tuesday 11th	Polo	Prince Of Wales Trophy Begins	*Windsor*	
Wednesday 12th	Football	UEFA Cup - Final	*Luzhniki Stadium, Moscow, Russia*	(BBC)
	Rallying	Rallye De France - Tour De Corse Finishes	*Ajaccio, France*	
Thursday 13th	Equestrian	British Nations Cup Begins	*Windsor*	(BBC)
	Golf	Benson & Hedges International (Round 1)	*Oxfordshire, Thame*	(BBC)
Friday 14th	Cricket	Cricket World Cup - England V Sri Lanka	*Lords*	(BSkyB)
	Golf	Benson & Hedges International (Round 2)	*Oxfordshire, Thame*	(BBC)
Saturday 15th	Badminton	6th Sudirman Cup Finishes	*Copenhagen, Denmark*	
	Cricket	Cricket World Cup - India V South Africa	*Hove*	(BSkyB)
	Cricket	Cricket World Cup - Zimbabwe V Kenya	*Taunton*	
	Cycling	Giro D'Italia Begins	*Various, Italy*	(Eurosport)
	Golf	Benson & Hedges International (Round 3)	*Oxfordshire, Thame*	(BBC)
	Rugby Union	Tetley's Bitter Cup Final	*Twickenham, London*	(BSkyB)
Sunday 16th	Badminton	11th World Championships Begin	*Copenhagen, Denmark*	
	Cricket	Cricket World Cup - Australia V Scotland	*Worcester*	(BBC)
	Cricket	Cricket World Cup - West Indies V Pakistan	*Bristol*	
	Equestrian	British Nations Cup Finishes	*Windsor*	(BBC)
	Football	End of The 1998/1999 Carling Premiership Season	*Various*	(BSkyB)
	Golf	Benson & Hedges International (Round 4)	*Oxfordshire, Thame*	(BBC)
	Ice Hockey	World Championships Finish	*Oslo, Hamar, Lillehammer, Norway*	(Eurosport)
	Lawn Tennis	Mercedes Super 9 - TIM Cup Finishes	*Rome, Italy*	(Eurosport)
	Motor Racing	Monaco Grand Prix	*Monte Carlo, Monaco*	(ITV)
	Rugby Union	Allied Dunbar Premiership 1 - Saracens V Newcastle Falcons	*Watford*	(BSkyB)
	Football	Arsenal V Aston Villa	*Highbury, London*	(BSkyB)

May 1999

	Sport	Event	Location	Broadcast
Monday 17th	Cricket	Cricket World Cup - New Zealand V Bangladesh	*Chelmsford*	(BSkyB)
Tuesday 18th	Cricket	Cricket World Cup - England V Kenya	*Canterbury*	(BBC)
Wednesday 19th	Cricket	Cricket World Cup - India V Zimbabwe	*Leicester*	
	Cricket	Cricket World Cup - Sri Lanka V South Africa	*Northampton*	(BSkyB)
	Cricket	Middlesex V tbc	*tbc*	(Ch4)
	Football	European Cup Winners Cup Final	*Villa Park, Birmingham*	(BBC)
Thursday 20th	Cricket	Cricket World Cup - Australia V New Zealand	*Cardiff*	(BBC)
	Cricket	Cricket World Cup - Pakistan V Scotland	*Chester-le-Street*	
Friday 21st	Cricket	Cricket World Cup - West Indies V Bangladesh	*Dublin, Ireland*	(BSkyB)
	Golf	Deutsche Bank-SAP Open Begins	*Heidelberg, Germany*	(BSkyB)
Saturday 22nd	Cricket	Cricket World Cup - England V South Africa	*The Oval*	(BBC)
	Cricket	Cricket World Cup - Zimbabwe V Sri Lanka	*Worcester*	
	Football	118th AXA Sponsored FA Cup Final	*Wembley Stadium*	(BBC)
	Rugby Union	Tetley's Bitter County Championship Finals	*Twickenham, London*	(BSkyB)
Sunday 23rd	Badminton	11th World Championships Finish	*Copenhagen, Denmark*	
	Cricket	Cricket World Cup - Australia V Pakistan	*Headingley*	
	Cricket	Cricket World Cup - Kenya V India	*Bristol*	(BSkyB)
	Cycling	The Prutour Begins	*Various*	(BSkyB)
	Polo	Prince Of Wales Trophy Finishes	*Windsor*	
	Rallying	Rally Argentina Begins	*Cordoba, Argentina*	
	Rugby Union	The Sanyo Cup	*Twickenham, London*	(BSkyB)
	Motor Cycling	French Grand Prix	*Paul Ricard*	(Eurosport)

Notes

145

	Sport	Event	Location	Broadcast
Monday 24th	Cricket	Cricket World Cup - Scotland V Bangladesh	*Edinburgh*	
	Cricket	Cricket World Cup - West Indies V New Zealand	*Southampton*	(BBC)
	Golf	Deutsche Bank-SAP Open Finishes	*Heidelburg, Germany*	(BSkyB)
	Lawn Tennis	French Open Championships - Roland Garros (Day 1)	*Roland Garros, Paris, France*	(BBC/Eurosport)
Tuesday 25th	Cricket	Cricket World Cup - England V Zimbabwe	*Trent Bridge, Nottingham*	(BSkyB)
	Lawn Tennis	French Open Championships - Roland Garros (Day 2)	*Roland Garros, Paris, France*	(BBC/Eurosport)
	Polo	Queens Cup Begins	*Little Budworth*	
Wednesday 26th	Cricket	Cricket World Cup - South Africa V Kenya	*Amstelveen, Netherlands*	
	Cricket	Cricket World Cup - Sri Lanka V India	*Taunton*	(BBC)
	Football	UEFA Champions League Final	*Nou Camp, Barcelona, Spain*	(ITV)
	Lawn Tennis	French Open Championships - Roland Garros (Day 3)	*Roland Garros, Paris, France*	(BBC/Eurosport)
	Rallying	Rally Argentina Finishes	*Cordoba, Argentina*	
Thursday 27th	Cricket	Cricket World Cup - Australia V Bangladesh	*Chester-le-street*	
	Cricket	Cricket World Cup - West Indies V Scotland	*Leicester*	(BSkyB)
	Equestrian	The Chubb Insurance Windsor International Horse Trials Begin	*Windsor*	
	Lawn Tennis	French Open Championships - Roland Garros (Day 4)	*Roland Garros, Paris, France*	(BBC/Eurosport)
Friday 28th	Cricket	Cricket World Cup - New Zealand V Pakistan	*Derby*	(BSkyB)
	Golf	Volvo PGA Championship (Round 1)	*Wentworth*	(BBC)
	Lawn Tennis	French Open Championships - Roland Garros (Day 5)	*Roland Garros, Paris, France*	(BBC/Eurosport)
Saturday 29th	Cricket	Cricket World Cup - England V India	*Edgbaston, Birmingham*	(BSkyB)
	Cricket	Cricket World Cup - Zimbabwe V South Africa	*Chelmsford*	
	Cycling	The Prutour Finishes	*Various*	(BSkyB)
	Football	Scottish FA Cup Final	*tbc*	(BSkyB)
	Golf	Volvo PGA Championship (Round 2)	*Wentworth*	(BBC)
	Horse Racing	VISA Triple Crown Challenge - Belmont Stakes	*Elmont, USA*	
	Lawn Tennis	French Open Championships - Roland Garros (Day 6)	*Roland Garros, Paris, France*	(BBC/Eurosport)
	Rugby Union	Middlesex Sevens	*Twickenham, London*	(BSkyB)
Sunday 30th	Cricket	Cricket World Cup - Sri Lanka V Kenya	*Southampton*	(BBC)
	Cricket	Cricket World Cup - West Indies V Australia	*Old Trafford, Manchester*	
	Equestrian	The Chubb Insurance Windsor International Horse Trials Finish	*Windsor*	
	Golf	Volvo PGA Championship (Round 3)	*Wentworth*	(BBC)
	Lawn Tennis	French Open Championships - Roland Garros (Day 7)	*Roland Garros, Paris, France*	(BBC/Eurosport)
	Motor Racing	Spanish Grand Prix	*Barcelona, Spain*	(ITV)

Venus Williams of the US stretches for a shot from Spain's Virginia Ruano-Pascual during their Singles match at Wimbledon •**Alastair Grant** ★30/6/98

★4 Jun	Horse Racing.	The Vodafone Oaks. *Epsom*
★5 Jun	Football	England V Sweden. *Wembley, London*
★5 Jun	Football	Faroe Islands V Scotland. *TBC, Faroe Islands*
★5 Jun	Horse Racing	The Vodafone Derby. *Epsom*
★7 Jun - 13 Jun	Lawn Tennis	The Stella Artois Grass Court Championships. *Queen's Club, London*
★9 Jun	Football	Bulgaria V England *TBC, Bulgaria*
★9 Jun	Football	Czech Republic V Scotland. *TBC, Czech Republic*
★9 Jun	Football	Wales V Denmark. *TBC*
★17 Jun - 20 Jun	Golf	US Open. *Pinehurst, USA*
★17 Jun	Horse Racing	The Gold Cup. *Ascot*
★19 Jun - 20 Jun	Athletics	European Cup Super League. *Paris, France*
★20 Jun	Cricket	Cricket World Cup Final. *Lords, London*
★21 Jun - 4 Jul	Lawn Tennis	The Wimbledon Lawn Tennis Championships. *All England Lawn Tennis Club, Wimbledon*
★24 Jun - 27 Jun	Golf	Compaq European Grand Prix. *Slaley Hall, Hexham*
★30 Jun - 4 Jul	Rowing	Henley Royal Regatta. *Henley*

May/June **1999**

	Sport	Event	Location	Broadcast
Monday 31st	Cricket	Cricket World Cup - Pakistan V Bangladesh	*Northampton*	
	Cricket	Cricket World Cup - Scotland V New Zealand	*Edinburgh*	(BSkyB)
	Golf	British Amateur Championships Begin	*Newcastle*	
	Golf	Volvo PGA Championship (Round 4)	*Wentworth*	(BBC)
	Lawn Tennis	French Open Championships - Roland Garros (Day 8)	*Roland Garros, Paris, France*	(BBC/Eurosport)
	Motorcycling	Isle Of Man TT Races Begin	*Isle Of Man*	
Tuesday 1st	Lawn Tennis	French Open Championships - Roland Garros (Day 9)	*Roland Garros, Paris, France*	(BBC/Eurosport)
Wednesday 2nd	Lawn Tennis	French Open Championships - Roland Garros (Day 10)	*Roland Garros, Paris, France*	(BBC/Eurosport)
Thursday 3rd	Golf	English Open (Round 1)	*tbc*	(BBC)
	Lawn Tennis	French Open Championships - Roland Garros (Women's Semi–Finals)	*Roland Garros, Paris, France*	(BBC/Eurosport)
Friday 4th	Cricket	Cricket World Cup - Group A Second V Group B Second	*The Oval*	(BSkyB)
	Golf	English Open (Round 2)	*tbc*	(BBC)
	Horse Racing	The Vodafone Oaks	*Epsom*	(Ch4)
	Lawn Tennis	French Open Championships - Roland Garros (Men's Semi–Finals)	*Roland Garros, Paris, France*	(BBC/Eurosport)
Saturday 5th	Cricket	Cricket World Cup - Group A First V Group B First	*Trent Bridge, Nottingham*	(BBC)
	Football	England V Sweden	*Wembley Stadium*	(BSkyB)
	Football	Faroe Islands V Scotland	*Toftir, Faroe Islands*	(Ch5)
	Football	Italy V Wales	*tbc, Italy*	(Ch5)
	Golf	British Amateur Championships Finish	*Newcastle*	
	Horse Racing	The Vodafone Derby	*Epsom*	(Ch4)
	Lawn Tennis	French Open Championships - Roland Garros (Women's Final)	*Roland Garros, Paris, France*	(BBC/Eurosport)
Sunday 6th	Cricket	Cricket World Cup - Group A Third V Group B Third	*Headingley, Leeds*	(BSkyB)
	Cycling	Giro D'Italia Finishes	*Various, Italy*	(Eurosport)
	Golf	English Open (Round 4)	*tbc*	(BBC)
	Lawn Tennis	French Open Championships - Roland Garros (Men's Final)	*Roland Garros, Paris, France*	(BBC/Eurosport)
	Rallying	Acropolis Rally Begins	*Athens, Greece*	
	Motor Cycling	Italian Grand Prix	*Mugello*	(Eurosport)

Notes

June 1999

	Sport	Event	Location	Broadcast
Monday **7th**	Lawn Tennis	DFS Classic (Day 1)	Birmingham	(BSkyB)
	Lawn Tennis	The Stella Artois Grass Court Championships (Day 1)	Queen's Club, London	(BBC)
Tuesday **8th**	Cricket	Cricket World Cup - Group A Second V Group B First	Old Trafford, Manchester	(BSkyB)
	Lawn Tennis	DFS Classic (Day 2)	Birmingham	(BSkyB)
	Lawn Tennis	The Stella Artois Grass Court Championships (Day 2)	Queen's Club, London	(BBC)
	Polo	Royal Windsor Cup Begins	Little Budworth	
Wednesday **9th**	Cricket	Cricket World Cup - Group A Third V Group B Second	Lords	(BBC)
	Football	Bulgaria V England	Sofia, Bulgaria	(Ch5)
	Football	Czech Republic V Scotland	Prague, Czech Republic	(Ch5)
	Football	Wales V Denmark	tbc	(BBC)
	Lawn Tennis	DFS Classic (Day 3)	Birmingham	(BSkyB)
	Lawn Tennis	The Stella Artois Grass Court Championships (Day 3)	Queen's Club, London	(BBC)
	Rallying	Acropolis Rally Finishes	Athens, Greece	
Thursday **10th**	Cricket	Cricket World Cup - Group A First V Group B Third	Edgbaston, Birmingham	(BSkyB)
	Equestrian	Bramham International Horse Trials Begin	Bramham	
	Golf	German Open Begins	Berlin, Germany	(BSkyB)
	Hockey	21st Men's Champions Trophy Begins	Brisbane, Australia	
	Hockey	7th Women's Champions Trophy Begins	Brisbane, Australia	
	Lawn Tennis	DFS Classic (Day 4)	Birmingham	(BSkyB)
	Lawn Tennis	The Stella Artois Grass Court Championships (Day 4)	Queen's Club, London	(BBC)
Friday **11th**	Cricket	Cricket World Cup - Group A Third V Group B First	The Oval	(BBC)
	Lawn Tennis	DFS Classic (Day 5)	Birmingham	(BSkyB)
	Lawn Tennis	The Stella Artois Grass Court Championships (Day 5)	Queen's Club, London	(BBC)
	Motorcycling	Isle Of Man TT Races Finish	Isle Of Man	
Saturday **12th**	Cricket	Cricket World Cup - Group A Second V Group B Third	Trent Bridge, Nottingham	(BBC)
	Horse Racing	The William Hill Trophy	York	(Ch4)
	Lawn Tennis	DFS Classic (Semi-finals)	Birmingham	(BSkyB)
	Lawn Tennis	The Stella Artois Grass Court Championships (Semi-finals)	Queen's Club, London	(BBC)
Sunday **13th**	Cricket	Cricket World Cup - Group A First V Group B Second	Headingley, Leeds	(BSkyB)
	Equestrian	Bramham International Horse Trials Finish	Bramham	
	Golf	German Open Finishes	Berlin, Germany	(BSkyB)
	Horse Racing	The William Hill Stakes	York	(Ch4)
	Lawn Tennis	DFS Classic (Final)	Birmingham	(BSkyB)
	Lawn Tennis	The Stella Artois Grass Court Championships (Final)	Queen's Club, London	(BBC)
	Motor Racing	Canadian Grand Prix	Montreal, Canada	(ITV)
	Polo	Queens Cup Finishes	Little Budworth	

June **1999**

Sport	Event	Location	Broadcast

Monday
14th

Sport	Event	Location	Broadcast
Lawn Tennis	The Nottingham Open (Day 1)	Nottingham	(BSkyB)

Tuesday
15th

Horse Racing	The Prince Of Wales's Stakes	Ascot	(BBC)
Horse Racing	The Queen Anne Stakes	Ascot	(BBC)
Lawn Tennis	Direct Line Insurance Championships (Day 1)	Eastbourne	(BBC)
Lawn Tennis	The Nottingham Open (Day 2)	Nottingham	(BSkyB)

Wednesday
16th

Cricket	Cricket World Cup - Semi Final 1	Old Trafford, Manchester	(BBC/BSkyB)
Horse Racing	The Queen Mary Stakes	Ascot	(BBC)
Lawn Tennis	Direct Line Insurance Championships (Day 2)	Eastbourne	(BBC)
Lawn Tennis	The Nottingham Open (Day 3)	Nottingham	(BSkyB)

Thursday
17th

Cricket	Cricket World Cup - Semi Final 2	Edgbaston, Birmingham	(BBC/BSkyB)
Golf	US Open (Round 1)	Pinehurst, USA	(BSkyB)
Horse Racing	The Gold Cup	Ascot	(BBC)
Lawn Tennis	Direct Line Insurance Championships (Day 3)	Eastbourne	(BBC)
Lawn Tennis	The Nottingham Open (Day 4)	Nottingham	(BSkyB)

Friday
18th

Golf	US Open (Round 2)	Pinehurst, USA	(BSkyB)
Horse Racing	The King Edward VII Stakes	Ascot	(BBC)
Lawn Tennis	Direct Line Insurance Championships (Day 4)	Eastbourne	(BBC)
Lawn Tennis	The Nottingham Open (Day 5)	Nottingham	(BSkyB)

Saturday
19th

Athletics	European Cup Super League Begins	Paris, France	(BBC/Eurosport)
Golf	US Open (Round 3)	Pinehurst, USA	(BSkyB)
Horse Racing	The Ladbroke	Ascot	(BBC)
Lawn Tennis	Direct Line Insurance Championships (Day 5)	Eastbourne	(BBC)
Lawn Tennis	The Nottingham Open (Final)	Nottingham	(BSkyB)

Sunday
20th

Athletics	European Cup Super League Finishes	Paris, France	(BBC/Eurosport)
Cricket	Cricket World Cup Final	Lords	(BBC/BSkyB)
Golf	US Open (Round 4)	Pinehurst, USA	(BSkyB)
Hockey	21st Men's Champions Trophy Finish	Brisbane, Australia	
Hockey	7th Women's Champions Trophy Finishes	Brisbane, Australia	
Lawn Tennis	Direct Line Insurance Championships (Final)	Eastbourne	(BBC)
Polo	Royal Windsor Cup Finishes	Little Budworth	
Motor Cycling	Catalunya Grand Prix	Catalunya	(Eurosport)

Notes

June **1999**

Sport	Event	Location	Broadcast

Monday 21st

Sport	Event	Location	Broadcast
Lawn Tennis	The Wimbledon Lawn Tennis Championships (Day 1)	*All England Lawn Tennis Club, Wimbledon*	(BBC)

Tuesday 22nd

Sport	Event	Location	Broadcast
Lawn Tennis	The Wimbledon Lawn Tennis Championships (Day 2)	*All England Lawn Tennis Club, Wimbledon*	(BBC)

Wednesday 23rd

Sport	Event	Location	Broadcast
Cricket	Natwest Trophy 3rd Round	*Various*	(Ch4)
Lawn Tennis	The Wimbledon Lawn Tennis Championships (Day 3)	*All England Lawn Tennis Club, Wimbledon*	(BBC)

Thursday 24th

Sport	Event	Location	Broadcast
Golf	Compaq European Grand Prix (Round 1)	*Hexham*	(BSkyB)
Lawn Tennis	The Wimbledon Lawn Tennis Championships (Day 4)	*All England Lawn Tennis Club, Wimbledon*	(BBC)

Friday 25th

Sport	Event	Location	Broadcast
Cricket	Super Cup Quarter Final 1	*tbc*	(BSkyB)
Golf	Compaq European Grand Prix (Round 2)	*Hexham*	(BSkyB)
Lawn Tennis	The Wimbledon Lawn Tennis Championships (Day 5)	*All England Lawn Tennis Club, Wimbledon*	(BBC)

Saturday 26th

Sport	Event	Location	Broadcast
Cricket	Super Cup Quarter Final 2	*tbc*	(BSkyB)
Games	1999 ESPN X Summer Games Begin	*tbc, USA*	
Golf	Compaq European Grand Prix (Round 3)	*Hexham*	(BSkyB)
Greyhound Racing	The Greyhound Derby Final	*Wimbledon, London*	
Lawn Tennis	The Wimbledon Lawn Tennis Championships (Day 6)	*All England Lawn Tennis Club, Wimbledon*	(BBC)
Motor Cycling	Dutch Grand Prix / Pays-Bas	*Assen*	(Eurosport)

Sunday 27th

Sport	Event	Location	Broadcast
Cricket	Super Cup Quarter Final 4	*tbc*	(BSkyB)
Golf	Compaq European Grand Prix (Round 4)	*Hexham*	(BSkyB)
Lawn Tennis	The Wimbledon Lawn Tennis Championships (Day 7)	*All England Lawn Tennis Club, Wimbledon*	(BBC)
Motor Racing	French Grand Prix	*Magny Cours, France*	(ITV)

Notes

June/July 1999

Sport	Event	Location	Broadcast

Monday 28th

Sport	Event	Location	Broadcast
Lawn Tennis	The Wimbledon Lawn Tennis Championships (Day 8)	All England Lawn Tennis Club, Wimbledon	(BBC)

Tuesday 29th

Sport	Event	Location	Broadcast
Lawn Tennis	The Wimbledon Lawn Tennis Championships (Day 9)	All England Lawn Tennis Club, Wimbledon	(BBC)
Polo	Veuve Clicquot Gold Cup Begins	Cowdray Park	

Wednesday 30th

Sport	Event	Location	Broadcast
Lawn Tennis	The Wimbledon Lawn Tennis Championships (Day 10)	All England Lawn Tennis Club, Wimbledon	(BBC)
Rowing	Henley Royal Regatta Begins	Henley	

Thursday 1st

Sport	Event	Location	Broadcast
Cricket	1st Test Match - England V New Zealand (Day 1)	Edgbaston, Birmingham	(Ch4/BSkyB)
Games	Universiade Begins	Palma De Mallorca, Spain	
Golf	Murphys Irish Open Begins	Druids Glen, Ireland	(BSkyB)
Lawn Tennis	The Wimbledon Lawn Tennis Championships (Women's Semi-finals)	All England Lawn Tennis Club, Wimbledon	(BBC)
Netball	England Test Series V South Africa Begins	Various	

Friday 2nd

Sport	Event	Location	Broadcast
Cricket	1st Test Match - England V New Zealand (Day 2)	Edgbaston, Birmingham	(Ch4/BSkyB)
Lawn Tennis	The Wimbledon Lawn Tennis Championships (Men's Semi-finals)	All England Lawn Tennis Club, Wimbledon	(BBC)

Saturday 3rd

Sport	Event	Location	Broadcast
Cricket	1st Test Match - England V New Zealand (Day 3)	Edgbaston, Birmingham	(Ch4/BSkyB)
Cycling	Tour De France Begins	Various, France	(Eurosport)
Lawn Tennis	The Wimbledon Lawn Tennis Championships (Women's Final)	All England Lawn Tennis Club, Wimbledon	(BBC)

Sunday 4th

Sport	Event	Location	Broadcast
Cricket	1st Test Match - England V New Zealand (Day 4)	Edgbaston, Birmingham	(Ch4/BSkyB)
Games	1999 ESPN X Summer Games Finish	tbc, USA	
Golf	Murphys Irish Open Finishes	Druids Glen, Ireland	(BSkyB)
Lawn Tennis	The Wimbledon Lawn Tennis Championships (Men's Final)	All England Lawn Tennis Club, Wimbledon	(BBC)
Rowing	Henley Royal Regatta Finishes	Henley	
Motor Cycling	British Grand Prix	Donington Park	(Eurosport)

Notes

A French fan at France's semi-final match with Croatia during France 98 •**Russell Cheyne** ★14/7/98

★1 Jul - 15 Jul	Games	Universiade. *Palma De Mallorca, Spain*
★1 Jul - 5 Jul	Cricket	1st Test Match - England V New Zealand. *Edgbaston, Birmingham*
★3 Jul - 25 Jul	Cycling	Tour De France. *Various, France*
★7 Jul - 10 Jul	Golf	Standard Life Loch Lomond. *Loch Lomond*
★11 Jul	Motor Racing	RAC British Grand Prix. *Silverstone, Towcester*
★13 Jul	Baseball	70th All-star Game. *Boston, USA*
★15 Jul - 18 Jul	Golf	128th British Open. *Carnoustie*
★22 Jul - 26 Jul	Cricket	2nd Test Match - England V New Zealand. *Lords, London*
★23 Jul - 8 Aug	Swimming	European Championships. *Istanbul, Turkey*
★24 Jul	Horse Racing	The King George VI And The Queen Elizabeth Diamond Stakes. *Ascot*
★31 Jul	Cricket	Super Cup Final. *TBC*

July **1999**

	Sport	Event	Location	Broadcast
Monday **5th**	Cricket	1st Test Match - England V New Zealand (Day 5)	Edgbaston, Birmingham	(Ch4/BSkyB)
Tuesday **6th**	Horse Racing	The Princess of Wales's Stakes	Newmarket	(Ch4)
Wednesday **7th**	Cricket Equestrian Golf	Natwest Trophy 4th Round Royal International Horse Show Begins Standard Life Loch Lomond (Round 1)	tbc Hickstead Loch Lomond	(Ch4) (BBC) (BBC)
Thursday **8th**	Golf	Standard Life Loch Lomond (Round 2)	Loch Lomond	(BBC)
Friday **9th**	Golf Motor Racing Rowing	Standard Life Loch Lomond (Round 3) RAC British Grand Prix Qualifying Begins FISA World Cup Begins	Loch Lomond Silverstone, England Lucerne, Switzerland	(BBC) (BBC/Eurosport)
Saturday **10th**	Cricket Golf	Super Cup Semi Final 1 Standard Life Loch Lomond (Round 4)	tbc Loch Lomond	(BSkyB) (BBC)
Sunday **11th**	Cricket Equestrian Motor Racing Rowing	Super Cup Semi Final 2 Royal International Horse Show Finishes RAC British Grand Prix FISA World Cup Finishes	tbc Hickstead Silverstone Lucerne, Switzerland	(BSkyB) (BBC) (ITV) (Eurosport/BBC)

Notes

July **1999**

Sport	Event	Location	Broadcast

Monday 12th

Sport	Event	Location	Broadcast
Modern Pentathlon	World Championships Begin	*Budapest, Hungary*	(Eurosport)

Tuesday 13th

Sport	Event	Location	Broadcast
Baseball	70th All-Star Game	*Boston, USA*	(Ch5)

Wednesday 14th

Thursday 15th

Sport	Event	Location	Broadcast
Games	Universiade Finishes	*Palma De Mallorca, Spain*	
Golf	128th British Open (Round 1)	*Carnoustie*	(BBC)

Friday 16th

Sport	Event	Location	Broadcast
Golf	128th British Open (Round 2)	*Carnoustie*	(BBC)
Lawn Tennis	Davis Cup By NEC Round 2 (First Day Singles)	*tbc*	(BBC)
Netball	England Test Series V South Africa Finishes	*tbc*	
Rallying	Rally Of New Zealand Begins	*Auckland, New Zealand*	

Saturday 17th

Sport	Event	Location	Broadcast
Golf	128th British Open (Round 3)	*Carnoustie*	(BBC)
Lawn Tennis	Davis Cup By NEC Round 2 (Middle Day Doubles)	*tbc*	(BBC)

Sunday 18th

Sport	Event	Location	Broadcast
Golf	128th British Open (Round 4)	*Carnoustie*	(BBC)
Lawn Tennis	Davis Cup By NEC Round 2 (Final Day Singles)	*tbc*	(BBC)
Modern Pentathlon	World Championships Finish	*Budapest, Hungary*	(Eurosport)
Polo	Veuve Clicquot Gold Cup Finishes	*Cowdray Park*	
Rallying	Rally Of New Zealand Finishes	*Auckland, New Zealand*	
Motor Cycling	German Grand Prix	*Sachenring*	(Eurosport)

Notes

July **1999**

Sport	Event	Location	Broadcast

Monday 19th

Tuesday 20th

Wednesday 21st

Sport	Event	Location	Broadcast
Football	UEFA Champions League 1st Qualifying Round 1st Leg	*tbc*	
Football	UEFA Cup 1st Qualifying Round 1st Leg	*tbc*	

Thursday 22nd

Sport	Event	Location	Broadcast
Cricket	2nd Test Match - England V New Zealand (Day 1)	*Lords*	(Ch4/BSkyB)
Golf	TNT Dutch Open Begins	*Hilversum, Netherlands*	(BSkyB)
Golf	US Womens Open (Round 1)	*Libertyville, USA*	(BSkyB)

Friday 23rd

Sport	Event	Location	Broadcast
Cricket	2nd Test Match - England V New Zealand (Day 2)	*Lords*	(Ch4/BSkyB)
Cycling	National Track Championships Begin	*Manchester Velodrome*	
Golf	US Womens Open (Round 2)	*Libertyville, USA*	(BSkyB)
Swimming	European Championships Begin	*Istanbul, Turkey*	(BBC/Eurosport)

Saturday 24th

Sport	Event	Location	Broadcast
Cricket	2nd Test Match - England V New Zealand (Day 3)	*Lords*	(Ch4/BSkyB)
Golf	US Womens Open (Round 3)	*Libertyville, USA*	(BSkyB)
Horse Racing	The King George VI And The Queen Elizabeth Diamond Stakes	*Ascot*	(BBC)
Lawn Tennis	KB Fed Cup - Semi-finals Begin	*tbc*	

Sunday 25th

Sport	Event	Location	Broadcast
Cricket	2nd Test Match - England V New Zealand (Day 4)	*Lords*	(Ch4/BSkyB)
Cycling	Tour De France Finishes	*Various, France*	(Eurosport)
Golf	TNT Dutch Open Finishes	*Hilversum, Netherlands*	(BSkyB)
Golf	US Womens Open (Round 4)	*Libertyville, USA*	(BSkyB)
Lawn Tennis	KB Fed Cup - Semi-finals Finish	*tbc*	
Motor Racing	Austrian Grand Prix	*A1-Ring Circuit, Spielberg, Austria*	(ITV)
Polo	International Day Sponsored By Cartier	*Little Budworth*	

Notes

July/August 1999

	Sport	Event	Location	Broadcast
Monday 26th	Cricket	2nd Test Match - England V New Zealand (Day 5)	*Lords*	(Ch4/BSkyB)
Tuesday 27th				
Wednesday 28th	Cricket	Natwest Trophy Quarter Finals	*tbc*	(Ch4)
	Football	UEFA Champions League 1st Qualifying Round 2nd Leg	*tbc*	
	Football	UEFA Cup 1st Qualifying Round 2nd Leg	*tbc*	
Thursday 29th	Horse Racing	The Goodwood Cup	*Goodwood*	(BBC)
Friday 30th	Cycling	National Track Championships Finish	*Manchester Velodrome*	
	Golf	Smurfit European Open Begins	*Dublin, Ireland*	(BSkyB)
Saturday 31st	Cricket	Super Cup Final	*tbc*	(BSkyB)
Sunday 1st	Motor Racing	German Grand Prix	*Hockenheim, Germany*	*(ITV)*

Notes

Tour-de-France leader Marco Pantani rides among the pack during the 19th stage •**AFP** ★31/7/98

★5 Aug - 9 Aug	Cricket	3rd Test Match - England V New Zealand. *Old Trafford, Manchester*
★12 Aug - 15 Aug	Golf	81st PGA Championship. *Medinah, USA*
★19 Aug - 23 Aug	Cricket	4th Test Match - England V New Zealand. *The Oval, London*
★20 Aug - 29 Aug	Athletics	IAAF 7th World Championships In Athletics. *Seville, Spain*
★22 Aug - 29 Aug	Rowing	FISA World Championships. *St Catherines, Canada*
★24 Aug - 30 Aug	Equestrian	European Jumping Championship. *Hickstead*
★26 Aug - 29 Aug	Golf	World Golf Championships - The NEC World Golf Invitational. *Akron, USA*
★28 Aug	Cricket	Natwest Trophy Final. *Lords, London*
★30 Aug - 12 Sep	Lawn Tennis	US Open Championships. *Flushing Meadows, New York, USA*

August **1999**

Sport	Event	Location	Broadcast

Monday
2nd

Golf	Smurfit European Open Finishes	*Dublin, Ireland*	(BSkyB)

Tuesday
3rd

Polo	National 15 Goal Championships Begin	*Cirencester*	

Wednesday
4th

Thursday
5th

Cricket	3rd Test Match - England V New Zealand (Day 1)	*Trent Bridge, Nottingham*	(Ch4/BSkyB)
Golf	Volvo Scandinavian Masters Begins	*Malmo, Sweden*	(BSkyB)

Friday
6th

Cricket	3rd Test Match - England V New Zealand (Day 2)	*Trent Bridge, Nottingham*	(Ch4/BSkyB)

Saturday
7th

Cricket	3rd Test Match - England V New Zealand (Day 3)	*Trent Bridge, Nottingham*	(Ch4/BSkyB)

Sunday
8th

Cricket	3rd Test Match - England V New Zealand (Day 4)	*Trent Bridge, Nottingham*	(Ch4/BSkyB)
Golf	Volvo Scandinavian Masters Finishes	*Malmo, Sweden*	(BSkyB)
Swimming	European Championships Finish	*Istanbul, Turkey*	(BBC/Eurosport)

Notes

August **1999**

	Sport	Event	Location	Broadcast
Monday **9th**	**Cricket**	3rd Test Match - England V New Zealand (Day 5)	*Trent Bridge, Nottingham*	(Ch4/BSkyB)
Tuesday **10th**	**Football**	UEFA Cup 2nd Qualifying Round 1st Leg	*tbc*	
Wednesday **11th**	**Football**	UEFA Champions League 2nd Qualifying Round 1st Leg	*tbc*	
Thursday **12th**	**Football** **Golf**	European Cup Winners Cup 1st Qualifying Round 1st Leg 81st PGA Championship (Round 1)	*tbc* *Medinah, USA*	(BSkyB)
Friday **13th**	**Golf**	81st PGA Championship (Round 2)	*Medinah, USA*	(BSkyB)
Saturday **14th**	**Cricket** **Golf**	Natwest Trophy Semi Finals 81st PGA Championship (Round 3)	*tbc* *Medinah, USA*	(Ch4) (BSkyB)
Sunday **15th**	**Cricket** **Golf** **Motor Racing** **Polo**	Natwest Trophy Semi Finals 81st PGA Championship (Round 4) Hungarian Grand Prix National 15 Goal Championships Finish	*tbc* *Medinah, USA* *Hungaroring, Budapest, Hungary* *Cirencester*	(Ch4) (BSkyB) (ITV)

Notes

August **1999**

	Sport	Event	Location	Broadcast
Monday 16th				
Tuesday 17th				
Wednesday 18th				
Thursday 19th	**Cricket** **Golf**	4th Test Match - England V New Zealand (Day 1) BMW International Open Begins	*The Oval* *Munich, Germany*	(Ch4/BSkyB) (BSkyB)
Friday 20th	**Athletics** **Cricket** **Rallying**	IAAF 7th World Championships In Athletics Begin 4th Test Match - England V New Zealand (Day 2) Neste Rally Finland Begins	*Seville, Spain* *The Oval* *Jyvakyla, Finland*	(BBC/Eurosport) (Ch4/BSkyB)
Saturday 21st	**Cricket**	4th Test Match - England V New Zealand (Day 3)	*The Oval*	(Ch4/BSkyB)
Sunday 22nd	**Cricket** **Golf** **Rallying** **Rowing** **Motor Cycling**	4th Test Match - England V New Zealand (Day 4) BMW International Open Finishes Neste Rally Finland Finishes FISA World Championships Begin Czechoslovakian Grand Prix	*The Oval* *Munich, Germany* *Jyvakyla, Finland* *St Catherines, Canada* *BMO*	(Ch4/BSkyB) (BSkyB) (BBC/Eurosport) (Eurosport)

Notes

August 1999

Sport	Event	Location	Broadcast

Monday

23rd

Cricket	4th Test Match - England V New Zealand (Day 5)	*The Oval*	(Ch4/BSkyB)

Tuesday

24th

Equestrian	European Show Jumping Championships Begin	*Hickstead*	(BBC)
Football	UEFA Cup 2nd Qualifying Round 2nd Leg	*tbc*	

Wednesday

25th

Football	UEFA Champions League 2nd Qualifying Round 2nd Leg	*tbc*	

Thursday

26th

Football	European Cup Winners Cup 1st Qualifying Round 2nd Leg	*tbc*	
Golf	World Golf Championships	*Akron, USA*	(BSkyB)
	- The NEC World Golf Invitational (Round 1)		

Friday

27th

Golf	World Golf Championships	*Akron, USA*	(BSkyB)
	- The NEC World Golf Invitational (Round 2)		

Saturday

28th

Cricket	Natwest Trophy Final	*Lords*	(Ch4)
Golf	World Golf Championships	*Akron, USA*	(BSkyB)
	- The NEC World Golf Invitational (Round 3)		

Sunday

29th

Athletics	IAAF 7th World Championships In Athletics Finish	*Seville, Spain*	(BBC/Eurosport)
Golf	World Golf Championships	*Akron, USA*	(BSkyB)
	- The NEC World Golf Invitational (Round 4)		
Motor Racing	Belgian Grand Prix	*Spa-Francorchamps, Belgium*	*(ITV)*
Rowing	FISA World Championships Finish	*St Catherines, Canada*	(BBC/Eurosport)

Notes

England's Jane Smith performs a forward somersault at the Commonwealth Games in Kuala Lumpur •Reuters ★18/9/98

★4 Sep - 26 Sep	Cycling	Vuelta A España. *Various, Spain*
★4 Sep	Football	Belarus V Wales. *Minsk, Belarus*
★4 Sep	Football	Bosnia & Herzegovina V Scotland. *TBC, Bosnia & Herzegovina*
★4 Sep	Football	England V Luxembourg. *TBC*
★4 Sep	Footballl	Northern Ireland V Turkey. *Windsor Park, Belfast*
★8 Sep	Football	Estonia V Scotland. *TBC, Estonia*
★8 Sep	Football	Germany V Northern Ireland. *Dortmund, Germany*
★8 Sep	Football	Poland V England. *TBC, Poland*
★9 Sep - 12 Sep	Golf	One-2-One British Masters. *TBC*
★11 Sep - 12 Sep	Golf	The Walker Cup. *Nairn*
★11 Sep	Horse Racing	The Pertemps St Leger Stakes. *Doncaster*
★13 Sep - 19 Sep	Lawn Tennis	The Samsung Open. *Bournemouth*
★18 Sep - 19 Sep	Lawn Tennis	KB Fed Cup Final. *TBC*
★21 Sep - 6 Oct	Netball	World Championships. *Christchurch, New Zealand*
★24 Sep - 26 Sep	Golf	33rd Ryder Cup.*Brookline, USA*
★27 Sep - 3 Oct	Lawn Tennis	Compaq Grand Slam Cup. *Munich, Germany*
★28 Sep	Cricket	County Championship Finishes. *Various*

August/September 1999

Sport	Event	Location	Broadcast

Monday 30th

Equestrian	European Show Jumping Championships Finish	*Hickstead*	(BBC)
Lawn Tennis	US Open Championships (Day 1)	*Flushing Meadows, New York, USA*	(BSkyB)

Tuesday 31st

Lawn Tennis	US Open Championships (Day 2)	*Flushing Meadows, New York, USA*	(BSkyB)

Wednesday 1st

Lawn Tennis	US Open Championships (Day 3)	*Flushing Meadows, New York, USA*	(BSkyB)

Thursday 2nd

Equestrian	Burghley Pedigree Chum Horse Trials Begin	*Burghley*	
Golf	Canon European Masters Begin	*Crans Sur Sierre, Switzerland*	(BSkyB)
Lawn Tennis	US Open Championships (Day 4)	*Flushing Meadows, New York, USA*	(BSkyB)

Friday 3rd

Lawn Tennis	US Open Championships (Day 5)	*Flushing Meadows, New York, USA*	(BSkyB)

Saturday 4th

Cycling	Vuelta A España Begins	*Various, Spain*	(Eurosport)
Football	Belarus V Wales	*Minsk, Belarus*	(Ch5)
Football	Bosnia & Herzegovina V Scotland	*Sarajevo, Bosnia & Herzegovina*	(Ch5)
Football	England V Luxembourg	*tbc*	(BSkyB)
Football	Northern Ireland V Turkey	*Windsor Park, Belfast*	(BBC)
Ice Hockey	Sekonda Superleague Season Starts	*Various*	(BSkyB)
Lawn Tennis	US Open Championships (Day 6)	*Flushing Meadows, New York, USA*	(BSkyB)

Sunday 5th

Equestrian	Burghley Pedigree Chum Horse Trials Finish	*Burghley*	
Golf	Canon European Masters Finish	*Crans Sur Sierre, Switzerland*	
Lawn Tennis	US Open Championships (Day 7)	*Flushing Meadows, New York, USA*	(BSkyB)
Motor Cycling	San Marino Grand Prix	*tbc*	(Eurosport)

Notes

September 1999

	Sport	Event	Location	Broadcast
Monday 6th	Lawn Tennis	US Open Championships (Day 8)	*Flushing Meadows, New York, USA*	(BSkyB)
Tuesday 7th	Lawn Tennis	US Open Championships (Day 9)	*Flushing Meadows, New York, USA*	(BSkyB)
Wednesday 8th	Football	Estonia V Scotland	*Kadriorg, Estonia*	(Ch5)
	Football	Germany V Northern Ireland	*Dortmund, Germany*	(BBC)
	Football	Poland V England	*Chorzow, Poland*	(Ch5)
	Lawn Tennis	US Open Championships (Day 10)	*Flushing Meadows, New York, USA*	(BSkyB)
Thursday 9th	Equestrian	Blenheim International Horse Trials Begin	*Woodstock*	
	Golf	One-2-One British Masters (Round 1)	*tbc*	(BSkyB)
	Lawn Tennis	US Open Championships (Women's Semi-finals)	*Flushing Meadows, New York, USA*	(BSkyB)
Friday 10th	Golf	One-2-One British Masters (Round 2)	*tbc*	(BSkyB)
	Lawn Tennis	US Open Championships (Men's Semi-finals)	*Flushing Meadows, New York, USA*	(BSkyB)
Saturday 11th	Basketball	Start Of 1999/2000 Budweiser Championship Season	*Various*	(BSkyB)
	Golf	One-2-One British Masters (Round 3)	*tbc*	(BSkyB)
	Golf	The Walker Cup Begins	*Nairn*	
	Horse Racing	The Pertemps St Leger Stakes	*Doncaster*	(Ch4)
	Lawn Tennis	US Open Championships (Women's Final)	*Flushing Meadows, New York, USA*	(BSkyB)
Sunday 12th	Equestrian	Blenheim International Horse Trials Finish	*Woodstock*	
	Golf	One-2-One British Masters (Round 4)	*tbc*	(BSkyB)
	Golf	The Walker Cup Finishes	*Nairn*	
	Lawn Tennis	US Open Championships (Men's Final)	*Flushing Meadows, New York, USA*	(BSkyB)
	Motor Racing	Italian Grand Prix	*Monza, Italy*	(ITV)

Notes

September **1999**

Sport	Event	Location	Broadcast

Monday 13th

Sport	Event	Location	Broadcast
Lawn Tennis	The Samsung Open (Day 1)	*Bournemouth*	(BBC)

Tuesday 14th

Sport	Event	Location	Broadcast
Lawn Tennis	The Samsung Open (Day 2)	*Bournemouth*	(BBC)
Football	UEFA Cup 1st Round 1st Leg	*tbc*	

Wednesday 15th

Sport	Event	Location	Broadcast
Lawn Tennis	The Samsung Open (Day 3)	*Bournemouth*	(BBC)
Football	UEFA Champions League Group Match 1	*tbc*	

Thursday 16th

Sport	Event	Location	Broadcast
Football	European Cup Winners Cup 1st Round 1st Leg	*tbc*	
Golf	Lancome Trophy Begins	*Paris, France*	(BSkyB)
Lawn Tennis	The Samsung Open (Day 4)	*Bournemouth*	(BBC)

Friday 17th

Sport	Event	Location	Broadcast
Lawn Tennis	The Samsung Open (Day 5)	*Bournemouth*	(BBC)

Saturday 18th

Sport	Event	Location	Broadcast
Lawn Tennis	KB Fed Cup Final Begins	*tbc*	
Lawn Tennis	The Samsung Open (Day 6)	*Bournemouth*	(BBC)

Sunday 19th

Sport	Event	Location	Broadcast
Cricket	National One-Day League Finishes	*Various*	(BSkyB)
Golf	Lancome Trophy Finishes	*Paris, France*	(BSkyB)
Lawn Tennis	KB Fed Cup Final Finishes	*tbc*	
Lawn Tennis	The Samsung Open (Final)	*Bournemouth*	(BBC)
Rallying	555 China Rally Begins	*Beijing, PR China*	
Motor Cycling	Comunidad Valencia Grand Prix -SPA	*Valencia*	(Eurosport)

Notes

September **1999**

Sport	Event	Location	Broadcast

Monday
20th

Tuesday
21st

Netball	World Championships Begin	*Christchurch, New Zealand*	
Rallying	555 China Rally Finishes	*Beijing, PR China*	

Wednesday
22nd

Thursday
23rd

Friday
24th

Golf	33rd Ryder Cup (Day 1)	*Brookline, USA*	(BSkyB)
Lawn Tennis	Davis Cup By NEC Round 3 - Semi-Finals (First Day Singles)	*tbc*	(BBC)

Saturday
25th

Golf	33rd Ryder Cup (Day 2)	*Brookline, USA*	(BSkyB)
Horse Racing	The Queen Elizabeth II Stakes	*Ascot*	(BBC)
Lawn Tennis	Davis Cup By NEC Round 3 - Semi-Finals (Middle Day Doubles)	*tbc*	(BBC)

Sunday
26th

Cycling	Vuelta A España Finishes	*Various, Spain*	(Eurosport)
Golf	33rd Ryder Cup (Day 3)	*Brookline, USA*	(BSkyB)
Lawn Tennis	Davis Cup By NEC Round 3 - Semi-Finals (Final Day Singles)	*tbc*	(BBC)
Motor Racing	European Grand Prix	*Nurburg, Germany*	(ITV)

Notes

September/October 1999

	Sport	Event	Location	Broadcast
Monday 27th	Lawn Tennis	Compaq Grand Slam Cup Begins	Munich, Germany	(BSkyB)
Tuesday 28th	Cricket	County Championship Finishes	*Various*	(BSkyB)
	Football	UEFA Cup 1st Round 2nd Leg	*tbc*	
Wednesday 29th	Equestrian	Horse Of The Year Show Begins	*Wembley Arena*	
	Football	UEFA Champions League Group Match 2	*tbc*	
Thursday 30th	Football	European Cup Winners Cup 1st Round 2nd Leg	*tbc*	
	Golf	Linde German Masters Begins	*Cologne, Germany*	(BSkyB)
Friday 1st	Rugby Union	Fiji V Namibia	*Beziers, France*	(ITV)
	Rugby Union	Wales V Argentina	*Millennium Stadium, Cardiff*	(ITV)
	Rugby Union	World Cup Opening Ceremony	*Millennium Stadium, Cardiff*	(ITV)
Saturday 2nd	Horse Racing	The Tote Cambridgeshire Handicap Stakes	*Newmarket*	(Ch4)
	Rugby Union	Europe 1 V USA	*Lansdowne Rd, Dublin, Ireland*	(ITV)
	Rugby Union	Europe 2 V Europe 5	*Twickenham, London*	(ITV)
	Rugby Union	Europe 4 V Repechage 2	*Galashiels*	(ITV)
	Rugby Union	France V Canada	*Beziers, France*	(ITV)
Sunday 3rd	Equestrian	Horse Of The Year Show Finishes	*Wembley Arena*	
	Golf	Linde German Masters Finishes	*Cologne, Germany*	(BSkyB)
	Horse Racing	Prix De L'Arc De Triomphe	*Longchamp, Paris, France*	(BBC)
	Lawn Tennis	Compaq Grand Slam Cup Finishes	*Munich, Germany*	(BBC)
	Rallying	Rallye Sanremo - Rallye D'Italia Begins	*San Remo, Italy*	
	Rugby Union	Australia V Europe 6	*Belfast*	(ITV)
	Rugby Union	Europe 3 V South Africa	*Murrayfield, Edinburgh*	(ITV)
	Rugby Union	New Zealand V Repechage 1	*Bristol*	(ITV)
	Rugby Union	Western Samoa V Asia 1	*Wrexham*	(ITV)
	Motor Cycling	Australian Grand Prix	*Phillip Island*	(Eurosport)

Tiger Woods misses a birdie at the seventh during the Dunhill Cup •**Russell Cheyne** ★8/10/98

★1 Oct	**Rugby Union**	Wales V Argentina. *Millennium Stadium, Cardiff*
★1 Oct	**Rugby Union**	World Cup Opening Ceremony. *Millennium Stadium, Cardiff*
★3 Oct	**Horse Racing**	Prix De L'Arc De Triomphe. *Longchamp, Paris, France*
★5 Oct - 10 Oct	**Cycling**	World Road Championships. *Verona/Trevise, Italy*
★7 Oct - 10 Oct	**Golf**	Alfred Dunhill Cup. *St Andrews, Fife*
★8 Oct - 16 Oct	**Gymnastics**	34th World Championships. *Tianjin, PR China*
★9 Oct	**Football**	Finland V Northern Ireland. *Helsinki, Finland*
★9 Oct	**Football**	Scotland V Lithuania. *TBC*
★9 Oct	**Football**	Wales V Switzerland. *TBC*
★9 Oct	**Rugby League**	JJB Super League Grand Final. *TBC*
★14 Oct - 17 Oct	**Golf**	Cisco World Match Play Championship Presented By Diners Club. *Wentworth*
★20 Oct - 24 Oct	**Cycling**	World Track Championships. *Berlin, Germany*
★30 Oct	**Rugby Union**	World Cup - Semi-final 1. *Twickenham, London*
★31 Oct	**Rugby Union**	World Cup - Semi-final 2. *Twickenham, London*

October 1999

Sport	Event	Location	Broadcast

Monday 4th

Tuesday 5th

Cycling	World Road Championships Begin	*Verona/Trevise, Italy*	(Eurosport)

Wednesday 6th

Netball	World Championships Finish	*Christchurch, New Zealand*	
Rallying	Rallye Sanremo - Rallye D'Italia Finishes	*San Remo, Italy*	

Thursday 7th

Golf	Alfred Dunhill Cup (Day 1)	*Fife*	(BSkyB)
Judo	World Championships Begin	*NIA, Birmingham*	

Friday 8th

Golf	Alfred Dunhill Cup (Day 2)	*Fife*	(BSkyB)
Gymnastics	34th World Championships Begin	*Tianjin, PR China*	
Rugby Union	Europe 3 V Repechage 2	*Murrayfield, Edinburgh*	(ITV)
Rugby Union	France V Namibia	*Bordeaux, France*	(ITV)

Saturday 9th

Football	Finland V Northern Ireland	*Helsinki, Finland*	(BBC)
Football	Scotland V Lithuania	*tbc*	(BSkyB)
Football	Wales V Switzerland	*tbc*	(BBC)
Golf	Alfred Dunhill Cup (Day 3)	*Fife*	(BSkyB)
Rugby League	JJB Super League Grand Final	*Old Trafford*	(BSkyB)
Rugby Union	Europe 2 V New Zealand	*Twickenham, London*	(ITV)
Rugby Union	Fiji V Canada	*Bordeaux, France*	(ITV)
Rugby Union	USA V Europe 6	*Dublin, Ireland*	(ITV)
Rugby Union	Wales V Asia 1	*Millennium Stadium, Cardiff*	(ITV)

Sunday 10th

Cycling	World Road Championships Finish	*Verona/Trevise, Italy*	(Eurosport)
Golf	Alfred Dunhill Cup (Day 4)	*Fife*	(BSkyB)
Judo	World Championships Finish	*NIA, Birmingham*	
Rugby Union	Argentina V Western Samoa	*Llanelli*	(ITV)
Rugby Union	Europe 1 V Australia	*Dublin, Ireland*	(ITV)
Rugby Union	South Africa V Europe 4	*Murrayfield, Edinburgh*	(ITV)
Motor Cycling	South African Grand Prix	*Welkom*	(Eurosport)

October **1999**

	Sport	Event	Location	Broadcast
Monday 11th				
Tuesday 12th				
Wednesday 13th				
Thursday 14th	Golf	Cisco World Match Play Championship Presented By Diners Club (Day 1)	Wentworth	(BBC)
	Rugby Union	Australia V USA	Limerick, Ireland	(ITV)
	Rugby Union	Canada V Namibia	Toulouse, France	(ITV)
	Rugby Union	Europe 5 V Repechage 1	Leicester	(ITV)
	Rugby Union	New Zealand V Europe 5	Huddersfield	(ITV)
	Rugby Union	Wales V Western Samoa	Millennium Stadium, Cardiff	(ITV)
Friday 15th	Golf	Cisco World Match Play Championship Presented By Diners Club (Day 2)	Wentworth	(BBC)
	Rugby Union	Europe 1 V Europe 6	Dublin, Ireland	(ITV)
	Rugby Union	Europe 2 V Repechage 1	Twickenham, London	(ITV)
	Rugby Union	South Africa V Repechage 2	Glasgow	(ITV)
Saturday 16th	Golf	Cisco World Match Play Championship Presented By Diners Club (Day 3)	Wentworth	(BBC)
	Gymnastics	34th World Championships Finish	Tianjin, PR China	
	Rugby Union	Argentina V Asia 1	Millennium Stadium, Cardiff	(ITV)
	Rugby Union	Europe 3 V Europe 4	Murrayfield, Edinburgh	(ITV)
	Rugby Union	France V Fiji	Toulouse, France	(ITV)
Sunday 17th	Golf	Cisco World Match Play Championship Presented By Diners Club (Day 4)	Wentworth	(BBC)
	Motor Racing	Malaysian Grand Prix	Kuala Lumpur, Malaysia	(ITV)
Notes				

October **1999**

Sport	Event	Location	Broadcast

Monday 18th

Tuesday 19th

Sport	Event	Location	Broadcast
Football	UEFA Cup 2nd Round 1st Leg	*tbc*	

Wednesday 20th

Sport	Event	Location	Broadcast
Cycling	World Track Championships Begin	*Berlin, Germany*	(Eurosport)
Football	UEFA Champions League Group Match 3	*tbc*	
Rugby Union	Quarter Final Play Offs - Runner Up A V Runner Up D	*Murrayfield, Edinburgh*	(ITV)
Rugby Union	Quarter Final Play Offs - Runner Up B V Runner Up C	*Twickenham, London*	(ITV)
Rugby Union	Quarter Final Play Offs - Runner Up E V 3rd Best	*Lens, France*	(ITV)

Thursday 21st

Sport	Event	Location	Broadcast
Football	European Cup Winners Cup 2nd Round 1st Leg	*tbc*	
Golf	Belgacom Open Begins	*tbc, Belgium*	(BSkyB)

Friday 22nd

Saturday 23rd

Sport	Event	Location	Broadcast
Rugby Union	Quarter Final 1	*Millennium Stadium, Cardiff*	(ITV)

Sunday 24th

Sport	Event	Location	Broadcast
Cycling	World Track Championships Finish	*Berlin, Germany*	(Eurosport)
Golf	Belgacom Open Finishes	*tbc, Belgium*	(BSkyB)
Rugby Union	Quarter Final 2	*Lens, France*	(ITV)
Rugby Union	Quarter Final 3	*Murrayfield, Edinburgh*	(ITV)
Rugby Union	Quarter Final 4	*Dublin, Ireland*	(ITV)
Motor Cycling	Rio Grand Prix	*Jacarepaguá*	(Eurosport)

Notes

October 1999

	Sport	Event	Location	Broadcast

Monday 25th
| Lawn Tennis | Mercedes Super 9 - Eurocard Open Begins | Stuttgart, Germany | |

Tuesday 26th

Wednesday 27th

Thursday 28th
| Golf | Volvo Masters Begins | Jerez, Spain | (BSkyB) |

Friday 29th

Saturday 30th
| Rugby Union | Semi Final 1 | Twickenham, London | (ITV) |

Sunday 31st
Golf	Volvo Masters Finishes	Jerez, Spain	(BSkyB)
Lawn Tennis	Mercedes Super 9 - Eurocard Open Finishes	Stuttgart, Germany	
Motor Racing	Japanese Grand Prix	Suzuka, Japan	(ITV)
Rugby Union	Semi Final 2	Twickenham, London	(ITV)
Motor Cycling	Argentinian Grand Prix	Buenos Aires	(Eurosport)

Notes

Damon Hill at the Hungarian Grand Prix •**Reuters** ★18/9/98

★4 Nov - 7 Nov	Golf	World Golf Championships - The American Express World Golf Strokeplay. *Valderrama, Sottogrande, Spain*
★4 Nov	Rugby Union	World Cup - 3rd/4th Place Play Off. *Millennium Stadium, Cardiff*
★6 Nov	Rugby Union	World Cup Final. *Millennium Stadium, Cardiff*
★13 Nov	Football	Euro 2000 Play-offs. *TBC.*
★15 Nov - 21 Nov	Lawn Tennis	ATP Tour World Doubles Championship. *Hartford, USA*
★15 Nov - 21 Nov	Lawn Tennis	Chase Championships Of The Corel WTA Tour. *Madison Square Gardens, New York, USA*
★17 Nov	Football	Euro 2000 Play-offs. *TBC.*
★18 Nov - 21 Nov	Golf	World Cup Of Golf. *Kuala Lumpur, Malaysia*
★20 Nov - 23 Nov	Rallying	Network Q RAC Rally. *Cheltenham*
★22 Nov - 28 Nov	Lawn Tennis	ATP Tour World Championship. *Hannover, Germany*
★30 Nov	Football	FIFA Toyota Cup - World Club Championship. *Tokyo, Japan*

November 1999

	Sport	Event	Location	Broadcast
Monday 1st	**Lawn Tennis**	Mercedes Super 9 - 14th Open De Paris Begins	*Paris, France*	(Eurosport)
Tuesday 2nd	**Football**	UEFA Cup 2nd Round 2nd Leg	*tbc*	
Wednesday 3rd	**Football**	UEFA Champions League Group Match 4	*tbc*	
Thursday 4th	**Football**	European Cup Winners Cup 2nd Round 2nd Leg	*tbc*	
	Golf	The American Express World Golf Strokeplay (Round 1)	*Sottogrande, Spain*	(BSkyB)
	Rallying	API Rally Australia Begins	*Perth, Australia*	
	Rugby Union	3rd/4th Place Play Off	*Millennium Stadium, Cardiff*	(ITV)
Friday 5th	**Golf**	The American Express World Golf Strokeplay (Round 2)	*Sottogrande, Spain*	(BSkyB)
Saturday 6th	**Golf**	The American Express World Golf Strokeplay (Round 3)	*Sottogrande, Spain*	(BSkyB)
	Horse Racing	Breeders' Cup	*Hallandale, USA*	
	Netball	International Test Series	*Wembley Arena*	
	Rugby Union	World Cup Final	*Millennium Stadium, Cardiff*	(ITV)
Sunday 7th	**Golf**	The American Express World Golf Strokeplay (Round 4)	*Sottogrande, Spain*	(BSkyB)
	Lawn Tennis	Mercedes Super 9 - 14th Open De Paris Finishes	*Paris, France*	(Eurosport)
	Rallying	API Rally Australia Finishes	*Perth, Australia*	

Notes

175

November **1999**

Sport	Event	Location	Broadcast

Monday
8th

Tuesday
9th

Wednesday
10th

Thursday
11th

Friday
12th

Saturday
13th

Sport	Event	Location	Broadcast
Football	Euro 2000 Play-offs	*tbc*	

Sunday
14th

Notes

November **1999**

Sport	Event	Location	Broadcast

Monday

15th

Golf	1999 Mastercard PGA Grand Slam Of Golf Begins	*tbc, USA*	
Lawn Tennis	ATP Tour World Doubles Championship Begins	*Hartford, USA*	(Eurosport)
Lawn Tennis	Chase Championships Of The Corel WTA Tour Begin	*New York, USA*	(Eurosport)

Tuesday

16th

Wednesday

17th

Football	Euro 2000 Play-offs	*tbc*	
Golf	1999 Mastercard PGA Grand Slam Of Golf Finishes	*tbc, USA*	

Thursday

18th

Golf	World Cup of Golf Begins	*Kuala Lumpur, Malaysia*	(BSkyB)

Friday

19th

Saturday

20th

Rallying	Network Q RAC Rally Begins	*Cheltenham*	

Sunday

21st

Golf	World Cup of Golf Finishes	*Kuala Lumpur, Malaysia*	(BSkyB)
Lawn Tennis	ATP Tour World Doubles Championship (Final)	*Hartford, USA*	(Eurosport)
Lawn Tennis	Chase Championships of The Corel WTA Tour (Final)	*New York, USA*	(Eurosport)

Notes

November **1999**

	Sport	Event	Location	Broadcast
Monday **22nd**	**Lawn Tennis**	ATP Tour World Championships Begin	*Hannover, Germany*	(Eurosport)
Tuesday **23rd**	**Football** **Rallying**	UEFA Cup 3rd Round 1st Leg Network Q RAC Rally Finishes	*tbc* *Cheltenham*	
Wednesday **24th**	**Football**	UEFA Champions League Group Match 5	*tbc*	
Thursday **25th**				
Friday **26th**				
Saturday **27th**				
Sunday **28th**	**Lawn Tennis**	ATP Tour World Championships Finish	*Hannover, Germany*	(Eurosport)

Notes

It's a funny old game... Nigel Martin and Paul Merson share a joke during a Leeds and Aston Villa Premiership match •**Frank Coppi** ★20/9/98

★3 Dec - 5 Dec	**Lawn Tennis**	Davis Cup By NEC World Group Final. *TBC,*
★4 Dec	**Horse Racing**	The William Hill Handicap Hurdle. *Sandown Park, Esher*
★4 Dec	**Ice Hockey**	Benson & Hedges Cup Final. *Sheffield*
★11 Dec	**Horse Racing**	The Tripleprint Gold Cup. *Cheltenham*
★16 Dec - 20 Dec	**Equestrian**	Olympia International Championships. *Olympia, London*
★16 Dec - 19 Dec	**Swimming**	British Swimming Championships. *Sheffield*

November/December 1999

Sport	Event	Location	Broadcast
Monday 29th			
Football	FIFA Toyota Cup - World Club Championship	*Tokyo, Japan*	
Tuesday 30th			
Wednesday 1st			
Thursday 2nd			
Friday 3rd			
Lawn Tennis	Davis Cup By NEC Final (First Day Singles)	*tbc*	(BBC)
Saturday 4th			
Ice Hockey	Benson & Hedges Cup Final	*Sheffield*	(BBC)
Lawn Tennis	Davis Cup By NEC Final (Middle Day Doubles)	*tbc*	(BBC)
Lawn Tennis	Davis Cup By NEC Final (Final Day Singles)	*tbc*	(BBC)
Sunday 5th			

Notes

December **1999**

Sport	Event	Location	Broadcast

Monday
6th

Tuesday
7th

Sport	Event	Location	Broadcast
Football	UEFA Cup 3rd Round 2nd Leg	*tbc*	

Wednesday
8th

Sport	Event	Location	Broadcast
Badminton	1999 World Grand Prix Finals Begin	*Jakarta, Indonesia*	
Football	UEFA Champions League Group Match 6	*tbc*	

Thursday
9th

Friday
10th

Saturday
11th

Sunday
12th

Sport	Event	Location	Broadcast
Badminton	1999 World Grand Prix Finals Finish	*Jakarta, Indonesia*	

Notes

December **1999**

Sport	Event	Location	Broadcast

Monday

13th

Tuesday

14th

Wednesday

15th

Thursday

Sport	Event	Location	Broadcast
Equestrian	Olympia International Championships Begin	*Olympia, London*	(BBC)
Swimming	British Championships Begin	*Sheffield*	(BBC)

16th

Friday

17th

Saturday

18th

Sunday

Sport	Event	Location	Broadcast
Swimming	British Championships Finish	*Sheffield*	(BBC)

19th

Notes

December **1999**

Sport	Event	Location	Broadcast
Equestrian	Olympia International Championships Finish	*Olympia, London*	(BBC)

Monday

20th

Tuesday

21st

Wednesday

22nd

Thursday

23rd

Friday

24th

Saturday

25th

Sunday

26th

Notes

December 1999

Sport	Event	Location	Broadcast
Horse Racing	The Pertemps King George VI Steeple Chase	*Kempton Park, Sunbury-on-Thames*	
Ice Hockey	Sekonda Superleague All Stars 99	*London*	(BSkyB)

Monday

27th

Tuesday

28th

Wednesday

29th

Thursday

30th

Friday

31st

Notes

Sportcal Online
The Future of World Sport

The Daily Telegraph Sports Yearbook 1999 is the essential reference guide for all sports enthusiasts who want to know when and where an event is taking place. But what happens when the date of an event changes or the event itself is yet to be announced?
The answer is *Sportcal Online*.

Sportcal Online is a daily updated sports events information service with all the latest news on when and where events are taking place. Covering over 14,000 national and international sports events from now until 2008, it really is the most comprehensive guide to the future of world sport.

All events listed in The Daily Telegraph Sports Yearbook 1999 have been provided by us but if you would like to keep up to date with new event information during 1999 visit our website at: http://www.sportcal.co.uk.
Contact us at:
Sportcal Global Communications Ltd, Hill Place House,
55a High Street, Wimbledon Village,
London SW19 5BA
Telephone: 0181 944 8786
Fax: 0181 944 8740
email: info@sportcal.co.uk

• **Picture courtesy of Reuters**

Angus Loughran

A good bet

Domestic sport fans have a year to savour in 99 as the British Isles hosts both the Cricket and Rugby World Cups. In rugby I expect New Zealand available at 11-4 with Corals to improve dramatically on their desperately disappointing showing last year and rate them the value to lift the Rugby World Cup in the autumn in Cardiff. The top price about the holders, South Africa, is 2-1 with Ladbrokes while Australia is available at 11-4, France the shortest price of the Europeans at 8-1 and England unfancied at 16-1.

In cricket the World Cup as you would expect is extremely open with bookmakers struggling to name a favourite. In a 50-over knock-out competition luck comes into it and the West Indies available at 13-2 look better value than the holders Sri Lanka and South Africa at 7-2. The World Cup Cricket will dominate the sporting summer before the Test series, covered for the first time by Channel 4, takes priority in the latter part of the summer.

Michael Schumacher is hot favourite at evens to win the world title but the value may be in Hills quote of 12-1 for Alex Zanadi recently recruited to the McLaren team to win the title at the first attempt. 12-1 could look a very fair wager come the final event in Japan in November.

The fight everyone has been waiting for will at last happen in 1999 with Evander Holyfield and Lennox Lewis clashing for the undisputed heavyweight championship of the world. This looks a tough fight to call for both the punter and the bookmaker but I take Lewis to dethrone Holyfield and become the unified champion. Expect Tyson to be amongst the first opponents for Lewis if he wins the crown, and a football stadium with a 60,000 capacity a likely venue.

Tiger Woods will once again be the man to beat in the US Masters and the 6-1 with Corals looks fair for the runaway winner of this event two years ago. David Duval who should have won it last year is a generous 14-1 while Lee Westwood who is destined surely to be the next European major winner is 25-1 to win at Augusta and 6-1 to win a major during 1999.

··

The fight everyone has been waiting for will at last happen in 1999 with Evander Holyfield and Lennox Lewis clashing for the undisputed heavyweight championship of the world

··

Victor Chandler offer a generous 20-1 on Tim Henman winning Wimbledon. 1999 could be the year that Henman makes the grand slam breakthrough and if he is to win one of the four major titles it will surely either be at Wimbledon in June or Flushing Meadow, New York in September. Greg Rusedski is only 8-1 to win Wimbledon and the tennis event to look forward to, apart from the grand slams, will be the GB v USA Davis Cup clash in April.

In football the pressure will be on England to qualify for Euro 2000 with Hills offering evens on whether Glen Hoddle's side fail to make it after their disappointing start to the Euro 2000 qualifying campaign. With a defeat in Sweden and a 0-0 draw at home to Bulgaria last October there can be no further slip ups.

The National Hunt Festival at Cheltenham in March is the most eagerly awaited event for followers of the jumpers with Istabraq the defending champion in the Champion Hurdle available at 3-1 and the one they all have to beat again this year. David Nicholson has a Gold Cup prospect in Escartafigue who won impressively at Liverpool last year. For the Classics the 2000 Guineas was blown wide open after the surprise defeat of Stravinsky and Enrique in the Dewhurst and looks wide open, while Bionic is the filly to keep on your side for the 1000 Guineas having only raced once when scoring in a maiden at Goodwood last summer.

Ronnie O'Sullivan has the potential to finally lift the World Snooker Crown at the Crucible Theatre in April and is top price of 5-1 to do so while watch out for Marco Fu, the best young prospect from Asia since James Wattana. Fu beat O'Sullivan in the Grand Prix at Preston last October and could well challenge for many of the games' top honours during 1999.

The golfing highlight aside from the majors will be the Ryder Cup at Brookline in September where the Americans are 4-7 with Hills and the Europeans top price at 5-2 to win the trophy. The Ryder Cup has provided so many close finishes over the last decade that the odds of 10-1 a tie, which would be good enough for Europe to retain the Cup, are quite appealing.

There may be no Olympics, World Cup or European Football Championships this year, but followers of golf, cricket and rugby union will have plenty to savour and to bet on throughout a golden year of sport.

★21/10/98

1999
Fixtures by Sport

Lucy Cope of Slough has her opponent on the hop •**Philip Brown** ★12/4/98

Fixtures 1999

American Football

2-3 Jan	AFC & NFC Wild-card Play-off Games, tbc, USA
9-10 Jan	AFC & NFC Divisional Play-off Games, tbc, USA
17 Jan	AFC & NFC Championship Games, tbc, USA
31 Jan	Superbowl XXXIII, Miami, USA
7 Feb	AFC/NFC Pro Bowl, Honolulu, USA
17 Apr	Start Of 1999 NFL-Europe League Season, Various
27 Jun	World Bowl 99 Presented By Holsten Pilsener, Dusseldorf, Germany
5 Sep	NFL Season Begins, Various, USA

Angling

3 Jul	National Championships Division 5 Peterborough
10 Jul	Junior National Championships Bridgewater
10 Jul	National Championships Intermediate Bridgewater
17 Jul	National Championships Division 3, Woodhall Spa
Aug	Shore Angling World Junior Championships tbc, Italy
7 Aug	National Womens Championships, Shrewsbury
18 Aug	Veterans National Event, Littleport
21 Aug	National Championships Division 2, Stainforth
22 Aug	National Disabled Championships, Holbeach
Sep	Boatangling World Championships, tbc, France
11 Sep	National Championships Division 4, Keadby
25 Sep	National Championships Division 1, Burnham On Sea
Oct	Shore Angling World Championships, tbc, Portugal
Dec	Big Game Fishing World Championships tbc, Croatia

Archery

21 Feb	English Field Archery Indoor Championships Bury St Edmonds
7-12 Mar	5th World Indoor Target Championship Havana, Cuba
19-21 Mar	2nd World Ski-Archery Championships Bessans, France
1-2 May	English Field Archery Spring Shoot, Rushden
29-30 May	All British And Open Field Championships Worthing
Jun	UK Blind Sport Archery Championships Lilleshall
5-6 Jun	UK Masters, Lilleshall
12-13 Jun	English Field Archery Bowhunter Championships, tbc
3 Jul-4 Jul	UK Field Archery Championships Inverness
22-29 Jul	40th World Target Championships, Riom, France
24-25 Jul	National Archery Championships, Rugby
7-14 Aug	World And European 3D Championships, Irrel, Germany
11-14 Aug	Junior European Target Archery Championships, Lilleshall
20-27 Aug	European Field Archery Championships tbc
11-12 Sep	English Field Archery Championships Bury St Edmonds

Athletics

Feb	Africa Invitational, Johannesberg, South Africa
Feb	Engen Grand Prix Final, Cape Town, South Africa
Feb	IAAF Grand Prix 2 Meet, Melbourne, Australia
Feb	Optus Grand Prix, Canberra, Australia
Feb	Optus Grand Prix & Trident Relays, Hobart, Australia
Feb	Optus Grand Prix Final, Brisbane, Australia
14 Feb	Bupa Indoor Grand Prix - Ricoh Tour Birmingham
19 Feb	Flanders Indoors, Ghent, Belgium
21 Feb	Meeting Vittel Du Pas De Calais, Lievin, France
25 Feb	DN Games, Stockholm, Sweden
1 Mar	7 International Grand Prix De Rio Maior Em Marcha Atletica, Rio Maior, Portugal
5-7 Mar	IAAF 7th World Indoor Championships Maebashi, Japan
27-28 Mar	IAAF 27th World Cross Country Championships, Belfast
11 Apr	Berlin Half Marathon, Berlin, Germany
18 Apr	Flora London Marathon, London
19 Apr	Boston Marathon, Hopkinton To Boston, USA
22-24 Apr	Penn Relays, Philadelphia, USA
28 Apr-2 May	The Womens Global Challenge, Various, USA
May	5 Oder-neisse Grand Prix, Eisenhuttenstadt, Germany
May	Grand Prix Brazil De Atletismo, Sao Paulo, Brazil
May	Grand Prix Cantones De La Coruna, La Coruna, Spain
May	Grand Prix Im Gehen Naumburg, Naumburg, Germany
1-2 May	IAAF 19th World Race Walking Cup, Deauville/Mezidon, France
May	Japan Grand Prix, Osaka, Japan
May	Prefontaine Classic, Eugene, USA
May	Softeland Grand Prix, Bergen, Norway
Jun	Mobil Bislett Games, Oslo, Norway
Jun	UK Blind Sport Athletics Championships Solihull
Jun	Znamensky Memorial, Moscow, Russia
12 Jun	Stockholm Marathon, Stockholm, Sweden
19-20 Jun	European Cup Super League, Paris, France
25-27 Jun	USA Track & Field Championships tbc, USA
26 Jun-2 Jul	1999 Island Games, Gotland, Sweden
26-27 Jun	Spar European Cup, tbc
Jul	13th Asian Athletic Championships, Jakarta, Indonesia
Jul	Golden Gala, Rome, Italy
Jul	Meeting Gaz De France, Paris, France
Jul	Nikaia Meeting, Nice, France
Jul	US Open, Edwardsville, USA
Jul	Weltklasse In Koln, Cologne, Germany
1-15 Jul	Universiade, Palma De Mallorca, Spain
3-4 Jul	National Junior Athletics Championships, Blackpool
16-18 Jul	World Youth Championships, Bydgoszcz, Poland
17-18 Jul	National Open Athletics Championships, Birmingham
24 Jul-8 Aug	13th Pan American Games, Winnipeg, Canada
Aug	Athletissima 99, Lausanne, Switzerland
Aug	British Grand Prix, Sheffield
Aug	DN Galan, Stockholm, Sweden
Aug	Herculis Zepter 99, Monte Carlo, Monaco
Aug	Memorial Ivo Van Damme, Brussels, Belgium
Aug	Weltklasse In Zurich, Zurich, Switzerland
20-29 Aug	IAAF 7th World Championships In Seville, Spain
Sep	15th IAAF Grand Prix Final, Sydney, Australia
Sep	IAAF Golden League / Grand Prix Final, Moscow, Russia
Sep	ISTAF'99, Berlin, Germany
26 Sep	26th Berlin Marathon, Berlin, Germany
Oct	IAAF 8th World Half Marathon Championships, tbc
9-16 Dec	Pacific Ocean Games, Santiago, Chile

Badminton

12-17 Jan	World Grand Prix - Korean Open, Seoul, Korea
19-24 Jan	World Grand Prix - Chinese Taipei Open, Taipei, Chinese Taipei
18-21 Feb	1998 World Grand Prix Finals, Jakarta, Indonesia
3-7 Mar	World Grand Prix - Swedish Open, Borlange, Sweden
9-14 Mar	Yonex All England Championships, Birmingham
18-21 Mar	World Grand Prix - Swiss Open, Basel, Switzerland
22-28 Mar	World Grand Prix - Polish Open, Woytek Cicharski, Poland
6-11 Apr	World Grand Prix - Japan, Tokyo, Japan
12-18 Apr	World Grand Prix - Brunei Open, Darussalam, Brunei
10-15 May	6th Sudirman Cup, Copenhagen, Denmark
16-23 May	11th World Championships, Copenhagen, Denmark
1-4 Jul	World Grand Prix - Malaysia
7-11 Jul	World Grand Prix - Thailand
24-8 Aug	13th Pan American Games, Winnipeg, Canada
24-29 Aug	World Grand Prix - Konica Cup, Singapore
26-29 Aug	World Grand Prix - Moscow, Russia,
1-5 Sep	World Grand Prix - Indonesia
8-12 Sep	World Grand Prix - USA
1-4 Oct	World Grand Prix - Netherlands
7-10 Oct	World Grand Prix - Germany
14-17 Oct	World Grand Prix - Denmark
27-31 Oct	World Grand Prix - India
4-7 Nov	World Grand Prix - Chinese Taipei
18-21 Nov	World Grand Prix - China
25-28 Nov	World Grand Prix - Hong Kong
8-12 Dec	1999 World Grand Prix Finals, Jakarta, Indonesia

Baseball

30 Mar	Start Of The Major League Baseball Season, Various, USA
13 Jul	70th All-Star Game, Boston, USA
4-5 Sep	British Baseball Federation National Finals, Brighton
16-24 Oct	Major League Baseball World Series, tbc, USA

Basketball

10 Jan	Sainsbury's Classic Cola National Cup Finals, Sheffield
11-14 Feb	NBA All Star Weekend, Philadelphia, USA
24 Feb	England V Belarus, Plymouth
27 Feb	Dairylea Dunkers All Star Game, Newcastle
13 Mar	Uni-ball Trophy Final, Birmingham
20-22 Apr	Final Four Of The Euro League For Men, Munich, Germany
1-2 May	Budweiser Championships Finals, Wembley, London
28-6 Jun	27th European Championships For Women, Poznan, Pruszkow & Warsaw, Poland
21 Jun-3 Jul	31st European Championships For Men, Various, France
1-15 Jul	Universiade, Palma De Mallorca, Spain
11 Sep	Start Of 1999/2000 Budweiser Championship Season, Various
14-16 Oct	1999 Mcdonalds Championship, tbc
29 Dec	Eurostars 1999 - East V West, tbc

Biathlon

8-10 Jan	Ruhrgas World Cup, Oberhof, Germany
13-17 Jan	Ruhrgas World Cup, Ruhpolding, Germany

22-24 Jan	Ruhrgas World Cup, Antholz, Italy
1-7 Feb	European Championships, Izhevsk, Russia
6-14 Feb	35th World Biathlon Championships Kontiolahti, Finland
23-28 Feb	33rd World Junior Championships, Pokljuka, Slovenia
25-28 Feb	Ruhrgas World Cup, Lake Placid, USA
4-6 Mar	Ruhrgas World Cup, Valcartier, Canada
11-14 Mar	Ruhrgas World Cup Final, Holmenkollen, Norway

Billiards

1-5 Mar	World Matchplay, Bath
8-11 Mar	British Open, Liverpool

Bobsleigh

12-17 Jan	World Cup & European Championships, Winterberg, Germany
18-24 Jan	European Cup, St. Moritz, Switzerland
19-24 Jan	World Cup, Igls, Austria
26-31 Jan	World Cup, St. Moritz, Switzerland
28-31 Jan	Skeleton World Cup, Igls, Austria
1-7 Feb	European Cup, Winterberg, Germany
2-14 Feb	World Championships, Cortina D'Ampezzo, Italy
3-6 Feb	Skeleton World Cup, Konigssee, Germany
8-14 Feb	World Junior Championships, Altenberg, Germany
9-14 Feb	Skeleton World Championships, Altenberg, Germany

Bowls(Lawn/Green)

25-5 Mar	English Womens Indoor Bowls Championship, Exeter
8-12 Mar	British Isles Indoor Bowls Championship, Bournemouth
14-18 Mar	British Isles Womens Indoor Championships Belfast
Apr	UK Indoor Blind Sport Singles Championships, Basingstoke
3-4 Apr	National Short Mat Bowls Championships, Gateshead
10-17 Apr	English Indoor Bowls Championship, Melton
8-9 May	National Bowls Championships, Harlow
17-22 Jun	British Isles Womens International Series, Belfast
5-9 Jul	British Isles Championships, Jersey
4-14 Aug	Womens National Championships, Leamington Spa
15-21 Aug	EBA Championships, Worthing
22-23 Aug	British Isles Junior Womens International Series, Ayr

Boxing

23 Apr	ABA Senior Championships - Finals, Barnsley
8 May	ABA Junior Championships - Finals, Birmingham
24 Jul-8 Aug	13th Pan American Games, Winnipeg, Canada
17 Aug-1 Sep	World Championships, Manila, Philippines
6-16 Nov	World Junior Championships, Tunis, Tunisia
7-16 Dec	Pacific Ocean Games, Santiago, Chile

Canoeing

3-4 Apr	Slalom International, Grandtully
7-9 May	19th Olympic Regatta, Hazewinkel, Belgium
12-13 Jun	Slalom - Bala, Bala
18-20 Jun	Slalom World Cup 1, Tacen, Slovenia
25-27 Jun	Slalom World Cup 2, Skopje, Macedonia
25-27 Jun	XVIII International Regatta, Duisburg, Germany
27 Jun-3 Jul	Canoe Sailing World Championships, Nynaeshamn, Sweden
22-25 Jul	Flatwater Racing World Junior Championships, Zagreb, Croatia
24 Jul-8 Aug	13th Pan American Games, Winnipeg, Canada
31 Jul-1 Aug	Marathon World Championships, Gyor, Hungary
7-8 Aug	International Regatta - Capris '99, Koper Zusterna, Slovenia
13-15 Aug	Slalom World Cup 3, Bratislava, Slovenia
20-22 Aug	Slalom World Cup 4, Augsburg, Germany
26-29 Aug	30th Flatwater Racing World Championships, Milan, Italy
28-29 Aug	Slalom International- Danubia Cup, Bratislava, Slovenia
3-5 Sep	2nd European Championships, Zagreb, Croatia
4-5 Sep	Slalom International- 46th Pieniny Slalom, Pieniny, Slovenia
9-12 Sep	Slalom World Championships For Seniors, La Seu D'Urgell, Spain
11-12 Sep	International Regatta - Adria '99, Koper Ankara, Slovenia
26-28 Sep	Pre Olympic Regatta, Sydney, Australia
30 Sep-3 Oct	Slalom World Cup 5 Finals, Sydney, Australia
30-31 Oct	Slalom International, Llangollen
1-5 Dec	Rodeo World Championships, Taupo, New Zealand

Cricket

1 Jan	Bradman XI V England, Bowral, Australia
2-6 Jan	3rd Test Match - New Zealand V India, Hamilton, New Zealand
2-6 Jan	4th Test Match - South Africa V West Indies, Cape Town, South Africa
2-6 Jan	Fifth Ansett Australia Test - Australia V England, Sydney, Australia
8 Jan	Queensland V England, Brisbane, Australia
9 Jan	1st One Day International - New Zealand V India, Auckland, New Zealand
10 Jan	Carlton & United Series - Australia V England, Brisbane, Australia
11 Jan	Carlton & United Series - Sri Lanka V England, Brisbane, Australia
12 Jan	2nd One Day International - New Zealand V India, Napier, New Zealand
13 Jan	Carlton & United Series - Sri Lanka V Australia, Sydney, Australia
14 Jan	3rd One Day International - New Zealand V India, Wellington, New Zealand
15-19 Jan	5th Test Match - South Africa V West Indies, Pretoria, South Africa
15 Jan	Carlton & United Series - England V Australia, Melbourne, Australia
16 Jan	4th One Day International - New Zealand V India, Auckland, New Zealand
17 Jan	Carlton & United Series - England V Australia, Sydney, Australia
19 Jan	5th One Day International - New Zealand V India, Christchurch, New Zealand
19 Jan	Carlton & United Series - England V Sri Lanka, Melbourne, Australia
21 Jan	Carlton & United Series - Australia V Sri Lanka, Hobart, Australia
22 Jan	1st One Day International - South Africa V West Indies, Johannesburg, South Africa
23 Jan	Carlton & United Series - England V Sri Lanka, Adelaide, Australia
24 Jan	2nd One Day International - South Africa V West Indies, East London, South Africa
24 Jan	Carlton & United Series - Australia V Sri Lanka, Adelaide, Australia
26 Jan	Carlton & United Series - Australia V England, Adelaide, Australia
27 Jan	3rd One Day International - South Africa V West Indies, Durban, South Africa
28 Jan	Carlton & United Series - Australia V Sri Lanka, Sydney, Australia
29 Jan	Carlton & United Series - Sri Lanka V England, Perth, Australia
30 Jan	4th One Day International - South Africa V West Indies, Port Elizabeth, South Africa
31 Jan	Carlton & United Series - Sri Lanka V Australia, Perth, Australia
2-6 Feb	1st Unofficial Test - Zimbabwe V England A, Harare, Zimbabwe
2-5 Feb	1st Youth Test - New Zealand U-19 V England U-19, New Plymouth, New Zealand
2 Feb	5th One Day International - South Africa V West Indies, Cape Town, South Africa
3 Feb	Carlton & United Series - Sri Lanka V England, Sydney, Australia
5 Feb	6th One Day International - South Africa V West Indies, Bloemfontein, South Africa
5 Feb	Carlton & United Series - Australia V England, Sydney, Australia
7 Feb	7th One Day International - South Africa V West Indies, Centurion, South Africa
7 Feb	Carlton & United Series - Sri Lanka V Australia, Perth, Australia
8-11 Feb	2nd Youth Test - New Zealand U-19 V England U-19, Wellington, New Zealand
9-13 Feb	2nd Unofficial Test - Zimbabwe V England A, Bulawayo, Zimbabwe
10 Feb	Carlton & United Series First Final, Sydney, Australia
12 Feb	Carlton & United Series Second Final, Melbourne, Australia
14 Feb	1st One Day International - New Zealand V South Africa, Dunedin, New Zealand
14 Feb	Carlton & United Series Third Final, Melbourne, Australia
16 Feb	1st One Day International - Zimbabwe V England A, Bulawayo, Zimbabwe
17 Feb	2nd One Day International - New Zealand V South Africa, Christchurch, New Zealand
18 Feb	2nd One Day International - Zimbabwe V England A, Harare, Zimbabwe
18-21 Feb	3rd Youth Test - New Zealand U-19 V England U-19, Dunedin, New Zealand
20 Feb	3rd One Day International - New Zealand V South Africa, Auckland, New Zealand
20 Feb	3rd One Day International - Zimbabwe V England A, Harare, Zimbabwe
25 Feb	1st Youth One Day International - New Zealand U-19 V England U-19, Christchurch, New Zealand
27 Feb-3 Mar	1st Test Match - New Zealand V South Africa, Auckland, New Zealand
27 Feb	2nd Youth One Day International - New Zealand U-19 V England U-19, Hamilton, New Zealand
1 Mar	3rd Youth One Day International - New Zealand U-19 V England U-19, Hamilton, New Zealand
5-9 Mar	1st Test Match - West Indies V Australia, Port Of Spain, Trinidad And Tobago

189

Fixtures 1999

11-15 Mar	2nd Test Match - New Zealand V South Africa, Christchurch, New Zealand	8 May	1999 World Cup Warm-up Match - Australia V Glamorgan, Cardiff	19 May	Nat West Trophy 2nd Round - Herefordshire V tbc, tbc
13-17 Mar	2nd Test Match - West Indies V Australia, Kingston, Trinidad And Tobago	8 May	1999 World Cup Warm-up Match - Bangladesh V Essex, Chelmsford	19 May	Nat West Trophy 2nd Round - Lancashire V tbc, tbc
18-22 Mar	3rd Test Match - New Zealand V South Africa, Wellington, New Zealand	8 May	1999 World Cup Warm-up Match - New Zealand V Hampshire, Southampton	19 May	Nat West Trophy 2nd Round - Middlesex V tbc, tbc
25 Mar	4th One Day International - New Zealand V South Africa, Napier, New Zealand	8 May	1999 World Cup Warm-up Match - Pakistan V Derbyshire, Derby	19 May	Nat West Trophy 2nd Round - Shropshire V tbc, tbc
26-30 Mar	3rd Test Match - West Indies V Australia, Bridgetown, Barbados	8 May	1999 World Cup Warm-up Match - Scotland V Durham, Chester-le-Street	19 May	Nat West Trophy 2nd Round - Somerset V tbc, tbc
27 Mar	5th One Day International - New Zealand V South Africa, Auckland, New Zealand	8 May	1999 World Cup Warm-up Match - West Indies V Gloucestershire, Bristol	19 May	Nat West Trophy 2nd Round - tbc V Buckinghamshire, tbc
30 Mar	6th One Day International - New Zealand V South Africa, Wellington, New Zealand	9 May	1999 World Cup Warm-up Match - England V Essex, Chelmsford	19 May	Nat West Trophy 2nd Round - tbc V Cheshire, tbc
1 Apr	Sharjah Cup, Sharjah, United Arab Emirates	9 May	1999 World Cup Warm-up Match - India V Yorkshire, Leeds	19 May	Nat West Trophy 2nd Round - tbc V Dorset, tbc
3-7 Apr	4th Test Match - West Indies V Australia, St John's, Antigua	9 May	1999 World Cup Warm-up Match - Kenya V Gloucestershire, Bristol	19 May	Nat West Trophy 2nd Round - tbc V Essex, tbc
11 Apr	1st One Day International - West Indies V Australia, tbc, St Vincent	9 May	1999 World Cup Warm-up Match - South Africa V Kent, Canterbury	19 May	Nat West Trophy 2nd Round - tbc V Staffordshire, tbc
13 Apr	County Championship begins, Various	9 May	1999 World Cup Warm-up Match - Sri Lanka V Nottinghamshire, Nottingham	19 May	Nat West Trophy 2nd Round - tbc V Sussex, tbc
14 Apr	2nd One Day International - West Indies V Australia, tbc, Grenada	9 May	1999 World Cup Warm-up Match - Zimbabwe V Derbyshire, Derby	19 May	Nat West Trophy 2nd Round - tbc V Worcestershire, tbc
17 Apr	3rd One Day International - West Indies V Australia, tbc, Trinidad and Tobago	10 May	1999 World Cup Warm-up Match - Australia V Worcestershire, Worcester	20 May	Cricket World Cup - Australia V New Zealand, Cardiff
17 Ap	National One-day League begins, Various	10 May	1999 World Cup Warm-up Match - Bangladesh V Middlesex, London	20 May	Cricket World Cup - Pakistan V Scotland, Chester-le-Street
18 Apr	4th One Day International - West Indies V Australia, tbc, Trinidad And Tobago	10 May	1999 World Cup Warm-up Match - New Zealand V Surrey, Kennington, London	21 May	Cricket World Cup - West Indies V Bangladesh, tbc, Ireland
21 Apr	5th One Day International - West Indies V Australia, tbc, Guyana	10 May	1999 World Cup Warm-up Match - Pakistan V Durham, Chester-le-Street	22 May	Cricket World Cup - England V South Africa, London
24 Apr	6th One Day International - West Indies V Australia, tbc, Barbados	10 May	1999 World Cup Warm-up Match - Scotland V Lancashire, Manchester	22 May	Cricket World Cup - Zimbabwe V Sri Lanka, Worcester
25 Apr	7th One Day International - West Indies V Australia, tbc, Barbados	10 May	1999 World Cup Warm-up Match - West Indies V Warwickshire, Birmingham	23 May	Cricket World Cup - Australia V Pakistan, Leeds
4 May	Nat West Trophy 1st Round - Bedfordshire V Huntingdonshire, tbc	11 May	1999 World Cup Warm-up Match - England V Hampshire, Southampton	23 May	Cricket World Cup - Kenya V India, Bristol
4 May	Nat West Trophy 1st Round - Berkshire V Warwickshire, tbc	11 May	1999 World Cup Warm-up Match - India V Nottinghamshire, Nottingham	23 May	Natwest Trophy 3rd Round, tbc
4 May	Nat West Trophy 1st Round - Cumbria V Cornwall, tbc	11 May	1999 World Cup Warm-up Match - Kenya V Glamorgan, Cardiff	24 May	Cricket World Cup - Scotland V Bangladesh, Edinburgh
4 May	Nat West Trophy 1st Round - Durham V Oxfordshire, tbc	11 May	1999 World Cup Warm-up Match - South Africa V Middlesex, London	24 May	Cricket World Cup - West Indies V New Zealand, Southampton
4 May	Nat West Trophy 1st Round - Gloucestershire V Yorkshire, tbc	11 May	1999 World Cup Warm-up Match - Sri Lanka V Leicestershire, Leicester	25 May	Cricket World Cup - England V Zimbabwe, Nottingham
4 May	Nat West Trophy 1st Round - Hertfordshire V Leicestershire, tbc	11 May	1999 World Cup Warm-up Match - Zimbabwe V Warwickshire, Birmingham	26 May	Cricket World Cup - South Africa V Kenya, Amstelveen, Netherlands
4 May	Nat West Trophy 1st Round - Kent V Denmark, tbc	12 May	1999 World Cup Warm-up Match - Australia V Somerset, Taunton	26 May	Cricket World Cup - Sri Lanka V India, Taunton
4 May	Nat West Trophy 1st Round - Lincolnshire V Wales, tbc	12 May	1999 World Cup Warm-up Match - Bangladesh V Northamptonshire, Northampton	27 May	Cricket World Cup - Australia V Bangladesh, Chester-le-Street
4 May	Nat West Trophy 1st Round - Netherlands V Cambridgeshire, The Hague, Netherlands	12 May	1999 World Cup Warm-up Match - New Zealand V Sussex, Hove	27 May	Cricket World Cup - West Indies V Scotland, Leicester
4 May	Nat West Trophy 1st Round - Northamptonshire V Wiltshire, tbc	12 May	1999 World Cup Warm-up Match - Pakistan V Lancashire, Manchester	28 May	Cricket World Cup - New Zealand V Pakistan, Derby
4 May	Nat West Trophy 1st Round - Northumberland V Ireland, tbc	12 May	1999 World Cup Warm-up Match - Scotland V Yorkshire, Leeds	29 May	Cricket World Cup - England V India, Birmingham
4 May	Nat West Trophy 1st Round - Scotland V Nottinghamshire, tbc	12 May	1999 World Cup Warm-up Match - West Indies V Surrey, Kennington, London	29 May	Cricket World Cup - Zimbabwe V South Africa, Chelmsford
4 May	Nat West Trophy 1st Round - Suffolk V Hampshire, tbc	14 May	Cricket World Cup - England V Sri Lanka, London	30 May	Cricket World Cup - Sri Lanka V Kenya, Southampton
4 May	Nat West Trophy 1st Round - Surrey V Norfolk, tbc	15 May	Cricket World Cup - India V South Africa, Hove	30 May	Cricket World Cup - West Indies V Australia, Manchester
7 May	1999 World Cup Warm-up Match - England V Kent, Canterbury	15 May	Cricket World Cup - Zimbabwe V Kenya, Taunton	31 May	Cricket World Cup - Pakistan V Bangladesh, Northampton
7 May	1999 World Cup Warm-up Match - India V Leicestershire, Leicester	16 May	Cricket World Cup - Australia V Scotland, Worcester	31 May	Cricket World Cup - Scotland V New Zealand, Edinburgh
7 May	1999 World Cup Warm-up Match - Kenya V Somerset, Taunton	16 May	Cricket World Cup - West Indies V Pakistan, Bristol	4 Jun	Cricket World Cup - Group A Second V Group B Second, London
7 May	1999 World Cup Warm-up Match - South Africa V Sussex, Hove	17 May	Cricket World Cup - New Zealand V Bangladesh, Chelmsford	5 Jun	Cricket World Cup - Group A First V Group B First, Nottingham
7 May	1999 World Cup Warm-up Match - Sri Lanka V Northamptonshire, Northampton	18 May	Cricket World Cup - England V Kenya, Canterbury	6 Jun	Cricket World Cup - Group A Third V Group B Third, Leeds
7 May	1999 World Cup Warm-up Match - Zimbabwe V Worcestershire, Worcester	19 May	Cricket World Cup - India V Zimbabwe, Leicester	8 Jun	Cricket World Cup - Group A Second V Group B First, Manchester
		19 May	Cricket World Cup - Sri Lanka V South Africa, Northampton	9 Jun	Cricket World Cup - Group A Third V Group B Second, London
		19 May	Nat West Trophy 2nd Round - Derbyshire V tbc, tbc	10 Jun	Cricket World Cup - Group A First V Group B Third, Birmingham
		19 May	Nat West Trophy 2nd Round - Devon V tbc, tbc		

11 Jun	Cricket World Cup - Group A Third V Group B First, London
12 Jun	Cricket World Cup - Group A Second V Group B Third, Nottingham
13 Jun	Cricket World Cup - Group A First V Group B Second, Leeds
16 Jun	Cricket World Cup - Semi Final 1, Manchester
17 Jun	Cricket World Cup - Semi Final 2, Birmingham
20 Jun	Cricket World Cup Final, London
25 Jun	Super Cup Quarter Final 1, tbc
26 Jun	Super Cup Quarter Final 2, tbc
26 Jun	Super Cup Quarter Final 3, tbc
27 Jun	Super Cup Quarter Final 4, tbc
1-5 Jul	1st Test Match - England V New Zealand, Birmingham
7 Jul	Natwest Trophy 4th Round, tbc
10 Jul	Super Cup Semi Final 1, tbc
11 Jul	Super Cup Semi Final 2, tbc
22-26 Jul	2nd Test Match - England V New Zealand, London
28 Jul	Natwest Trophy Quarter Finals, tbc
31 Jul	Super Cup Final, tbc
1 Aug	UK Blind Sport Knockout Finals, London
5-9 Aug	3rd Test Match - England V New Zealand, Manchester
14 Aug	Natwest Trophy Semi Final 1, tbc
15 Aug	Natwest Trophy Semi Final 2, tbc
19-23 Aug	4th Test Match - England V New Zealand, London
28 Aug	Natwest Trophy Final, London
19 Sep	National One-day League finishes, Various
28 Sep	County Championship begins, Various

Croquet

5-6 Jun	Home Internationals, Budleigh Salterton
7-13 Jun	Mens & Womens Championships, Cheltenham
1-4 Jul	Senior Championships, Surbiton
4-11 Jul	Open Championships, London
19-25 Jul	Veterans Championships, Southwick
22-25 Jul	Challenge & Gilbey, Nottingham
25-29 Aug	Barlow Bowl, Southwick
25-29 Aug	Longman Bowl, Southwick
8-12 Sep	Spencer ELL Cup, Parkstone
9-12 Sep	Chairmans Salver, Southport
9-12 Sep	Presidents Cup, Bowdon
18-19 Sep	All England Final, Pendle
2-3 Oct	CA Finals Weekend, Cheltenham

Curling

19-21 Mar	RCCC Rink Championships, Aviemore
20-28 Mar	World Junior Curling Championships, Ostersund, Sweden
2-11 Apr	Ford World Curling Championships, New Brunswick, Canada
Dec	European Curling Championships, Chamonix, France

Cycling

20 Mar	World Cup - Milano-San Remo, Italy
21 Mar	Premier Road Race - Grand Prix Of Essex, Halstead
27-28 Mar	Premier Road Race - Europa 2 Day, Meonstoke
3-5 Apr	Premier Road Race - Girvan 3 Day, Girvan
5 Apr	World Cup - Tour Des Flandres, Belgium
11 Apr	Premier Road Race - Archer International GP, Beaconsfield
18 Apr	Premier Road Race - Lancaster-Hertford GP, Welwyn Garden City
18 Apr	World Cup - Liege-Bastogne-Liege, Belgium

24-25 Apr	Premier Road Race - East Riding Classic, Hull
24 Apr	World Cup - Amstel Gold Race, Heerlen - Mastrich, Netherlands
29 Apr-3 May	Premier Road Race - Travelwise Tour, tbc
9 May	Premier Road Race - Lincoln International GP, Lincoln
15 May-6 Jun	Giro D'Italia, Various, Italy
15-16 May	Premier Road Race - Silver Spoon 2 Day, Ollerton
23-29 May	The Prutour, Various
29-30 May	Premier Road Race - Tour Of The Kingdom, Dunfermline
25 Jun	Premier Road Race - Manx International, Isle Of Man
27 Jun	Elite Road Race, Solihull
3 Jul-25 Jul	Tour De France, Various, France
3 Jul	Tour De France - Prologue, Puy De Fou, France
4 Jul	Tour De France - 1st Stage, Montaigu - Challans, France
11 Jul	Premier Road Race - Five Valleys RR, Port Talbot
23-30 Jul	National Track Championships, Manchester
24 Jul-8 Aug	13th Pan American Games, Winnipeg, Canada
30 Jul	Gala International, Manchester
1 Aug	Premier Road Race - International Tour Of The Cottswolds, Gloucester
7 Aug	World Cup - San Sebastian, Spain
8 Aug	Premier Road Race - Havant Grand Prix, Havant
22 Aug	World Cup - GP Suisse, Switzerland
4-26 Sep	Vuelta A España, Various, Spain
5 Sep	Premier Road Race - Rourke Grand Prix, Stafford
12 Sep	Premier Road Race - Tour Of The Peak, Buxton
22-26 Sep	UCI World Masters Championships, Manchester
1 Oct	World Time Trial Championships, Avoriaz, France
3 Oct	World Cup - Paris-Tours, Paris, France
5-10 Oct	World Road Championships, Verona/Trevise, Italy
16 Oct	World Cup - Giro Di Lombardia, Italy
20-24 Oct	World Track Championships, Berlin, Germany

Cyclo-cross

30-31 Jan	World Championships, Poprad, Slovakia

Darts

3 Jan	PDC Skol World Championships, Purfleet
2-10 Jan	Embassy World Darts Championship, Frimley Green
1 Feb	5th Scottish Open, tbc
5-7 Feb	Eastbourne Festival, Eastbourne
27 Feb	British Internationals, Frimley Green, Surrey
20-21 Mar	German Open, Bochum, Germany
23-25 Apr	Antwerp Open, Antwerp, Belgium
1 May	Welsh Open, tbc
20-23 May	Golden Harvest North American Open, Saskatoon, Canada
1 Jun	English Open, Camber Sands
4-6 Jun	Pontins Festival, Prestatyn
25-31 Jul	World Matchplay, Blackpool
13-15 Aug	North American Open, Las Vegas, USA
6-9 Oct	World Cup XII, Durban, South Africa
8-10 Oct	Chicago Open, Chicago, USA
13-17 Oct	World Grand Prix, Rochester
12-14 Nov	Boston Witch City Open, Boston, USA
19-21 Nov	Belgian Masters, Honthalen, Belgium
Dec	British Open, tbc
Dec	Winmau World Masters, tbc
27 Dec	PDC Skol World Championships, Purfleet

Diving

12-16 Jan	11th FINA Diving World Cup & Diving Grand Prix 1, Wellington, New Zealand
19-21 Jan	Diving Grand Prix 2, Sydney, Australia
5-7 Mar	Diving Grand Prix 3, Gelsenkirchen, Germany
11-14 Mar	Diving Grand Prix 4, Electrostal, Russia
28 Apr-2 May	The Womens Global Challenge, Various, USA
29 Apr-2 May	Diving Grand Prix 5, Montreal, Canada
6-9 May	Diving Grand Prix 6, tbc, USA
6-9 May	Diving Grand Prix 7, Juarez City, Mexico
27-30 May	Diving Grand Prix 8, Hong Kong, PR China
3-6 Jun	Diving Grand Prix 9, tbc, PR China
10-12 Jun	Diving Grand Prix 10, Glasgow
18-20 Jun	Diving Grand Prix 11, Madrid, Spain
27-29 Jun	Diving Grand Prix 12, Budapest, Hungary
27-29 Jun	Diving Grand Prix 13, Ronneby, Sweden
2-4 Jul	Diving Grand Prix 14, Vienna, Austria
2-13 Jul	Universiade, Palma De Mallorca, Spain
7-9 Jul	Diving Grand Prix 15, Rome, Italy
24 Jul-8 Aug	13th Pan American Games, Winnipeg, Canada
18-22 Aug	FINA XI Junior Diving World Championships, Partubice, Czech Republic
11-12 Sep	Diving Grand Prix Super Final, tbc
7-11 Dec	Pacific Ocean Games, Santiago, Chile

Equestrian

1-4 Apr	Danish International Horse Show, Aarhus, Denmark
23-25 Apr	National Winter Dressage Championships, Addington
24-25 Apr	World Cup Jumping Final, Gothenburg, Sweden
3-6 May	The Albert E Sharp Horse Trials, Sansaw Park
6-9 May	Mitsubishi Motors Badminton Horse Trials, Badminton
13-16 May	British Nations Cup & Grand Prix, Windsor
27-30 May	The Chubb Insurance Windsor International Horse Trials, Windsor
10-13 Jun	Bramham International Horse Trials, Bramham, Wetherby, Yorks
10-13 Jun	International Jumping Event, Helsinki, Finland
17-20 Jun	Macallan Burgie Horse Trials, Elgin
6-11 Jul	Canadian FEI Jumper Competition, Blainville, Canada
7-11 Jul	Royal International Horse Show, Hickstead
8-11 Jul	International Dressage Event, Falsterbo, Sweden
8-11 Jul	International Jumping Event, Falsterbo, Sweden
24 Jul-8 Aug	13th Pan American Games, Winnipeg, Canada
5-9 Aug	International Jumping Event, Dublin, Ireland
21-24 Aug	International Dressage Event, Rotterdam, Netherlands
21-24 Aug	International Jumping Event, Rotterdam, Netherlands
24-30 Aug	European Jumping Championship, Hickstead
26-29 Aug	Blair Castle International Horse Trials, Blair Athol
26-29 Aug	World Driving Championships, Bordeaux, France
2-5 Sep	Burghley Pedigree Chum Horse Trials, Burghley
8-12 Sep	Canadian FEI Jumper Competition, Spruce Meadows, Canada
9-12 Sep	Blenheim International Horse Trials, Woodstock
10-12 Sep	International Driving Event, Targu Secuiesc, Romania
16-19 Sep	International Jumping Event, Linz, Austria
17-19 Sep	BD National Dressage Championships, tbc

Fixtures 1999

23-26 Sep	International Jumping Event, Prague, Czech Republic
29 Sep-3 Oct	Horse Of The Year Show, Wembley, London
7-10 Oct	Weston Park Horse Trials, Shifnal
21-24 Oct	International Three Day Event, Le Lion D'Angers, France
24-31 Oct	International Jumping Event - Washington International Horse Show, Landover, USA
12-14 Nov	International Dressage Event, Brussels, Belgium
12-14 Nov	International Jumping Event, Brussels, Belgium
6-17 Dec	Pacific Ocean Games, Santiago, Chile
16-20 Dec	Olympia International Championships, Olympia, London

Fencing

15-16 Jan	Coppa De Brasil - Grand Prix FIE, Rio De Janeiro, Brazil
30-31 Jan	C.I.P. - Grand Prix FIE, Paris, France
30-31 Jan	Coupe Martini - Grand Prix FIE, Budapest, Hungary
6-7 Feb	Coupe Gerevich - Grand Prix FIE, Budapest, Hungary
27-28 Feb	Candidature A - Grand Prix FIE, Seoul, Korea
27-28 Feb	T. Daewoo - Grand Prix FIE, Seoul, Korea
13-14 Mar	Coupe Akropolis - Grand Prix FIE, Athens, Greece
13-14 Mar	Reinhold Wurth Cup - Grand Prix FIE, Tauberbischofsheim, Germany
27 Mar	British Sabre Championship, Taunton
9-10 Apr	Grand Prix Heidenheim, Heidenheim, Germany
30 Apr-1 May	Trophee Esperia - Grand Prix FIE, Come, Italy
8 May	British Foil Championship, Milton Keynes
8-9 May	Tournoi International - Grand Prix FIE, Buenos Aires, Argentina
15 May	British Epee Championship, London
15-16 May	Villa De Madrid - Grand Prix FIE, Madrid, Spain
22-23 May	Tournoi International - Grand Prix FIE, Espinho, Portugal
28-29 May	Trophee Luxardo - Grand Prix FIE, Abano Terme, Italy
4-5 Jun	Tournoi International - Grand Prix FIE, Rochester, USA
11-12 Jun	Candidature A - Grand Prix FIE, Bucharest, Romania
19-20 Jun	Coppa Villa La Habana - Grand Prix FIE, Havana, Cuba
19-20 Jun	Tournoi International - Grand Prix FIE, Havana, Cuba
1-15 Jul	Universiade, Palma De Mallorca, Spain
24 Jul-8 Aug	13th Pan American Games, Winnipeg, Canada
4-5 Sep	Challenge Bernadotte - Grand Prix FIE, Stockholm, Sweden
11-12 Sep	C.Cidade De Lisboa - Grand Prix FIE, Lisbon, Portugal
Oct	World Championships, Seoul, Korea
2-3 Oct	Grand Prix Tractorul, Brasov, Romania
7-12 Dec	Pacific Ocean Games, Santiago, Chile

Fives

20-21 Mar	National Open Doubles Championships, London
17-18 Apr	National Clubs Championships, London
1-2 May	Scottish Championships, Edinburgh
4-5 Dec	National Open Singles Championships, tbc

Football

FA Carling Premiership

9 Jan	Arsenal V Liverpool, Highbury, London
9 Jan	Blackburn Rovers V Leeds United, Ewood Park, Blackburn
9 Jan	Coventry City V Nottingham Forest, Highfield Rd, Coventry
9 Jan	Everton V Leicester City, Goodison Park, Liverpool
9 Jan	Manchester United V West Ham United, Old Trafford, Manchester
9 Jan	Middlesbrough V Aston Villa, Cellnet Stadium, Middlesbrough
9 Jan	Newcastle United V Chelsea, St James' Park, Newcastle
9 Jan	Sheffield Wednesday V Tottenham Hotspur, Hillsborough, Sheffield
9 Jan	Southampton V Charlton Athletic, The Dell, Southampton
9 Jan	Wimbledon V Derby County, Selhurst Park, London
16 Jan	Aston Villa V Everton, Villa Park, Birmingham
16 Jan	Charlton Athletic V Newcastle United, The Valley, London
16 Jan	Chelsea V Coventry City, Stamford Bridge, London
16 Jan	Derby County V Blackburn Rovers, Pride Park, Derby
16 Jan	Leeds United V Middlesbrough, Elland Rd, Leeds
16 Jan	Leicester City V Manchester United, Filbert Street, Leicester
16 Jan	Liverpool V Southampton, Anfield, Liverpool
16 Jan	Nottingham Forest V Arsenal, City Ground, Nottingham
16 Jan	Tottenham Hotspur V Wimbledon, White Hart Lane, London
16 Jan	West Ham United V Sheffield Wednesday, Upton Park, London
30 Jan	Arsenal V Chelsea, Highbury, London
30 Jan	Blackburn Rovers V Tottenham Hotspur, Ewood Park, Blackburn
30 Jan	Charlton Athletic V Manchester United, The Valley, London
30 Jan	Coventry City V Liverpool, Highfield Rd, Coventry
30 Jan	Everton V Nottingham Forest, Goodison Park, Liverpool
30 Jan	Middlesbrough V Leicester City, Cellnet Stadium, Middlesbrough
30 Jan	Newcastle United V Aston Villa, St James' Park, Newcastle
30 Jan	Sheffield Wednesday V Derby County, Hillsborough, Sheffield
30 Jan	Southampton V Leeds United, The Dell, Southampton
30 Jan	Wimbledon V West Ham United, Selhurst Park, London
6 Feb	Aston Villa V Blackburn Rovers, Villa Park, Birmingham
6 Feb	Charlton Athletic V Wimbledon, The Valley, London
6 Feb	Chelsea V Southampton, Stamford Bridge, London
6 Feb	Derby County V Everton, Pride Park, Derby
6 Feb	Leeds United V Newcastle United, Elland Rd, Leeds
6 Feb	Leicester City V Sheffield Wednesday, Filbert Street, Leicester
6 Feb	Liverpool V Middlesbrough, Anfield, Liverpool
6 Feb	Nottingham Forest V Man. United, City Ground, Nottingham
6 Feb	Tottenham Hotspur V Coventry City, White Hart Lane, London
6 Feb	West Ham United V Arsenal, Upton Park, London
13 Feb	Aston Villa V Leeds United, Villa Park, Birmingham
13 Feb	Charlton Athletic V Liverpool, The Valley, London
13 Feb	Chelsea V Blackburn Rovers, Stamford Bridge, London
13 Feb	Everton V Middlesbrough, Goodison Park, Liverpool
13 Feb	Leicester City V Derby County, Filbert Street, Leicester
13 Feb	Manchester United V Arsenal, Old Trafford, Manchester
13 Feb	Newcastle United V Coventry City, St James' Park, Newcastle
13 Feb	Sheffield Wednesday V Wimbledon, Hillsborough, Sheffield
13 Feb	Tottenham Hotspur V Southampton, White Hart Lane, London
13 Feb	West Ham United V Nottingham Forest, Upton Park, London
20 Feb	Arsenal V Leicester City, Highbury, London
20 Feb	Blackburn Rovers V Sheffield Wednesday, Ewood Park, Blackburn
20 Feb	Coventry City V Manchester United, Highfield Rd, Coventry
20 Feb	Derby County V Charlton Athletic, Pride Park, Derby
20 Feb	Leeds United V Everton, Elland Rd, Leeds
20 Feb	Liverpool V West Ham United, Anfield, Liverpool
20 Feb	Middlesbrough V Tottenham Hotspur, Cellnet Stadium, Middlesbrough
20 Feb	Nottingham Forest V Chelsea, City Ground, Nottingham
20 Feb	Southampton V Newcastle United, The Dell, Southampton
20 Feb	Wimbledon V Aston Villa, Selhurst Park, London
27 Feb	Aston Villa V Coventry City, Villa Park, Birmingham
27 Feb	Charlton Athletic V Nottingham Forest, The Valley, London
27 Feb	Chelsea V Liverpool, Stamford Bridge, London
27 Feb	Everton V Wimbledon, Goodison Park, Liverpool
27 Feb	Leicester City V Leeds United, Filbert Street, Leicester
27 Feb	Manchester United V Southampton, Old Trafford, Manchester
27 Feb	Newcastle United V Arsenal, St James' Park, Newcastle
27 Feb	Sheffield Wednesday V Middlesbrough, Hillsborough, Sheffield
27 Feb	Tottenham Hotspur V Derby County, White Hart Lane, London
27 Feb	West Ham United V Blackburn Rovers, Upton Park, London
6 Mar	Arsenal V Sheffield Wednesday, Highbury, London
6 Mar	Blackburn Rovers V Everton, Ewood Park, Blackburn
6 Mar	Coventry City V Charlton Athletic, Highfield Rd, Coventry
6 Mar	Derby County V Aston Villa, Pride Park, Derby
6 Mar	Leeds United V Tottenham Hotspur, Elland Rd, Leeds
6 Mar	Liverpool V Manchester United, Anfield, Liverpool
6 Mar	Middlesbrough V Chelsea, Cellnet Stadium, Middlesbrough
6 Mar	Nottingham Forest V Newcastle United, City Ground, Nottingham
6 Mar	Southampton V West Ham United, The Dell, Southampton
6 Mar	Wimbledon V Leicester City, Selhurst Park, London
13 Mar	Chelsea V West Ham United, Stamford Bridge, London
13 Mar	Coventry City V Blackburn Rovers, Highfield Rd, Coventry
13 Mar	Derby County V Liverpool, Pride Park, Derby
13 Mar	Everton V Arsenal, Goodison Park, Liverpool

Fixtures 1999

13 Mar	Leicester City V Charlton Athletic	Filbert Street, Leicester
13 Mar	Middlesbrough V Southampton	Cellnet Stadium, Middlesbrough
13 Mar	Newcastle United V Manchester United	St James' Park, Newcastle
13 Mar	Sheffield Wednesday V Leeds United	Hillsborough, Sheffield
13 Mar	Tottenham Hotspur V Aston Villa	White Hart Lane, London
13 Mar	Wimbledon V Nottingham Forest	Selhurst Park, London
20 Mar	Arsenal V Coventry City	Highbury, London
20 Mar	Aston Villa V Chelsea	Villa Park, Birmingham
20 Mar	Blackburn Rovers V Wimbledon	Ewood Park, Blackburn
20 Mar	Charlton Athletic V Tottenham Hotspur	The Valley, London
20 Mar	Leeds United V Derby County	Elland Rd, Leeds
20 Mar	Liverpool V Leicester City	Anfield, Liverpool
20 Mar	Manchester United V Everton	Old Trafford, Manchester
20 Mar	Nottingham Forest V Middlesbrough	City Ground, Nottingham
20 Mar	Southampton V Sheffield Wednesday	The Dell, Southampton
20 Mar	West Ham United V Newcastle United	Upton Park, London
3 Apr	Aston Villa V West Ham United	Villa Park, Birmingham
3 Apr	Blackburn Rovers V Middlesbrough	Ewood Park, Blackburn
3 Apr	Charlton Athletic V Chelsea	The Valley, London
3 Apr	Derby County V Newcastle United	Pride Park, Derby
3 Apr	Leeds United V Nottingham Forest	Elland Rd, Leeds
3 Apr	Liverpool V Everton	Anfield, Liverpool
3 Apr	Sheffield Wednesday V Coventry City	Hillsborough, Sheffield
3 Apr	Southampton V Arsenal	The Dell, Southampton
3 Apr	Tottenham Hotspur V Leicester City	White Hart Lane, London
3 Apr	Wimbledon V Manchester United	Selhurst Park, London
5 Apr	Arsenal V Blackburn Rovers	Highbury, London
5 Apr	Chelsea V Leeds United	Stamford Bridge, London
5 Apr	Coventry City V Southampton	Highfield Rd, Coventry
5 Apr	Everton V Sheffield Wednesday	Goodison Park, Liverpool
5 Apr	Leicester City V Aston Villa	Filbert Street, Leicester
5 Apr	Manchester United V Derby County	Old Trafford, Manchester
5 Apr	Middlesbrough V Wimbledon	Cellnet Stadium, Middlesbrough
5 Apr	Newcastle United V Tottenham Hotspur	St James' Park, Newcastle
5 Apr	Nottingham Forest V Liverpool	City Ground, Nottingham
5 Apr	West Ham United V Charlton Athletic	Upton Park, London
10 Apr	Aston Villa V Southampton	Villa Park, Birmingham
10 Apr	Blackburn Rovers V Manchester United	Ewood Park, Blackburn
10 Apr	Derby County V Nottingham Forest	Pride Park, Derby
10 Apr	Everton V Coventry City	Goodison Park, Liverpool
10 Apr	Leeds United V Liverpool	Elland Rd, Leeds
10 Apr	Leicester City V West Ham United	Filbert Street, Leicester
10 Apr	Middlesbrough V Charlton Athletic	Cellnet Stadium, Middlesbrough
10 Apr	Sheffield Wednesday V Newcastle United	Hillsborough, Sheffield
10 Apr	Tottenham Hotspur V Arsenal	White Hart Lane, London
10 Apr	Wimbledon V Chelsea	Selhurst Park, London
17 Apr	Arsenal V Wimbledon	Highbury, London
17 Apr	Charlton Athletic V Leeds United	The Valley, London
17 Apr	Chelsea V Leicester City	Stamford Bridge, London
17 Apr	Coventry City V Middlesbrough	Highfield Rd, Coventry
17 Apr	Liverpool V Aston Villa	Anfield, Liverpool
17 Apr	Manchester United V Sheffield Wednesday	Old Trafford, Manchester
17 Apr	Newcastle United V Everton	St James' Park, Newcastle
17 Apr	Nottingham Forest V Tottenham Hotspur	City Ground, Nottingham
17 Apr	Southampton V Blackburn Rovers	The Dell, Southampton
17 Apr	West Ham United V Derby County	Upton Park, London
24 Apr	Aston Villa V Nottingham Forest	Villa Park, Birmingham
24 Apr	Blackburn Rovers V Leicester City	Ewood Park, Blackburn
24 Apr	Derby County V Southampton	Pride Park, Derby
24 Apr	Everton V Charlton Athletic	Goodison Park, Liverpool
24 Apr	Leeds United V Manchester United	Elland Rd, Leeds
24 Apr	Leicester City V Coventry City	Filbert Street, Leicester
24 Apr	Middlesbrough V Arsenal	Cellnet Stadium, Middlesbrough
24 Apr	Sheffield Wednesday V Chelsea	Hillsborough, Sheffield
24 Apr	Tottenham Hotspur V West Ham United	White Hart Lane, London
24 Apr	Wimbledon V Newcastle United	Selhurst Park, London
1 May	Arsenal V Derby County	Highbury, London
1 May	Charlton Athletic V Blackburn Rovers	The Valley, London
1 May	Chelsea V Everton	Stamford Bridge, London
1 May	Coventry City V Wimbledon	Highfield Rd, Coventry
1 May	Liverpool V Tottenham Hotspur	Anfield, Liverpool
1 May	Manchester United V Aston Villa	Old Trafford, Manchester
1 May	Newcastle United V Middlesbrough	St James' Park, Newcastle
1 May	Nottingham Forest V Sheffield Wednesday	City Ground, Nottingham
1 May	Southampton V Leicester City	The Dell, Southampton
1 May	West Ham United V Leeds United	Upton Park, London
8 May	Aston Villa V Charlton Athletic	Villa Park, Birmingham
8 May	Blackburn Rovers V Nottingham Forest	Ewood Park, Blackburn
8 May	Derby County V Coventry City	Pride Park, Derby
8 May	Everton V West Ham United	Goodison Park, Liverpool
8 May	Leeds United V Arsenal	Elland Rd, Leeds
8 May	Leicester City V Newcastle United	Filbert Street, Leicester
8 May	Middlesbrough V Manchester United	Cellnet Stadium, Middlesbrough
8 May	Sheffield Wednesday V Liverpool	Hillsborough, Sheffield
8 May	Tottenham Hotspur V Chelsea	White Hart Lane, London
8 May	Wimbledon V Southampton	Selhurst Park, London
16 May	Arsenal V Aston Villa	Highbury, London
16 May	Charlton Athletic V Sheffield Wednesday	The Valley, London
16 May	Chelsea V Derby County	Stamford Bridge, London
16 May	Coventry City V Leeds United	Highfield Rd, Coventry
16 May	End of The 1998/1999 Premiership Season	Various
16 May	Liverpool V Wimbledon	Anfield, Liverpool
16 May	Manchester United V Tottenham Hotspur	Old Trafford, Manchester
16 May	Newcastle United V Blackburn Rovers	St James' Park, Newcastle
16 May	Nottingham Forest V Leicester City	City Ground, Nottingham
16 May	Southampton V Everton	The Dell, Southampton
16 May	West Ham United V Middlesbrough	Upton Park, London

Scottish Premier League

1 Jan	Motherwell V Kilmarnock	Fir Park, Motherwell
2 Jan	Dundee V Dundee Utd	Dens Park Stadium, Dundee
2 Jan	Dunfermline Athletic V Heart Of Midlothian	East End Park, Dunfermline
2 Jan	St Johnstone V Aberdeen	McDiarmid Park, Perth
3 Jan	Rangers V Celtic	Ibrox Stadium, Glasgow
6 Jan	Dundee V Motherwell	Dens Park Stadium, Dundee
30 Jan	Aberdeen V Rangers	Pittodrie Stadium, Aberdeen
30 Jan	Dundee United V Dunfermline Athletic	Tannadice Park, Dundee
30 Jan	Heart Of Midlothian V Motherwell	Tynecastle Park, Edinburgh
30 Jan	Kilmarnock V Dundee	Rugby Park, Kilmarnock
31 Jan	Celtic V St Johnstone	Celtic Park, Glasgow
6 Feb	Aberdeen V Kilmarnock	Pittodrie Stadium, Aberdeen
6 Feb	Celtic V Heart Of Midlothian	Celtic Park, Glasgow
6 Feb	St Johnstone V Dundee United	McDiarmid Park, Perth
7 Feb	Dunfermline Athletic V Rangers	East End Park, Dunfermline
13 Feb	Aberdeen V Celtic	Pittodrie Stadium, Aberdeen
20 Feb	Dundee United V Aberdeen	Tannadice Park, Dundee
20 Feb	Heart Of Midlothian V St Johnstone	Tynecastle Park, Edinburgh
20 Feb	Kilmarnock V Dunfermline Athletic	Rugby Park, Kilmarnock
20 Feb	Motherwell V Celtic	Fir Park, Motherwell
20 Feb	Rangers V Dundee	Ibrox Stadium, Glasgow
27 Feb	Celtic V Dundee United	Celtic Park, Glasgow
27 Feb	Dundee V St Johnstone	Dens Park Stadium, Dundee
27 Feb	Heart Of Midlothian V Aberdeen	Tynecastle Park, Edinburgh
27 Feb	Motherwell V Dunfermline	Fir Park, Motherwell
13 Mar	Dundee United V Heart of Midlothian	Tannadice Park, Dundee

Fixtures 1999

13 Mar	Dunfermline Athletic V Dundee East End Park, Dunfermline
13 Mar	Rangers V Motherwell Ibrox Stadium, Glasgow
13 Mar	St Johnstone V Kilmarnock McDiarmid Park, Perth
20 Mar	Dundee V Heart of Midlothian Dens Park Stadium, Dundee
20 Mar	Dunfermline Athletic V St Johnstone East End Park, Dunfermline
20 Mar	Kilmarnock V Celtic Rugby Park, Kilmarnock
20 Mar	Motherwell V Aberdeen Fir Park, Motherwell
20 Mar	Rangers V Dundee United Ibrox Stadium, Glasgow
28 Mar	Kilmarnock V Rangers Rugby Park, Kilmarnock
3 Apr	Aberdeen V Dunfermline Athletic Pittodrie Stadium, Aberdeen
3 Apr	Celtic V Dundee Celtic Park, Glasgow
3 Apr	Dundee United V Motherwell Tannadice Park, Dundee
3 Apr	Heart Of Midlothian V Kilmarnock Tynecastle Park, Edinburgh
3 Apr	St Johnstone V Rangers McDiarmid Park, Perth
10 Apr	Dundee United V St Johnstone Tannadice Park, Dundee
10 Apr	Heart Of Midlothian V Celtic Tynecastle Park, Edinburgh
10 Apr	Kilmarnock V Aberdeen Rugby Park, Kilmarnock
10 Apr	Motherwell V Dundee Fir Park, Motherwell
10 Apr	Rangers V Dunfermline Athletic Ibrox Stadium, Glasgow
17 Apr	Aberdeen V Dundee United Pittodrie Stadium, Aberdeen
17 Apr	Celtic V Motherwell Celtic Park, Glasgow
17 Apr	Dundee V Rangers Dens Park Stadium, Dundee
17 Apr	Dunfermline Athletic V Kilmarnock East End Park, Dunfermline
17 Apr	St Johnstone V Heart of Midlothian McDiarmid Park, Perth
24 Apr	Dundee V Kilmarnock Dens Park Stadium, Dundee
24 Apr	Dunfermline Athletic V Dundee United East End Park, Dunfermline
24 Apr	Motherwell V Heart of Midlothian Fir Park, Motherwell
24 Apr	Rangers V Aberdeen Ibrox Stadium, Glasgow
24 Apr	St Johnstone V Celtic McDiarmid Park, Perth
1 May	Aberdeen V St Johnstone Pittodrie Stadium, Aberdeen
1 May	Dundee United V Dundee Tannadice Park, Dundee
1 May	Heart Of Midlothian V Dunfermline United Tynecastle Park, Edinburgh
1 May	Kilmarnock V Motherwell Rugby Park, Kilmarnock
2 May	Celtic V Rangers Celtic Park, Glasgow
8 May	Aberdeen V Dundee Pittodrie Stadium, Aberdeen
8 May	Dundee United V Kilmarnock Tannadice Park, Dundee
8 May	Dunfermline Athletic V Celtic East End Park, Dunfermline
8 May	Rangers V Heart of Midlothian Ibrox Stadium, Glasgow
8 May	St Johnstone V Motherwell McDiarmid Park, Perth
15 May	Celtic V Aberdeen Celtic Park, Glasgow
15 May	Dundee V Dunfermline Athletic Dens Park Stadium, Dundee
15 May	Heart Of Midlothian V Dundee United Tynecastle Park, Edinburgh
15 May	Kilmarnock V St Johnstone Rugby Park, Kilmarnock
15 May	Motherwell V Rangers Fir Park, Motherwell
22 May	Aberdeen V Heart of Midlothian Pittodrie Stadium, Aberdeen
22 May	Dundee United V Celtic Tannadice Park, Dundee
22 May	Dunfermline Athletic V Motherwell East End Park, Dunfermline
22 May	Rangers V Kilmarnock Ibrox Stadium, Glasgow
22 May	St Johnstone V Dundee McDiarmid Park, Perth

....

Football
Other Major Events

2 Jan	118th AXA Sponsored FA Cup Third Round Various
8 Jan	Confederations Cup - Brazil V France Guadalajara, Mexico
9 Jan	Confederations Cup - Bolivia V Egypt Mexico City, Mexico
9 Jan	Confederations Cup - Mexico V Saudi Arabia Mexico City, Mexico
10 Jan	Confederations Cup - New Zealand V USA Guadalajara, Mexico
12 Jan	Confederations Cup - Mexico V Egypt Mexico City, Mexico
12 Jan	Confederations Cup - Saudi Arabia V Bolivia Mexico City, Mexico
13 Jan	Confederations Cup - Brazil V USA Guadalajara, Mexico
13 Jan	Confederations Cup - France V New Zealand Guadalajara, Mexico
14 Jan	Confederations Cup - Mexico V Bolivia Mexico City, Mexico
15 Jan	Confederations Cup - Brazil V New Zealand Guadalajara, Mexico
15 Jan	Confederations Cup - France V USA Guadalajara, Mexico
17 Jan	Confederations Cup - Semi Finals Mexico City, Mexico
17 Jan	Confederations Cup - Semi Finals Guadalajara, Mexico
19 Jan	Confederations Cup - Third Place Game Guadalajara, Mexico
20 Jan	Confederations Cup - Final Mexico City, Mexico
23 Jan	118th AXA Sponsored FA Cup Fourth Round Various
27 Jan	Worthington Cup Semi Final 1st Leg Various
13 Feb	118th AXA Sponsored FA Cup Fifth Round Various
17 Feb	Worthington Cup Semi Final 2nd Leg Various
2 Mar	UEFA Cup Quarter Final 1st Leg tbc
3 Mar	UEFA Champions League Quarter Final 1st Leg tbc
4 Mar	European Cup Winners Cup Quarter Final 1st Leg tbc
6 Mar	118th AXA Sponsored FA Cup Sixth Round Various
16 Mar	UEFA Cup Quarter Final 2nd Leg tbc
17 Mar	UEFA Champions League Quarter Final 2nd Leg tbc
18 Mar	European Cup Winners Cup Quarter Final 2nd Leg tbc
21 Mar	Worthington Cup Final Wembley, London
27 Mar	England V Poland Wembley, London
27 Mar	Northern Ireland V Germany Belfast
27 Mar	Scotland V Bosnia & Herzegovina tbc
31 Mar	Moldova V Northern Ireland Kishinev, Moldova
31 Mar	Scotland V Czech Republic tbc
31 Mar	Switzerland V Wales tbc, Switzerland

3 Ap	
24 Apr	FIFA World Youth Championship (Under-20) - The FIFA/Coca-Cola Cup Various, Nigeria
6 Apr	UEFA Cup Semi Final 1st Leg tbc
7 Apr	UEFA Champions League Semi Final 1st Leg tbc
8 Apr	European Cup Winners Cup Semi Final 1st Leg tbc
10 Apr	118th AXA Sponsored FA Cup Semi Finals Various
20 Apr	UEFA Cup Semi Final 2nd Leg, tbc
21 Apr	UEFA Champions League Semi Final 2nd Leg tbc
22 Apr	European Cup Winners Cup Semi Final 2nd Leg tbc
12 May	UEFA Cup - Final Moscow, Russia
19 May	European Cup Winners Cup - Final Birmingham
22 May	118th AXA Sponsored FA Cup Final Wembley, London
26 May	UEFA Champions League - Final Barcelona, Spain
29 May	Scottish FA Cup Final tbc
5 Jun	England V Sweden Wembley, London
5 Jun	Faroe Islands V Scotland tbc, Faroe Islands
5 Jun	Italy V Wales tbc, Italy
9 Jun	Bulgaria V England tbc, Bulgaria
9 Jun	Czech Republic V Scotland tbc, Czech Republic
9 Jun	Wales V Denmark tbc
1 Jul-18 Jul	1999 Copa America Various, Paraguay
1 Jul-15 Jul	Universiade Palma De Mallorca, Spain
21 Jul	UEFA Cup 1st Qualifying Round 1st Leg tbc
21 Jul	UEFA Champions League 1st Qualifying Round 1st Leg tbc
28 Jul	UEFA Cup 1st Qualifying Round 2nd Leg tbc
28 Jul	UEFA Champions League 1st Qualifying Round 2st Leg tbc
10 Aug	UEFA Cup 2nd Qualifying Round 1st Leg tbc
11 Jul	UEFA Champions League 2nd Qualifying Round 1st Leg, tbc
12 Aug	European Cup Winners Cup 1st Qualifying Round 1st Leg tbc
24 Aug	UEFA Cup 2nd Qualifying Round 2nd Leg tbc
21 Jul	UEFAChampions League 2nd Qualifying Round 2nd Leg, tbc
26 Aug	European Cup Winners Cup 1st Qualifying Round 2nd Leg tbc
27 Aug	European Super Cup tbc
4 Sep	Belarus V Wales, Minsk, Belarus
4 Sep	Bosnia & Herzegovina V Scotland tbc, Bosnia & Herzegovina
4 Sep	England V Luxembourg tbc
4 Sep	Northern Ireland V Turkey Belfast
8 Sep	Estonia V Scotland tbc, Estonia
8 Sep	Germany V Northern Ireland Dortmund, Germany
8 Sep	Poland V England tbc, Poland
14 Sep	UEFA Cup 1st Round 1st Leg tbc
15 Sep	UEFA Champions League Group Match 1 tbc
16 Sep	European Cup Winners Cup 1st Round 1st Leg tbc
28 Sep	UEFA Cup 1st Round 2nd Leg tbc

29 Sep	UEFA Champions League Group Match 2 tbc
30 Sep	European Cup Winners Cup 1st Round 2nd Leg tbc
9 Oct	Finland V Northern Ireland Helsinki, Finland
9 Oct	Scotland V Lithuania tbc
9 Oct	Wales V Switzerland tbc
19 Oct	UEFA Cup 2nd Round 1st Leg tbc
20 Oct	UEFA Champions League Group Match 3 tbc
21 Oct	European Cup Winners Cup 2nd Round 1st Leg tbc
2 Nov	UEFA Cup 2nd Round 2nd Leg tbc
3 Nov	UEFA Champions League Group Match 4 tbc
4 Nov	European Cup Winners Cup 2nd Round 2nd Leg tbc
10 - 27 Nov	FIFA World Under-17 Championship- The FIFA/JVC Cup tbc, New Zealand
13 Nov	Euro 2000 Play-Offs tbc
17 Nov	Euro 2000 Play-Offs tbc
23 No	UEFA Cup 3rd Round 1st Leg tbc
24 Nov	UEFA Champions League Group Match 5 tbc
30 Nov	FIFA Toyota Cup - World Club Championship. Tokyo, Japan
7 Dec	UEFA Cup 3rd Round 2nd Leg tbc
8 Dec	UEFA Champions League Group Match 6 tbc

Gaelic Football

26 Sep	Bank of Ireland All Ireland Football Final, Dublin, Ireland

Games

1 Jan-1 Feb	Fespic Games, Bangkok, Thailand
14-15 May	National Disability Sport Mini Games, Aylesbury

Gliding

22 May-6 Jun	11th European Gliding Championships For Women, Leszno, Poland
11-24 Jul	1st World Junior Gliding Championships, Terlet, Netherlands
31 Jul-15 Aug	26th World Gliding Championships, Bayreuth, Germany
17-27 Oct	World Solar Gliding Challenge, Darwin - Adelaide, Australia

Greyhound Racing

3 Apr	Grand National, Wimbledon, London
24 Apr	Regal Scotish Derby Final, Glasgow
26 Jun	The Greyhound Derby Final, Wimbledon, London
16 Jul	Champion Stakes Final, Romford
9 Oct	Laurent Perrier Champagne Grand Prix Final, Walthamstow, London
23 Oct	1999 Breeders Forum Produce Stakes Final, Birmingham
13 Nov	St Leger Final, Wembley, London
11 Dec	The Oaks Final, Wimbledon, London

Golf
EPGA

14-17 Jan	Alfred Dunhill South African PGA Championship, Johannesburg, South Africa
21-24 Jan	South African Open, Cape Town, South Africa
28-31 Jan	Heineken Classic Perth, Perth, Australia
4-7 Feb	Malaysian Open, Kuala Lumpur, Malaysia

11-14 Feb	Dubai Desert Classic, Dubai, United Arab Emirates
17-20 Feb	Qatar Masters, Doha, Qatar
4-7 Mar	Portuguese Algarve Open, tbc, Portugal
11-14 Mar	Turespana Masters, tbc, Spain
18-21 Mar	Moroccan Open, Agadir, Morocco
25-28 Mar	Madeira Island Open, Madeira, Portugal
22-25 Apr	Peugeot Spanish Open, tbc, Spain
29 Apr-2 May	The 56th FIAT and FILA Italian Open, Turin, Italy
6-9 May	French Open, tbc, France
13-16 May	Benson & Hedges International, Thame
21-24 May	Deutsche Bank-SAP Open, Heidelburg, Germany
28-31 May	Volvo PGA Championship, Wentworth
3-6 Jun	English Open, tbc
10-13 Jun	German Open, Berlin, Germany
24-27 Jun	COMPAQ European Grand Prix, Hexham
1-4 Jul	Murphys Irish Open, Druids Glen, Ireland
7-10 Jul	Standard Life Loch Lomond, Loch Lomond
15-18 Jul	128th British Open, Carnoustie
22-25 Jul	TNT Dutch Open, Hilversum, Netherlands
22-25 Jul	US Womens Open, Libertyville, USA
30 Jul-2 Aug	Smurfit European Open, Dublin, Ireland
Aug	McDonald's Championship Of Europe Gleneagles
Aug	Weetabix Women's British Open, Woburn, Milton Keynes
5-8 Aug	Volvo Scandinavian Masters, Malmo, Sweden
19-22 Aug	BMW International Open, Munich, Germany
2-5 Sep	Canon European Masters, Crans Sur Sierre, Switzerland
9-12 Sep	One-2-One British Masters, tbc
16-19 Sep	Lancome Trophy, Paris, France
30 Sep-3 Oct	Linde German Masters, Cologne, Germany
14-17 Oct	Cisco World Match Play Championship Presented By Diners Club, Wentworth
14-17 Oct	Open Novotel Perrier, Bordeaux, France
21-24 Oct	Belgacom Open, tbc, Belgium
28-31 Oct	Volvo Masters, Jerez, Spain
18-23 Nov	EPGA Tour Qualifying School Final, San Roque & Sotogrande, Spain

Golf: USPGA

4-10 Jan	Mercedes Championships, Maui, USA
11-17 Jan	SONY Open in Hawaii, Honolulu, USA
20-24 Jan	Bob Hope Chrysler Classic, Indian Wells, USA
28-31 Jan	Motorola Phoenix Open, Scottsdale, USA
4-7 Feb	AT&T Pebble Beach National Pro-Am, Pebble Beach, USA
11-14 Feb	Buick Invitational, Lajolla, USA
18-21 Feb	Nissan Open, Pacific Palisades, USA
24-28 Feb	Tucson Chrysler Classic, Tucson, USA
4-7 Mar	Doral-Ryder Open, Miami, USA
11-14 Mar	Honda Classic, Coral Springs, USA
18-21 Mar	Bay Hill Invitational, Orlando, USA
25-28 Mar	The Players Championship, Ponte Vedra Beach, USA
1-4 Apr	Bellsouth Classic, Duluth, USA
8-11 Apr	The Masters, Augusta, USA
15-18 Apr	MCI Classic, Hilton Head Island, USA
22-25 Apr	Greater Greensboro Chrysler Classic, Greensboro, USA
29 Apr-2 May	Shell Houston Open, The Woodlands, USA
6-9 May	Entergy Classic, New Orleans, USA
13-16 May	GTE Byron Nelson Classic, Irving, USA
20-23 May	Mastercard Colonial, Ft. Worth, USA
27-30 May	Kemper Open, Potomac, USA
3-6 Jun	Memorial Tournament, Dublin, USA
10-13 Jun	Fedex St. Jude Classic, Memphis, USA
17-20 Jun	US Open, Pinehurst, USA
24-27 Jun	Buick Classic, Rye, USA

1-4 Jul	Motorola Western Open, Lemont, USA
8-11 Jul	Greater Milwaukee Open By LITE, Milwaukee, USA
15-18 Jul	Southern Farm Bureau Insurance Golf Classic, Annandale, USA
22-25 Jul	John Deere Classic Coal Valley, USA
29 Jul-1 Aug	Canon Greater Hartford Open, Cromwell, USA
5-8 Aug	Buick Open, Grand Blanc, USA
12-15 Aug	81st PGA Championship, Medinah, USA
19-22 Aug	The Sprint International, Castle Rock, USA
26-29 Aug	Reno Open, Reno, USA
2-5 Sep	Air Canada Championship, Surrey, Canada
9-12 Sep	Bell Canadian Open, Oakville, Canada
16-19 Sep	BC Open, Endicott, USA
23-26 Sep	Westin Texas Open, San Antonio, USA
30 Sep-3 Oct	Buick Challenge, Pine Mountain, USA
7-10 Oct	Michelob Championship at Kingsmill, Williamsburg, USA
13-17 Oct	Las Vegas Invitational, Las Vegas, USA
21-24 Oct	National Car Rental Golf Classic at Walt Disney World Resort, Lake Buena Vista, USA
28-31 Oct	The Tour Championship Presented By Mercedes-Benz & Southern Company, Houston, USA
12-14 Nov	Franklin Templeton Shark Shootout, Thousand Oaks, USA
27-28 Nov	Skins Game, La Quinta, USA
2-5 Dec	JC Penney Classic, Palm Harbor, USA
6-12 Dec	Diners Club Matches, tbc, USA
18-19 Dec	Wendys Three Tour Challenge, Henderson, USA

Golf: Other Major Events

24-28 Feb	World Golf Championships-The Anderson Consulting World Golf Matchplay, Carlsbad, USA
31 May-5 Jun	British Amateur Championships, Newcastle
26-29 Aug	World Golf Championships - The NEC World Golf Invitational, Akron, USA
11-12 Sep	The Walker Cup, Nairn
24-26 Sep	33rd Ryder Cup, Brookline, USA
7-10 Oct	Alfred Dunhill Cup, Fife
4-7 Nov	World Golf Championships - The American Express World Golf Strokeplay, Sottogrande, Spain
15-17 Nov	1999 Mastercard PGA Grand Slam Of tbc, USA
18-21 Nov	World Cup Of Kuala Lumpur, Malaysia

Gymnastics

28 Apr-2 May	The Womens Global Challenge, Various, USA
2-4 Jul	Womens British Championships, Guildford
4-10 Jul	11th World Gymnaestrada, Gothenburg, Sweden
24 Jul-8 Aug	13th Pan American Games, Winnipeg, Canada
4-5 Sep	Mens British Championships, Stoke
8-16 Oct	34th World Championships (artistic), Tianjin, PR China
6-7 Nov	British Age Group Championships, Guildford

Horse Racing: Flat Racing

28 Mar	The Dubai World Cup, Nad Al Sheba, United Arab Emirates
1 May	The Sagitta 2000 Guineas Stakes, Newmarket
1 May	VISA Triple Crown Challenge - Kentucky Derby, Louisville, USA
2 May	The Sagitta 1000 Guineas Stakes, Newmarket
8 May	VISA Triple Crown Challenge - Preakness Stakes, Baltimore, USA
29 May	VISA Triple Crown Challenge - Belmont Stakes, Elmont, USA

Fixtures 1999

4 Jun	The Vodafone Coronation Cup, Epsom
4 Jun	The Vodafone Oaks, Epsom
5 Jun	The Vodafone Derby, Epsom
5 Jun	The Vodafone Diomed Stakes, Epsom
15 Jun	The Prince Of Wales's Stakes, Ascot
15 Jun	The Queen Anne Stakes, Ascot
15 Jun	The St James's Palace Stakes, Ascot
16 Jun	The Coronation Stakes, Ascot
16 Jun	The Queen Mary Stakes, Ascot
17 Jun	The Gold Cup, Ascot
18 Jun	The King Edward VII Stakes, Ascot
18 Jun	The Kings Stand Stakes, Ascot
24 Jul	The King George VI and The Queen Elizabeth Diamond Stakes, Ascot
24 Jul	The Princess Margaret Stakes, Ascot
29 Jul	The Goodwood Cup, Chichester
11 Sep	The Pertemps St Leger Stakes, Doncaster
25 Sep	The Meon Valley Stud Fillies' Mile, Ascot
25 Sep	The Queen Elizabeth II Stakes, Ascot
26 Sep	The Mail On Sunday Final, Ascot
26 Sep	The Sunday Special Handicap, Ascot
3 Oct	Prix De L'Arc De Triomphe, Longchamp - Paris 16e, France
9 Oct	The McGee Autumn Stakes, Ascot
9 Oct	The Princess Royal Stakes, Ascot
17 Oct	Canadian International, Rexdale, Canada
6 Nov	Breeders' Cup, Hallandale, USA
28 Nov	Japan Cup, Tokyo, Japan
12 Dec	Hong Kong International Races, Sha Tin, Hong Kong

Horse Racing: National Hunt

16-18 Mar	Cheltenham Festival, Cheltenham
18 Mar	The Tote Cheltenham Gold Cup Steeple Chase, Cheltenham
8 Apr	The Martell Cup Steeple Chase, Liverpool
9 Apr	The Mumm Melling Steeple Chase, Liverpool
10 Apr	The Martell Grand National Steeple Chase, Liverpool
10 Apr	The Martell Red Rum Steeple Chase, Liverpool
17 Apr	The Stakis Casinos Scottish Grand National, Ayr
24 Apr	The 43rd Whitbread Gold Cup Handicap Steeple Chase, Esher
13 Nov	The Murphys Gold Cup Handicap Steeple Chase, Cheltenham
19 Nov	The Coopers & Lybrand Ascot Hurdle, Ascot
27 Nov	The Hennessy Cognac Gold Cup Handicap Steeple Chase, Newbury
27 Dec	The Pertemps King George VI Steeple Chase, Kempton Park, Sunbury-on-Thames
28 Dec	The Welsh National Handicap Steeple Chase, Chepstow

Hang Gliding

26 Jul-7 Aug	World Hang Gliding Championship, Monte Cucco, Italy

Hockey

22-24 Jan	9th Mens European Indoor Nations Cup Division A, Slagelse, Denmark
22-24 Jan	9th Mens European Indoor Nations Cup Division B, Oporto, Portugal
29-31 Jan	4th Junior Womens European Indoor Nations Cup, Prague, Czech Republic
19-21 Feb	10th Mens European Indoor Club Championship Division A, Lille, France
19-21 Feb	10th Mens European Indoor Club Championship Division B, Prague, Czech Republic
19-21 Feb	10th Mens European Indoor Club Championship Division C, Budapest, Hungary
26-28 Feb	10th Womens European Indoor Club Championship Division A, Glasgow
26-28 Feb	10th Womens European Indoor Club Championship Division B, tbc, Czech Republic
26-28 Feb	10th Womens European Indoor Club Championship Division C, Poznan, Poland
28 Feb-1 Mar	British Aerospace U16 & U18 Schools Championship, Milton Keynes
2-5 Apr	10th Mens European Cup Winners Cup, tbc
2-5 Apr	9th Womens European Cup Winners Cup, tbc
3 May	EHL Premiership Final, Milton Keynes
21-24 May	26th Mens European Club Championship, tbc
21-24 May	26th Womens European Club Championship, tbc
10-20 Jun	21st Mens Champions Trophy, Brisbane, Australia
10-20 Jun	7th Womens Champions Trophy, Brisbane, Australia
17 Jul	England V Wales, tbc
24 Jul-8 Aug	13th Pan American Games, Winnipeg, Canada
4 Aug	Four Nations Senior International Tournament, Milton Keynes
18-29 Aug	5th Womens European Nations Cup, Hurth, Germany
1-12 Sep	8th Mens European Nations Cup, Padova, Italy
29 Sep-3 Oct	4 Nations Tournament, Sydney, Australia

Ice Hockey

12 Jan	SKODA European Hockey League - Play-Off Round, tbc
22-24 Jan	49th NHL All Star Weekend, Tampa Bay, USA
22-24 Jan	SKODA European Hockey League - Semi Final Round, tbc
13 Feb	SKODA European Hockey League - Top Four Finals - Semi Final 1, tbc
14 Feb	SKODA European Hockey League - Top Four Finals - 1st/2nd Place, tbc
21 Feb	Superleague Challenge Cup Semi Final, tbc
7 Mar	Superleague Challenge Cup Semi Final, tbc
8-14 Mar	Womens World Championship Pool A, Espoo, Kerava & Vantaa, Finland
10-16 Mar	World Championship Pool D, Krugerdorp & Pretoria, South Africa
21 Mar	Superleague Challenge Cup Final, tbc
21-28 Mar	Womens World Championship Pool B, Colmar & Strasbourg, France
3 Apr	Sekonda Superleague Play-off Championships - Semi Final 1, Manchester
4 Apr	Sekonda Superleague Play-off Championships - Final, Manchester
5-11 Apr	World Championship Pool C, Eindhoven & Tilburg, Netherlands
8-17 Apr	World Championship Pool B, Copenhagen & Odense, Denmark
21 Apr	Start Of Stanley Cup Play-offs, Various, USA
1-16 May	World Championship Pool A, Oslo, Hamar, Lillehammer, Norway
4 Sep	Sekonda Superleague Season Starts, Various
Oct	Start Of 1999/2000 NHL Season, Various, USA
4 Dec	Benson & Hedges Cup Final, Sheffield
27 Dec	Sekonda Superleague All Stars 99, London

Ice Skating

1-2 Feb	Slough Open, Slough
3-6 Feb	4th Winter Asian Games - Figure Skating, Yongpyong, Korea
21-28 Feb	Four Continents Figure Skating Championships, Halifax, Canada
4-7 Mar	ISU Grand Prix - Final, St Petersburg, Russia
17-18 Mar	Bristol Open, Bristol
21-28 Mar	World Figure Skating Championship, Helsinki, Finland
22-25 Apr	Scottish Championships, Aberdeen
28 Apr-2 May	The Womens Global Challenge, Various, USA
22-26 Jun	Basingstoke Open, Basingstoke

Judo

24-25 Apr	British Open Championships, Birmingham
24-25 Apr	Senior Blind European Championships, Birmingham
20-23 May	EJU Championships, Bratislava, Slovakia
3-13 Jul	Universiade, Palma De Mallorca, Spain
24 Jul-8 Aug	13th Pan American Games, Winnipeg, Canada
7-10 Oct	World Judo Championships, Birmingham
23-24 Oct	Team EJU Championships, Istanbul, Turkey
4 Dec	A Tournament, Basle, Switzerland
7-10 Dec	Pacific Ocean Games, Santiago, Chile

Karate

14 Mar	EKGB National Senior Karate Championships, Birmingham
May	European Championships, Portugal
May	PUKO Senior Championships, tbc, Chile
Jun	European Club Championships, France
24 Jul-8 Aug	13th Pan American Games, Winnipeg, Canada
13-14 Aug	7th Annual Summer Invitational Championships, tbc, Barbados
17 Oct	EKGB National Childrens Karate Championships, Birmingham
7-10 Dec	Pacific Ocean Games, Santiago, Chile

Lacrosse

10-11 Apr	Festival Weekend, tbc
24-31 Jul	European Championships, Manchester

Lawn Tennis
ATP

4-10 Jan	Australian Men's Hardcourt Championships, Adelaide, Australia
4-10 Jan	Qatar Mobil Open '99, Doha, Qatar
10-16 Jan	Adidas International, Sydney, Australia
11-17 Jan	Bellsouth Open, Auckland, New Zealand
1-7 Feb	Croatian Indoors, Split, Croatia
1-7 Feb	Open 13 - Marseille, Marseille, France
8-14 Feb	Dubai Tennis Open 1999, Dubai, United Arab Emirates
8-14 Feb	St Petersburg Open, St Petersburg, Russia
8-14 Feb	Sybase Open, San Jose, USA
15-21 Feb	Kroger St. Jude, Memphis, USA
22-28 Feb	Guardian Direct London
1-7 Mar	ABN/AMRO World Tennis Tournament, Rotterdam, Netherlands
1-7 Mar	Franklin Templeton Tennis Classic, Scottsdale, USA
8-14 Mar	Copenhagen Open, Copenhagen, Denmark
8-14 Mar	Mercedes Super 9 - Newsweek Champions Indian Wells, USA
18-28 Mar	Mercedes Super 9 - The Lipton Championships, Key Biscayne, USA
22-28 Mar	Grand Prix Hassan II, Casablanca, Morocco
5-11 Apr	Estoril Open, Lisbon, Portugal
5-11 Apr	Gold Flake Open, Chennai, India
6-12 Apr	Salem Open - Hong Kong
12-18 Apr	Japan Open '99, Tokyo, Japan
12-18 Apr	Open SEAT- Godo '99, Barcelona, Spain
19-25 Apr	Mercedes Super 9 - Monte Carlo Open '99, Monte Carlo, Monaco
19-25 Apr	U.S. Clay Court Championships, Orlando, USA
26 Apr-2 May	AT&T Challenge, Atlanta, USA
26 Apr-2 May	Paegas Czech Open, Prague, Czech Republic
27 Apr-3 May	BMW Open 1999, Munich, Germany

3-9 May	America's Red Clay Tennis Championship, Coral Springs, USA
3-9 May	Mercedes Super 9 - Licher German Open, Hamburg, Germany
10-16 May	Mercedes Super 9 - Campionati Internazionali D'italia - TIM Rome, Italy
17-23 May	Internationaler Raiffeisen Grand Prix, St Polten, Austria
5-13 Jun	Gerry Weber Open '99, Halle In Westfalen, Germany
7-13 Jun	Internazionali Di Tennis Carisbo, Bologna, Italy
7-13 Jun	The Stella Artois Grass Court Championships, London
14-20 Jun	Heineken Trophy, Hertogenbosch, Netherlands
14-19 Jun	The Nottingham Open Nottingham
5-11 Jul	Miller Lite Hall Of Fame Tennis Championships, Newport, USA
5-11 Jul	Rado Swiss Open, Gstaad, Switzerland
6-12 Jul	Investor Swedish Open - Bastad, Sweden
19-25 Jul	1999 Mercedes Cup - Stuttgart, Germany
19-25 Jul	Legg Mason Tennis Classic, Washington, USA
26 Jul-1 Aug	Croatia Open Umag, Croatia
26 Jul-1 Aug	Generali Open 1999, Kitzbuhel, Austria
26 Jul-1 Aug	Mercedes-Benz Los Angeles, USA
2-8 Aug	Grolsch Open '99, Amsterdam, Netherlands
2-8 Aug	Mercedes Super 9 - Du Maurier Open, Montreal, Canada
9-15 Aug	Internazionali Di Tennis Di San Marino, San Marino, San Marino
9-15 Aug	Mercedes Super 9 - Great American Insurance ATP Championship, Cincinnati, USA
16-22 Aug	Pilot Pen International Tennis Tournament, New Haven, USA
16-22 Aug	RCA Championships, Indianapolis, USA
23-29 Aug	MFS Pro Championships, Boston, USA
23-29 Aug	Waldbaum's Hamlet Long Island, USA
13-19 Sep	Open Romania, Bucharest, Romania
13-19 Sep	Presidents Cup - Tashkent, Tashkent, Uzbekistan
13-19 Sep	The Samsung Open, Bournemouth
27 Sep-3 Oct	Grand Prix De Tennis De Toulouse, Toulouse, France
27 Sep-3 Oct	Mallorca Open, tbc, Spain
4-10 Oct	Campionati Internazionali Di Sicilia, Palermo, Italy
4-10 Oct	Davidoff Swiss Indoors Basel, Basel, Switzerland
4-10 Oct	Shanghai Open '99, Shanghai, Pr China
11-17 Oct	CA Tennis Trophy,Vienna, Austria
11-17 Oct	Heineken Open - Singapore,
18-24 Oct	Grand Prix De Tennis De Lyon, Lyon, France
18-24 Oct	IPB Czech Indoor, Ostrava, Czech Republic
25-31 Oct	Abierto Mexicano De Tenis, Mexico City, Mexico
25-31 Oct	Mercedes Super 9 - Eurocard Open, Stuttgart, Germany
1-7 Nov	Cerveza Club Colombia Open, Bogota, Colombia
1-7 Nov	Mercedes Super 9 - 14th Open De Paris, Paris, France
8-14 Nov	Chevrolet Cup, Santiago, Chile
8-14 Nov	Kremlin Cup '99, Moscow, Russia
8-14 Nov	Scania Stockholm Open, Stockholm, Sweden
15-21 Nov	ATP Tour World Doubles Championship, Hartford, USA
22-28 Nov	ATP Tour World Championship, Hannover, Germany

Lawn Tennis: National Championships

Nov	The National Tennis Championships, Telford

Davis Cup

2-4 Apr	Davis Cup By NEC World Group Round 1, tbc
2-4 Apr	Davis Cup World Group Round 1 - Belgium V Czech Republic, tbc, Belgium
2-4 Apr	Davis Cup World Group Round 1 - France V Netherlands, tbc, France
2-4 Apr	Davis Cup World Group Round 1 - Germany V Russia, tbc, Germany
2-4 Apr	Davis Cup World Group Round 1 - Great Britain V USA, tbc
2-4 Apr	Davis Cup World Group Round 1 - Spain V Brazil, tbc, Spain
2-4 Apr	Davis Cup World Group Round 1 - Sweden V Slovak Republic, tbc, Sweden
2-4 Apr	Davis Cup World Group Round 1 - Switzerland V Italy, tbc, Switzerland
2-4 Apr	Davis Cup World Group Round 1 - Zimbabwe V Australia, tbc, Zimbabwe
16-18 Jul	Davis Cup By NEC World Group Round 2, tbc
24-26 Sep	Davis Cup By NEC World Group Round 3 - Semi Finals, tbc
3-5 Dec	Davis Cup By NEC World Group Final. tbc

Fed Cup

17-18 Apr	KB Fed Cup - 1st Round, tbc
24-25 Jul	KB Fed Cup - Semi Finals/World Group Playoffs, tbc
18-19 Sep	KB Fed Cup - Finals, tbc

Grand Slam

18-31 Jan	Australian Open Championships, Melbourne, Australia
24 May-6 Jun	French Open Championships - Roland Garros, Paris, France
21 Jun-4 Jul	The Wimbledon Lawn Tennis Championships, Wimbledon, London
30 Aug-12 Sep	US Open Championships, New York, USA

WTA

4-10 Jan	A.S.B. Bank Classic, Auckland, New Zealand
4-10 Jan	Thalgo Australian Womens Hardcourt Championships, Gold Coast, Australia
11-17 Jan	Adidas International, Sydney, Australia
11-17 Jan	ANZ Tasmania International, Hobart, Australia
1-7 Feb	Toray Pan Pacific Open, Tokyo, Japan
8-14 Feb	Nokia Cup, Prostejov, Czech Republic
15-21 Feb	Copa Colsanitas, Bogota, Colombia
15-21 Feb	Faber Grand Prix, Hannover, Germany
22-28 Feb	IGA Tennis Classic, Oklahoma City, USA
22-28 Feb	Open Gaz De France, Paris, France
1-14 Mar	Evert Cup, Indian Wells, USA
15-28 Mar	The Lipton Championships, Key Biscayne, USA
29 Mar-4 Apr	Family Circle Magazine Hilton Head Island, USA
5-11 Apr	Bausch & Lomb Championships, Amelia Island, USA
12-18 Apr	Japan Open, Tokyo, Japan
19-25 Apr	Beijing Open, Beijing, Pr China
19-25 Apr	Budapest Lotto Ladies Open, Budapest, Hungary
26 Apr-2 May	Croatian Bol Ladies Open, Bol, Croatia
26 Apr-2 May	Intersport Ladies Grand Prix, Hamburg, Germany
26 Apr-2 May	Presidents Cup Women's Open, Tashkent, Uzbekistan
3-9 May	Italian Open, Rome, Italy
3-9 May	Warsaw Cup By Heros, Warsaw, Poland
10-16 May	Antwerp Open, Antwerp, Belgium
10-16 May	German Open, Berlin, Germany
17-23 May	Internationaux De Strasbourg. Strasbourg, France
17-23 May	Open Paginas Amarillas Villa De Madrid, Madrid, Spain
7-13 Jun	DFS Classic, Birmingham
14-20 Jun	Heineken Trophy, Hertogenbosch, Netherlands
15-20 Jun	Direct Line Insurance Championships, Eastbourne
5-11 Jul	Skoda Czech Open, Karlovy Vary, Czech Republic
5-11 Jul	Styria Open Maria Lankowitz, Maria Lankowitz, Austria
12-18 Jul	Prokom Polish Open, Soppot, Poland
12-18 Jul	Torneo Internazionale, Palermo, Italy
26 Jul-1 Aug	Bank Of The West Classic, Stanford, USA
2-8 Aug	Senex Trophy, Knokke-zoute, Belgium
2-8 Aug	Toshiba Tennis Classic, San Diego, USA
9-15 Aug	Acura Classic, Los Angeles, USA
9-15 Aug	Boston Cup, Boston, USA
16-22 Aug	Du Maurier Open, Montreal, Canada
23-29 Aug	Pilot Pen International Women's Championship, New Haven, USA
20-26 Sep	SEAT Open Luxembourg Kockelscheuer, Luxembourg,
20-26 Sep	Toyota Princess Tokyo, Japan
27 Sep-3 Oct	Wismilak International, Surabaya, Indonesia
4-10 Oct	Porsche Tennis Grand Prix, Filderstadt, Germany
11-17 Oct	European Championships, Zurich-kloten, Switzerland
18-24 Oct	Ladies Kremlin Cup, Moscow, Russia
25-31 Oct	Bell Challenge, Quebec City, Canada
25-31 Oct	Generali Ladies Linz, Linz, Austria
1-7 Nov	Sparkasen Cup International Grand Prix, Leipzig, Germany
8-14 Nov	Advanta Championships, Philadelphia, USA
8-14 Nov	Wismilak Open, Jakarta, Indonesia
15-21 Nov	Chase Championships Of The Corel WTA Tour, New York, USA
15-21 Nov	Volvo Womens Open, Pattya City, Thailand

Modern Pentathlon

20-21 Feb	British Modern Tetrathlon & Pentathlon Championship, Bracknell
4-7 Mar	World Cup 1, San Antonio, USA
11-14 Mar	World Cup 2, Mexico City, Mexico
8-11 Apr	World Cup 3, Rome, Italy
14-15 Apr	British Modern Open Pentathlon, Millfield
22-25 Apr	World Cup 4, Darmstadt, Germany
23-26 Apr	World Cup 5 - Women, Aix-en-Provence, France
10-13 Jun	World Cup 5 - Men, Budapest, Hungary
10-13 Jun	World Cup 6 - Women, Szekesfehervar, Hungary
10-11 Jul	British Modern Junior & Youth Pentathlon Championship, Millfield
12-18 Jul	World Championships, Budapest, Hungary
24 Jul-8 Aug	13th Pan American Games, Winnipeg, Canada
2-8 Aug	World Junior Championships, Chieti, Italy
4-5 Sep	Pentathlon 1999 World Tour 1, Las Vegas, USA
4-5 Sep	World Youth Championships, Bayreuth, Germany
18-19 Sep	Pentathlon 1999 World Tour 2, Arcachon, France
2-3 Oct	Pentathlon 1999 World Tour 3, Rome, Italy
16-17 Oct	World Cup Finals, Sydney, Australia
23-24 Oct	Pentathlon 1999 World Tour 4, Sydney, Australia

Motor Cycling

4 Apr	World Superbike Championship, Kyalami, South Africa
18 Apr	Malaysian Grand Prix, Sepang, Malaysia
18 Apr	World Superbike Championship, Philip Island, Australia
25 Apr	Japanese Grand Prix, Twin Ring Motegi, Japan

Fixtures 1999

2 May	World Superbike Championship, Donington Park, Great Britain
9 May	Spanish Grand Prix, Jerez de la frontera, Spain
16 May	World Superbike Championship, Albacete, Spain
23 May	French Grand Prix, Paul Ricard, France
30 May	World Superbike Championship, Monza, Italy
31 May-11 Jun	Isle Of Man TT Races, Isle Of Man
6 Jun	Italian Grand Prix, Mugello, Italy
20 Jun	Catalunya Grand Prix, Catalunya, Spain
13 Jun	World Superbike Championship, Nürburgring, Germany
26 Jun	Dutch Grand Prix, Assen, Netherlands
27 Jun	World Superbike Championship, San Marino, tbc
4 Jul	British Grand Prix, Donington Park, Great Britain
11 Jul	World Superbike Championship, Laguna, Seca
18 July	German Grand Prix, Sachsenring, Germany
11 Aug	World Superbike Championship, Brands Hatch, Great Britain
22 Aug	Czechoslovakian Grand Prix, Bmo, Czech Republic
5 Sep	San Marino Grand Prix, tbc, San Marino
5 Sep	World Superbike Championship, Assen, Netherlands
19 Sep	Comunidad Valenciana Grand Prix, Valencia, Spain
26 Sep	World Superbike Championship, tbc
3 Oct	Australian Grand Prix, Phillip Island, Australia
10 Oct	South African Grand Prix, Welkom, South Africa
10 Oct	World Superbike Championship, Sugo, Japan
24 Oct	Brazilian Grand Prix, Jacarepaguá, Rio, Brazil
31 Oct	Argentinian Grand Prix, Buenos Aires, Argentina

Motor Racing: Cart

21 Mar	Marlboro Grand Prix of Miami, Homestead, USA
10 Apr	Japan 500, Motegi, Japan
18 Apr	Toyota Grand Prix of Long Beach, Long Beach, USA
2 May	Bosch Spark Plug Grand Prix Presented By Toyota, Nazareth, USA
15 May	Rio 400, Rio De Janeiro, Brazil
29 May	Motorola 300, Madison, USA
6 Jun	Miller Lite 200, West Allis, USA
20 Jun	Budweiser/GI Joe's 200 Presented By Texaco/Havoline, Portland, USA
27 Jun	Medic Drug Grand Prix of Cleveland Presented by Star Bank, Cleveland, USA
11 Jul	Texaco/Havoline 200, Elkhart Lake, USA
18 Jul	Molson Indy, Toronto, Canada
25 Jul	US 500 Presented By Toyota, Brooklyn, USA
8 Aug	Grand Prix Detroit, Detroit, USA
15 Aug	Miller Lite 200, Lexington, USA
22 Aug	Chicago Grand Prix, Cicero, USA
5 Sep	Molson Indy Vancouver, Vancouver, Canada
12 Sep	Honda Grand Prix of Monterey Featuring The Texaco/Havoline 300, Monterey, USA
26 Sep	Texaco Grand Prix of Houston, Houston, USA
17 Oct	1999 Honda Indy, Gold Coast, Australia
31 Oct	Marlboro 500 Presented by Toyota, Fontana, USA

Motor Racing: RAC Touring Cars

4-5 Apr	Auto Trader RAC Touring Car Championship, Castle Donington, Derby
17-18 Apr	Auto Trader RAC Touring Car Championship, Silverstone, Towcester
2-3 May	Auto Trader RAC Touring Car Championship, Thruxton, Andover
15-16 May	Auto Trader RAC Touring Car Championship, Brands Hatch, Dartford
30-31 May	Auto Trader RAC Touring Car Championship, Oulton Park, Tarporley
19-20 Jun	Auto Trader RAC Touring Car Championship, Castle Donington, Derby
3-4 Jul	Auto Trader RAC Touring Car Championship, Croft On Tees, Darlington
17-18 Jul	Auto Trader RAC Touring Car Championship, Snetterton, Norwich
31 Jul-1 Aug	Auto Trader RAC Touring Car Championship, Thruxton, Andover
14-15 Aug	Auto Trader RAC Touring Car Championship, Dunfermline
29-30 Aug	Auto Trader RAC Touring Car Championship, Brands Hatch, Dartford
11-12 Sep	Auto Trader RAC Touring Car Championship, Oulton Park, Tarporley
18-19 Sep	Auto Trader RAC Touring Car Championship, Silverstone, Towcester

Motor Racing: Formula One

7 Mar	Qantas Australian Grand Prix, Melbourne, Australia
21 Mar	China Grand Prix, Zhuhai, Pr China
11 Apr	Brazilian Grand Prix, Sao Paulo, Brazil
2 May	San Marino Grand Prix, Imola, Italy
16 May	Monaco Grand Prix, Monte Carlo, Monaco
30 May	Spanish Grand Prix, Barcelona, Spain
13 Jun	Canadian Grand Prix, Montreal, Canada
27 Jun	French Grand Prix, France
11 Jul	RAC British Grand Prix, Silverstone, Towcester
25 Jul	Austrian Grand Prix, Spielberg, Austria
1 Aug	German Grand Prix, Hockenheim, Germany
15 Aug	Hungarian Grand Prix, Budapest, Hungary
29 Aug	Belgian Grand Prix, Francorchamps, Belgium
12 Sep	Italian Grand Prix, Monza, Italy
26 Sep	Europe Grand Prix, Nurburg, Germany
17 Oct	Malaysia Grand Prix, Kuala Lumpur, Malaysia
31 Oct	Japanese Grand Prix, Suzuka, Japan

Motor Racing: British Formula Three

21 Mar	Autosport British Formula 3 Championship, Castle Donington, Derby
27-28 Mar	Autosport British Formula 3 Championship, Silverstone, Towcester
11 Apr	Autosport British Formula 3 Championship, Thruxton, Andover
24-25 Apr	Autosport British Formula 3 Championship, Brands Hatch, Dartford
2-3 May	Autosport British Formula 3 Championship, Oulton Park, Tarporley
30-31 May	Autosport British Formula 3 Championship, Snetterton, Norwich
19-20 Jun	Autosport British Formula 3 Championship, Brands Hatch, Dartford
8-10 Jul	Autosport British Formula 3 Championship, Silverstone, Towcester
14-15 Aug	Autosport British Formula 3 Championship, Pembrey
29 Aug	Autosport British Formula 3 Championship, Castle Donington, Derby
4-5 Sep	Autosport British Formula 3 Championship, Croft On Tees, Darlington
25-26 Sep	Autosport British Formula 3 Championship, Spa, Belgium
9-10 Oct	Autosport British Formula 3 Championship, Silverstone, Towcester
17 Oct	Autosport British Formula 3 Championship, Thruxton, Andover

Motor Racing: Formula 3000

15 May	FIA Formula 3000 International Championship, Monte Carlo, Monaco
29 May	FIA Formula 3000 International Championship, Barcelona, Spain
26 Jun	FIA Formula 3000 International Championship, Magny-cours, France
10 Jul	FIA Formula 3000 International Championship, Silverstone, Towcester
24 Jul	FIA Formula 3000 International Championship, Spielberg, Austria
31 Jul	FIA Formula 3000 International Championship, Hockenheim, Germany
14 Aug	FIA Formula 3000 International Championship, Budapest, Hungary
28 Aug	FIA Formula 3000 International Championship, Francorchamps, Belgium
11 Sep	FIA Formula 3000 International Championship, Monza, Italy
25 Sep	FIA Formula 3000 International Championship, Nurburg, Germany

Motor Racing: Indy Racing League

24 Jan	Pep Boys IRL- Indy 200, Orlando, USA
28 Mar	Pep Boys IRL - Phoenix 200, Phoenix, USA
1 May	Pep Boys IRL - Charlotte - Visionaire 500, Concord, USA
30 May	Pep Boys IRL - Indianapolis 500, Indianapolis, USA
12 Jun	Pep Boys IRL - Texas - True Value 500, Fort Worth, USA
27 Jun	Pep Boys IRL - Pikes Peak, Colorado Springs, USA
17 Jul	Pep Boys IRL - Atlanta 500 Classic, Hampton, USA
1 Aug	Pep Boys IRL - Dover Downs - Pep Boys 400, Dover, USA
29 Aug	Pep Boys IRL - Pikes Peak - Radisson 200, Colorado Springs, USA
17 Oct	Pep Boys IRL - Las Vegas 500k, Las Vegas, USA
17 Oct	Pep Boys IRL - Texas - Lone Star 500, Fort Worth, USA

Motor Racing: NASCAR

7 Feb	1999 NASCAR Winston Cup Series - Bud Shootout, Daytona Beach, USA
14 Feb	1999 NASCAR Winston Cup Series - Daytona 500, Daytona Beach, USA
21 Feb	1999 NASCAR Winston Cup Series - GM Goodwrench Service Plus 400, Rockingham, USA
7 Mar	1999 NASCAR Winston Cup - Las Vegas 400, Las Vegas, USA
14 Mar	1999 NASCAR Winston Cup - Primestar 500, Atlanta, USA
21 Mar	1999 NASCAR Winston Cup Series - Transouth Financial 400, Darlington, USA
28 Mar	1999 NASCAR Winston Cup Series - Texas 500, Royce City, USA
11 Apr	1999 NASCAR Winston Cup Series - Food City 500, Bristol, USA
18 Apr	1999 NASCAR Winston Cup Series - Goody's 500, Martinsville, USA
25 Apr	1999 NASCAR Winston Cup Series - Diehard 500, Talladega, USA
2 May	1999 NASCAR Winston Cup Series - California 500 Presented by NAPA, Fontana, USA
15 May	1999 NASCAR Winston Cup Series - Pontiac Excitement 400, Richmond, USA
22 May	1999 NASCAR Winston Cup Series - The Winston, Concord, USA
30 May	1999 NASCAR Winston Cup Series - Coca-Cola 600, Concord, USA
6 Jun	1999 NASCAR Winston Cup Series - MBNA Platinum 400, Dover, USA

13 Jun	1999 NASCAR Winston Cup Series - Miller Lite 400, Brooklyn, USA
20 Jun	1999 NASCAR Winston Cup Series - Pocono 500, Long Pond, USA
27 Jun	1999 NASCAR Winston Cup Series - Save Mart/Kargen 300, Sonoma, USA
3 Jul	1999 NASCAR Winston Cup Series - Pepsi 400, Daytona Beach, USA
11 Jul	1999 NASCAR Winston Cup Series - Jiffy Lube 300, Louden, USA
25 Jul	1999 NASCAR Winston Cup Series - Pennsylvania 500, Long Pond, USA
7 Aug	1999 NASCAR Winston Cup Series - Brickyard 400, Indianapolis, USA
15 Aug	1999 NASCAR Winston Cup Series - The Bud at The Glen, Watkins Glen, USA
22 Aug	1999 NASCAR Winston Cup Series - Devilbiss 400, Brooklyn, USA
28 Aug	1999 NASCAR Winston Cup Series - Goody's Headache Powder 500, Bristol, USA
5 Sep	1999 NASCAR Winston Cup Series - Southern 500, Darlington, USA
11 Sep	1999 NASCAR Winston Cup Series - Exide Nascar Select Batteries 400, Richmond, USA
19 Sep	1999 NASCAR Winston Cup Series - New Hampshire 300, Louden, USA
26 Sep	1999 NASCAR Winston Cup Series - MBNA Gold 400, Dover, USA
3 Oct	1999 NASCAR Winston Cup Series - NAPA Autocare 500, Martinsville, USA
10 Oct	1999 NASCAR Winston Cup Series - UAW-GM Quality 500, Concord, USA
17 Oct	1999 NASCAR Winston Cup Series - Winston 500, Talladega, USA
24 Oct	1999 NASCAR Winston Cup Series - Acdelco 400, Rockingham, USA
7 Nov	1999 NASCAR Winston Cup Series - Dura Lube 500, Tolleson, USA
14 Nov	1999 NASCAR Winston Cup Series - Jiffy Lube Miami 400, Miami, USA
21 Nov	1999 NASCAR Winston Cup Series - NAPA 500, Hampton, USA

Netball

16-30 Jan	South Pacific Games, tbc, Guam
6-7 Mar	FENA Under 16 Tournament, tbc
26-28 Mar	FENA U17 Tournament, tbc
1-16 Jul	England Test Series V South Africa, tbc
21 Sep-6 Oct	World Championships, Christchurch, New Zealand
6 Nov	International Test Series, Wembley, London

Orienteering

20 Feb	British Night Championships
2-4 Apr	Jan Kellstrom International Orienteering Festival, Surrey
8 May	British Orienteering Championships, North Yorkshire
9 May	British Relay Championships, North Yorkshire
18-23 Jul	World Masters Orienteering Championships 1999, Aarhus, Denmark
31 Jul-6 Aug	Highland '99 - Scottish 6 Days
1-8 Aug	World Orienteering Championships 1999, Inverness
5-7 Nov	World Junior Orienteering Championships 1999, Varna, Bulgaria

Point To Point

3 Apr	Ashford Valey Foxhounds at Charing
3 Apr	Cattlestock Hunt at Little Windsor
3 Apr	Cleveland Hunt at Stainton
3 Apr	Curre Hunt at Howick
3 Apr	Essex Hunt at High Easter
3 Apr	Ledbury Hunt at Maisemore Park
3 Apr	North Staffordshire at Sandon
3 Apr	Percy Hunt at Alnwick

3 Apr	Spooners & West Dartmoor Foxhounds at Cherry Brook
3 Apr	Tedworth Hunt at Barbury Castle
3 Apr	United Pack at Brampton Bryan
3 Apr	Vale of Aylesbury at Kimble
3 Apr	Vale of Lune at Whittington
3 Apr	Woodland Pytchley at Dingley
5 Apr	East Kent Hunt at Aldington
5 Apr	Eggesford Hunt at Bishopsleigh
5 Apr	Essex Farmers & Union at Marks Tey
5 Apr	Four Burrow Foxhounds at Trebudonnin
5 Apr	Morpeth Hunt at Tranwell
5 Apr	North Cotswold Hunt at Paxford
5 Apr	Old Berkshire Hunt at Lockinge
5 Apr	South Notte Hunt at Thorpe
5 Apr	South Pembrokeshire at Lydstep
5 Apr	South Shropshire at Eyton on Severn
5 Apr	Southdown & Bridge Hunt at Heathfield
5 Apr	Staintondale Hunt at Charm Park
5 Apr	Taunton Vale Foxhounds at Kingston St Mary
5 Apr	Vine & Craven at Hackwood Park
1 May	Albrighton Hunt at Weston Park
1 May	Berkeley Hunt at Woodford
1 May	Devon & Somerset Staghounds at Holnicote
1 May	Gelligaer Farmers Hunt at Honvilston
1 May	Modbury Harriers at Flete Park
1 May	Pendle Forest & Craven Hunt at Gisburn
1 May	Surrey Union Hunt at Peper Harrow
2 May	Fernie at Dingley
2 May	Lauderdale at Mosshouses
2 May	Radnor & West Herefordshire at Cursneh Hill
3 May	Banwen Miners Hunt at Pantyderi
3 May	Cotley Hunt at Cotley
3 May	Enfield Chace Foxhounds at Northam
3 May	North Shropshire at Byton on Severn
3 May	Stevestone Foxhounds at High Bickington
3 May	Warwickshire Hunt at Ashorne
3 May	West Street Tickam at Aldington
3 May	Zetland Hunt at Witton Castle
29 May	Exmoor Foxhounds at Bratton Down
30 May	Berks & Bucks Draghounds at Kingston Blount
30 May	Harborough Hunts Club at Dingley
31 May	Albrighton Woodland Hunt at Chaddesley Corbett
31 May	South Tetcott Foxhounds at Lifton

Polo

22-24 Jan	IV International Trophy Jumping And Polo On Snow, Megeve, France
29-31 Jan	15th Cartier Polo World Cup On Snow, St Moritz, Switzerland
15-21 Feb	10th Cortina Dampezzo Polo On Snow, Cortina D'ampezzo, Italy
15-18 Apr	Ambassadors Cup, Chantilly, France
11-23 May	Prince Of Wales Trophy, Windsor
18-23 May	Dollar Cup, Midhurst
18-30 May	Gerald Balding Cup, Cirencester
25 May-13 Jun	Queens Cup, Little Budworth
29 May-6 Jun	Arthur Lucas Cup, Beaufort
8-20 Jun	Royal Windsor Cup, Little Budworth
14-27 Jun	Archie David Cup, Little Budworth
15 Jun-4 Jul	Eduardo Moore Tournament, Windsor
15-27 Jun	Warwickshire Cup, Cirencester
19-26 Jun	Prince Of Wales Cup, Beaufort
29 Jun-18 Jul	Cirencester 12 Goal Championship, Cirencester
29 Jun-18 Jul	Veuve Clicquot Gold Cup, Midhurst
6-11 Jul	Duke Of Beaufort's Cup, Beaufort
12-17 Jul	RCBPC 8 Goal Tournament, Windsor
20-31 Jul	Harrison Cup, Midhurst

25 Jul	International Day Sponsored By Cartier, Little Budworth
26 Jul-1 Aug	Holden White Challenge Cup, Midhurst
28 Jul-1 Aug	Cowdray Park Challenge Cup, Midhurst
3-15 Aug	National 15 Goal Championships, Cirencester
13-15 Aug	4th Cartier Trophy/Polo Silver Cup, Gstaad, Switzerland
17-29 Aug	Cheltenham Cup, Cirencester
17-28 Aug	Duke Of Wellington Trophy, Windsor
24 Aug-5 Sep	12-15 Goal Championship, Windsor
28 Aug-12 Sep	Autumn Tournament Nations Cup, Little Budworth

Rackets

9 Jan	World Championship Challenge 1st Leg, Chicago, USA
16 Jan	World Championship Challenge 2nd Leg, London

Rallying

17-20 Jan	Rallye Automobile Monte Carlo, Monte Carlo, Monaco
12-14 Feb	International Swedish Rally, Karlstad, Sweden
26-28 Feb	Safari Rally Kenya, Nairobi, Kenya
13-14 Mar	Mobil British Rally Championship - Vauxhall Rally Of Wales, Bromborough
21-24 Mar	Rallye Du Portugal, Oporto, Portugal
18-21 Apr	Rallye De Espana, Lloret De Mar, Spain
24-25 Apr	Mobil British Rally Championship - Pirelli International Rally, Carlisle
9-12 May	Rallye De France - Tour De Corse, Ajaccio, France
23-26 May	Rally Argentina, Cordoba, Argentina
6-9 Jun	Acropolis Rally, Athens, Greece
11-12 Jun	Mobil British Rally Championship - RSAC Scottish Rally, Dumfries
2-4 Jul	Mobil British Rally Championship - SEAT Jim Clark Memorial Rally, Duns
16-18 Jul	Rally Of New Zealand, Auckland, New Zealand
30-31 Jul	Mobil British Rally Championship - Stena Line Ulster Rally, Belfast
20-22 Aug	Neste Rally Finland, Jyvaskyla, Finland
10-12 Sep	Mobil British Rally Championship - Manx International Rally, Douglas
19-21 Sep	555 China Rally, Beijing, PR China
3-6 Oct	Rallye Sanremo - "Rallye D'Italia", San Remo, Italy
4-7 Nov	API Rally Australia, Perth, Australia
20-23 Nov	Network Q RAC Rally, Cheltenham

Real Tennis

19-25 Apr	Ladies British Open Singles Championship, Holyport
26 Apr-2 May	Ladies World Championship, Hampton Court

Rhythmic Gymnastics

6-7 Mar	British Championships, Dewsbury
17 Apr	British Group Championships, Hinckley
27-30 May	European Championships, Budapest, Hungary
24 Jul-8 Aug	13th Pan American Games, Winnipeg, Canada
28 Sep-3 Oct	23rd World Rhythmic Championships, Osaka, Japan

Rowing

27 Mar	Head Of The River, London
3 Apr	Oxford V Cambridge Boat Race, London
28-30 May	FISA World Cup, Munich, Germany
18-20 Jun	FISA World Cup, Vienna, Austria
30 Jun-4 Jul	Henley Royal Regatta, Henley
9-11 Jul	FISA World Cup, Lucerne, Switzerland
16-18 Jul	National Championships, Nottingham

Fixtures 1999

24 Jul-8 Aug	13th Pan American Games, Winnipeg, Canada
4-8 Aug	World Junior Championships, Plovdiv, Bulgaria
22-29 Aug	FISA World Championships, St Catherines, Canada
9-12 Sep	FISA Masters Regatta, Seville, Spain
29 Sep-1 Oct	Pre Olympic Regatta, Sydney, Australia
Oct	8th Asian Championships, Naganuma, Japan
23-24 Oct	Head Of The Charles, Boston, USA

Rugby League

Jan	World Club Championship, Johannesburg, South Africa
5 Mar	Start Of JJB Super League, Various
1 May	Silk Cut Challenge Cup Final, Wembley, London
Oct	Tri Nation Test Series, tbc, Australia
9 Oct	JJB Super League Grand Final, tbc

Rugby Union: Domestic Cup Competitions

24 Apr	The Willis Corroon Trophy - Royal Navy V Army, Twickenham, London
15 May	Tetley's Bitter Cup Final, Twickenham, London
22 May	Tetley's Bitter County Championship Finals, Twickenham, London

Rugby: Five Nations

6 Feb	Lloyds TSB Five Nations - Ireland V France, Dublin, Ireland
6 Feb	Lloyds TSB Five Nations - Scotland V Wales, Edinburgh
20 Feb	Lloyds TSB Five Nations - England V Scotland, Twickenham, London
20 Feb	Lloyds TSB Five Nations - Wales V Ireland, Wembley, London
6 Mar	Lloyds TSB Five Nations - France V Wales, Paris, France
6 Mar	Lloyds TSB Five Nations - Ireland V England, Dublin, Ireland
20 Mar	Lloyds TSB Five Nations - England V France, Twickenham, London
20 Mar	Lloyds TSB Five Nations - Scotland V Ireland, Edinburgh
10 Apr	Lloyds TSB Five Nations - France V Scotland, Paris, France
11 Apr	Lloyds TSB Five Nations - Wales V England, Wembley, London

Rugby: Internationals

6 Mar	Scotland V Italy, Edinburgh
21 Mar	Italy V Wales, tbc, Italy
10 Apr	Ireland V Italy, Dublin, Ireland
17 Apr	Argentina V Rest Of The World, tbc, Argentina
3 Jun	Argentina V Wales, Buenos Aires, Argentina
10 Jun	Argentina V Wales, Buenos Aires, Argentina
12 Jun	Australia V Ireland, tbc, Australia
12 Jun	Tonga V France, tbc, Tonga
16 Jun	Western Samoa V France, tbc, Western Samoa
19 Jun	Australia V Ireland, tbc, Australia
20 Jun	New Zealand A V France, tbc, New Zealand
26 Jun	New Zealand V France, tbc, New Zealand
Aug	Ireland V Argentina, Dublin, Ireland
28 Aug	Wales V Canada, Cardiff

Rugby: Pacific Rim Championship

1 May	Japan V Hong Kong, Tokyo, Japan
8 May	Hong Kong V USA, Hong Kong,
8 May	Japan V Fiji, Tokyo, Japan
15 May	Canada V Tonga, Vancouver, Canada
15 May	Hong Kong V Fiji, Hong Kong,
15 May	Japan V USA, Tokyo, Japan
22 May	Hong Kong V Western Samoa, Hong Kong
22 May	USA V Tonga, tbc, USA
29 May	Fiji V Canada, Suva, Fiji
29 May	Tonga V Western Samoa, tbc, Tonga
5 Jun	Tonga V Japan, tbc, Tonga
5 Jun	Western Samoa V Canada, tbc, Western Samoa
12 Jun	Fiji V Tonga, Suva, Fiji
12 Jun	Western Samoa V Japan, tbc, Western Samoa
19 Jun	Canada V Japan, Vancouver, Canada
19 Jun	Fiji V USA, Suva, Fiji
19 Jun	Tonga V Hong Kong, tbc, Tonga
26 Jun	Canada V Hong Kong, Vancouver, Canada
26 Jun	USA V Western Samoa, tbc, USA
3 Jul	USA V Canada, tbc, USA
3 Jul	Western Samoa V Fiji. tbc, Western Samoa

Rugby: Sevens

9-10 Jan	Punta Del Este Sevens, Punta Del Este, Uruguay
26-28 Mar	Credit Suisse First Boston Hong Kong Rugby Sevens, Hong Kong
29 May	Middlesex Sevens, Twickenham, London

Rugby: Tri-Nations

10 Jul	New Zealand V South Africa, tbc, New Zealand
17 Jul	Australia V South Africa, tbc, Australia
24 Jul	Bledisoe Cup - New Zealand V Australia, tbc, New Zealand
7 Aug	South Africa V New Zealand, tbc, South Africa
14 Aug	South Africa V Australia, tbc, South Africa
28 Aug	Bledisoe Cup - Australia V New Zealand, tbc, Australia

Rugby: Varsity

Dec	The Bowring Bowl - Oxford V Cambridge Varsity Match, Twickenham, London

Rugby: Youth Championships

24-4 Apr	IRB/FIRA World Youth Championship, Various

Rugby: World Cup

1 Oct	Fiji V Namibia, Beziers, France
1 Oct	Wales V Argentina, Cardiff
1 Oct	World Cup Opening Ceremony, Cardiff
2 Oct	Europe 1 V USA, Dublin, Ireland
2 Oct	Europe 2 V Europe 5, Twickenham, London
2 Oct	Europe 4 V Repechage 2, Galashiels
2 Oct	France V Canada, Beziers, France
3 Oct	Australia V Europe 6, Belfast
3 Oct	Europe 3 V South Africa, Edinburgh
3 Oct	New Zealand V Repechage 1, Bristol
3 Oct	Western Samoa V Asia 1, Wrexham
8 Oct	Europe 3 V Repechage 2, Edinburgh
8 Oct	France V Namibia, Bordeaux, France
9 Oct	Europe 2 V New Zealand, Twickenham, London
9 Oct	Fiji V Canada, Bordeaux, France
9 Oct	USA V Europe 6, Dublin, Ireland
9 Oct	Wales V Asia 1, Cardiff
10 Oct	Argentina V Western Samoa, Llanelli
10 Oct	Europe 1 V Australia, Dublin, Ireland
10 Oct	South Africa V Europe 4, Edinburgh
14 Oct	Australia V USA, Limerick, Ireland
14 Oct	Canada V Namibia, Toulouse, France
14 Oct	Europe 5 V Repechage 1, Leicester
14 Oct	New Zealand V Europe 5, Huddersfield
14 Oct	Wales V Western Samoa, Cardiff

15 Oct	Europe 1 V Europe 6, Dublin, Ireland
15 Oct	Europe 2 V Repechage , Twickenham, London
15 Oct	South Africa V Repechage 2, Glasgow
16 Oct	Argentina V Asia 1, Cardiff
16 Oct	Europe 3 V Europe 4, Edinburgh
16 Oct	France V Fiji, Toulouse, France
20 Oct	Quarter Final Play Offs - Runner Up A V Runner Up D, Edinburgh
20 Oct	Quarter Final Play Offs - Runner Up B V Runner Up C, Twickenham, London
20 Oct	Quarter Final Play Offs - Runner Up E V 3rd Best, Lens, France
23 Oct	Quarter Final 1, Cardiff
24 Oct	Quarter Final 2, Lens, France
24 Oct	Quarter Final 3, Edinburgh
24 Oct	Quarter Final 4, Dublin, Ireland
30 Oct	Semi Final 1, Twickenham, London
31 Oct	Semi Final 2, Twickenham, London
4 Nov	3rd/4th Place Play Off, Cardiff
6 Nov	World Cup Final, Cardiff

Shooting

12-14 Feb	National Air Pistol Championships, Wolverhampton
20-25 Mar	World Cup In Trap Skeet, Lima, Peru
8-15 May	World Cup In Trap Skeet, Kumamoto City, Japan
17-24 May	World Cup In Rifle & Pistol, Munich, Germany
24-31 May	World Cup In Rifle & Pistol, Milan, Italy
26 Jun-2 Jul	1999 Island Games, Gotland, Sweden
27 Jun-4 Jul	World Cup In Rifle & Pistol, Atlanta, USA
1-12 Jul	World Shotgun Championships, Tampere, Finland
23 Jul-1 Aug	European Championships In 300m, 50m, And 25m, Bordeaux, France
23 Jul-1 Aug	European Championships In Clay Target, Montpellier, France
24 Jul-8 Aug	13th Pan American Games, Winnipeg, Canada
Nov	World Shoot XII, Cebu, Philippines
10-15 Dec	Pacific Ocean Games, Santiago, Chile

Skiing - Alpine

1-3 Jan	Cafe De Colombia Alpine World Cup, Maribor, Slovenia
5-6 Jan	Cafe De Colombia Alpine World Cup, Kranjska Gora, Slovenia
7-9 Jan	Cafe De Colombia Alpine World Cup, Schladming, Austria
7-9 Jan	Cafe De Colombia Alpine World Cup, Berchtesgaden, Germany
10 Jan	Cafe De Colombia Alpine World Cup, Flachau, Austria
10-16 Jan	The FIS British Land British Senior Championships, Tignes, France
12 Jan	31. Herren-Weltcup Riesenslalom, Adelboden, Switzerland
15-17 Jan	Cafe De Colombia Alpine World Cup, St Anton, Austria
16-17 Jan	68. Internationale Lauberhornrennen, Wengen, Switzerland
22-24 Jan	Cafe De Colombia Alpine World Cup, Kitzbuhel, Austria
22-24 Jan	Cafe De Colombia Alpine World Cup, Cortina D'ampezzo, Italy
31 Jan-5 Feb	4th Winter Asian Games - Alpine Skiing, Yongpyong, Korea
1-14 Feb	FIS World Alpine Championships, Vail, USA
20-21 Feb	Cafe De Colombia Alpine World Cup, Garmisch Partenkirchen, Germany
22-27 Feb	Cafe De Colombia Alpine World Cup, Are, Sweden
27-28 Feb	Cafe De Colombia Alpine World Cup - Rennen Herren, Ofterschwang, Germany
5-6 Mar	Cafe De Colombia Alpine World Cup, St.Moritz, Switzerland

6-14 Mar	14th Winter World Games For The Deaf, Davos, Switzerland
6-7 Mar	Cafe De Colombia Alpine World Cup, Kvitfjell, Norway
10-14 Mar	Cafe De Colombia Alpine World Cup - Final, Sierra Nevada, Spain
10-14 Mar	Cafe De Colombia Alpine World Cup - Final, Sierra Nevada, Spain
28 Mar-2 Apr	English Ski Council Alpine Race Championships 1999, tbc
12-16 Apr	Scottish Senior FIS Championships & K McGibbon Memorial Races, Nevis Range

Skiing - Freestyle

9-10 Jan	FIS Freestyle World Cup, Mt.Tremblant, Canada
15-17 Jan	FIS Freestyle World Cup, Steamboat, USA
22-24 Jan	FIS Freestyle World Cup, Heavenly Valley, USA
30-31 Jan	FIS Freestyle World Cup, Whistler, Canada
6-7 Feb	FIS Freestyle World Cup, Chatel, France
11-12 Feb	FIS Freestyle World Cup, Altenmarkt, Austria
17 Feb	FIS Freestyle World Cup, Inawashiro, Japan
20-21 Feb	FIS Freestyle World Cup, Madarao, Japan
20-21 Feb	FIS Freestyle World Cup, Piancavallo, Italy
25-27 Feb	FIS Freestyle World Cup - Finals, La Plagne, France
6-14 Mar	FIS Freestyle World Championships, Meiringen-Hasliberg, Switzerland

Skiing - Jumping

1 Jan	Ruhrgas FIS Ski Jumping World Cup, Garmisch-Partenkirchen, Germany
3 Jan	Ruhrgas FIS Ski Jumping World Cup, Innsbruck, Austria
6 Jan	Ruhrgas FIS Ski Jumping World Cup, Bischofshofen, Austria
9 Jan	Ruhrgas FIS Ski Jumping World Cup, Engelberg, Switzerland
10 Jan	Ruhrgas FIS Ski Jumping World Cup, Engelberg, Switzerland
16 Jan	Ruhrgas FIS Ski Jumping World Cup, Zakopane, Poland
17 Jan	Ruhrgas FIS Ski Jumping World Cup, Zakopane, Poland
23 Jan	Ruhrgas FIS Ski Jumping World Cup, Sapporo Okura, Japan
24 Jan	Ruhrgas FIS Ski Jumping World Cup, Sapporo Okura, Japan
30 Jan	Ruhrgas FIS Ski Jumping World Cup, Willingen, Germany
31 Jan	Ruhrgas FIS Ski Jumping World Cup, Willingen, Germany
6 Feb	Ruhrgas FIS Ski Jumping World Cup, Harrachov, Czech Republic
7 Feb	Ruhrgas FIS Ski Jumping World Cup, Harrachov, Czech Republic
18-28 Feb	Ruhrgas FIS World Championships, Ramsau, Austria
4 Mar	Ruhrgas FIS Ski Jumping World Cup, Kuopio, Finland
5-7 Mar	Ruhrgas FIS Ski Jumping World Cup - Lahti Ski Games, Lahti, Finland
9 Mar	Ruhrgas FIS Ski Jumping World Cup, Trondheim/granasen, Norway
11 Mar	Ruhrgas FIS Ski Jumping World Cup, Falun, Sweden
14 Mar	Ruhrgas FIS Ski Jumping World Cup, Holmenkollen, Oslo, Norway
20 Mar	Ruhrgas FIS Ski Jumping World Cup - Ski Flying - Final, Planica, Slovenia
21 Mar	Ruhrgas FIS Ski Jumping World Cup Final - Ski Flying, Planica, Slovenia

Skiing - Nordic

2-3 Jan	Warsteiner FIS World Cup Nordic Combined, Schonach, Germany
5 Jan	Warsteiner FIS World Cup Nordic Combined, Reit Im Winkl, Germany

9-10 Jan	Warsteiner FIS World Cup Nordic Combined, Strbske Pleso, Slovakia
16-17 Jan	Warsteiner FIS World Cup Nordic Combined, Liberec, Czech Republic
24 Jan	Warsteiner FIS World Cup Nordic Combined, St Moritz, Switzerland
26-27 Jan	Warsteiner FIS World Cup Nordic Combined, Predazzo, Italy
30-31 Jan	Warsteiner FIS World Cup Nordic Combined (Cross Country), Le Brassus, Switzerland
30-31 Jan	Warsteiner FIS World Cup Nordic Combined (Jumping), Chaux Neuve, France
2-7 Feb	Nordic Junior World Ski Championships, Saalfelden, Austria
18-28 Feb	Warsteiner FIS World Cup Nordic Combined, WSC Ramsau, Austria
18-28 Feb	World Championships, Bischofshofen, Austria
5-7 Mar	Warsteiner FIS World Cup Nordic Combined - Lahti Ski Games, Lahti, Finland
6-14 Mar	14th Winter World Games For The Deaf, Davos, Switzerland
10 Mar	Warstiener FIS World Cup Nordic Combined, Falun, Sweden
12-13 Mar	Warsteiner FIS World Cup Nordic Combined, Oslo, Norway
20-21 Mar	Warsteiner FIS World Cup Nordic Combined - Final, Zakopane, Poland

Snooker

2-21 Jan	Qualifying For Regal Scottish, British Open & Embassy World Championships, Blackpool
16-24 Jan	Nations Cup, Newcastle
25-31 Jan	Regal Welsh, Cardiff
7-14 Feb	Benson & Hedges Masters, Wembley, London
15-21 Feb	Regal Scottish Open, Aberdeen
25-28 Feb	Liverpool Victoria Charity Challenge, Derby
23-28 Mar	Benson & Hedges Irish Masters, County Kildare, Ireland
29 Mar-2 Apr	Embassy Final Qualifying Round, Telford
4-11 Apr	British Open, Plymouth
17 Apr-3 May	Embassy World Championships, Sheffield
Aug	Champions Cup, tbc
16-17 Oct	National Snooker Championships, Swindon

Speed Skating

8-11 Jan	Speed Skating - European Championship, Heerenveen, Netherlands
22-24 Jan	Short Track Speed Skating - European Championship, Oberstdorf, Germany
31 Jan-1 Feb	4th Winter Asian Games - Short Track, Yongpyong, Korea
2-5 Feb	4th Winter Asian Games - Chunchon, Korea
5-7 Feb	Speed Skating - World Championship, Hamar, Norway
12-14 Feb	Speed Skating - World Junior Championship, Geithus, Norway
20-21 Feb	World Sprint Speed Skating Championships, Calgary, Canada
5-7 Mar	Short Track Speed Skating - World Team Championship, St Louis, USA
10-12Mar	Short Track Speed Skating - World Championships, Sheffield
2-14 Mar	World Speed Distance Skating Championships, Heerenveen, Netherlands
19-21 Mar	Short Track Speed Skating - World Championship, Sofia, Bulgaria

Squash

23-28 Jan	Tournament Of Champions, New York, USA
17-28 Mar	British Open, Birmingham
15-16 May	National Clubs Grand Finals Weekend, Nottingham

11-15 Aug	Mens World Cup, 's-Hertogenbosch, Netherlands
24-26 Sep	12th European Club Championships Helsinki, Finland

Swimming

5-6 Jan	FINA Swimming World Cup, Beijing, PR China
9-10 Jan	FINA Swimming World Cup, tbc, Hong Kong
15-16 Jan	FINA Swimming World Cup, Sydney, Australia
18-19 Jan	FINA Swimming World Cup, Hobart, Australia
24 Jan	Salvador De Bahia - FINA Marathon Swimming World Cup, Salvador, Brazil
24 Jan	Tapes-Rio Grande Do Sul - FINA Marathon Swimming World Cup, Salvador, Brazil
29-31 Jan	British Swimming Grand Prix, Swansea
13-14 Feb	FINA Swimming World Cup, Glasgow
16-17 Feb	FINASwimming World Cup, Malmo, Sweden
19-21 Feb	British Swimming Grand Prix, Leeds
20-21 Feb	FINA Swimming World Cup, Paris, France
27-28 Feb	FINA Swimming World Cup, Gelsenkirchen, Germany
27-28 Feb	National Junior Swimming Championships, Darlington
3-4 Mar	FINA Swimming World Cup, Imperia, Italy
20-22 Mar	National Masters Diving Competitions, Sheffield
1-4 Apr	FINA World Swimming Championships (25m), Hong Kong
Apr	UK Blind Sport Swimming Championships, Mansfield
3-4 Apr	8 Nations Junior, tbc
16-18 Apr	British Swimming Grand Prix, tbc
28 Apr-2 May	The Womens Global Challenge, Various, USA
28-30 May	British Swimming Grand Prix Super Final, Sheffield
4-6 Jun	National Long Course Swimming Championships, Sheffield
26 Jun-2 Jul	1999 Island Games, Gotland, Sweden
2-13 Jul	Universiade, Palma De Mallorca, Spain
23 Jul-8 Aug	European Championships, Istanbul, Turkey
24 Jul-8 Aug	13th Pan American Games, Winnipeg, Canada
19-22 Aug	Pan Pacific Championships, Sydney, Australia
Dec	European Sprints, Lisbon, Portugal
8-13 Dec	Pacific Ocean Games, Santiago, Chile
15-17 Dec	13th Asian Games, Bangkok, Thailand
16-19 Dec	British Swimming Championships, Sheffield

Synchronized Swimming

7-8 Mar	National Synchro Championships, Halifax
7-11 Jul	6th Junior World Championships, Cali, Colombia
24 Jul-8 Aug	13th Pan American Games, Winnipeg, Canada
27 Jul-8 Aug	VIII FINA World Masters Championships, Munich, Germany
8-12 Sep	World Cup A, Seoul, Korea
Nov	National Masters Synchro Competition, Leicester
13-16 Dec	Pacific Ocean Games, Santiago, Chile

Table Tennis

7-10 Jan	ITTF Pro Tour Finals 1998, Paris, France
15-17 Jan	English Senior Nationals, Bath
22-26 Feb	ITTF Pro Tour - Qatar Open, Doha, Qatar
11-14 Mar	ITTF Pro Tour - English Open, Hopton-On-Sea
18-21 Mar	ITTF Pro Tour - Croatian Open, Zagreb, Croatia

Fixtures 1999

26 Apr-9 May	45th World Championships, Belgrade, Yugoslavia
27-30 May	ITTF Pro Tour - Netherlands Open, Eindhoven, Netherlands
29-30 May	Grand Prix Finals, Bath
3-6 Jun	ITTF Pro Tour - Lebanon Open, Beirut, Lebanon
12-13 Jun	National Team Finals, Bury St Edmunds
24-27 Jun	ITTF Pro Tour - Brazilian Open, Rio De Janeiro, Brazil
26 Jun-2 Jul	1999 Island Games, Gotland, Sweden
24 Jul-8 Aug	13th Pan American Games, Winnipeg, Canada
19-22 Aug	ITTF Pro Tour - Australian Open, Melbourne, Australia
26-29 Aug	ITTF Pro Tour - Taipei Open, Taipei, Chinese Taipei
10-12 Sep	ITTF Women's World Cup, tbc
16-19 Sep	ITTF Pro Tour - China Open, tbc, PR China
18-19 Sep	National Table Tennis Championships, Hull
23-26 Sep	ITTF Pro Tour - Japan Open, Kobe, Japan
14-17 Oct	ITTF Pro Tour - German Open, Bremen, Germany
21-24 Oct	ITTF Pro Tour - Austrian Open, Linz, Austria
28-31 Oct	ITTF Men's World Cup, tbc
11-14 Nov	ITTF Pro Tour - French Open, tbc, France
18-21 Nov	ITTF Pro Tour - Swedish Open, tbc, Sweden
7-16 Dec	Pacific Ocean Games, Santiago, Chile
9-12 Dec	ITTF Pro Tour - Czech Open, Prague, Czech Republic

Ten Pin Bowling
| 1 Mar | UK Blind Sport Ten-Pin Bowling Championships, tbc |

Triathlon
8 May	British Modern Triathlon Championships, Milton Keynes Or Wolverhampton
10 Jul	World Long Distance Triathlon Championships, Sater, Sweden
24 Jul-8 Aug	13th Pan American Games, Winnipeg, Canada
31 Jul	World Triathlon Championships, Munich, Germany
7 Aug	National Relay Championships, Nottingham
4 Sep	European Long Distance Triathlon Championships, Almere, Netherlands
19 Sep	ETU Prestige Races - The London
16 Dec	Pacific Ocean Games, Santiago, Chile

Volleyball
12-17 Jul	World League Finals, tbc, Argentina
22-24 Jul	FIVB Beach Volleyball World Championships 1999 - Women, Marseille, France
23-25 Jul	FIVB Beach Volleyball World Championships 1999 - Men, Marseille, France
13 Aug-5 Sep	World Grand Prix, Various
4-5 Sep	World Grand Prix Finals, Various
2 Nov-2 Dec	Mens & Womens World Cups, tbc, Japan
17 Dec	England V Scotland, tbc
18 Dec	England V Scotland, tbc
19 Dec	England V Scotland, tbc

Water Polo
16 May	Championship Finals, Sheffield
24-30 May	12th Womens Water Polo World Cup, Winnipeg, Canada
1-15 Jul	Universiade, Palma De Mallorca, Spain
24 Jul-8 Aug	13th Pan American Games, Winnipeg, Canada
27 Jul-8 Aug	3rd Junior Womens World Championships, Catania, Italy
2-11 Sep	European Water Polo World Championships, Florence, Italy
28 Sep-3 Oct	11th Mens Water Polo World Cup, Sydney, Australia
9-18 Oct	10th Junior Mens World Championships, Kuwait

Waterskiing
24 Jul-8 Aug	13th Pan American Games, Winnipeg, Canada
13-19 Sep	World Tournament Championships, Milan, Italy
7-10 Dec	Pacific Ocean Games, Santiago, Chile

Yachting
1-26 Jan	1999 World Sailing Championship, Melbourne, Australia
2-8 Jan	1999 Europe Class Open Week, Melbourne, Australia
2-8 Jan	1999 Europe Class World Championship, Melbourne, Australia
2-4 Jan	Int 14 Team Racing World Championship, Sandringham, Melbourne, Australia
4-13 Jan	1999 Laser World Championships, Melbourne, Australia
6-17 Jan	1999 Finn Gold Cup, Melbourne, Australia
6-17 Jan	1999 Soling World Championship, Melbourne, Australia
6-16 Jan	Junior Finn Championship, Melbourne, Australia
7-17 Jan	1999 470 Open World Championship, Melbourne, Australia
7-17 Jan	1999 470 Women's World Championship, Melbourne, Australia
7-13 Jan	1999 Hobie 17 And Hobie 18 World Championship, Melbourne, Australia
7-16 Jan	1999 Int A-Division Catamaran World Championship, Melbourne, Australia
7-14 Jan	Int 14 World Championship, Melbourne, Australia
8-17 Jan	49er World Championship, Melbourne, Australia
11-16 Jan	Sail Melbourne, Melbourne, Australia
15-22 Jan	1999 Laser Masters World Championships, Melbourne, Australia
18-22 Jan	Infanta Cristina Trophy, Melbourne, Australia
26-30 Jan	Miami Olympic Classes Regatta, Miami, USA
15-23 Apr	Semaine Olympique Francaise, Hyeres, France
26-30 May	Spa Regatta, Medemblik, Netherlands
31 May-5 Jun	Sydney 40 Class Association, Hamble
5-11 Jun	Finn Europeans, Oostende, Belgium
7-12 Jun	Hoya Royal Lymington Cup, Lymington
11-13 Jun	British National Melges 24 Championships, Hayling Island
19-27 Jun	Kiel Week, Kiel, Germany
1-10 Jul	Star European Championship, Helsinki, Finland
1 Jul	UK National Women's Match Race Championship, tbc
1-15 Jul	Universiade, Palma De Mallorca, Spain
12-25 Jul	Champagne Mumm Admirals Cup, Cowes
15-23 Jul	Europe Dinghy European Championship, Hayling Island
23-31 Jul	FD World Championship, Lee On Solent
23-30 Jul	Laser European Championship, Finland
24-31 Jul	International Flying Dutchman Open World Champs, Lee On Solent
25-31 Jul	Soling European Championship, Sandefjord, Norway
31 Jul-7 Aug	Cowes Week, Cowes
5-14 Aug	470 European Championship, Zadar, Croatia
7-13 Aug	420 Junior European Championship, Plymouth
20-29 Aug	Mistral European And Youth European Championship, Puck, Poland
21-29 Aug	Cork And Laser II World Championship, Kingston, Canada
13-18 Sep	Mumm 30 World Championships, Hamble, Southampton
16-26 Sep	Sydney Harbour Regatta, Sydney Harbour, Australia
17-20 Dec	Sydney International Regatta, Sydney Harbour, Australia

General

English Sports Council
+44 (0) 171 273 1500
+44 (0) 171 383 5740

United Kingdom Sports Council
+44 (0) 171 380 8000
+44 (0) 171 380 0927

Aerobatics

Fédération Aeronautique Internationale
+33 1 49 54 38 92
+33 1 49 54 38 88
http://www.fai.org/

Royal Aero Club of the United Kingdom
+44 (0) 1162 531051
+44 (0) 1162 531939
http://www.u-net.com/icarus/royal.aero.club/aviation/

American Football

NFL Europe
+44 (0) 171 629 2992
+44 (0) 171 629 4005
http://www.nfl.com/

NFL International
+1 212 450 2000
+1 212 681 7582
http://www.nfl.com/

Angling

Confederation Internationale de la Peche Sportive
+39 06 368 58239
+39 06 368 58109

National Federation of Anglers
+44 (0) 1283 734735
+44 (0) 1283 734799

Salmon and Trout Association
+44 (0) 171 283 5838
+44 (0) 171 626 5137

Archery

English Field Archery Society
+44 (0) 1905 358957
+44 (0) 1905 359246
http://www.fieldarcher.com

Fédération Internationale de Tir à l'Arc
+41 21 614 3050
+41 21 614 3055
http://www.archery.org

Grand National Archery Society
+44 (0) 1203 696631
+44 (0) 1203 419662

Athletics

Athletics UK
+44 (0) 121 456 5098
+44 (0) 121 456 4998
http://www.british-athletics.co.uk

International Amateur Athletic Federation
+377 93 10 88 88
+377 93 15 95 15
http://www.iaaf.org/

Badminton

Badminton Association of England Ltd.
+44 (0) 1908 268400
+44 (0) 1908 268412

International Badminton Federation
+44 (0) 1242 234904
+44 (0) 1242 221030
http://www.intbadfed.org

Scottish Badminton Union
+44 (0) 141 445 1218
+44 (0) 141 425 1218

Welsh Badminton Association
+44 (0) 1222 222 082
+44 (0) 1222 394 282

Baseball

British Baseball Federation
+44 (0) 1482 643551
+44 (0) 1482 640224
http://www.bbf.org/

International Baseball Association
+41 21 311 18 63
+41 21 311 18 64
http://monviso2.alpcom.it/digesu/

Major League Baseball
+1 212 350 8300
+1 212 826 2230
http://www.majorleaguebaseball.com

National League of Professional Baseball Clubs
+1 212 339 7700
+1 212 935 5069
http://www.majorleaguebaseball.com

The American League of Professional Baseball Clubs
+1 212 339 7600
+1 212 593 7138
http://www.majorleaguebaseball.com

Basketball

Budweiser Basketball League
+44 (0) 121 749 1355
+44 (0) 121 749 5355
http://www.basketball-league.co.uk/

English Basketball Association
+44 (0) 113 236 1166
+44 (0) 113 236 1022
http://www.basketballengland.org.uk

FIBA Basketball Promotion
+49 89 74 81 58-0
+49 89 7481 58-88
http://www.fiba.com

National Basketball Association (NBA)
+1 212 407 8500
+1 212 371 8129
http://www.nba.com

Clubs

Birmingham Bullets
+44 (0) 121 246 6022
+44 (0) 121 246 6033
http://www.members.aol.com/bpbullets

Chester Jets
+44 (0) 1829 751413
+44 (0) 1829 751413
http://www.btinternet.com/~jets

Derby Storm
+44 (0) 1332 340 484
+44 (0) 1332 340 484
http://www.dspace.dial.pipex.com/derbystorm

Edinburgh Rocks
+44 (0) 131 447 1737
+44 (0) 131 220 3550

Greater London Leopards
+44 (0) 171 224 1992
+44 (0) 171 486 8450
http://www.leopards.force9.co.uk

Leicester Riders
+44 (0) 116 270 3761
+44 (0) 116 233 3172
http://www.leicesterriders.com/riders/index.htm

London Towers
+44 (0) 171 722 0109
+44 (0) 171 586 1422
http://www.london-towers.demon.co.uk

Manchester Giants
+44 (0) 161 950 7000
+44 (0) 161 950 7007
http://www.giants.co.uk

Milton Keynes Lions
+44 (0) 1442 825760

Newcastle Eagles
+44 (0) 191 496 1100
+44 (0) 191 488 0900
http://www.newcastle-eagles.com

Sheffield Sharks
+44 (0) 114 257 1994
+44 (0) 114 257 1993
http://www.members.aol.com/shefsharks

Thames Valley Tigers
+44 (0) 1344 300185
+44 (0) 1344 409855
http://www.uk.oracle.com/tvtigers/

Worthing Bears
+44 (0) 1903 213806
+44 (0) 1903 236552
http://www3.mistral.co.uk/markf/

BMX

Great Britain BMX Association
+44 (0) 1706 621193
+44 (0) 1706 621193

Bowls

English Bowling Association
+44 (0) 1903 820222
+44 (0) 1903 820444

English Indoor Bowling Association
+44 (0) 1664 481900
+44 (0) 1664 481901

English Women's Indoor Bowling Association
+44 (0) 1604 494163
+44 (0) 1604 494434

English Women's Bowling Association
+44 (0) 1297 21317
+44 (0) 1297 21317

World Bowls Board
+44 (0) 1903 247468
+44 (0) 1903 502616

Boxing

Amateur Boxing Association
+44 (0) 181 778 0935
+44 (0) 181 778 9324

Association Internationale de Boxe Amateur
+49 30 423 6766
+49 30 423 5943
http://www.uni-leipzig.de/~iat/aiba/aiba1.htm

Canoeing

British Canoe Union
+44 (0) 115 982 1100
+44 (0) 115 982 1797

International Canoe Federation
+36 1 363 48 32
+36 1 157 56 43
http://www.worldsport.com/sports/canoeing/home.html

Chess

British Chess Federation
+44 (0) 1424 442500
+44 (0) 1424 718372

Directory

International Chess Federation (FIDE)
+41 21 310 3900
+41 21 310 3905
http://www.fide.com

Cricket Governing Bodies and Associations

Australian Cricket Board
+61 3 9653 9999
+61 3 9653 9911

Board of Control for Cricket in Sri Lanka
+94 1 69 1459
+94 1 69 7405

England & Wales Cricket Board
+44 (0) 171 432 1200
+44 (0) 171 289 5619
http://www.lords.org/

Pakistan Cricket Board Of Control
+92 42 575 4737
+92 42 571 1860

The Board of Control for Cricket In India
+91 265 431 233
+91 265 428 833

The International Cricket Council
+44 (0) 171 266 1818
+44 (0) 171 266 1777
http://lords.msn.com/admin/email/con_s05.htm

New Zealand Cricket Inc.
+64 3 366 2964
+64 3 365 7491

United Cricket Board of South Africa
+27 11 880 2810
+27 11 880 6578
http://www-rsa.cricket.org

West Indies Cricket Board of Control
+1 268 460 5462
+1 268 460 5452

Women's Cricket Association
+44 (0) 121 440 0567
+44 (0) 121 440 0520

Zimbabwe Cricket Union
+263 4 704616
+263 4 729370

British Clubs

Derbyshire County Cricket Club
+44 (0) 1332 383211
+44 (0) 1332 290251

Durham County Cricket Club
+44 (0) 191 387 1717
+44 (0) 191 387 1616
http://www.durham-ccc.org.uk/

Essex County Cricket Club
+44 (0) 1245 252420
+44 (0) 1245 491607

Glamorgan County Cricket Club
+ 44 1222 343 478
+ 44 1222 377 044
http://wwwuk.cricket.org/link_to_database/NATIONAL/ENG/FC_TEAMS/GLAM/

Gloucestershire Cricket Club
+44 (0) 117 924 5216
+44 (0) 117 924 1193

Hampshire County Cricket Club
+44 (0) 1703 333788
+44 (0) 1703 330121
http://www.hampshire.cricket.org

Kent County Cricket Club
+44 (0) 1227 456886
+44 (0) 1227 762168

Lancashire County Cricket Club
+44 (0) 161 282 4000
+44 (0) 161 282 4100

Leicestershire Cricket Club
+44 (0) 116 283 2128
+44 (0) 116 244 0363

Middlesex County Cricket Club
+44 (0) 171 289 1300
+44 (0) 171 289 5831

Northamptonshire Cricket Club
+44 (0) 1604 632917
+44 (0) 1604 232855

Nottinghamshire Cricket Club
+44 (0) 115 982 1525
+44 (0) 115 937 4315

Somerset County Cricket Club
+44 (0) 1823 272946
+44 (0) 1823 332395

Surrey County Cricket Club
+44 (0) 171 582 6660
+44 (0) 171 735 7769
http://www.surreyccc-oval.co.uk

Sussex County Cricket Club
+44 (0) 1273 732161
+44 (0) 1273 771917

Warwickshire Cricket Club
+44 (0) 121 466 4422
+44 (0) 121 446 4544
http://www.warwickshireccc.org.uk

Worcestershire Cricket Club
+44 (0) 1905 748474
+44 (0) 1905 748005

Yorkshire County Cricket Club
+44 (0) 113 278 7394
+44 (0) 113 278 4099
http://www.yorkshireccc.org.uk

Croquet

The Croquet Association
+44 (0) 171 736 3148
+44 (0) 171 731 3148
http://users.ox.ac.uk/~croquet/cahtml.html

World Croquet Association
+44 (0) 1270 820296

Cycling

British Cycling Federation
+44 (0) 161 230 2301
+44 (0) 161 231 0591

Union Cycliste Internationale
+41 21 622 05 80
+41 21 622 05 88
http://www.uci.ch

Darts

British Darts Organisation - HQ
+44 (0) 181 883 5544
+44 (0) 181 883 0109

PDC
+44 (0) 1482 565444
+44 (0) 1482 353635

World Darts Federation
+44 (0) 181 883 5055
+44 (0) 181 883 0109

Disabled Sport

British Blind Sport
+44 (0) 1788 536142
+44 (0) 1788 536676

British Deaf Sports Council
+44 (0) 1943 850081
+44 (0) 1943 850828

British Paralympics Association
+44 (0) 181 681 9655
+44 (0) 181 681 9650

British Sports Association for the Disabled
+44 (0) 171 490 4919
+44 (0) 171 490 4914

Cerebral Palsy Sport
+44 (0) 115 940 1202
+44 (0) 115 940 2984

International Blind Sports Association (IBSA)
+33 1 40 31 45 00
+33 1 40 31 45 42
http://www.ibsa.es

International Paralympic Committee
+32 5 038 9340
+32 5 039 0119
http://info.lut.ac.uk/research/paad/ipc/ipc.html

Special Olympics
+44 (0) 171 416 7551
+44 (0) 171 735 4639

Special Olympics International (SOI)
+1 202 628 36 30
+1 202 824 02 00
http://www.specialolympics.org

Dragon Boat Racing

British Dragon Boat Racing Association
+44 (0) 1295 770629
+44 (0) 1295 770629
http://easyweb.easynet.co.uk/~colenorton/bda.html

Equestrian

British Equestrian Federation
+44 (0) 1203 698871
+44 (0) 1203 696484

British Horse Society
+44 (0) 1926 707700
+44 (0) 1926 707800
http://www.brucepub.com/bhs

Fédération Equestre Internationale
+41 21 312 5656
+41 21 312 8677
http://210.116.176.1/samsung/snc/ver3/sub6/index.html

Fencing

Amateur Fencing Association
+44 (0) 181 742 3032
+44 (0) 181 742 3033
http://www.netlink.co.uk/users/afa

FédérationInternationale d'Escrime
+41 21 32 03 115
+41 21 32 03 116
http://fie.ch

Field Hockey

Federation Internationale de Hockey
+32 2 219 4537
+32 2 219 2761
http://www.fihockey.org

The English Hockey Association
+ 44 1908 544644
+ 44 1908 241106

Football Federations and Associations

Federation Internationale de Football Associations
+41 1 384 9595
+41 1 384 9696
http://www.fifa.com

The Football Association
+44 (0) 171 402 7151
+44 (0) 171 402 0486

The Football Association of Ireland
+353 1 676 6864
+353 1 661 0931

The Football Association of Wales
+44 (0) 1222 372325
+44 (0) 1222 343961
http://www.faw.co.uk

The Football League Limited
+44 (0) 1253 729421
+44 (0) 1253 724786

The Irish Football Association Ltd
+44 (0) 1232 669458
+44 (0) 1232 667620

The Scottish Football Association
+44 (0) 141 332 6372
+44 (0) 141 332 7559
http://www.scottshfa.co.uk

The Scottish Football League
+44 (0) 141 248 3844
+44 (0) 141 221 7450

The Scottish Premier League
+44 (0) 141 649 6962
+44 (0) 141 649 6963

UEFA
+41 22 994 44 44
+41 22 994 44 88

FA Carling Premiership

Arsenal Football Club
+44 (0) 171 704 4000
+44 (0) 171 704 4001
http://www.arsenal.co.uk

Aston Villa Football Club
+44 (0) 121 327 2299
+44 (0) 121 322 2107

Blackburn Rovers Football Club
+44 (0) 1254 698888
+44 (0) 1254 671042
http://www.rovers.co.uk

Charlton Athletic Football Club
+44 (0) 181 333 4000
+44 (0) 181 333 4001

Chelsea Football Club
+44 (0) 171 385 5545
+44 (0) 171 381 4831
http://www.chelseafc.co.uk

Coventry City Football Club
+44 (0) 1203 234000
+44 (0) 1203 234099
http://www.ccfc.co.uk

Derby County Football Club
+44 (0) 1332 667503
+44 (0) 1332 667519

Everton Football Club
+44 (0) 151 521 2020
+44 (0) 151 286 9112
http://www.evertonfc.com

Leeds United Football Club
+44 (0) 113 226 6000
+44 (0) 113 226 6050
http://www.lufc.co.uk

Leicester City Football Club
+44 (0) 116 291 5000
+44 (0) 116 247 0585
http://www.lcfc.co.uk

Liverpool Football Club
+44 (0) 151 263 2361
+44 (0) 151 260 8813

Manchester United Football Club
+44 (0) 161 872 1661
+44 (0) 161 876 5502
http://www.sky.co.uk

Middlesbrough Football Club
+ 44 1642 877700
+ 44 1642 877840

Newcastle United Football Club
+44 (0) 191 201 8400
+44 (0) 191 201 8600
http://www.newcastle-utd.co.uk

Nottingham Forest Football Club
+44 (0) 115 982 4444
+44 (0) 115 982 4466

Sheffield Wednesday Football Club
+44 (0) 114 221 2121
+44 (0) 114 221 2122

Southampton Football Club
+44 (0) 1703 220505
+44 (0) 1703 330360
http://www.soton.ac.uk

Tottenham Hotspur Football Club
+44 (0) 181 365 5000
+44 (0) 181 365 5005
http://www.spurs.co.uk

West Ham United Football Club
+44 (0) 181 548 2748
+44 (0) 181 548 2758
http://www.westhamunited.co.uk

Wimbledon Football Club
+44 (0) 181 771 2233
+44 (0) 181 768 0641

Scottish Premier League

Aberdeen Football Club
+44 (0) 1224 650400
+44 (0) 1224 644173

Celtic Football Club
+44 (0) 141 556 2611
+44 (0) 141 551 8106
http://www.celtic.co.uk

Dundee Football Club
+44 (0) 1382 826106
+44 (0) 1382 832284

Dundee United Football Club
+44 (0) 1382 833126
+44 (0) 1382 889398

Dunfermline Football Club
+44 (0) 1383 724295
+44 (0) 1383 723468

Heart of Midlothian Football Club
+44 (0) 131 200 7200
+44 (0) 131 200 7222
http://www.hearts.co.uk

Motherwell Football Club
+44 (0) 1698 333333
+44 (0) 1698 276333

Kilmarnock Football Club
+44 (0) 1563 525184
+44 (0) 1563 522181

Rangers Football Club
+44 (0) 141 427 8500
+44 (0) 141 427 8947

St Johnstone Football Club
+44 (0) 1738 626961
+44 (0) 1738 625771

Gaelic Football

Gaelic Athletic Association
00 353 1 836 3222
00 353 1 836 6420
http://www.gaa.ie/

Gliding

British Gliding Association
+44 (0) 116 251 5939

Golf

English Golf Union
+44 (0) 1526 354500
+44 (0) 1526 354020

English Ladies Golf Union
+44 (0) 1334 475818
+44 (0) 1334 472818

European Ladies PGA Golf Tour
+ 44 (0) 1625 611444
+ 44 (0) 1625 610406

PGA European Tour
+44 (0) 1344 842881
+44 (0) 1344 842929
http://www.europeantour.com/defaulty.asp

The Professional Golfers Association of America
+1 561 624 8400
+1 561 624 8430
http://www.pga.com

The Professional Golfers Association-UK HQ
+44 (0) 1675 470333
+44 (0) 1675 470674
http://www.pga.com

USPGA
+1 904 285 3700
+1 904 285 7913
http://www.pgatour.com/index2.html

Greyhound Racing

National Greyhound Racing Club Ltd
+44 (0) 171 267 9256
+44 (0) 171 482 1023

Gymnastics

British Gymnastics Association
+44 (0) 1952 820330
+44 (0) 1952 820621
http://www.baga.co.uk

Fédération Internationale de Gymnastique
+41 32 494 64 10
+41 32 494 64 19
http://www.worldsport.com/sports/gymnastics/home.html

Handball

British Handball Association
+44 (0) 1706 229354
+44 (0) 1706 229354

International Handball Federation
+41 61 272 1300
+41 61 272 1344

Horse-Racing

International Racing Bureau
+44 (0) 1638 668881
+44 (0) 1638 665032

The British Horse-Racing Board
+44 (0) 171 396 0011
+44 (0) 171 935 3626

Ice Hockey

British Ice Hockey Federation
+44 (0) 1 202 303 946
+44 (0) 1 202 398 005
http://wkweb1.cableinet.co.uk/stan/biha/

Directory

International Ice Hockey Federation
+41 1 289 8600
+41 1 289 8622
http://www.iihf.com

Sekonda Ice Hockey Superleague
+44 (0) 1530 838899
+44 (0) 1530 830055

Clubs

Ayr Scottish Eagles
+44 (0) 1292 281 311
+44 (0) 1292 618 328

Bracknell Bees
+44 (0) 1344 860 033
+44 (0) 1344 409 855

Cardiff Devils
+44 (0) 1222 811823
+44 (0) 1222 811823
http://www.cwtc.co.uk/devils

London Knights
+44 (0) 171 536 2600
+44 (0) 171 536 2603

Manchester Storm
+44 (0) 161 950 5335
+44 (0) 161 950 6000

Newcastle Riverkings
+44 (0) 191 260 2327
+44 (0) 191 260 2328

Nottingham Panthers
+44 (0) 115 941 3103
+44 (0) 115 941 8754
http://www.ccc.nottingham.ac.uk/~nozjs

Sheffield Steelers
+44 (0) 114 494 723
+44 (0) 114 490 099
http://www.steelers.co.uk

Judo

British Judo Association
+44 (0) 116 255 9669
+44 (0) 116 255 9660

International Judo Federation
+82 2 759 6936
+82 2 754 1075
http://www.ijf.org/

Karate

English Karate Governing Body
+44 (0) 1225 834008
+44 (0) 1225 834008

World Karate Federation
+30 1 27 17 563
+30 1 27 17 564
http://www.wkf.net/html/wkf.html

Lawn Tennis

ATP Tour - America's International Headquarters
+1 904 285 8000
+1 904 285 5966
http://www.atptour.com

Corel WTA Tour
+1 203 978 1740
+1 203 978 1702
http://www.corelwtatour.com/

International Tennis Federation
+44 (0) 181 878 6464
+44 (0) 181 878 7799
http://www.itftennis.com/

Lawn Tennis Association
+44 (0) 171 381 7000
+44 (0) 171 381 5965
http://www.itftennis.com

Life Saving

International Life Saving Federation
+32 16 35 35 00
+32 16 35 01 02
http://www.worldsport.com/worldsport/sports/life_saving/home.html

Royal Life Saving Federation
+44 (0) 1789 773994
+44 (0) 1789 773995

Motor Cycling

Auto-Cycle Union
+44 (0) 1788 540519
+44 (0) 1788 573585

Fédération Internationale de Motocyclisme
+41 22 950 9500
+41 22 950 9501
http://www.fim.ch/

Motor Racing

Fédération Internationale Du Sport Autombile
+33 1 43 12 44 55
+33 1 43 12 44 66

R.A.C. Motor Sports Association Ltd
+44 (0) 1753 681736
+44 (0) 1753 682938

Tracks

Brands Hatch
+44 (0) 1474 872331
+44 (0) 1474 874766

Donington Park
+44 (0) 1332 810048
+44 (0) 1332 850422

Knockhill
+44 (0) 1383 723337
+44 (0) 1383 620167

Silverstone
+44 (0) 1327 857271
+44 (0) 1327 857663

Snetterton
+44 (0) 1953 887303
+44 (0) 1953 888220

Thruxton
+44 (0) 1264 772696
+44 (0) 1264 773794

Netball

All England Netball Association
+44 (0) 1462 442344
+44 (0) 1462 443243

International Federation of Netball Associations
+44 (0) 121 446 4451
+44 (0) 121 440 2408
http://www.netball.org/

Polo

Hurlingham Polo Association
+44 (0) 1869 350044
+44 (0) 1869 350625

International Polo Federation
+1 310 557 9259
+1 310 472 5220
http://www.worldsport.com/worldsport/sports/polo/home.html

Powerboating

Union Internationale Motonautique
+377 92052522

+377 92052523
http://www.worldsport.com/worldsport/sports/powerboating/home.html

Rowing

Amateur Rowing Association
+44 (0) 181 748 3632
+44 (0) 181 741 4658

Fédération Internationale des Sociétés d'Aviron
+41 21 617 8373
+41 21 617 8375
http://www.fisa.org/

Rugby League

Rugby League International Federation
+61 7 4632 3024
+61 2 9339 8501

Super League Europe
+44 (0) 113 244 1114
+44 (0) 113 244 1110
http://www.sporting-life.com/rleague/

The Rugby League Ltd
+44 (0) 113 232 9111
+44 (0) 113 232 9666
http://www.sporting-life.com/rleague/

Clubs

Bradford Bulls
+44 (0) 1274 733899
+44 (0) 1274 724730
http://www.bradfordbulls.co.uk

Castleford Tigers
+44 (0) 1977 552674
+44 (0) 1977 518007

Gateshead
+44 (0) 1484 530710
+44 (0) 1484 531712

Halifax Blue Sox
+44 (0) 1422 250600
+44 (0) 1422 349607

Huddersfield Giants
+44 (0) 1484 530710
+44 (0) 1484 531712

Hull Sharks
+44 (0) 1482 327200
+44 (0) 1482 320338

Leeds Rhinos
+44 (0) 113 278 6181
+44 (0) 113 275 4284
http://www.sporting-life.com/rleague/leeds

London Broncos
+44 (0) 181 410 5000
+44 (0) 181 410 5001
http://www.koppanet.com/broncos/

Salford Reds
+44 (0) 161 737 6654
+44 (0) 161 745 8072
http://www.reds.co.uk

Sheffield Eagles
+44 (0) 114 261 0326
+44 (0) 114 261 0303

St Helens
+44 (0) 1744 23697
+44 (0) 1744 451302
http://saints.merseyworld.com

Warrington
+44 (0) 1925 635338
+44 (0) 1925 571744

Wigan Warriors
+44 (0) 1942 231321
+44 (0) 1942 820111

Rugby Union

Fédération Française de Rugby
+33 1 5321 1515
+33 1 5321 1547

International Rugby Board
+353 1662 5444
+353 1676 9334
http://www.irfb.com

Irish Rugby Football Union
+353 1 668 4601
+353 1 660 5640
http://www.bathrugby.co.uk

Rugby Football Union
+44 (0) 181 892 2000
+44 (0) 181 892 9816
http://www.rfu.com/

The Scottish Rugby Union
+44 (0) 131 346 5000
+44 (0) 131 346 5001

Welsh Rugby Union
+44 (0) 1222 390111
+44 (0) 1222 781722
http://www.wru.com

Clubs

Bath Rugby Football Club
+44 (0) 1225 469230
+44 (0) 1225 325201

Bedford Rugby Football Club
+44 (0) 1234 347980
+44 (0) 1234 347511

Gloucester Rugby Football Club
+44 (0) 1452 381087
+44 (0) 1452 383321
http://www.glawster.demon.co.uk

Harlequins Rugby Football Club
+44 (0) 181 410 6000
+44 (0) 181 410 6001
http://www.quins.co.uk

Leicester Rugby Football Club
+44 (0) 116 254 1607
+44 (0) 116 285 4766
http://www.le.ac.uk/leicester/tigers/indexLondon

London Irish Rugby Football Club
+44 (0) 1932 783034
+44 (0) 1932 784462

London Scottish Rugby Football Club
+44 (0) 181 410 6002
+44 (0) 181 410 6003

NEC Harlequins Rugby Football Club
+44 (0) 181 410 6000
+44 (0) 181 410 6001
http://www.quins.co.uk

Newcastle Rugby Football Club
+44 (0) 191 496 1100
+44 (0) 191 488 0900

Northampton Rugby Football Club
+44 (0) 1604 751543
+44 (0) 1604 599110

Richmond Rugby Football Club
+44 (0) 181 332 7112
+44 (0) 181 332 7113
http://richmond.uk.oracle.com

Saracens Rugby Football Club
+44 (0) 1923 496200
+44 (0) 1923 496201
http://www.saracens©rfu.co.uk

Wasps Rugby Football Club
+44 (0) 181 743 0262
+44 (0) 181 740 2508

West Hartlepool Rugby Football Club
+44 (0) 1429 233149

+44 (0) 1429 261857

Skating

International Skating Union
+41 21 612 66 66
+41 21 612 66 77
http://virtserv.interhop.net/~isu/

National Skating Association of Great Britain
+44 (0) 171 613 1188
+44 (0) 171 613 4616

Skiing

British Ski Federation
+44 (0) 1506 884343
+44 (0) 1506 882952
http://alpha.communicata.co.uk/BSF/homepage.

The International Ski Federation
+41 33 244 6161
+41 33 243 5353
http://www.zip.com.au/~birdman/fis.html

Speedway

Speedway Control Board Ltd
+44 (0) 1788 540096
+44 (0) 1788 552308
http://www.british-speedway.co.uk

Squash

Squash Rackets Association
+44 (0) 181 746 1616
+44 (0) 181 746 0580

Women's International Squash Players' Association
+44 (0) 171 222 1667
+44 (0) 171 976 8778
http://www.squash.org

World Squash Federation
+44 (0) 1424 429245
+44 (0) 1424 429250
http://www.squash.org

Swimming

Amateur Swimming Association
+44 (0) 1509 618700
+44 (0) 1509 618701

Fédération Internationale de Natation Amateur
+41 21 312 6602
+41 21 312 6610
http://www.fina.org

Table Tennis

English Table Tennis Association
+44 (0) 1424 722525
+44 (0) 1424 422103

International Table Tennis Federation
+44 (0) 1424 721414
+44 (0) 1424 431871
http://www.ittf.com/

Taekwondo

British Taekwondo Council
+44 (0) 1604 581933
+44 (0) 1604 581933

The World Taekwondo Federation
+82 2 566 2505
+82 2 553 4728
http://www.worldsport.com/sports/taekwondo

Triathlon

British Triathlon Association

+44 (0) 1530 414234
+44 (0) 1530 563340

International Triathlon Union
+1 604 926 7250
+1 604 926 7260
http://triathlon.org

Tug-of-war

Tug-of-war Association
+44 (0) 1494 783057
+44 (0) 1494 792040

Tug-of-war International Federation
+1 608 879 2869
+1 608 879 2103

Volleyball

English Volleyball Association
+44 (0) 115 981 6324
+44 (0) 115 945 5429

Fédération Internationale de Volleyball
+ 41 21 345 35 35
+ 41 21 345 35 45
http://www.fivb.ch

Weightlifting

British Amateur Weight Lifters Association
+44 (0) 1865 200339
+44 (0) 1865 790096

International Weightlifting Federation
+36 1 353 0530
+36 1 153 0199
http://www.worldsport.com/sports/weightlifting/home.html

Wrestling

British Amateur Wrestling Association
+44 (0) 161 832 9209
+44 (0) 161 833 1120

Fédération Internationale des Luttes Associées
+41 21 312 8426
+41 21 323 6073
http://www.uni-leipzig.de/~iat/fila/fila1.htm

Yachting

International Sailing Federation
+44 (0) 1703 635111
+44 (0) 1703 635789
http://www.sailing.org

Royal Yachting Association
+44 (0) 1703 627400
+44 (0) 1703 629924http://www.sailing.org

Out for a duck... looking forward to an English summer of cricket in 1999 •**Frank Coppi, Edgbaston** ★**2/6/98**

With grateful thanks to:

Members of the Daily Telegraph Sports Department: David Welch, Russell Cheyne, Wayne Caba, Joanna Lloyd, all the writers and photographers and special thanks to Martin Smith

The design team at Wherefore Art?: David Costa, Rachel Godfrey, Martin Buckwell, Sian Rance, Emma Smilie and not forgetting Fiona Andreanelli

At Sportcal Global Communications: Mike Laflin, Luke Boyle and Philip Davies

At Dig.It Design: Tony Peacock

Production Consultant: Lyn Corson. At PDQ: Paul Dossett